Endorsements

Charlie Barnes is a master storyteller and entertainer, and a great Seminole. In *The Bowden Dynasty: A Story of Faith, Family, and Football*, he covers the whole field—all the personalities, issues, and events that defined Seminole football in the 1990s.

—COACH BOBBY BOWDEN

I shouted "touchdown, Florida State" on the radio more times in the 1990s than in any other decade. It was an epic time to be a Seminole, and Charlie Barnes covers the 1990s dynasty era completely ... with a little good humor thrown in too. Now that's another "touchdown, FSU!"

—GENE DECKERHOFF
The "Voice of the Seminoles"

I began my term as president the very day we won our first national championship. And, throughout my time as president, it was Charlie Barnes who continued to chronicle the FSU sports program and put the success of the dynasty period into perspective, demonstrating how important the sports program was to the university. Charlie has been the Boswell of our sports era, helping us understand and appreciate all that has been achieved.

—SANDY D'ALEMBERTE
President, Florida State University 1994–2003

It was an incredible time, and it changed my life. In my four years on the team, we never lost a game in Doak Campbell Stadium. Thanks to Charlie Barnes for refreshing all those wonderful memories.

—CHRIS WEINKE
2000 Heisman Trophy Winner

A STORY OF FAITH, FAMILY & FOOTBALL

An Insider's Account

CHARLIE BARNES
AND BOBBY BOWDEN

BroadStreet
PUBLISHING

BroadStreet Publishing Group, LLC
Racine, Wisconsin, USA
BroadStreetPublishing.com

THE BOWDEN DYNASTY: A STORY OF FAITH, FAMILY & FOOTBALL
An Insider's Account

ISBN-13: 978-1-4245-5435-5 (softcover)
ISBN-13: 978-1-4245-5463-2 (e-book)

Stock or custom editions of BroadStreet Publishing titles may be purchased in bulk for educational, business, ministry, fundraising, or sales promotional use. For information, please e-mail info@ broadstreetpublishing.com.

Cover design by Chris Garborg at www.garborgdesign.com
Typesetting by Katherine Lloyd at www.theDESKonline.com

Printed in the United States of America

17 18 19 20 21 5 4 3 2 1

Contents

Introduction

The film *The Bowden Dynasty* and this companion book are a fusion of dreams, serendipity, and faith all coming together. I first met Charlie Barnes when he was an older FSU alumnus supervising his fraternity's opening rush night in 1980. I had been on campus for no more than a week, and this was the first rush party I had been to. My roommate and I were flattered that Charlie was so outgoing and welcoming. Unlike the dozens of other people we met that week, I didn't forget Charlie's name and how enthusiastic of a salesperson he was. Later I would recognize him as an up-and-coming executive with the Seminole Boosters.

The Seminole Boosters realized early on that given Tallahassee's remote location in the state of Florida, if they were to begin raising serious funds to help build a top-level football program, then they were going to have to go where the money was—in cities and towns all over the Southeast. Charlie Barnes was for many Boosters the face of the organization, traveling every year with Coach Bobby Bowden from town to town. They hosted banquets, golf tournaments, pep rallies—anything they could do to help build the Seminole Boosters organization. Charlie did it all: he drove Bobby and Ann Bowden in the Boosters' van; he was the master of ceremonies; he slapped every back he could; and he regaled anyone who would listen with one Seminole tale after another. Coach Bowden would stay late and sign autographs, and then it was on to the next town.

Charlie was one of the most impressive public speakers at FSU, and few people had more enthusiasm for what was happening at Florida State during the Bowden era. At the same time, Charlie was a print voice of authenticity for the Boosters, sharing his insights in Booster reports, magazine articles, and newspaper columns. In those days, before the Internet, that was how most of us who followed the FSU football team got our "insider" news—via first-class mail, in Booster magazines.

For many of us fans, Charlie Barnes' Booster columns were as insightful in the 1990s as the sports news we'd get in the *Osceola*, a Seminole sports newspaper run by Jerry Kutz. If you were a die-hard fan back then, chances are you subscribed to the *Osceola* for the most candid news and inside stories about the program. A good friend from the FSU Foundation, Pat Ramsey, introduced me to Jerry Kutz back in 2006 and said she thought we might have something in common. None of us had any idea of what was to come.

It was my good fortune to meet up with Charlie Barnes as I began imagining our film *The Bowden Dynasty*. The year was 2012 and Charlie mentioned he was culling his best articles and columns for a possible book he had in mind that focused on the same topic of the dynasty. He offered to let me read the manuscript, and when I did, I couldn't put it down. Unfortunately, the timing wasn't right for the film to come together and it would be a few more years before I could talk to Charlie about combining our film with his written accounts of the dynasty years.

In 2013, I took a chance meeting with Seminole Booster executives Andy Miller and Jerry Kutz to discuss the idea of a documentary on the dynasty years and Coach Bowden's life story. Jerry bought into the idea so much that by the time lunch was finished, he had already scheduled a meeting with Coach Bowden—an hour later! Before I knew it, Jerry was driving me across town to Bobby Bowden's home.

I wasn't prepared for this, and I was about as apprehensive about the meeting as I could ever be. Over the years, I've worked with a number of military generals, and had the opportunity to direct some amazing talents, including actors George C. Scott and Charlton Heston. I even had the opportunity of four meetings with President Ronald Reagan. But an appointment with Bobby Bowden loomed larger to me, perhaps because he has always been a larger-than-life hero. He had been so iconic to everyone else who shared the FSU experience with him as a head coach. And I was just a fan! As we drove toward his house, I wasn't sure what to say, or even where to begin. The film was just a few sentences of description at the time, a set of goals really, because documentaries are often journeys of discovery—they rarely start with scripts.

Jerry pulled up to Coach's front door, and Bobby came right out and greeted us personally. With a firm handshake, he looked me in the eye and asked with a smile, "How are you doing, boy?" It was like meeting an old friend, and I instantly felt at home. I had posed for a picture with Coach once at a 1993 golf tournament in Los Angeles, and before then my only time shared with Bobby Bowden was on an elevator ride in the FSU stadium ten years before. Even then, he walked into the elevator with a number of his staff members, and the first thing he did was ask me how my day was going! Imagine how that single act of kindness made me feel back then when I was just a junior in school. Coach Bowden made me feel like the most important person on that elevator that day. I will never forget that moment, because it speaks volumes about the man.

So here I am, thirty years later, sitting in Coach's home discussing a potential documentary. Coach Bowden asked where people would eventually see the film, and, at the risk of alienating him, I had to be honest. "I don't really know, Coach," I said. "I can take this concept to a number of television networks first, but the minute we do that we've lost editorial control." Coach just listened and didn't say anything. I told him I wasn't interested in doing a retrospective of his thirty-four years at Florida State, and I didn't want to get tied down in the X's and O's either.

With Jerry Kutz looking on, I shared my desire to shine a light on one of the most important sports records of all time—Florida State football's fourteen years of top-5 AP finishes and ten-or-more wins from 1987 to 2000. To me, it is one of the greatest sports stories never told. Bowden's '90s teams had been recognized by ESPN as the team of the decade (in any sport), and many other accolades had been bestowed on Bowden's teams over the years for their achievements. But the record Coach Bowden and his teams set in those fourteen years is a true marvel. I wanted to dig for details and tell the story of how he and his staff pulled it off.

As I explained these points to Coach Bowden, his eyes seemed to light up. He remarked that the fourteen-year dynasty was the record he was most proud of, because of both the adversity the teams faced and overcame and the consistency with which they had to play to stay at such a high level year in and year out.

It's not easy to be a top-5 college football team for even a few years. When you are a top-rated team, every school on your schedule is going to prepare all summer for that meeting, and you are going to get their very best shot. Over the years, we've seen teams peak for a while. USC, Ohio State, Florida, Alabama, Miami, and Oregon come to mind as schools that looked like dynasties in the making, but eventually fell out of the top 5 at the end of a given year. The closest a team has ever come to FSU's fourteen-year, top-5 dynasty streak is the University of Oklahoma, with seven straight years—in the 1950s.

Another fact makes the dynasty all the more astonishing. There is only one team in the country that plays in two "conferences." For the past several decades, Florida State has played in the "Florida Conference," as well as the ACC. In those fourteen dynasty years, the University of Miami and the University of

Florida were also top-level teams, and were always on the Noles' schedule. (Those two teams stopped playing each other annually years ago.) As Mickey Andrews says in the film, "If you can win the state championship in Florida, there's a pretty good chance you can win the national championship."

No documentary had ever explored the details on how Coach Bowden and his staff pulled off the dynasty feat, and Coach seemed grateful I wanted to tell that side of the story. I then shared with Coach another reason why I wanted to make the film independently, and that was to be able to tell the story of his faith. That seemed to be the clincher for him, and he was the most enthusiastic about that opportunity.

For decades Coach Bowden has been preaching all over the country to groups large and small on Sundays with little fanfare. The idea of a film that could reach many more people with his message and be a lasting testament to his Christian faith appealed to him. Neither of us could think of a network that would greenlight our documentary production and still allow us to have the final word in the edit room. By the time Jerry and I left, Coach Bowden gave his word on a handshake that if I could fund it, he was on board.

Given that I was already working full time on a long-term project, I needed to find a team to help produce the vision Bobby and I now shared. Watching the SEC channel one night, I came across a terrific documentary about Will Clark and Rafael Palmeiro (who formed the imposing one-two hitting punch known as "Thunder and Lightning") on the best team never to win the College World Series—the 1985 Mississippi State Bulldogs.

After tracking down the credits, making a few phone calls, and booking a flight to Charlotte, I met producer Rob Harvell and editor Brian Goodwin in person. Rob and Brian like to share the director credit and they helped produce ESPN Films' favorites such as *The Book of Manning* and *I Hate Christian Laettner*. I had the basic story beats already worked out, and they loved the idea of creating a long-form documentary without commercial breaks and interference. They convinced me that if I raised some initial funding, then they could do a lot of the shooting in the fall of 2015, and then make a short video to help raise the rest of the budget. It was an idea that required a lot of faith and trust on all fronts.

The last big step was a letter I wrote to a few friends I knew from my days in the Sigma Chi Fraternity at FSU. Brothers Rick Brawner, Scott Davis, and Mike Ortoll were the first to step up and help launch the project, and then others followed. Had Rick, Scott, and Mike not done so, this project would never have gotten off the ground. And I would have had to tell Coach the project was a no-go.

By the time Rob Harvell and Brian Goodwin finished our production in the fall of 2016, they had crisscrossed the country and conducted over sixty-five extensive two-camera interviews. The film's all-star cast includes Chuck Amato, Mickey Andrews, Fred Biletnikoff, the Bowden family, Peter Boulware, Derrick Brooks, Mack Brown, Kenny Chesney, Lee Corso, Gene Deckerhoff, Vince Dooley, Warrick Dunn, Jimbo Fisher, Lou Holtz, Jimmy Johnson, Jim Kelly, Burt Reynolds, Mark Richt, Nick Saban, Deion Sanders, Howard Schnellenberger, Bart Starr, Andre Wadsworth, Charlie Ward, Peter Warrick, Chris Weinke, and Danny Wuerffel.

The Bowden Dynasty will eventually make it to television, but before then it will be a film experience to be enjoyed without commercial interruptions as we take our measure of the dynasty years. It's a story too big for the small screen, so it begins as a theatrical feature release in over 450 theaters across the USA. With the help of Fathom Events, on a single night Bobby Bowden fans all over the country will join together in a communal experience of the film's premiere. Eventually, *The Bowden Dynasty* will make its way to DVD, Blu-ray, and digital release.

Our hope is that people will be inspired by the film, and turn to the pages in this book to learn more. These insider accounts from Charlie Barnes were written with the emotion and energy of the moment, not years later with filters of hindsight applied. Coach Bowden and his son Steve also worked to collaborate on this book, adding Coach's insight and some handpicked Scripture verses to help frame each of the years of the dynasty.

On a long drive home after a fateful meeting with the University of Alabama's athletic department, Coach Bobby Bowden made a monumental decision on January 2, 1987. He decided to stay at Florida State. No one could have known it then, but that day was the beginning of perhaps the most incredible record in sports history—the FSU dynasty. I believe the delays in making this film were no coincidence, and all glory goes to God. *The Bowden Dynasty* and this companion book are being released on the thirtieth anniversary of the week Coach Bowden simply said, "I'm staying at FSU."

All of us involved in the film's (and the book's) production, marketing, and distribution are doing so with an eye toward honoring and thanking Coach Bowden for everything he did for Florida State University and for college football in general. In the thirty-four years he was at FSU, there was unrelenting growth and constant change. Coaches, players, and staff came and went. The football program transitioned from being Independent to joining the ACC. The college football game became a major television draw, and FSU played in numerous "games of the century." Doak Campbell Stadium went from being the butt of jokes as a steel "erector set" to the largest continuous brick structure in the world (with the Great Wall of China being the only exception). But during all these transformations, there was one constant: Coach Bobby Bowden. He kept the program together and did it his way, emphasizing three priorities: faith, family, and football—in that order.

Millions of people have been inspired by Coach Bowden's faith and leadership over the years, and we trust that our film and this companion book will continue to inspire others for years to come. There are so many lessons to be learned from the dynasty years, and we look forward to telling those stories for some time. Come join us as the story continues at www.BowdenDynasty.com and at www.Facebook.com/BowdenDynasty.

Finally, I want to express a special thank you to my wife, Patty, for her steady support and encouragement to me to keep after this project when, at times, it didn't seem possible to pull off or even complete.

—JOHN CORRY
Executive Producer,
The Bowden Dynasty: A Story of Faith, Family & Football

Better Than
the Most Wonderful Time

You may remember it as the most wonderful time. But it was much better than that.

These fourteen Seminole teams—1987 through 2000—won at least ten games a year and never finished a season ranked lower than No. 4 until the final 2000 season, when they finished No. 5. They won every conference title after they began Atlantic Coast Conference play in 1992. In fact, in fourteen years, the Seminoles' conference record was an incredible 72–2.

In fourteen seasons, the Seminoles played for the national championship five times, winning two of those championships. They were victorious in eleven of fourteen bowl games, including nine in a row between 1987 and 1995. Not only that, but they vanquished numerous bowl opponents, including some of the brightest stars in the college football skies: Ohio State, Penn State, Notre Dame, Nebraska, Auburn, Florida, and Texas A&M. In those days, only five bowls (Cotton, Rose, Fiesta, Sugar, and Orange) were considered to be "major bowls." The dynasty teams played in the Cotton Bowl, four Orange Bowls, five Sugar Bowls, and the three Fiesta Bowls. The Seminoles conquered all of them except the Rose Bowl, for which we were not eligible to play. In 2013, Florida State's third national championship came in Pasadena.

It was a glorious run for Seminole quarterbacks, led by Heisman Trophy winners Charlie Ward and Chris Weinke. Casey Weldon was the Heisman runner-up in 1991. In addition to their

Heisman honors, Charlie Ward won the Davey O'Brien Award, the Johnny Unitas Golden Arm Award, and the Maxwell Award. In fact, in his time, Charlie was the most decorated college football player in history. Chris Weinke won the Davey O'Brien Award and the Johnny Unitas Golden Arm Award. And Casey Weldon won the Johnny Unitas Golden Arm Award too.

Among the defensive stars of the dynasty were Jim Thorpe Award winners Deion Sanders and Terrell Buckley. Linebackers Marvin Jones and Paul McGowan each won a Butkus Award. Jones picked up the Vince Lombardi Trophy as well, as did Jamal Reynolds. Corey Simon and Andre Wadsworth were each runners-up for the Lombardi Trophy. And Sebastian Janikowski won the Lou Groza Award twice.

For Florida State, it was the era of giants on the field. There have been lots of All-American teams, but to be named a consensus All-American, a player must be selected first team on at least three of the five officially recognized lists: Associated Press, American Football Coaches Association, Football Writers Association, the Walter Camp Foundation, and the Sporting News. As rare as such honors are, dynasty era Seminole stars were routinely distinguished as consensus All-Americans. During the fourteen-year dynasty, no fewer than twenty individual Seminole players were named consensus All-Americans.

Underscoring FSU's reputation as "Cornerback U," six of the twenty consensus All-Americans were Seminole corners: Deion Sanders (twice), Leroy Butler, Terrell Buckley, Corey Sawyer, Clifton Abraham, and Tay Cody. Other consensus All-Americans on defense included linebackers Marvin Jones (twice), Sam Cowart, and Derrick Brooks (twice). Brooks was also an Academic All-American.

Five Seminole defensive linemen who earned consensus honors were defensive ends Peter Boulware, Reinhard Wilson, Jamal Reynolds, Andre Wadsworth, and noseguard Corey Simon.

Wadsworth had been a walk-on player.

The list of offensive stars, led by Heisman Trophy winner Charlie Ward, is similarly impressive. A pair of offensive linemen, center Clay Shiver and guard Jason Whittaker, were consensus All-Americans, as was flanker Snoop Minnis. Flanker Peter Warrick's spectacular touchdown catch to seal the national championship victory in 1999 is legend. Warrick was twice named consensus All-American.

Between 1987 and 2000, a total of sixty-eight individual Seminole football players were named to one recognized All-American team or another. In addition, Chris Hope, Derrick Brooks, and Daryl Bush were named academic All-Americans.

Florida State athletics has officially retired either the numbers or the jerseys of only ten former players. Seven of these—Ward, Sanders, Brooks, Weinke, Buckley, Dunn, and Marvin Jones—are from the dynasty era.

From this quick overview, anyone can see an astonishing level of talent was concentrated in these fourteen Seminoles teams. Deion Sanders and Derrick Brooks were inducted into both the Pro and College Halls of Fame. Charlie Ward is in the College Hall of Fame, while Walter Jones is featured in the Pro Hall of Fame.

Along the way, our Seminoles won more football games in that one glorious decade of the 1990s than any team in any other decade in college football history. And the 1999 national champions were the first ever to go wire-to-wire, preseason to postseason, ranked No. 1. Coach Bobby Bowden was inducted into the College Hall of Fame in 2006.

The unique successes and culture of the dynasty was much more of a reflection on Bobby Bowden's character and leadership than any other single factor. He surrounded himself with a cadre of men who shared his beliefs, his faith, and his methods. As staff, they recruited the collection of student-athletes who were among the finest young men to play college football in the 1980s and '90s.

The era of Bobby Bowden's dynasty was a rich landscape of stories, issues, and personalities. And no other program in America captured the public's imagination like the Seminoles and their old rascal coach who became a legend.

Sections were chosen from among hundreds of published stories, columns, and essays by Charlie Barnes. Much additional new material was written exclusively for this book, and some of the previously published material has been edited by the author. His articles have appeared in the *Report to Boosters*, *Unconquered Magazine*, the *Florida State Times*, the *Overtime Times*, the *Tallahassee Democrat*, and the *Scalping Knife*.

These essays spotlight the extraordinary strength of Coach Bobby Bowden's leadership and character, providing entertaining insight into the national landscape surrounding Florida State football in the dynasty era. The glories of the dynasty include five national championship games in seven years between 1993 and 2000, and nine consecutive ACC Championships with only two losses (72–2) since starting league play in 1992. The range of personalities, all the controversies, and all the triumphs are recorded in these pages.

Charlie Barnes served as executive director and senior vice president of the Seminole Boosters until his retirement in 2012. He and Coach Bowden traveled together on the annual Seminole Booster banquet-and-golf circuit ("Bobby Bowden Tour") for more than thirty years. He remains a popular writer and speaker, and his columns appear in the Seminole Boosters' *Unconquered Magazine*. In 2016, he was inducted into the Florida State Athletic Hall of Fame. He and his wife, Connie, are alumni of Florida State University.

A Lasting Legacy

by Coach Bobby Bowden

Keep your heart with all vigilance,
for from it flow the springs of life.
—PROVERBS 4:23

I've often been asked what I hope my legacy will be. That question is best left for football aficionados, not me. The best I can answer, however, and the legacy for which I hope to leave, is that I served God's purposes in my life. That I might have achieved an honorable legacy within the context of football would be the best of both worlds for me, because I wanted to coach football since childhood.

I believe my successes at FSU are inseparable from my faith in God. God equipped me with a perspective on life and a skill set that I never would've possessed without his wisdom and strength. Football is not just about athletic talent or X's and O's. It's also about relationships. And fighting through adversity. It is about character, heart, forgiveness, and love of one another. It's about transcending ourselves and giving our best each and every day. My job was to practice what I preached. And I leaned heavily on God for his help.

The most amazing thing about our dynasty years is how consistent we were. There was never a drop-off from one year to the next. I loved winning championships. I would have loved to have won three or four more than I did. But what makes those dynasty years so ridiculously satisfying is that we ended each season ranked no lower than No. 4 in the polls, won two national championships, played for three others, and won eleven bowl games, including nine in a row. None of us thought about these things at the time, nor did we plan for them. In hindsight, I realize we accomplished something unique in college football history. On my own, I would have thought it was impossible. And yet it happened.

Ultimately, I attribute that success to God. This is not to say that he rigged games for us. If so, he must've been asleep at the wheel during some of our games with Miami and Florida! What I do believe, however, is that God gave me more strength and wisdom than I ever would have possessed on my own. He enabled me to keep football in perspective. And life in perspective. He required of me what I asked of my players and coaches—namely, to go out and give their best. And that is what we did.

—BOBBY BOWDEN

1987 Season

We were ranked No. 1 and Miami was ranked No. 2 when we lined up to play one another on October 3, 1987, in Tallahassee. With only seconds remaining in the fourth quarter, we scored a touchdown to pull within 1 point. An extra point would tie the game, but 2 points would give us the win. We decided to go for 2. A pass was called into the corner of the end zone. The pass was underthrown, however, and was batted down by their defender. We lost 25–26. It was the only game we lost that year. All other things being equal, if I had decided to kick the extra point and settle for a tie, we probably would have remained No. 1 that next week.

At the end of the regular season, Miami finished No. 1 and FSU No. 2. Miami played for the national championship and won, while we played Nebraska in the Fiesta Bowl and won. The 1987 season proved to be a valuable eye-opener. It convinced me that FSU had arrived as a major football program. We could have been national champions that year, and we could be in the hunt for that title in the years to come. The 1987 season confirmed it.

—Bobby Bowden

1987 Season

Began the season ranked No. 8
Ended the season ranked No. 2
Record 11–1
Fiesta Bowl Champions

September 5, defeated Texas Tech in Tallahassee 40–16

September 12, defeated East Carolina in Greenville 44–3

September 19, defeated Memphis State in Tallahassee 41–24

September 26, defeated Michigan State in East Lansing 31–3

October 3, lost to Miami in Tallahassee 25–26

October 10, defeated Southern Mississippi in Hattiesburg 61–10

October 17, defeated Louisville in Tallahassee 32–9

October 31, defeated Tulane in Tallahassee 73–14

November 7, defeated Auburn in Auburn 34–6

November 14, defeated Furman in Tallahassee 41–10

November 28, defeated Florida in Gainesville 28–14

January 1, 1988, defeated Nebraska in the Fiesta Bowl 31–28

In the Beginning

Bobby Bowden's Seminole dynasty began with the 1987 season and continued its incredible progression through the 2001 Orange Bowl. Without Bowden there would have been no dynasty for FSU. However, toward the end of 1986, there was increasing doubt that Bowden would remain the Seminole head coach. Events transpired in those last weeks of 1986 to convince Bobby and Ann Bowden to stay in Tallahassee.

It has been said that the speed of light is relative to the observer. So it seems is the speed of time. Bobby Bowden's Seminole dynasty lasted for fourteen years. There has now, as of 2016, been a greater distance in time—fifteen seasons—since the dynasty ended. For fans whose memories are forever enriched by the glories of that breathtaking run of consecutive ten-win seasons and top-4 finishes, it feels hardly possible that we have to look back nearly three decades to find its beginning.

When did the seeds of the dynasty take root, and will we ever see that wondrous tree bloom again? So far no one has been able to duplicate the astonishing run of fourteen seasons, and the 1999 Seminoles were the first to earn a flawless, wire-to-wire No. 1 ranking, from preseason through national championship.

Bobby Bowden was fifty-eight years old when the dynasty began and seventy-one when it ended. Nick Saban, at sixty-five, certainly seems to have the Alabama program well in hand. But

I believe fifty-year-old Jimbo Fisher will prove to be perhaps the best head coach of his generation. How difficult would it be to reproduce or surpass the dynasty record? I'd say either Saban or Fisher has the best chance of doing it. And recruiting Jimbo Fisher to his staff in 2007 might rival the dynasty as Bobby Bowden's greatest legacy to Seminole football.

In duplicating the dynasty, the ten-win threshold is no longer the challenge it was thirty years ago. More teams today play twelve, thirteen, fourteen, and possibly even fifteen games in a season. But the top-4 finish is the killer. That record eliminates any other contender.

No analogy is exact, but here's one I like: In any given PGA tournament, a touring pro has a 5 percent chance of sinking a forty-foot putt. When one does go in, there's a loud whoop from the crowd (golfing spectators aren't prone to do a lot of cheering). As explained by my good Seminole friend Doug Russell:

> Most greens are not flat, so negotiating a long putt requires incredible skill and course knowledge. There are so many variables that go into the calculation of reading a green, especially for a long putt: multiple speeds, many different slopes, angles, lines. Different grasses have different grains and impact the roll and break. Line, aim, speed, and stroke. You need some luck too. Coach Bowden often said you need a certain amount of luck to win it all, and the same is true in a long putt.

The 1987 season was the first of Bobby Bowden's forty-foot putts. That year we were No. 3 when we lost to No. 4 Miami in October on a failed 2-point conversion. In the Fiesta Bowl, FSU came from two touchdowns back to edge out No. 5 Nebraska 31–28 and win a No. 2 final ranking behind national champion Miami. It was the first New Year's Day bowl the Seminoles had ever won. And it was only the beginning.

Here's the remarkable question: What do you think the chances are of making fourteen of those forty-foot putts in a row? That is in effect what Bowden did during the dynasty era. He sank fourteen consecutive putts without missing one.

Perhaps you remember the intermittent chaos of those years: The Foot Locker affair, the conflict over Osceola as a symbol, the controversy over ACC officiating, the Peter Warrick business, brawls on the field vs. the Gators, the hostility of media, and the ravings of Steve Spurrier. The fact is that the landscape was much different each year when Bowden lined up for his "putt." Sometimes it was raining, while at other times it was windy. Sometimes people were screaming at him, while at other times idiots would run across the green and tear up the turf. It didn't matter, however. He never missed. He made fourteen forty-foot putts in a row.

John Corry, an FSU alumnus and award-winning documentary filmmaker, is producing a film about Coach Bowden, his character, and his achievements, and the faith that has defined his life. The work is called *The Bowden Dynasty: A Story of Faith, Family & Football.* Corry and his crew have spent long months interviewing all the coaches and principal figures of that era, searching, as he said, for "the seeds of the dynasty." Where are the seeds of the dynasty to be found?

In the early years of the Bobby Bowden Tour, it felt like we were traveling tent evangelists, except we also played golf. We drove from town to town late at night to spend all of the next day and share an

Bobby and Ann Bowden with Charlie Barnes on the Bobby Bowden Tour.

evening meal with the Seminole Booster clubs. Just like the tent preachers, there was singin', shoutin', preachin', and prayin' and it was all about the Seminoles.

One dark night when Coach Bowden and I were driving the highways and back roads in the spring of 1985, the conversation turned to his stellar recruiting class and the state of the program. We talked about the fact that all of us fans had been spoiled by Bowden's exhilarating success in the late 1970s.

By 1985, Bobby had been here almost a decade. After the back-to-back Orange Bowl years, the program had sort of flattened out. Oh, Florida State always had winning seasons, always went to a bowl game, and nearly always won those bowls. But for a while in the early 1980s we just couldn't seem to knock down Florida, Miami, or Auburn, and the fans were restless. He said, "I don't know how long it will take—but if I got another recruiting class like the one we got this spring—I don't care *who* we play."

I didn't understand it at the time, but of course we know the names now: Sammie, Deion, Odell, and Peter Tom. That class was so phenomenal that we didn't even have to use last names. Michael Tanks, Chip Ferguson, Pat Tomberlin, and Dedrick Dodge. FSU signed twenty-nine players altogether. That 1985 class must have contained the seeds of the dynasty. But if I had to point to a singularity, I would say the actual beginning of the dynasty was the worst bowl weekend that I had ever endured.

At the end of the 1986 season, we were 6–5 and invited to play in the All-American Bowl in Birmingham. Our opponent was 6–5 Indiana. That year we had lost to Miami and Florida again. We didn't play Auburn in 1986, but we had lost the three previous contests. The weather was ghastly—snow, followed by freezing rain and sleet. But even the black clouds that blanketed Birmingham were not as dark as the mood of the Seminole fans and the big Boosters who traveled to the game.

The University of Alabama was looking for a new coach

and Bobby Bowden had always been honest about his desire to go home if Alabama called. It seemed to Seminole fans that the deal was inevitable. Also stoking discontent was an awareness of our own athletic director's ambition to become athletic director at Alabama (which he eventually did). Fans speculated on whose behalf he might be working.

You have to understand the psychological history of Florida State fans. We were the second sons. For so long, we always got the hand-me-downs. We wore a chip on our shoulders. But Bobby Bowden changed all that. He became the national face of Florida State. His public personality was identified as ours, and for the first time we were a respected and envied program beyond the borders of our own state. We liked it, and we especially liked him.

Sure, we wanted to start beating Miami and Florida and Auburn again, but we wanted *him* to do it. And *he* was leaving. All the old insecurities came flooding back. It was dark and cold and miserable in Birmingham, and Bobby Bowden was leaving and we couldn't do a thing about it.

There's a story that may or may not be true, but I like to believe it is. Former Miami head coach Howard Schnellenberger was a good friend of Bowden and a favorite of Seminole fans. He was available and, so the story is told, was prepared to board a private jet in Opa-Locka and fly to Birmingham should the announcement come that Bowden had departed for Alabama. Our fans felt powerless in the face of sinister forces beyond their control, and Schnellenberger was the closest thing to Bobby Bowden. If Bobby left, the fans and big Boosters would take it on themselves to recruit a replacement.

Kickoff came at eight o'clock at night in a driving snowstorm that turned to frozen sleet by halftime. The game was sold out, but there wasn't a single human being in that stadium other than followers of FSU and Indiana. The people of Birmingham are great football fans, but they're not suicidal. Birmingham newspapers and television and radio stations all promoted the All-American Bowl as Bobby Bowden's final game as head coach of FSU.

At halftime, the snow turned to rain and then sleet. We just sat there. A character in the *Peanuts* cartoon series mourned, "It always rains on the unloved." There we were, squinting up into the black night sky, freezing, wet, unloved, bitter, and sad.

Sammie scored a pair of touchdowns, and we won the bowl game, 27–13. Afterward we walked back to the hotel, wondering what was going to become of us.

Bobby and Ann decided to drive back to Tallahassee from Birmingham. When they drove up to their home in Killearn, the front lawn was filled with trucks and cameras and television cables—so they kept on going. They meandered the long road around Killearn and talked about the future. They talked about their shared goals and dreams, about their long journey together since they were high school sweethearts at Woodlawn in Birmingham.

When they came to Tallahassee in 1976, the Bowdens estimated they would stay in Tallahassee for five years. He had seen the 1981 schedule featuring the "Octoberfest" away games in sequence against Nebraska, Ohio State, Notre Dame, Pitt, and LSU, one after another every week. He later joked, "I wondered who was going to be coaching here then."

He had always wanted to go home to coach in Alabama; to be the head coach of Alabama had been a lifelong dream. But he knew he had an experienced staff and a stable filled with extraordinarily talented players at Florida State. By the time he and Ann finally drove back to their home, they had decided to stay in Tallahassee.

The dynasty was a unique record. No one has ever achieved it before; certainly, no one has done it since. So the next time you're having a conversation with someone who wants to know what was so special about Bobby Bowden and the dynasty, answer them with this question: "How many national championships have been won by schools that didn't start playing football until after World

War II?" The answer is three. And all three of those trophies are available for your viewing in the football offices of the Moore Athletic Center at Florida State University.

In 1993 and 1999, Bowden coached the first two national championships won by any school that didn't start playing football until after World War II. And Florida State is still the only such school to have done so.[*]

---

[*] Much of this chapter's material was initially published in *Unconquered Magazine* (summer 2016).

Bernie and the Bandit

S uch was the love affair between Burt Reynolds and Seminole fans that one joke going around was a whimsical petition to rename Campbell Stadium and call it Sally Field. She, of course, was rumored to be more than just his costar in the wildly popular *Smokey and the Bandit* movies. *Smokey* debuted as the second-highest-grossing film of 1977, second only to *Star Wars*. Reynolds had begun in Hollywood as a stunt man, then progressed to the grim alpha male character in *Deliverance*. *Smokey* introduced America to the Burt Reynolds as Seminole fans knew him. His amiable, laughing, lovable, ornery character was not an act.

On September 5, 1987, we opened at home against Texas Tech. Burt Reynolds flew in to dedicate the brand-new Burt Reynolds Hall. He brought his wife, Lonnie Anderson, with him, along with actor pals Bernie Casey, Ricardo Montalban, and Dom DeLuise. A huge gathering at the Civic Center was headlined as "Bernie & the Bandit."

On that first day of the first weekend of the first year of the dynasty, it wasn't dark or snowing or raining. The sun was bright and the sky was clear. Burt Reynolds was, at that moment, the top male box-office draw in the world. And Bobby Bowden would go on to become the winningest head football coach in Division I history. It was a fabulous beginning.

Bernie of the "Bernie & the Bandit" was of course FSU president Bernard Sliger, the pool-shooting former army sergeant with a PhD in economics. Bernie was as popular with Seminole fans as was Burt Reynolds, and thousands of us packed into the massive exhibition hall to see the two of them, as well as other celebrities, together on stage.

Burt was dressed in his Bandit jacket with rolled-up sleeves; Lonnie Anderson was resplendent in garnet and gold game-day attire. President Bernie Sliger opted for his long academic robes. Jim King was the master of ceremonies.

When King introduced Florida State's distinguished university president, Sliger stood up and unzipped his academic gown to reveal a full sheriff's uniform and a striking transformation. Bernie was the image of Texas sheriff Buford T. Justice, the character played by Jackie Gleason in the *Bandit* movies. The crowd jumped to their feet, cheering.

Burt Reynolds and Florida State is, at its heart, the story of a love affair.

If Bobby Bowden's professional life is the story of Seminole football's ascent to greatness, then Burt Reynolds' is the story of the maturing of our alumni, and of their passion and lifelong commitment to FSU. Our fans and alumni know that Burt is an actor and an alumnus who has been involved with the university. Most have little idea who the man really is, however, and to what extent his life reflects all that is good and noble about FSU.

Burton "Buddy" Reynolds was a highly recruited high school star from West Palm who committed informally to Miami, but was turned toward FSU by Seminole coach Tom Nugent. Another man who influenced his decision was his close friend from high school, a Seminole baseball player named Dick Howser. Nugent jested with the young Reynolds that FSU wanted him so bad that they had named a freshman girls' dorm on campus in his honor. "Reynolds Hall—my own dorm filled with beautiful women!" he said, smiling at the memory.

Nugent was in his second season as the Seminole head coach, and FSU was quickly upgrading its schedule to that of a major college program. Our little Seminole team was truly a David against the Goliaths of the SEC, and Coach Nugent knew the Tribe needed a serious upgrade in talent. And his recruiting of halfback Buddy Reynolds and quarterback Lee Corso was part of that project.

Decades later, the smiling, graying men of that era still proudly referred to themselves as "Nugent's boys." The boys went 8–3 that year against tough competition, and, in fact, Nugent's innovative passing offense set what was then a national record for the number of touchdown passes in one season with 19.

Burt was a star from the first day he arrived on campus. He bypassed the freshman team directly to be made a member of the varsity and a starter. In recording a bitter loss to Auburn, the FSU yearbook, *Tally Ho*, described, "Freshman left halfback Buddy Reynolds almost turned the trick for the Seminoles in the third quarter. He broke through left tackle and dashed for 54 yards." Unfortunately, as he crossed the goal line, Burt was knocked cold by Tiger defensive back Fob James.

One day in spring practice, Burt went up to catch a ball and came down awkwardly on his knee. As simple as that, his football career was finished. He tried to rehabilitate and made an attempt to come back later, but the intricacies of knees were still a mystery in that day. It was over. He told me sometime later, "If I hadn't busted my knee, I'd be a high school football coach in West Palm today." He sounded as if that would have been a fine outcome as far as he was concerned. He is a man who is at peace with himself.

Those who've seen his movies know Reynolds is clever. However, few realize he is such a devoted academic and intellectual. As Coach Bowden's assistant through all of the 1980s and 1990s, Sue Hall developed a close relationship with Reynolds. "You would not believe the size of his personal library," she said. "Entire walls of shelves of books. It's not unusual for him to read a book a day.

Every night he falls asleep listening to books on tape, but don't ask me how I know that," she joked.

And what feeds that voracious appetite? History, art, architecture, social commentary, and the classics. "Burt told me he acquired his appreciation of fine art and literature from his close friend Dinah Shore," Sue said. "He has an amazing mind. I've been fortunate to be on movie sets while he's working. He reads the script at night, memorizes it, and knows it cold the next day. I've never seen him ask for a prompter. He's modest about it; says it's all due to the training, but I've never seen anyone who could absorb that amount of material that fast. He is an extremely gifted man in terms of his intellect."

Reynolds tries to come to at least one game a year, usually watching from Bobby Bowden's private office where he can see the action unfold and then watch the replays on television. "He's a real student of the game," Hall said. "I always try to send him media guides at the beginning of each season. He never needs a script for the Great Moments segments. He remembers just about everything that has ever happened in Seminole football."

Joel Padgett believes Reynolds was the first Hollywood star to aggressively promote his alma mater in film. If you think about it, he really is still the only one who does that to any extent at all. Hall remembers, "We used to send him boxes and boxes of stuff all the time. He wanted something in every movie. It might be coffee cups on the desk, or wastebaskets, or game jerseys, or sweatshirts; anything with FSU on it got crowded into the set. We just cleaned out the office whenever Burt called."

And it wasn't just FSU jerseys and sweatshirts that popped up across the landscape of Reynolds' signature series of movies. Reynolds once had his pal, actor Dom DeLuise, play a character named Doctor Victor Prinzi. Vic Prinzi, of course, was Florida State's longtime radio commentator, partner to Gene Deckerhoff. Prinzi was also one of Nugent's boys, and Burt's quarterback.

Hall recalled the Bobby Bowden episode of Reynolds' hit television series *Evening Shade*: "It got a lot more involved with television. I had to go find Tommy Wright here on campus and get notarized permission for Burt to use the FSU fight song."

Reynolds' relationship with Bowden goes much deeper than many realize. "Coach Bowden and Burt talk a lot about religion," Sue said. "I get the impression that Burt"—she searches for the right words—"used to have a reputation for enjoying parties." She believes Bowden's close relationship has made a substantial difference in Reynolds' spiritual life.

Bowden has mentioned that he and Reynolds designed the arrow helmet together. Monk Bonasorte, the former FSU safety and All-American who is now an athletic department executive, said, "Back in 1979, when I played, our uniforms were actually in kind of poor condition. They were patched up because uniforms were expensive and the school didn't have a lot of money. Burt bought the first set of gold pants—they were actually called Notre Dame gold. It was the first time we'd had new uniforms in a while." Reynolds bought the first set of all-garnet uniforms and had some of his Hollywood pals tweak the design.

Monk is still close to Reynolds. He describes Burt as unfailingly charming, a splendid-looking man. He still has quite a bit of the Bandit in his smile, but once in a while you can also see those dangerous eyes from his character in *Deliverance*. "He's a complicated guy," said Monk, "but he's the best."

Yes, the best.

Had Reynolds not been such a great football player out of high school, he and Bobby Bowden might have met sooner. The talented Reynolds bypassed FSU's freshman team entirely. In those days, the freshman squad plus walk-ons and whoever else could fill in from the varsity played its own schedule of games. One of their regular opponents was South Georgia Junior College in Douglas, a team whose new twenty-four-year-old head coach was also required by the school to drive the team bus and to coach basketball as well. But it was not yet time for Bowden and Reynolds to cross paths.

The 1987 season was a heady time for the Seminoles. But I also remembered the Baylor game back in 1974, a miserable night in a miserable season in which FSU defeated only one opponent: the equally hapless Miami Hurricanes. We played Baylor at home in October. *The Longest Yard*, had been released in the summer, and it was a huge hit. Burt was back in Tallahassee for the Baylor game. He was introduced to the wildly enthusiastic crowd, standing at midfield with his friend, the gigantic Richard Keil, another actor in the movie.

Burt Reynolds was pretty much all we had in those days. I don't think anyone knew at the time how important it was to Burt that he had us as well. In 2004, Reynolds was again introduced to the crowd in Doak Campbell Stadium before a collection of Seminole fans somewhat larger than the one thirty years prior to this. Once again, he brought fellow actors with him, including the gigantic fellow who plays the old Richard Keil character in this current remake of *The Longest Yard*.

At the "Bernie & the Bandit" show in 1987, Burt and I discussed the details of the weekend, including the dramatic pregame surprise where he would throw the flaming spear into the turf. I was impressed with his size; he's big. For some reason most Hollywood actors tend to be on the smaller side. Reynolds looked more like a bodyguard or stunt man than an actor. You can see the athlete.

He made quite a show of it. Chief Osceola handed him the burning spear at midfield. Reynolds stood facing the alumni side of the stadium, then raised the spear triumphantly overhead. The crowd roared. Then he turned to the student side and did the same. Fans were in a frenzy when he finally rammed the fiery point into the turf. At a distance, no one could see the emotion on his face. But whatever it meant to us, it meant even more to him.

I saw him years later in Palm Beach. He was a surprise visitor to the Palm Beach Seminole Club's annual Bobby Bowden Banquet. We were backstage getting ready for him to make his appearance. It wasn't the best time in his personal or professional life. He was holding his little son. He looked tired. I told him I didn't want to intrude, but I wanted him to know that there were a lot of us FSU alumni who love him and appreciate what he had done for the university, and that fans like the ones there that night would always be there for him. I told him, "You can always come home to Florida State."

His voice cracked a little bit. He said that his relationship with the fans gave him strength, and that was why he was there—he needed now to draw on that strength. Of course, once the curtain went up, hundreds of Seminoles whooped in surprise. Reynolds was the ultimate professional, the classic celebrity Burt, the personality so familiar to everyone. He and Coach Bowden shared the microphone.

After our traveling party packed in the van to drive to the airport, Burt stayed behind for nearly an hour, patiently taking photos, smiling, and talking about football and anything else his fans wanted. The fans crushed in to be close to him, and he wanted to be with them.

He loved FSU from the time he first saw the red bricks, the rolling hills, and the towering pines at age eighteen. He loved the cool, green campus, the scented spring breeze, and the pretty girls in their bright dresses. He loved football, Phi Delta Theta, and the food in the big dining hall where all Florida State students took their meals together. He liked knowing everyone and knowing that everyone liked him.

Burton Reynolds was a devoted Seminole long before he was Burt Reynolds of the movies, decades before he was the number one–ranked male box-office draw in the world. And now, in the afternoon of a celebrated career as an actor, teacher, and director, he remains a completely devoted son of Florida State University.

From time to time, something from him, always welcome, shows up in the mail. Most recently it was an autographed photo of him sporting the Mean Machine football uniform of his character from the 2005 version of *The Longest Yard*, charging full ahead with game-faced fury. He'd written: "Charlie—Do you know anybody that would like a mean, not fat but not too swift sixty-six-year-old running back?"

Well yes, pal. Yes, I do. And there are tens of thousands of us.

Miami, Auburn, and Florida

Three games in 1987 defined the regular season. Miami was in their glory days and would go on to win the 1987 national championship. The Seminoles had beaten Auburn only once in fourteen tries, and the last FSU victory was in 1977. The Gators were riding a six-game winning streak against the Noles. If there was to be a dynasty, it would first have to banish these old ghosts.

Miami came to Tallahassee on October 3, 1987, led by All-American quarterback Steve Walsh and future All-Pro receiver Michael Irvin. The Canes were ranked No. 3, the Seminoles No. 4. Some called it the game of the century, which was a bit much, but the phrase would become more commonly associated with Florida State games as the dynasty progressed.

Steve Walsh said that the "game-day atmosphere was incredible" in Tallahassee. Sixty future NFL players would face each other on that field that day. Hurricane coach Jimmy Johnson was well schooled in Florida State's talent, and that knowledge was underscored as the Seminoles jumped to a 19–2 halftime lead, which held until just one minute shy of the fourth quarter.

Neither team held back. Tempers flared. Millions of television viewers saw Deion Sanders and Miami's Melvin Bratton exchange a running commentary. Sammie Smith showed why he was one of the nation's top running backs. The game was a tribute to both talent and intensity.

Miami tied the game in the fourth quarter, and then went up 26–19 on a sensational 73-yard touchdown play by Michael Irvin. Danny McManus fought back with an 83-yard scoring drive, and the game stood Miami 26, Seminoles 25, with less than a minute on the clock.

Bobby Bowden called Derek Schmidt for the extra point to tie, but McManus pressed for the 2-point conversion. "We've got the play and I can make the throw," he said. Bowden agreed and went for the win. Film appears to show McManus' feet slipping just half a step as he dropped back. Tight end Pat Carter was waiting in the back of the end zone, but the ball was slightly underthrown and the Hurricanes knocked it down.

Later, Bowden said that if he had to do it all over again, he would have kicked the extra point, but the fans and national media were unanimous in their praise of Bowden for going for the win. In fact, in later years some pundits credited that failed 2-point conversion with establishing the now-familiar brand of Florida State football: No holding back, no half measures. Go for the win.

Another vignette took place that same afternoon on October 3 in Athens, Tennessee, far away from Tallahassee. The Samford Bulldogs were playing Tennessee Wesleyan. It wasn't much of a game; Samford won 59–7. But head coach Terry Bowden kept a radio on the bench in care of his quarterback. The radio was tuned to the Florida State-Miami game, and when the Samford defense was on the field, Terry would run back and ask, "How's Daddy doing?"

Terry's quarterback was a young man who liked to wear his Seminole hat, and, in fact, was wearing it that afternoon while taking a breather on the bench and listening to the game. Someone took a picture and put it in the Samford yearbook. In 2007, the former twenty-year-old quarterback, who was now a forty-year-old offensive coordinator at LSU, accompanied Terry to Tallahassee. Terry Bowden met with Bobby Bowden, and that's how Jimbo Fisher came to FSU.

November 7 was a Saturday, which was Bobby Bowden's birthday. He was fifty-eight and headed north to Jordan-Hare Stadium in Auburn. We had beaten Auburn only once before; the two unranked teams had fought to a 24–3 Seminole victory in 1977. Seminole fans shared an unspoken affinity, and even an affection, for the Tigers. When Florida State was a young pup struggling to gain recognition and respect in the 1950s, Auburn was one of the few big-name teams willing to play us. The first contest was that 1954 game in Burt Reynolds' freshman year.

As proud and as powerful as Auburn was, their fans still were bound to chafe in the shadow of Alabama's glory. Seminoles well understood what it was like to be the second son in our own state.

By the end of October 1987, we had regained our No. 4 ranking after the Miami loss and had dispatched the next three opponents by an average score of 55–11. The Auburn Tigers were ranked No. 6 and were very happy to be at home defending an undefeated season record and visions of competing for the national title.

Auburn had every reason to be confident. The Tiger defense had yielded no more than 15 points to any opponent, except Tennessee, which had managed to score 20. And they were in the middle of a string of four straight SEC titles that would stretch from 1986 through 1989. But that day started badly for the Tigers and it never got better.

On the first play from scrimmage, an Auburn pass was caught, then fumbled and recovered by the Seminoles. Deion Sanders and other Seminole defenders feasted on the rattled Tiger offense, forcing five turnovers in the first half alone. Seminole running backs Sammie Smith, Dexter Carter, and Edgar Bennet ran over, around, and through the exhausted Tiger defenders. In the end, it was a four-touchdown victory, 34–6 FSU.

After Bobby Bowden set the Florida Gators back on their heels with four straight wins in the late 1970s, Florida had come back with a vengeance in the early '80s and pummeled the Seminoles six consecutive seasons. The most recent loss in 1986, in the driving rain, was especially galling as many fans believed it was due to a biased flag by an SEC referee who had called back Sammie Smith's winning touchdown run.

In the spring of 1987, I received a call from a loyal Seminole Booster in Pensacola. He was part of a cadre of Seminole lawyers who followed the outcome of recruiting battles with passionate obsession. "Where is Emmitt going?" he asked. I had to tell him that USA Today and Parade All-American National Player of the Year Emmitt Smith from Pensacola was going to sign with Florida. "Well," he sighed grimly, "we just lost four more years to the Gators."

And so it was at the end of November that we took our No. 3 ranking and marched to Gainesville to face our nemesis. Emmitt Smith, the freshman, had already rushed for more than 1,000 yards and he was waiting for us. The Gators were a talented team and, at home, they had nothing to lose. But our visiting Seminoles had everything to lose. The throat can tighten and doubt creeps in through the mind's back door.

In the first quarter, the score was 7–3 on an Emmitt Smith touchdown. Later, between Florida's blocking of an FSU punt and Emmitt Smith scoring his second touchdown to make it 14–3, CBS announcer Dick Vermeil made much of the fact that Florida had won six in a row and speculated that Florida coaches were thinking, "If we can keep the game close until the end, FSU will find a way to lose it." Derek Schmidt hit a 53-yard field goal as time ran out to make it 14–9 at the half.

Wherever doubt was creeping, it was ejected from the Seminole locker room at halftime. FSU had more talent and had the better team. It was time to make that fact clear. Emmitt Smith would not score again. In fact, no Florida player scored again as the Seminoles drove in two more touchdowns and topped each one with a successful 2-point conversion. Just a way of shaking off cobwebs from the Miami game?

In the fourth quarter, Vermeil admitted, "FSU has assumed control of this game." The second announcer responded that FSU had been in control of the game since the second quarter. Indeed. Florida gained 93 yards in the first, but wasn't able to muster even 80 total yards for the final three quarters. Dexter Carter had over 100 yards, and Sammie Smith had over 100 yards and was the Chevy MVP. Not only that, but this was Bobby Bowden's one hundredth victory as head coach of the Seminoles.

To appreciate the full breadth of Florida State's achievements in 1987, consider that the Seminoles and the Hurricanes had only one loss between them, and that by 1 point. The Hurricanes went on to win the 1987 national championship. Miami and FSU finished the year ranked No. 1 and No. 2, respectively. Auburn remained undefeated in the SEC after the Florida State game, shutting out Alabama in the Iron Bowl to earn their spot as the SEC champion in the Sugar Bowl.

University of Florida freshman Emmitt Smith did not start the first two games of 1987. But by the seventh game, he had broken 1,000 yards, the fastest any rookie college running back had ever reached that number. He was named SEC and National Freshman of the Year. Emmitt made his mark as one of the greatest running backs in Gator history, ninth in the Heisman balloting as a freshman, and the NFL's all-time leading rusher during his playing career … but he never beat the Seminoles. Not even once.

Magic in the Desert

Many Seminole fans did not understand the significance of the Fiesta Bowl victory. At the time there were considered to be only five major bowl games, all known as the New Year's Day bowls. FSU had played in the Fiesta Bowl before, and in two Orange Bowls, but we had never won; we had never been a New Year's Day bowl champion. Victory was a major benchmark for the program. In addition, what was surely one of the strangest episodes in college football that season, or perhaps any season, transpired in the second half of Florida State's victory over Nebraska in the Fiesta Bowl. It was magic.

Do you believe in magic? Neither do I. But I came close to embracing the supernatural on a dead hot afternoon in the desert toward the end of a football game on New Year's Day, 1988. That victory might have been the figurative big bang of the Seminole dynasty.

A word about the magician, Michael J. Markowski, a Florida State graduate whose movie-star looks and genius for numbers made him one of the young lions of Wall Street in the 1980s. He became a leading authority on crowdfunding and financial analytics, but on this first day of 1988 he was not yet famous.

On New Year's Day, 1988, the Fiesta Bowl game started early to accommodate the Eastern television markets, around ten thirty in the morning. The slow moving all-nighters among our Seminole fans piled into the stadium with squinting eyes. Heat ate through the morning shadows quickly, then sat motionless in the air like a giant melting marshmallow. Florida State was ranked No. 3, and Nebraska No. 5. Our perfect season had been marred only by the 1-point loss to Miami.

Nebraska started fast, jumping to a two-touchdown lead before some Seminoles had time to find their seats. Seminole defenders rose up. A Deion Sanders interception and a Paul McGowan fumble recovery both led to touchdowns. At halftime, the Seminoles were up 21–14.

Florida State had never won eleven games in a season; we had never won a major bowl game. The dynasty would be decorated with those achievements and more, year after year, for the next fourteen years. But at two o'clock in the afternoon in the desert on that day, the dynasty had not quite yet arrived.

Nebraska scored twice in the third quarter, pulling ahead 28–24. In the fourth quarter, the Cornhuskers' punishing runners drove the field, eating up the clock. My friends and I were sitting on the Seminole goal line. We could look right down that line and see the Nebraska players, confident, poised to score.

Cornhuskers were in control. The ball was on the 2-yard line. First and goal. Television time-out. It was during the long time-out that Michael J. Markowski rose to his feet and surveyed our despondent Seminole fans. His voice thundered, "Everyone! Listen to me!" Markowski raised his arms and turned roundabout to see the faces. "I want you to focus," he said. "Focus your eyes and your minds on that goal line. Concentrate as hard as you can. Stare at the ball and think … *fumble*."

"Trust me," he commanded. "Think. Fumble."

Hundreds of Seminoles did exactly as we were told. Why not? We lowered our eyes and stared at the goal line and the ball—the ball that was so close to that line. No one made a sound. We concentrated with all our might. "Fumble," we pleaded. "Fumble!"

The ball was snapped, helmets cracked against each other, and the ball disappeared. Noseguard O'Dell Haggins got underneath the big Nebraska center, pushing him up and into the Cornhusker running back. The impact jarred loose the ball, and Eric Hayes found it on the ground beneath his belly. Magic! It was the Seminole's football on the 2-yard line.

When Seminole cheers subsided, fans were left to make what they would of the strange event. Some were uncomfortable with the thought that they had played a direct role in conjuring up forces of the supernatural. On the other hand, no one suggested giving the ball back to Nebraska.

Quarterback Danny McManus took his team 82 yards down the field in 10 plays to the Nebraska 15. On a fourth down play, with only minutes left in the game, McManus threw a frozen rope to Ronald Lewis for the score and victory. Even before the long drive at the end, Danny McManus had set a new Fiesta Bowl passing record.

Florida State finished the year with our first major bowl victory and a No. 2 national ranking. In 1987, the Noles did not give up even a touchdown by punt, by kickoff, or by interception return. Home attendance was the best in history. It would be another fifteen years before the Seminoles ranked any lower than No. 4 at season's end.[*]

---

[*] Portions of this chapter's material were initially published in the *Florida State Times*.

1988 Season

"Lord, help my words to be gracious and tender today, for tomorrow I may have to eat them." I have tried to heed that advice most of my adult life. And it might be the takeaway from the 1988 season. That was the year we were the nation's preseason No. 1 team. Everyone picked FSU to win it all that year.

While Ann and I were traveling in Europe that summer, the team back in Tallahassee decided to make a rap video, much like the NFL's Chicago Bears had done during their great winning streak. I wish my players had asked me first. Still, they were brimming with confidence and just wanted to have some fun. I learned about it when I got back in town. It didn't sit well with me, yet I didn't want to hurt their morale going into the season. So I agreed not to nix it. That was a bad decision on my part. We got routed 31–0 by Miami in our opening game. The video inspired them more than us. Miami went on to win the national championship that year. We won all our remaining games and came in at No. 3.

"He who restrains his words has knowledge, and he who has a cool spirit is a man of understanding. Even a fool who keeps silent is considered wise; when he closes his lips, he is deemed intelligent" (Proverbs 17:27–28). Scripture is full of wisdom and good advice, is it not?

—Bobby Bowden

1988 Season

Began the season ranked No. 1
Ended the season ranked No. 3
Record 11–1
Sugar Bowl Champions

September 3, lost to Miami in the Orange Bowl 0–31

September 10, defeated Southern Mississippi in Tallahassee 49–13

September 17, defeated Clemson in Clemson 24–21

September 24, defeated Michigan State in Tallahassee 30–7

October 1, defeated Tulane in the Superdome 48–28

October 8, defeated Georgia Southern in Tallahassee 28–10

October 15, defeated East Carolina in Tallahassee 45–21

October 22, defeated Louisiana Tech in Tallahassee 66–3

November 5, defeated South Carolina in Columbia 59–0

November 12, defeated Virginia Tech in Tallahassee 41–14

November 26, defeated Florida in Tallahassee 52–17

January 2, 1989, defeated Auburn in the Sugar Bowl 13–7

Summer Dreams and Fantasies

In the summer of 1988, for the first time the Seminoles were ranked No. 1 in preseason. Almost all the myriad preseason football magazines, all the pundits, and all the fans envisioned a national championship for Florida State. This 1988 Seminole team seemed to have all the parts in place. Would FSU accelerate unblemished through a tough schedule and win the title? Seminole fans looked for signs and good omens, and found them everywhere that summer.

Seminole fans remembered a football game they enjoyed watching on December 19, 1988. They said it was probably like watching Florida State football live in the late 1940s, or perhaps the undefeated Seminole team of 1950. The college band pounded out "Injun" music and the crowd rocked and swayed to the beat of its own "war chant." There were pretty girls decorated in war paint, and strong young football players walking the sidelines in their garnet-and-gold uniforms. It was the Northeast Louisiana Indians vs. the Marshall University Thundering Herd for the national championship of Division I-AA. "Our" team won 43–42. Seminole fans were more than willing to embrace this as a sign of our own championship season to come.

"Voice of the Seminoles" Gene Deckerhoff was in Tampa in July for the annual Bobby Bowden-Galen Hall square-off at the Citrus Club. The room held four hundred people, half of them fans from FSU and half from Florida. Deckerhoff said, "I think Bobby got his first taste of it today. ... These Seminole fans were already designing their national championship rings. The attitude is kind of scary."

That summer, Sammie Smith quietly arranged his academic schedule so he could graduate at the end of fall. Sammie was married, had a child, and wanted to get on with his profession, which, at the moment, was running faster and better than anyone else in college football. Fullback Dayne Williams told how he was struggling in the weight room that spring when Sammie showed up. "We were all shocked," Dayne said with a laugh. "Sammie Smith ain't *seen* the weight room since 1985."

The players wanted to know what he was doing there. Why now? Sammie smiled and replied, "I can smell the money, baby. I can smell the money."

Seminole players were not shy about making their own predictions for the season. Joey Ionata predicted that O'Dell Haggins would lead the country in sacks in 1988, and Dedrick Dodge chimed in, "O'Dell is going to be the soul of the defense in 1988. ... He's the inspiration for the players." Ionata said he believed the team would be heavily run oriented and that Sammie Smith would carry over 20 times per game and win the Heisman Trophy.

Toughest game? Ionata predicted it would be South Carolina. He thought both FSU and the Gamecocks would be undefeated on November 5 and looking for that Orange Bowl berth. Dedrick Dodge predicted if the Seminoles beat Clemson, then no one else could stop FSU. This was not to discount any of the other opponents, you must understand. He just felt that it was our year.

Never reticent, Deion Sanders was recorded after the Fiesta Bowl as saying, "After college maybe I'll become a big Seminole Booster and buy an Emmitt Smith, just like they did, and put him in the Seminole backfield." Of course, Deion said it all with good humor and a huge winning smile.

The annual spring game had been less than inspiring. The defense disrupted the sluggish offense as it had done all spring. Even though the final score was 31–20, the game was so boring that one sportswriter speculated, "The MVP on Saturday may well have been the press box official who sliced some time off the clock."

Punting seemed to be of concern. "This year [1988] we may just not punt at all," said Bowden. With departure of the poised and experienced Danny McManus, quarterback duties would fall to either senior Chip Ferguson or junior Peter Tom Willis. Nothing much was settled in the spring game. Ferguson was sacked twice. Willis and freshman Casey Weldon were sacked six times between the two of them. Freshman Brad Johnson was only 5 for 13 but was never sacked, and a kid at the bottom of the roster named Charlie Ward did not play.

But the offense could run. One sportswriter said, "Between Sammie Smith and Dexter Carter, [Chris] Parker, [Keith] Ross, and [Victor] Floyd, the Seminoles alone have more good tailbacks than many conferences do!"

The summer rumor mill also had it that Galen Hall would be dismissed as Gator coach to be replaced by Steve Spurrier in 1989. Conventional wisdom was that Spurrier was the shoe-in, but things may not be as they seemed. Rumors from the Gator camp indicated that offensive coordinator Len Amadee was fighting for the job from the inside. Maybe the scariest candidate of all would be one who had close ties to Florida's athletic director, Bill Arnsbarger. That would be Howard Schnellenberger. One prominent Booster remarked, "I'd hate to have to hate Howard. We really like him."

The successes of 1987 had boosted Seminole spirits. In the spring of 1988, so many bothersome clouds from the previous six years seemed to have disappeared. There was growing sentiment that unreasonable expectations on the part of fans and supporters were actually healthy for an ambitious program.

If you learn to accept losing, however gracefully, then losing is what you're likely to experience more often than not. After the rising optimism created in 1987, fans became even more unwilling to play Cinderella, perpetually scrubbing floors for her ugly stepsisters (Auburn, Miami, and Florida?).

In the spring and summer of 1988, no one had yet thought in terms of a dynasty, but there was pride and optimism. What was once a young Florida State program had managed to assemble the credentials to join our big rivals at the same table.

Here's one bit of summer research that made Seminoles smile: Florida State began playing football in 1947, and since that time had gone to sixteen bowl games where our record was 7–7–2. Miami began playing in 1926, and had gone to fifteen bowl games, emerging with an overall record of 6–9. Florida claims to have begun playing for real in 1906, also posting a fifteen bowl record of 7–8. By the spring of 1988, we had gone to more bowls than the others and were the only one of the three programs with a non-losing record.

Miami and the Rap Video

The Miami game was originally scheduled to take place in midseason. CBS approached both teams about moving it to the season opener and scheduled the kickoff for nine o'clock at night—late night, in the Orange Bowl, with a new quarterback, against Miami. The optimists saw it as a great opportunity to take our revenge on a national stage for the previous year's 1-point loss.

Bobby and Ann Bowden had spent a month in Europe lecturing at armed forces clinics in Germany, then touring France and the Baltic states. Bowden loves the Autobahn, where there is no speed limit and the big cars routinely cruise at speeds beyond a hundred miles per hour. Bill McGrotha said Bowden told him, "I rented me the best BMW you ever saw. Finally, I had me a car just like Deion Sanders!"

McGrotha said that Bowden also mused on the upcoming season, noting that Bowden's record in September games had been solid: Miami in the Orange Bowl, then Southern Mississippi, then Clemson away, and then back to Tallahassee for Michigan State. "We'll be in it or we'll be out of it by the end of September," Bowden said.

I first heard about the rap video from my good friend Griffin Siegel, the writer and producer. It sounded funny and entertaining, and evidently the players thoroughly enjoyed the process. In fact, the players were greatly amused at O'Dell Haggin's attempts to perform. In their minds, O'Dell's shortcomings were that he listened exclusively to country music, and he could not sing at all. They began calling him "Merle" Haggins, after the country singer Merle Haggard, who *could* in fact sing. Deion was appropriately flamboyant for his part, while Peter Tom and Chip seemed a little stiff with the rap format, but they were troopers.

After I saw the production, I thought our team had better be as good as advertised, and I hoped that the wrong people didn't get a hold of this. I told Griff, "You know, this is a first-class production. But if we somehow lose this game, your video will get all the blame." We knew we were going to win. We were ranked No. 1 in the country, while Miami was No. 8, and we owed them for the previous year's loss.

Twenty years later, when he was head coach at Georgia, Mark Richt remembered the rap in an interview with the *Savannah Morning News*. "It was like the Chicago Bears' Super Bowl Shuffle," he said. "The Seminoles stole their shuffle and the Miami Hurricanes stole their defense. [Miami] was working on football while our guys are working on theatrics. Miami beat the tar out of us that day."

Bowden had evidently given approval for "some video" before he went to Europe, but he had not seen the final product. "I went over there [to Europe] on vacation," Bowden recalled, "and when I got back it was done." Had he known, he never would have allowed it. "When I saw that, I knew we'd get in trouble, but it was one of those things where it was too late to do anything about it."

As the story goes, a pirate copy of the video found its way to Miami coach Jimmy Johnson's desk. The night before our game, he took his team to the movies as per their routine. After the movie, the theater went dark and up on screen came the Seminole rap. They played it not once but many times, over and over again, until the Miami players were screaming and running through the aisles.

Very little went our way in that awful game. The only Seminole player whose nose or pride didn't get bloodied was Deion's. Miami's goal seemed to be to defeat every Seminole player at every position on the field. They kept throwing at Deion over and over as if breaking him would be their biggest prize. But Deion never lost a step; he never let any man beat him.

Given the history, being a Seminole fan in the old Orange Bowl was too often bad enough. Being there *that night* was the worst fan experience in a long litany of dreadful Orange Bowl stories. Postgame, the pervasive feeling was that while this was once considered to be a friendly rivalry, it was not very friendly anymore.

We dropped from No. 1 to No. 10, and some felt that was a charitable ranking. We opened at home against Southern Mississippi a week later, dispatching them with anger in a 49–13 win. Miami vaulted to the No. 1 ranking after our game, but later on lost it on a failed 2-point conversion (31–30) to Notre Dame in South Bend in the infamous "Catholics vs. Convicts" game.

Clemson and the Puntrooskie

Not much has been written about the toughness and the strength of leadership required to hold a team together after a disastrous game like Miami. Players have to trust the experience of their coaches, and in turn the coaches have to be able to depend on the character of their players. Character is probably the only virtue that might explain how a humiliated team and their coaches were able to recover and rise to win every game the rest of the way and finish in the nation's top 3. Strength of character has been Bobby Bowden's signature throughout his fifty-six-year coaching career.

Clemson was good. They were ranked No. 3 in the country, and the hungry Tigers looked upon us as prey. We were a damaged team with a top-10 ranking, an easy victory to be used to pad their strength of schedule. Clemson had won the national championship in 1981, and now another trophy was just within reach.

To some in those days, being a nonconference team in the South was the same as being from the wrong side of the tracks. Clemson was the star of the Atlanta Coast Conference, and to the Tigers, Florida State was on a par with East Carolina. But their deepest hatred was reserved for South Carolina, former member of the ACC and was then a Southern Independent power.

To the Tiger faithful, Gamecocks were pretenders who thought far too much of themselves and looked down their noses at everyone else. The Gamecocks were especially dismissive of those they considered to be wild hillbillies from the western mountains of the state and who persisted in believing that Clemson was a real college. Nor were the Tigers overly impressed with Bobby Bowden. They had their own folk hero in Coach Danny Ford. Ford was an inelegant, tobacco-chewing good ole Alabama boy who brought Clemson five ACC titles and an undefeated national championship season, and who made Bowden look like Cary Grant. It was into this roiling, festive atmosphere that our Seminole's arrived on September 17.

The weather was miserable—drizzling and cold. Our Seminoles wore all white with gold helmets, a smart-looking set. Clemson media describes their "Howard's Rock" tradition as "the most exciting twenty-five seconds of college football from a color and pageantry standpoint." After the opposing team entered Death Valley, Clemson players gathered at the top of the end zone hill around a white rock mounted on a pedestal. They jumped up and down, whipping the crowd into frenzy. Then a cannon boomed and the Clemson players streamed down the hill into the stadium. The show served to inflame Tiger fans and intimidate the opponent.

But on this day, the opponent was not intimidated. The crowd was becoming more excited. Chants of "It's great to hate Florida State" began drifting down from the stands. Clemson players clustered around the mounted white rock, jumping and gesturing to the crowd, waiting for the signal. But no one really noticed tackle Eric Hayes and some other Florida State players drifting over to the base of the hill. There the Seminoles stood as if they owned the ground. Hayes raised his hand to the Clemson players, and with exaggerated motion waved them down. "Come on down!" he yelled. "We're ready to play. What are you waiting for?"

The Clemson radio network announcer said, "I been doing Clemson games for thirty years and I ain't never seen nothing like this!" while Alan Schmadtke, writing for the *Ft. Lauderdale Sun-Sentinel*, said that Hayes "nearly incited a riot."

Whatever confidence the Noles may have lost in Miami seemed to have caught back up with them. Late in the third quarter, as Clemson prepared to punt, Deion Sanders gestured to the Clemson crowd and pointed toward the end zone. If that weren't enough, Sanders then turned to the Clemson bench and yelled, "This one's coming back." And it did—76 yards for a touchdown and the lead.

The Seminoles seemed to have Clemson's number as well as their enmity. Schmadtke said, "Nobody stirs the blood here [in Death Valley] as do the Seminoles. ... No school has a better record at Death Valley than Florida State."

With just a minute and a half left in the game, the score was tied 21–21. It was fourth down and the Seminoles were barely out of their own end zone. Clemson fans *knew* the Tigers would get the punt return and then march down the field to victory, sending those upstart Seminoles back to the flatlands in defeat.

What happened next is the stuff of legend. Sportscaster Beano Cook called it "the greatest play since *My Fair Lady*." Punter Tim Corlew leaped into the air and sold the fake, running back toward his own end zone as if in a desperate attempt to cover the muffed snap. Leroy Butler froze in his stance and did not move—he kept looking at the ball that no Tiger defender had yet spied.

Then Butler took off around the corner and down the sideline. He ran and ran until he was knocked out of bounds a few yards shy of the goal. Danny Ford jerked his arms back and forth, signaling to the officials the play was no good. Not just the fans but the officials themselves seemed stunned.

Officials placed the ball on the Clemson 1-yard line. The first-down play went nowhere and Bowden called time-out. Apparently, the officials did not realize that FSU had no time-outs remaining. But Danny Ford knew, and so he kept screaming after the officials to penalize FSU.

On second down, Dayne Williams bulled across the line for

the touchdown, but the scoreboard stayed at 24–24 while the officials tried to sort out the chaos. Both coaches were furious as the officials scrambled to make sense of what had happened. Ford convinced the officials to call the touchdown back. On either second down, or third down, depending on your point of view, Bowden sent Ritchie Andrews in to kick the 19-yard field goal with only thirty-two seconds left on the clock.

In the winner's locker room, Bowden was soaked to the bone but smiling, laughing, and entertaining the sports media. He bent over, rump in the air, with his hands back between his legs to illustrate what Butler saw. "Puntrooskie," Bowden said, savoring the name of the play. The media was delighted. Leroy Butler was named Chevrolet Player of the Game.

On Monday at the weekly Booster luncheon, Bowden was asked, "Did you think about running run one more play and maybe try to score a touchdown?" Bowden shook his head. "Absolutely not," he said. "I saw [Coach Ford] kept trying to get the attention of the officials and I thought, *We gotta kick this thing and get out of here.*"

Clemson was a cathartic game for the Seminoles. They would spend the next month boosting both their reputation and their rankings. The Clemson Tigers would lose only one more game that season, to North Carolina State in Raleigh. They were crowned ACC champions and went on to defeat Oklahoma in the Citrus Bowl. Danny Ford would get his full measure of revenge the following year in Tallahassee.

South Carolina, Florida, and Auburn

In 1988, senior offensive tackle Joey Ionata was accorded Honorable Mention All-American honors by the Associated Press. It was he who in the summer speculated that the game against South Carolina in Columbia on November 5 presented the greatest likelihood of upsetting FSU's season. Ionata was not the only Seminole who may have looked past Miami, but few could imagine the resounding victories to come later against the Gamecocks in Columbia and against the Gators at home.

South Carolina began 1988 as a top-20 team and worked their way up to the top-10 club on the basis of six straight wins to start the season. After a disheartening 0–34 shutout at the hands of Georgia Tech, they bounced back and gave head coach Joe Morrison his hundredth win with a victory over NC State.

Florida State was ranked No. 5 and South Carolina No. 15 when they met the night of November 5. With Seminole quarterback Chip Ferguson nursing a separated shoulder, Gene Deckerhoff announced, "Peter Tom Willis will be introduced to the college football world tonight." Willis introduced himself to the Gamecocks on the second play from scrimmage, throwing long to Terry Anthony for a 44-yard touchdown. With an 85 percent completion mark in the 59–0 rout, Willis was named Casio Player of the

Game. Receivers Bruce LaSane and Lawrence Dawsey had at least 100 yards each. Dawsey, with two touchdowns, was also the Seminoles' leading rusher.

On Friday before the game, the local USC student newspaper published a long piece on a local controversy over steroid use by athletes. The article began, "No athlete has tested positive for steroids since USC instituted its drug-testing program in April, officials said Wednesday." On Monday, a cruel message was delivered in a cartoon published in the local Columbia paper. It showed a scoreboard with the 0–59 score and the caption: "Absolute, incontrovertible proof that Gamecock players do not use steroids or enhancing drugs of any kind."

Two weeks later, the Gamecocks lost to rival Clemson and then lost to Indiana in the Liberty Bowl, finishing 8–4 on the year. Head coach Joe Morrison died of a heart attack at age fifty-one, less than two months after the bowl game.

The Gators were off to a great start, winning their first five games of the 1988 season and rising to a No. 14 national ranking. Then the roof caved in. The roof was Emmitt Smith, who injured his knee in a shocking loss to Memphis State. Smith was sidelined for a month, in which time Florida's offense did not score even a single touchdown in the next three losses.

But Florida was not without strength; their defense was solid. Coordinator Gary Darnell could count on talent and depth. Florida was a 17-point underdog when the Gators came to Tallahassee on December 2. Gator players were intense and emotional, determined to salvage their season with a monumental upset of the No. 5-ranked Seminoles. The blood was up. Gators were flagged for a personal foul on the kickoff. On the first play from scrimmage, Florida was flagged again.

Chip Ferguson was finally back behind center for the Seminoles, and Emmitt Smith was finally back at running back for the Gators. Smith carried 15 times with one touchdown to tie the game in the first quarter, but counted for less than 60 yards on the night. Sammie Smith carried 20 times for 109 yards and a touchdown. Eight different Seminoles scored.

By the end of the third quarter, the score was 45–10. I walked down to the north end zone to watch from the ground. As the clock wound down with what would be the final 52–17 score posted high above, I thought back five years ago to a similar game, with a similar score, but that time we were on the opposite end of it.

At the Monday Booster luncheon, one Booster asked Coach Bowden why he called off the dogs at the end. "Why didn't you keep scoring?" he asked. Coach laughed and shrugged, and said, "Well, I guess I figured we had enough to win." The crowd made clear its sentiment that we could have never scored enough points in that game.

Florida lost five of its last six games before finally defeating Illinois in the All-American Bowl. Against the Illini, Emmitt Smith ran for a 55-yard touchdown on the first play from scrimmage and was named the game's MVP. But he never beat the Seminoles.

The festive atmosphere of New Orleans and "Prime Time" Deion Sanders were the perfect match. Deion showed up for the Sugar Bowl via limousine and wearing a tuxedo. Most FSU fans loved Deion's passion and devotion to the Seminoles, but some found his antics offensive. On the Bobby Bowden Spring Tour that May, Coach Bowden ran into someone at one of the banquets who asked him, "Are you bothered at all by Deion's behavior?" and, "Why would you recruit another player like him?"

Coach raised his back up a little and snapped back, "Do you want to go 7-4 every year?" Then he softened. "Look, you have to have the players if you want to win. Deion may be playful, but he's a man of good character and popular with his teammates."

Later, while driving one of those long dark roads that skirts the swamps, down through the south central part of the state, Coach said he shouldn't have reacted so strongly to the question. "There's a lot people don't understand," he said. "Truth is, if Deion was a problem, we'd dismiss him. Every week we coaches choose a pair of captains for each game. If the players got to vote, they'd name Deion a captain every week. Every day in the spring he comes over to football practice after he's already done with baseball practice, and he goes out there and rounds up all our young defensive backs and works with them. No one in the program outworks Deion Sanders."

Bowden had already been quoted as saying that Deion was the greatest athlete he had ever coached, but he never really talked much about Sanders' leadership. "You know, all of it is an act," Bowden said. "The players know it. They're in on it; they enjoy it. He's a great player, but there are always other great players. I think some of what he does is just a way to set him apart, to grab the attention of the pros." We both laughed at the joke about someone telling Deion that there is no "I" in team. "Yeah," he replied, "but there are three in millionaire."

Seminole fans surged on to New Orleans to meet mighty Auburn in the Sugar Bowl. Gone was the trauma of the Miami loss. We were ranked No. 4 and Auburn No. 7. The game was promoted nationally as one of the best bowl matchups of the 1980s. Auburn was king of the SEC in the late 1980s, and Florida State was becoming a consistent, recognized national power.

The game turned out to be brutal defensive battle. Each team managed only one touchdown. The score at the half was 13–7, Seminoles. Neither team would score any points in the second half. Even so, Sammie Smith got 115 yards on 24 carries.

The dramatic "movie ending" came when Auburn put together a long final drive from their own goal. The Tigers converted three straight fourth downs to get to the Seminoles' 22-yard line. Florida State was flagged for interference on Auburn's first pass to the end zone.

Auburn was so close. With five seconds left, Auburn passed to their receiver standing just inside the goal line. Deion flashed across from the left and took the ball away. Gene Deckerhoff shouted, "Prime Time will not let them in!" It was done.

Auburn's regular season record was 10–1, with just a 1-point loss to LSU. They were the SEC champions—again. They were ranked No. 7 coming into New Orleans, and they finished the year with the same rank. The Seminoles rose to No. 3 in the final standings. The first two years of the dynasty were complete.

1989 Season

The heat was sweltering in August as we prepared for the '89 season. Anyone who lives in the Deep South understands how one can almost suffocate in the heavy, humid days of August. I normally spent hours outdoors during June and July just to keep myself acclimated for what was coming. Once preseason camp started, our players fought through cramps, dehydration, and exhaustion. They paid the price to be ready for our season opener. We had a good team and a proven game plan. We knew how to win. Sacrifices were necessary. No one complained. And when camp ended, we all felt ready.

Then the worst happened. We lost our opening game to Southern Mississippi. Then we lost our second game to Clemson. Fortunately for us, however, our players didn't wilt. They didn't quit or throw away all hope. Instead, they bowed up and won all their remaining games, beat Nebraska in the Fiesta Bowl, and ended with a No. 3 national ranking. I'm proud of the indefatigable strength they displayed.

"The strongest steel is forged in the hottest fire." I don't know where that quote originated, but I've heard it all my life. We are wise to remind ourselves of it during difficult seasons in life. It points to a deeper and more promising spiritual truth: "For I know the plans I have for you, says the LORD, plans for welfare and not for evil, to give you a future and a hope" (Jeremiah 29:11).

—Bobby Bowden

1989 Season

Began the season ranked No. 6
Ended the season ranked No. 3
Record 10–2
Fiesta Bowl Champions

September 2, lost to Southern Mississippi in Jacksonville 26–30

September 9, lost to Clemson in Tallahassee 23–34

September 16, defeated LSU in Baton Rouge 31–21

September 23, defeated Tulane in Tallahassee 59–9

October 7, defeated Syracuse in the Carrier Dome 41–10

October 14, defeated Virginia Tech in Blacksburg 41–7

October 21, defeated Auburn in Tallahassee 22–14

October 28, defeated Miami in Tallahassee 24–10

November 4, defeated South Carolina in Tallahassee 35–10

November 18, defeated Memphis State in Tallahassee 57–20

December 2, defeated Florida in Gainesville 24–17

January 1, 1990, defeated Nebraska in the Fiesta Bowl 41–17

A Dreadful Beginning

Whatever dreams there had been of a dynasty seemed to evaporate in the smoke of two losses in the first two games of the season. It wasn't until midway through the schedule that the Seminoles were ranked at all, and then it was No. 25, just prior to the Syracuse game in October. No one who saw FSU drop two losses to start the year would have imagined that the Seminoles would end 1989 in triumph as Fiesta Bowl champions with a No. 3 national ranking. It was to be a rocky but exhilarating journey.

I may have been exposed to more intense heat, but I couldn't recall when. September 2, 1989, during the Gator Bowl on the banks of the St. Johns River in Jacksonville, was the hottest game I had ever experienced. It didn't take long for fans to realize that the heat was dangerous. A routine visit to concessions meant stepping over rows of people lying on the ground in the shadows beneath the stadium. It reminded me of that scene in the train yard with massive numbers of wounded in *Gone with the Wind*.

The Jacksonville Sports Authority had bought the home game from Southern Mississippi and television had scheduled the kick-off for noon. When the USM Golden Eagle players ran out for warm-ups, we saw they were wearing black uniforms and black helmets. Seminole fans assumed the game was as good as over. Heat would exhaust the black-clad Southerners who would collapse in heaps before halftime.

We came into Jacksonville ranked No. 6. Southern, of course, was unranked. We had never heard of quarterback Brett Favre before. USM was up 17–10 at the half, but the Seminoles seemed to take control in the third quarter. Peter Tom Willis combined with Lawrence Dawsey and Dexter Carter for two touchdowns and the defense shut out the Southerners. It all came down to the end. Behind 23–26, with only twenty-three seconds left in the game, Favre rolled left and found his receiver in the end zone. Our Seminoles lost 26–30.

Brett Favre was recruited to USM as a defensive back but he insisted on playing quarterback. Consequently, coaches designated him the seventh-string quarterback on the Southern depth chart. By the third game, Favre was the starter. He started ten games as a freshman, winning six of those games. Later an All-Pro and a Super Bowl Champion, upon his retirement in 2011 Favre held the all-time NFL records in passing yards and passing touchdowns.

In 1990, USM's Curley Hallman was hired to be the head coach at LSU. On a cold, late October night in 1991, in a driving rain storm in Baton Rouge, the No. 1-ranked Seminoles defeated Hallman's team 27–16. However, as many as six FSU players were knocked out of the game for at least one series, including quarterback Casey Weldon. It is firmly believed the appalling number of injuries to FSU players in that game directly contributed to back-to-back losses to Miami and Florida at the end of the 1991 season.

Hallman is the only LSU coach never to have posted a winning season or gone to a bowl game. He was fired midway through the 1994 season but was allowed to coach throughout the rest of the year. His last home game at LSU was a loss to Southern Mississippi.

After our loss to USM in Jacksonville, there was speculation among coaches that every available effort, every preparation by Southern Mississippi in the spring and preseason, had been devoted solely to winning this one game. The evidence cited was that Favre and USM lost their next four games and were only 6–5 on the season. But that made no difference. By the time we got back to Tallahassee, our ranking had dropped to No. 16. A week later, we'd be facing No. 10 Clemson at home.

Danny Ford and the Clemson faithful could not wait to get to Tallahassee. Somewhere around eighty thousand Tigers—loud, sassy, and looking for payback for Puntrooskie—clambered into Doak Campbell Stadium on Saturday night. It still counts as the largest number of Clemson fans ever to attend a game in Tallahassee. In fact, it still ranks as the largest fan contingent from any ACC school ever to visit Tallahassee.

Clemson piled it on from the beginning. A Tiger ran the kick-off back to midfield, and their big runners plowed into the end zone on the first drive. Clemson went up quickly, 28–10 at the half. Dexter Carter's only touchdown of the half came with less than two minutes left.

Our Seminoles seemed to get their footing in the second half, however. Running backs Paul Moore and Chris Parker scored a touchdown each. With minutes left, the Clemson band mocked the "war chant" and delighted Tiger fans joined in full throat. There were ten seconds left on the clock when Casey Weldon scrambled out of the pocket, then threw all the way across the field to Chris Parker for a touchdown. The final score was Clemson 34, FSU 23.[*]

As the crowd dispersed across Doak Campbell Stadium, I saw one figure wearing an orange coach's shirt standing in the middle of the darkening field, his head tilted, looking all around and up into the stands. It took me a moment to realize I recognized him. It was Rick Stockstill, Coach Bowden's three-year letterman quarterback and captain of the 1981 Seminoles. Now quarterback coach for the Clemson Tigers, Stockstill likely had not been back to Tallahassee since his playing days. He stood alone at midfield, searching the sweep of the stands, drinking in all the memories of

---

[*] Clemson finished the year 10–2 and defeated West Virginia in the Gator Bowl. That would be Danny Ford's last game as head coach of the Tigers.

those Seminole Saturday nights when his world was young.

Rick Stockstill had been Bowden's senior quarterback during the murderous "Octoberfest" schedule in 1981—back-to-back road games in October against Nebraska, Ohio State, Notre Dame, Pitt, and LSU. The most improbable result was the fact that the Seminoles won three of those games, defeating Ohio State, Notre Dame, and LSU.

After that season, at the annual football awards banquet in January, more than a thousand Seminole fans arose and thundered applause as Stockstill approached the stage. He seemed overcome with emotion, barely able to speak. "I'm sorry about six and five," he said. The crowd embraced him with their voices to say they were proud of him: *You're one of us, and you always will be.*

The Fooler from Paskagooler
and Other Stories

I t is almost impossible to know how to pronounce the name of this small Mississippi coastal town. Its spelled Pascagoula, but the locals pronounce it Papsa-goola. And Terrell Buckley added a new twist to the name. Buckley came to FSU with the 1989 freshman class, touted as one of the elite cornerbacks in the nation. He didn't disappoint. His senior year in high school he had intercepted ten passes and retuned seven for touchdowns. He had also collected thirty interceptions altogether and was an astonishingly prolific return man.

After the Clemson loss, our unranked Seminoles dispatched LSU and Tulane by a combined score of 90–30. Coach Bowden was not in a charitable frame of mind. After the Seminole victory at LSU, Coach Bowden praised the play of quarterback Peter Tom Willis, but with a caveat. He said, "Peter Tom has confidence. He made plays we haven't even practiced yet." Bowden was making a joking reference to his 1982 quarterback Kelly Lowrey, who also had a mind of his own. Bowden said, "I'd send plays in to Kelly, and he'd just wave me off."

By October 7, we had climbed back into the top 25 and headed to Syracuse, New York, where the No. 17-ranked Orangemen boasted a sixteen-game home winning streak in the Carrier Dome. Syracuse players were huge—big Northern kids who were brutal on defense. But the Seminoles were faster and much quicker. Our leading runner, Dexter Carter, carried 14 times for 83 hard-fought yards.

In the third quarter, Syracuse punted to freshman Terrell Buckley, who was standing alone on the 30. He caught the ball and stood, relaxed as if waiting for the official to come get the ball. The instant the Orange players seemed to pull up, Buckley took off running. He had given no fair catch signal and he sliced through the shocked Orangemen for a 70-yard touchdown. Three minutes later, Leroy Butler scored on an 88-yard interception return. The 41–10 final was Syracuse's worst home loss in seven years. Buckley said he didn't tell the coaches what he planned to do. He had done the same thing once in high school back in Mississippi. And so Gene Deckerhoff tagged him "the Fooler from Paskagooler."

On the Sunday afternoon *Coach's Show*, Syracuse coach Dick MacPherson said, "Those Florida State boys, they can strut. Oh, how they can really strut." It didn't sound like a compliment. But Buckley wasn't the only interesting character in 1989. The landscape of college football was richly adorned with personalities.

The Gators won big at Memphis State in September, avenging the loss from the previous year. Before the game, a sportswriter from the *Florida Times-Union*, interviewing Memphis Tigers' quarterback Tim Jones, asked him about the Gators' revenge motive. "Don't get them fired up on me!" said Jones. "I don't want to get hurt." *The Dallas Morning News* noted this: "After their 31–30 victory over the University of Connecticut, SMU fans tried, and failed, to tear down the goal posts."

In October, Ole Miss was in New Orleans to play Tulane. Somehow most of the offensive line became trapped in an elevator for an hour at the Hyatt Regency. A woman representing a travel agency was also on the elevator. One giant lineman reassured her, saying, "Coach Wickline will open the doors, if he wants us."

The 1989 Heisman Trophy was awarded to Houston quarterback Andre Ware. The Houston "Run & Shoot" offense was not universally respected. A *Sports Illustrated* writer opined that what was setting offensive records at the college level was viewed with contempt by the pros.

> The run and shoot, as all pro football fans are aware, is a half-baked backyard fire drill that features a wild-eyed scrambling quarterback tossing the ball constantly to a gang of pygmy receivers scurrying over the turf like ants on a honey spill. The attack pops up occasionally in the lower reaches of the football world, and flourishes there briefly, like a fungus, until its practitioners play decent teams, or until its coaches leave to become shoe reps. ... The run and shoot is the kind of thing pro coaches like to talk about over a beer or two, the way they talk about hang gliding or hair transplants—things that are intriguing to virile, aging men, but which those men would never be involved with.

After the Pitt Panthers lost badly to Notre Dame and Miami on back-to-back weekends, a Hurricane columnist asked Pittsburg players to compare the two teams. They declined. Gene Collier, writer for the *Pittsburg Press*, had the best answer: "It's like asking roadkill to distinguish between the front axle and the back axle."

During the 1989 season, the Associated Press discovered Edward J. Story, Notre Dame's oldest living alumnus at age one hundred. Did he have a secret to longevity? "I don't smoke, drink, gamble, chew, or run around," Story said with a sigh. "You wouldn't think I've had much fun and the truth is I sure haven't."

According to a story in the *Toledo Blade*, Dr. Allen Bohl, who was the athletic director at Toledo, announced the firing of his football coach Dan Simrell. Reaching for a historical allusion to put the decision into perspective, Dr. Bohl said, "There are many trying days in the life of an individual. Like when Truman decided to drop the bomb and take the lives of thousands of people."

The Stretch Run

By mid-October, Florida State was riding down the stretch of the third year of the dynasty. Old rivals were being vanquished like never before. But the schedule ahead was studded with a mine-field of top-10 teams like Miami, Auburn, and Nebraska, plus rival Florida. Given the early losses, it seemed unlikely that the Noles could finish the year with an unblemished record.

Auburn quarterback Reggie Slack's final pass in the Sugar Bowl had been intercepted by Deion Sanders. Now Slack and his teammates were on their way to Tallahassee for the rematch. Florida State at No. 9 vs. Auburn at No. 11 was being billed as one of the season's best matchups. Both Auburn and FSU were teams off to slow starts in 1989, but by midseason each team seemed to be emerging back out into the light. For Auburn and Slack, the motive was revenge for the Sugar Bowl loss. For Bobby Bowden, the Auburn game was a chance to continue to build momentum toward a signature bowl berth.

Edgar Bennet took control by shocking Auburn with a pair of touchdowns in the first half. Reggie Slack suffered five sacks in the first half; the Tiger offense was held to -8 total yards. Auburn outscored the Noles 11–3 in the second half. A Seminole fumble deep inside Auburn territory gave the Tigers a chance to drive the field and win. It was much the same scenario as the Sugar Bowl the year before.

This time, however, with Auburn 18 yards away from victory, Seminole linebacker Shelton Thompson tackled Slack at the 11-yard line as time ran out. The final score was 22–14, FSU. The 1989 victory evened Bowden's record against Auburn at 4–4 since his arrival in Tallahassee in 1976.

After years of cajoling and dealing, in order to get the annual game moved from Birmingham, Auburn coach Pat Dye and Tiger fans were ecstatic to finally welcome rival Alabama to Jordan-Hare Stadium. They beat No. 2-ranked Alabama at home, then went on to defeat Ohio State in the Hall of Fame Bowl, earning a No. 6 final ranking.

Bill McGrotha wrote that prior to being named Miami's starting quarterback, Gino Torretta said, "I'm just worried about beating Florida State. ... I'm anxious to go to Tallahassee, wherever that is, and have a good time and execute the offense." Gino Torretta's team was ranked No. 2 on that day; Florida State was ranked No. 6. Miami scored 10 in the first quarter and were shut out for the remainder of the game. Florida State never trailed in the 24–10 victory.

Linebacker Kirk Carruthers had a career high sixteen tackles against Miami. Dexter Carter had 21 carries for 142 yards. It was Miami's only loss of the year. But Miami recovered its No. 2 ranking with their victory over Notre Dame at season's end. And after upending Alabama in the Sugar Bowl, Miami was named 1989 national champion by both major polls.

A ranking service called the Billingsley Report handed the 1989 national championship to Florida State based on their victory over 11-1 Miami. The Billingsley Report was legit, being recognized by the NCAA since 1996 as one of the selectors of historic national champions. In 1999, the Billingsley Report became one of the seven mathematical formulae used to determine the Bowl Championship Series (BCS) rankings. It is interesting to note that Mr. Richard Billingsley is a retired minister.

Florida was unranked when we met on December 2 in Gaines-ville, but rankings are never a consideration when the Seminoles and Gators face off. Galen Hall was the Gator head coach in Sep-tember, but by the time the Seminoles arrived, Hall had been forced to resign midseason and was replaced by defensive coordi-nator Gary Darnell. Penn State's Joe Paterno stood up for his old assistant coach, and in truth it did not seem that the accusations against Hall amounted to a great deal. The speculation was that the NCAA had had enough of the earlier Charley Pell scandals and Florida would be punished again just on general principle. Florida's season record was 7–5, including a loss to Washington in California's Freedom Bowl.

Gary Darnell was an outstanding career defensive coordinator and lobbied hard to be considered for the permanent position as Gator head coach. But powerful forces had been moving behind the scenes for some time. Steve Spurrier was announced on Janu-ary 1, and the first true golden era for Gator football commenced immediately. In twelve seasons, Spurrier brought home six SEC titles and a national championship, along with a prickly personal-ity and a rivalry with Bobby Bowden that generated some of the most memorable stories in college football lore.

The game itself was tied 10–10 at the half. Florida State pulled away in the second half with touchdowns by Bruce LaSane and tight end Dave Roberts. LaSane and Roberts each bulled their way across the goal line in the grasp of three Gator defenders. Dexter Carter carried 21 times for 100 yards, while Emmitt Smith carried 30 times for 153 yards and a touchdown in his final game against Florida State.

The Fiesta Bowl (vs. Nebraska) was a matchup of No. 5 against No. 6. The scene was almost identical to the Fiesta Bowl two years previously, with the same teams matching No. 3 and No. 5. Dex-ter Carter was again the Seminole workhorse on the ground with 13 carries for 72 yards. However, most of the damage inflicted by

Florida State was from the air. Eight Seminole receivers caught passes in that game.

Nebraska got on the board first—and early. Then the Seminoles exploded in the second quarter. Terry Anthony, Reggie Johnson, and Dexter Carter all scored touchdowns. Ron Lewis caught five passes for 105 yards. Peter Tom Willis threw for five touchdowns and 422 yards on the night.

What had been a dreadful start with two consecutive losses on the season ended with the Seminoles ranked No. 3. The dynasty's third year was complete. FSU had finished three seasons ranked No. 2, No. 3, and No. 3 in a row.

1990 Season

This was the least experienced team I fielded during the dynasty years. They were young. Too few were sufficiently battle tested. Rough edges needed to be honed, and sharp edges needed to be properly trained. Was this team talented? Yes. But talent alone is rarely enough.

Steve Spurrier had just arrived as Florida's new head coach. He was an offensive wizard who knew how to exploit weaknesses. Other tough games also were on the schedule. As a coach, you learn to live with a certain measure of anxiety. This year I hoped my players had enough "heart" to make up for their lack of experience. Heart is not just a muscle in the body or an organ that pumps blood; *heart* also arises from deep within the soul, a resolute determination to succeed despite the odds. From this wellspring of strength arises the acclamation, "I can … I will … I must." Scripture claims that "out of the heart flow the springs of life" (see Proverbs 4:23). This truth is played out repeatedly on the battlefields of life. My 1990 squad was an example of it.

We won ten games that year, including victories over Virginia Tech, LSU, South Carolina, Florida, and Penn State. When the smoke cleared, my players were recognized as one of the four best teams in the country. They played with the heart of a champion.

—Bobby Bowden

1990 Season

Began the season ranked No. 3
Ended the season ranked No. 4
Record 10–2
Blockbuster Bowl Champions

September 8, defeated East Carolina in Tallahassee 45–24

September 15, defeated Georgia Southern in Tallahassee 48–6

September 22, defeated Tulane in New Orleans 31–13

September 29, defeated Virginia Tech in Tallahassee 39–28

October 6, lost to Miami in Miami 22–31

October 20, lost to Auburn in Auburn 17–20

October 27, defeated LSU in Tallahassee 42–3

November 3, defeated South Carolina in Columbia 41–10

November 10, defeated Cincinnati in Tallahassee 70–21

November 17, defeated Memphis State 35–3

December 1, defeated Florida in Tallahassee 45–30

December 29, defeated Penn State in the Blockbuster Bowl 24–17

The Decision:
Should FSU Join a Conference?

It was the year of the great realignment in college football. Penn State had joined the Big Ten and Arkansas abandoned the failing Southwest Conference for the SEC. Money from television contracts pushed established conferences to cultivate the most attractive independents. Weak leagues scrambled to lock in their strongest members and to build strength through expansion. At the end of the day, Notre Dame would remain the nation's only major Independent. In this fourth year of the dynasty, Florida State was a princess with many suitors.

"May you live in interesting times," is an ancient Chinese curse. Florida State's decision on whether or not to join a conference was supposed to be announced before the end of September. Probably the best news for FSU fans of that time had to do with the way in which the final decision was being reached.

There were four options from which to choose: remain Independent, join the Metro, the SEC, or the ACC. And there was a strong suspicion that if one could make Bernie Sliger, Bob Goin, and Bobby Bowden reveal their personal preferences, one would get three different answers. That difference probably also reflected the feelings of our thousands of fans and supporters. If the mail was any indicator, each of those four options enjoyed its own passionate following.

In an atmosphere where there was no clear consensus, the opportunity existed for one or more special interests to try to muscle their way to the front of the line. But that was not happening at Florida State. It was reassuring to watch the decision-making process get underway. All those involved (and that included faculty, administrators, athletic department leaders, and key alumni) were moving together carefully and deliberately to reach the most intelligent solution, and the one which would benefit the university the most.

What complicated things was that all the targets were moving. With major conference realignments and what appeared to be a major shift in the bowls, it would no longer be assumed that the 10–1 team would always get the nod for a New Year's Day bowl over an 8–3 team. What may have been more significant than Penn State joining the Big Ten was the fact that at the same time the Nittany Lions dropped their series with Notre Dame. Was the premier Independent going to have trouble putting together a quality schedule in the future? If so, what did that mean for others who choose to remain Independent?

No doubt the Seminoles' reputation and recruiting had gained from playing a national schedule against high-profile opponents. What could we lose by giving that up? And if the decision was to join a conference, then which one? Did we choose the one that allowed us to keep a bigger piece of the pie but didn't put more fans in the stadium, or did we go with the one that takes more of our money but gave us a schedule that was guaranteed to fill the house? It was dangerous ground. But we were certain that whatever the decision, there would be negative consequences.

While there was much for Florida State to gain, there was also much for Florida State to lose. Those most closely involved in the decision were sobered by that realization. That's why all Boosters were glad that people of integrity and good judgment, who would not put their personal leanings ahead of the interests of the university, would not allow politics to taint the choice. To get an idea of what was at stake, let's take a look at the negative.

There were advantages to remaining an Independent. But there were not many big-time high-profile national Independents, and with only a few more defections we could have found ourselves without influence in a new bowl structure. As conferences grew, teams would have fewer scheduling options. Could we count on Auburn or LSU or Clemson ever coming back to Tallahassee?

There were advantages to an expanded Metro-Eastern Seaboard League too. But the major conferences were social and political alliances, as well as athletic ones. Could a loose-knit assemblage put together for television have any real staying power? Was the cultural gulf between North and South too great to foster fan loyalty and long-term rivalries? What happened if the league broke up in a year or two and we had already burned our bridges?

There were also advantages to joining the Southeastern Conference. But we would enter this powerful league with one of the smallest athletic budgets in the conference, no seniority, and minimal political influence. The stands would be packed, but there would be no more back-to-back Ohio State/Notre Dame road wins, no more coming home the week after beating Nebraska and then whipping Pitt.

There were also advantages to joining the Atlantic Coast Conference. But with the exception of Clemson, ACC fans were used to driving thirty minutes or so to an "away" game. Great basketball package, but how many nationally televised football games could we count on against ACC opponents? Round-ball recruiting would be helped, but how about football recruiting?

The University of Miami would seem to be a key factor in how it all turned out for us, just as we were a key factor in how it turned out for them. Our two schools acting together could generate extraordinary benefits for both. But what if, say, Florida State joined the ACC and Miami was then quickly snapped up by the SEC? Could FSU and Georgia Tech, isolated in the Deep South interior, continue to recruit as effectively as before? One of our Orlando Boosters considered that scenario and wrote, "If that happens, you'll never see the word Seminole again in any newspaper south of Lake City."

Two key points emerged from all of this. First, the majority of us needed to be grateful that we were not the ones responsible for making that decision. There was simply no reliable map anymore that could tell us what was going to happen, or even what was likely to happen. As one of our athletic department officials said, "Ten years from now, our names are going to be hanging on the wall ... or our heads." We needed to be assured that great care was being taken, that nothing was being done quickly, and that the best interests of our university were being placed ahead of all other considerations.

The second point was that, in spite of the negatives, the potential benefits for Florida State were enormous. We seemed to have become the most attractive and desired entity at precisely the right time. Coach Bowden always said he'd rather be lucky than good. Luck and excellence both appeared to be in Florida State's corner. What was behind door number one? We didn't know. It could be the sports car and the world cruise, or it could be the year's supply of Alpo. But we had some pretty smart players who were giving those doors a long, close look before opening one.

It was going to be interesting indeed.[*]

---

[*] Much of this chapter's material was initially published in the *Report to Boosters* (September 1990).

"You'll Pay, FSU! You'll Pay!"

Fallout from the decision to join the ACC was immediate. A sort of gentlemen's agreement had been in place for a while between FSU and the SEC. The understanding was that if the invitation was offered, then we would accept. But when it finally became in the SEC's best interests to bring the Seminoles under their wing (or, under their thumb some said), the ACC was already standing on the front porch with a bouquet of flowers.

Think back for a moment to the 1989 season Syracuse game. Syracuse's offensive linemen were rated the best in the country. None were bigger and none were stronger. But the Seminoles were faster. Time after time, the Seminole's sleek defensive linemen slipped by those lumbering Syracuse giants to register a record number of sacks. Frustrated and losing, they hurled challenges at Eric Hayes and O'Dell Haggins. "You're wimps!" they said. "You're afraid to lock up with us, man to man."

After a particularly vigorous exchange, Eric Hayes responded, "Look, pal, I'm not interested in locking up with you. I want your quarterback!"

We had read the reactions of the Southeastern Conference the previous few weeks. A lot of it reminded me of the Syracuse linemen. One got the impression that the SEC felt insulted that FSU didn't accept their ring when it was finally offered. They shouldn't have felt that way, for surely no insult was intended. There was no doubt that some of the best football in the country was played in the SEC. Likewise, there was no doubt that Florida State's finances and fan support were both football driven. So why didn't the football school join the football conference?

Here's the most straightforward answer to that question: After looking carefully at all the information and all the variables, FSU officials determined that Seminole football would be helped more by joining the ACC rather than by remaining Independent or by joining the SEC. Football home-game attendance was one factor, and it was unlikely that ACC fans would travel in numbers to Tallahassee, as SEC fans would. But let's not sell ourselves short: Two of the largest crowds in Doak Campbell Stadium history came for games against East Carolina and Georgia Southern earlier that fall. And those were Florida State fans, not opponents.

Football would be helped. Don't read too much into the charges that FSU took the easy route. The Seminoles had never ducked a tough schedule or dropped a series because the opponent was too good. Competition in the SEC was such that a team's nonconference schedule had to include the likes of say, Montana State and Akron. With an ACC schedule, it was still possible for FSU to play national series games against schools like Notre Dame, Michigan, and Ohio State, as well as high-profile traditional rivals like Miami, Auburn, and Florida.

One of the things that appealed so strongly to FSU coaches, players, and fans was the high level of visibility we gained from playing all those national "names" during the 1980s. Plainly, the very thing that built our reputation, the very thing that made us so attractive to the SEC, was the very thing we would have lost upon joining the Southeastern Conference.

Football recruiting would be helped too. With the ACC's comprehensive television package, recruits would be exposed to a television market that extended from New York to Atlanta to Miami. Bill McGrotha pointed out that no SEC team would play

Miami in 1990. In fact, Florida State was the only team from the Deep South that would. That went for 1991 as well. It could have been 1995 before the Seminoles played a full ACC schedule, but 1990's recruits would benefit immediately in three ways.

First, they would be eligible at some point to compete for All-Conference honors. Second, they would likely be on television more, with concentrated exposure in the East where so many of the national sportswriters live. Third, an academic degree from Florida State would become more valuable simply because of FSU's association with the nation's most prestigious collection of academic institutions playing Division I football.

In the end, joining the ACC was a decision made exclusively by the Florida State family. Past Booster chairman Ken Cashin said, "This has been the most open, the most discussed issue I've seen at this university in years." And faculty leader Dr. Leo Sandon remarked, "There doesn't seem to have been much lobbying at all. … Over a period of time, all the parties seemed to come separately to the same conclusion."

There was no doubt that we were in for a rough time from our SEC friends. The day of the ACC announcement, the Birmingham newspaper shrieked like a banshee, promising, in effect, "You'll pay, FSU. You'll pay!" Think of it like boxing. The objective is to win the title, but before you choose that career, before you ever climb into the ring, you have to accept the knowledge that even when you beat an opponent, you're going to take a pounding.

We were heavyweights. And we were championship contenders. From that point on, we could expect a few punches thrown after the bell, and we could take some hits below the belt. But really and truly, wasn't that the way it had been for the previous forty-three years?[*]

---

[*] Much of this chapter's material was initially published in the *Report to Boosters* (October 1990).

We Are What We Are

There was an importance of Seminole football to the greater mission of our university. In 1990, much publicity and discussion was devoted to the question of conference affiliation. The Seminole Boosters organization was moving ahead with major construction on University Center, a visionary project that demanded much in the way of university attention and resources. Some voices complained about too much emphasis being placed on athletics. The case had to be made for the practical value of a winning collegiate athletics program.

"I'm just trying to improve myself," was the boxer's answer, his face bloody and swollen nearly beyond recognition. He had been asked why he boxed and he had answered honestly. Boxing was his way out, and it was his way up. Winning in the ring was a way of making enough money to achieve his dreams for a better life. And those who looked down their nose at the boxer more than likely had their own paths to the good life eased by privilege from the beginning.

It was honest to say that Florida State played Division I athletics because it was trying to better itself. If the essence of a university is the faculty, then the lifeblood of a university is its students. Better students are attracted by excellent faculty; better students are attracted by excellent facilities and programs; and, yes, better students—great numbers of them, in fact—are attracted by the aura of a successful big-time athletic program. Perhaps that ought not to be true, but the truth cares little for opinions.

It took money to improve our university. Florida State relied more than most on the generosity and support of alumni. It would have been swell if we could have raised twenty-five-million dollars a year for academics from foundations and corporations, but we were not to that point yet. Collegiate athletics touched a chord in the hearts of alumni, and it was a fact that many who began by donating to the athletic program quickly become contributors to the academic side as well.

We were what we were. We were a very good state university trying to become a great one. There was much in our favor. For one thing, Florida State University had been, throughout its relatively brief history, extraordinarily lucky. The average college president is in the office less than five years. For fifteen years, we had a president with impeccable academic credentials, Bernie Sliger, who knew that a whole lot of money for the classroom could be found on the way through the locker room. For fifteen years we had a football coach, Bobby Bowden, who had won and won and won with grace, good humor, and integrity. For fifteen years we had a CEO of the Seminole Boosters, Andy Miller, whose drive and vision brought us from a local pass-the-hat outfit to become the second largest collegiate Booster organization in America.

Bowden, Sliger, and Miller were only three, but there were many more: faculty, administrators, and volunteers. In 1989, over four hundred volunteers participated as fundraisers for the Boosters. The National Booster Chairman was elected annually, and that office had been held by a series of visionary, intensely dedicated volunteers.

Bobby Bowden's signature was winning with integrity, and he defined the standard for all coaches in all sports at FSU. The October 30 *Orlando Sentinel* reported that "Florida State University has the best graduation rates for football players during the three years the rates have been published." Also FSU ranked highest among all recruited female athletes, and second only to Central Florida among all recruited male athletes.

Florida State became a school of choice. Some folks deplored the fact that a winning athletic program attracted rafts of students with ever higher SAT scores. But there it was. At Florida State, we used our athletic success to help fuel other engines within the university. We didn't care much how we got the better students, as long as we came by them honestly. We were getting them, and that's what we wanted. We came up hard, like the boxer. We were just trying to better ourselves the best way we knew how.

When the boxer makes enough money, he'll retire from the ring and get on with his life. Did this mean that when Florida State reached a certain stage of academic success, it would drop collegiate athletics? We looked to some of the nation's great institutions for an answer: Notre Dame, Penn State, Texas, Virginia, North Carolina—all those would seem to be good company. Athletic director Bob Goin said, "I know exactly what the alumni and fans of Florida State want. They want a clean, wholesome program of excellence ... well funded, well run, and well led with a great amount of enthusiasm." So that's the way we did it. We won, and we won with integrity and grace.

And in the summer of '89 the Atlantic Coast Conference came to us and said, in effect, "You have a fine university, and a first-rate football program. We would like you to help us with football, and in return we will help you enhance your other sports, some of them dramatically. And, most importantly, we will let you in and accept you as one of us in an exclusive association of the most prestigious academic institutions in America at the Division I level. How about it?"

Luck. And a strong right hook.*

---

* Much of this chapter's material was initially published in the *Report to Boosters* (November 1990).

It's Not 1966 Anymore

When he arrived in Tallahassee for his first game against the Seminoles, newly minted Gators' head coach Steve Spurrier was so confident of victory that he arranged for a catered postgame banquet and celebration, which was to take place in our visitor's locker room. It proved unnecessary for that game or for any other for that matter. Steve Spurrier never won in Doak Campbell Stadium during his entire tenure as the Gators' head man.

Every underdog who knows how to win knows this trick: Never allow the upper dog to set the rules. How history would have been different if David had looked at Goliath and then turned to his soldiers and asked them to borrow a shield and a spear. But David knew the trick, and so he stood on a hill and flung rocks until Goliath fell down. Then he cut off his head for good measure, just to emphasize the final score.

Florida State had made a pretty fine career out of being the underdog who knew how to win. It was an attitude that happily permeated both the athletic and academic elements of our university. There was a perception—though a wrong one—that FSU football never was much before Bobby Bowden arrived. The truth was that some of the most significant innovations in the college game were born in Doak Campbell Stadium as Florida State searched for ways to knock down the Goliaths of the day.

In the twenty years before Bowden arrived, there were only three really bad seasons (1973–1975), and only five years elapsed between the 0–11 season of 1973 and the 11–0 season of 1979. In the season before the 1973 disaster, the Seminoles were 7–4; the year before that we were 8–3 with a Fiesta Bowl berth.

Among all the schools that began playing football after World War II, Florida State seemed to enjoy the most spectacular and enduring success. This underdog found ways to win big against the odds. Don Veller (1948–1952) lost only five games in his first four years as head coach. Then came Tom Nugent, the man who invented football's I formation as a way to give his outmanned Seminoles a competitive edge against the upper dogs.

Bill Peterson, who led the Tribe throughout the decade of the 1960s, deserves a special place in the heart of every loyal Seminole. In an era before recruiting caps, when large schools could use their resources to sign an unlimited number of players (sometimes taking prospects just to keep them from playing somewhere else), Bill Peterson whipped the upper dogs and changed the face of the game by introducing the pro-set passing offense to college football.

On a football weekend in Birmingham in 1967, ABC was shooting a documentary on Bear Bryant. Florida State was to be the sacrificial David to Alabama's Goliath. But Kim Hammond flung footballs with an accuracy worthy of David and his stones, and in a game that Bill McGrotha said rocked the football world, Alabama and the Tribe played to a 37–37 tie. ABC cameras recorded Bryant raging along the sidelines, yelling, "What's going on out there?" What was going on was that Florida State wasn't playing by Alabama's rules.

Seminole Boosters, Inc., would celebrate its fortieth anniversary in 1991. For the first several decades of Seminole football, the Boosters were a solid serviceable fundraising organization that contributed about sixty thousand per year to the athletic department. But after the winless 1973 season, football faced a six-hundred-thousand-dollar deficit and the Boosters were told to raise the money or football could be dropped altogether.

Andy Miller was hired to run the Boosters in 1975. By 1980, the Seminole Boosters ranked among the top six in the nation, with income of well over a million per year. In 1990, Booster income would reach almost $6.5 million, with over sixteen thousand contributors. Only Clemson's athletic program enjoyed greater support in numbers.

The Booster leadership knew the trick. Back then, all the upper dogs raised money by tying contributions to season tickets. But FSU was a long way from major population centers, and many of the alumni lived in South Florida. So instead of the people and the money coming to us, we went to them. In 1990, thousands of loyal fans and alumni who lived too far away to come to a game or buy season tickets contributed to the athletic program through the Boosters. As of 1999, Seminole Boosters, Inc., was the second-largest collegiate athletic fundraising organization in America.

We didn't achieve this success because we were smarter or prettier than our larger, older rivals. We did it because we *had* to. We *had* to find ways to raise money. As financial underdogs, we invented our own set of rules. And the creativity and aggressiveness that helped us to survive went on to be used to make FSU's athletic program competitive with any other in the nation.

The wonderful inventiveness that sparks the underdog to win on the field was present in Florida State's academic side as well. Have you heard about the a hundred-million-dollar National Magnet Research Laboratory that Florida State won away from the Massachusetts Institute of Technology? Newspapers wrote about FSU's aggressive and energetic pursuit of the lab, and about MIT's lack of the same, as well as their presumption that they would be handed the lab because of their status as an academic Goliath. When the decision was announced awarding the lab to FSU, MIT set up such a howl that one FSU official said he thought it might do MIT some good to join an athletic conference so they could have a better appreciation of sportsmanship.

But another and even more important milestone was quietly observed within the last few months of 1990. New York's prestigious *Barron's Compact Guide to Colleges* published their academic rankings of all major American colleges and universities. Rankings were based on admissions standards, strength of the faculty, number of outstanding program areas, and so forth. In the new edition that was to be published after the first of year (1991), Florida State would receive for the first time the rank of Very Competitive. That designation was exactly the same as that enjoyed by, among others, the University of Florida, Purdue University, Wake Forest, Michigan State, and Southern Cal.

U.S. News and World Report's annual review of colleges also made for interesting reading regarding their findings relative to Florida and Florida State, the ACC and the SEC. Don't allow anyone to tell you that FSU's academic credentials weren't as solid and impressive, and as highly rated, as any in the state of Florida.

What happens when an underdog becomes the upper dog? Well, an upper dog that retains the cunning, the instincts, and the aggressiveness of an underdog is a very dangerous beast indeed.

I was struck by the fact that Steve Spurrier seemed so shocked after the game. On his postgame radio show, and in the papers later, he continued saying, "I didn't realize the Florida State players were that talented," and, "I didn't think they could do that to us." The fact was that Florida State was no longer an underdog. Other than the Miami game of 1990, I cannot remember any football game since 1986 in which Florida State was not favored to win.

In September 1990, I received a letter from one of our Golden Chiefs down in Central Florida. He wrote, "Steve Spurrier is a fine gentleman and an excellent coach. I play golf with him, I know him, and I like him. But Steve sort of thinks not much has changed since 1966. Back then, all the great players wanted to go to Florida.

The media wasn't as adversarial as it is now. And Miami and Florida State could be a problem if you overlooked them, but they weren't really a threat." He then went on to say: "I believe that until Steve brings his team to Tallahassee on December 1, he won't really understand what Florida State has become. By the end of the game, I think he'll know."

Steve Spurrier learned firsthand about the Florida State of the '90s, that former underdog of 1966. I hoped they would sit him down before they told him about what Miami had become. Perhaps they already had. There had been rumblings out of Gainesville in the early part of December 1990 suggesting that maybe there wasn't room on the schedule for the Hurricanes after all.

Florida would do well. They had a great school and a great program, and now they had a great coach. But it was not 1966 anymore. There were other great schools, other great programs, and other great coaches. Perhaps Goliath's final thought was, "I didn't know he could do that to me." Believe it.*

Florida State Bowl Media Guide from the 1990 Blockbuster Bowl: No. 6 FSU vs. No. 7 Penn State. The 24–17 Seminole victory lifted the Tribe record to 10–2 in the fourth year of the dynasty. The young man is nine-month-old Jonathan Richt, son of the FSU quarterbacks coach Mark Richt. On January 10, 2014, Coach Richt announced that he was to become a grandfather thanks to his son Jon and his wife, Anna.

---

* Much of this chapter's material was initially published in the *Report to Boosters* (December 1990).

Pat Dye Drops the Seminoles

At the end of the 1990 season, Colorado and Georgia Tech shared a split national championship. Colorado won the AP title, but the UPI awarded their trophy to Georgia Tech by only one vote. That single vote was cast by Nebraska coach Tom Osborne, who was in the unique position of having played both teams during the season, losing to each.

Florida State fans were upset at the announcement by Auburn head coach Pat Dye that the Tigers would not renew their series with the Seminoles. Dye made the announcement following our loss to Auburn in October, and many felt that previous Seminole victories over the Tigers in 1987 and again in the 1989 Sugar Bowl had dampened Dye's enthusiasm for playing FSU.

"You've got to dance like nobody's watching," they say. What they mean, I think, is that your most un-self-conscious and totally committed effort will yield your very best performance. There are other ways to say it too: "Play with abandon," and "Put it all on the line," and "Play loose."

Anything you do well, you will do less well if you try too hard. That's what most students of human behavior contend, and I haven't seen too many exceptions to that rule. True in sports, and true in life: If you worry too much about fumbling the ball, you will fumble the ball. And, as the legendary Coach Heisman remarked earlier in the century, "It is better for a lad to die young than to fumble the football."

Put it all on the line and then go all-out. Trust your instincts. Trust your talents. Play with abandon. Deion Sanders, signaling to the Clemson crowd that he would run the punt back for a touchdown—and then doing it. Senior quarterback Steve Spurrier stepping into the Gator huddle with the game tied against Auburn, saying, "We're going to win this game with a field goal, and I'm going to kick it." And then doing it.

Coach Howard Schnellenberger, at a remarkable Seminole Boosters luncheon in Tallahassee, the Friday before the 1983 Miami game, saying, "If we can beat you Saturday, we will have the opportunity to win the national championship at the end of the season. This game tomorrow is the most important game in the history of University of Miami football." And then winning the game, and later the national title.

Bobby Bowden calling the Puntrooskie with his back to the goal line and the score tied against Clemson, because, as he said, "I made up my mind that *somebody* was going to win this game"— and then winning it. Joe Namath, hero and MVP of Super Bowl III, before his 21-point underdog Jets upset the Colts: "We'll win Sunday. I guarantee it."

Pat Kennedy, minutes before his debut as Seminole head coach in front of the largest crowd ever to see a basketball game in the state of Florida, telling his team, "I've spent my whole career preparing for tonight. All my life, I've dreamed of coaching a game like this, with this much on the line. I know that each one of you is going to go out there and play the best game you've ever played. I know that you are going to defeat the University of Florida." And then winning 80–76.

In one of the greatest upsets in modern sports, American coach Herb Brooks' youngsters defeated the heavily favored Soviet Army hockey team in the 1980 Olympics, 4–3. There was a long silence in the locker room before the game. Finally, Brooks addressed his team. His voice was soft, and he spoke only four sentences: "You were meant to be a player," he said. "You were meant for this moment. You were meant to be *here*. This is your time."

All these feats were done, not with arrogance, but with grace, good humor, and good sportsmanship. Every real sports fan appreciates the coach, the team, the player who puts it all on the line, who dances like nobody's watching, regardless of the outcome.

Every Monday following a Seminole football game, the Seminole Boosters hosted a luncheon in Tallahassee, which was open to the public. After 1990's Auburn game, Coach Bowden apologized to the house. "It's all my fault," he said honestly. "I called that trick play even though we were ahead because I felt we needed to score again to win. Our kids played great. I'm the one to blame."

Then something happened that had never happened before: The crowd laughed at Bobby Bowden. Over three hundred people laughed out loud at him. Then one fellow in the back stood up and said, "Coach, I think I can speak for most of us when I say that we've watched you win a lot of games with that kind of call. I guess we all knew it would cost us a game someday. Well, we've had our loss now, so I guess we'll win the rest of them." The crowd applauded. Then they stood up and applauded some more.

This brings us, roundabout, to the subject of Pat Dye.

Just after the announcement that Auburn ended the series with FSU, I got a letter from one of our Boosters in Pensacola. "I hope we never become like Pat Dye," she wrote. "He always seems to play like he's more afraid of losing than he is excited about trying to win." What she was saying was that Pat Dye dances like *everybody's* watching.

"Don't take chances," the thinking goes. "If you start having trouble with a particular step, just drop it from your routine. You'll never be Fred Astaire, but you can make a comfortable living as a valued member of the chorus line." As for the Seminoles and Florida State, we've never really been content to be in the chorus, even if it is more secure.

We had no national title yet to show that we could dance as well as Fred Astaire. Every once in a while, we came pretty close, and once in a while we tripped over our own feet into a pratfall. But we were not afraid to line up side by side with the best there was, match him step for step—maybe even try to outdo him with a few tricks of our own—and let the audience be the judge.

There was every indication that in the upcoming spring the Seminoles could be tagged by many publications and commentators as their choice for preseason No. 1. I was already starting to hear from fans who were unhappy about it: "Don't want a repeat of 1988," they said. "Much better to be ranked low at the beginning and then move up." Catch people by surprise, they advised, like Georgia Tech did.

Smart scheduling was important and necessary. But planning the season with the goal of sneaking in the back door of a national title game sounded like someone who was more afraid of losing than about trying to win. Georgia Tech didn't have a choice. Their coaches and players believed in themselves, even if the voters did not. Tech didn't plan to sneak up on people. The Yellow Jackets just went out and tried to beat every team they played. The fact is that if you want to be *the* champion, then you have to be willing to be *a* champion all of the time—every year.

In 1989, Colorado was the Cinderella team. In 1990, everybody was ready for them. But they won anyway. Everybody was always ready for Miami—they won anyway. This was not an endorsement of their behavior; it was just that those who would be champions are prepared to play their best every game. They don't run from the challenge that every champion must face. In fact, they seek it out.

In September of the '91 season, we were going to the dance.

When we walked into that room, they were going to put the spotlight on us. Everyone would be watching to see what they would have to beat in order to win. With grace, good humor, and good sportsmanship, we would pick up our hat and cane, flash our most elegant Fred Astaire smile, and then leave them all absolutely astonished.*

---

* Much of this chapter's material was initially published in the *Report to Boosters* (January 1991).

1991 Season

Our loss to Miami in 1991 was the low point of the season. After ten straight wins and an unblemished record, we faced them in Tallahassee for yet another "game of the century." Once again, we were ranked No. 1 and Miami was ranked No. 2. We had a great game plan.

We controlled the line of scrimmage up until the early fourth quarter, when we led 16–7. Our defense was playing well. Miami would need two scores to beat us. And in the fourth quarter, that's just what they did, scoring twice to take a 17–16 lead. We got the ball back with 3:01 to play. Casey Weldon led us on a drive deep into Miami territory. Time was running out. With seconds left in the game, I decided to go for a field goal on third and 9 at their 17-yard line. Victory, I believed, was at hand. Our kicker had never missed inside the 40. Moreover, he was three for three on the day. We both assumed the kick would go through the uprights. Well ... so much for assumptions. The kick drifted wide by inches. We lost by 1 point. Then we lost to Florida the following week.

By then the phrase "wide right" had entered football parlance. And by chance, 1991 was also the year the NCAA reduced the width of the college goal posts by almost five feet, to match the width in the NFL. For me, only one phrase mattered: "This too shall pass."

—Bobby Bowden

1991 Season

Began the season ranked No. 1
Ended the season ranked No. 4
Record 11–2
Cotton Bowl Champions

August 29, defeated Brigham Young in Jacksonville 44–28

September 7, defeated Tulane in Tallahassee 38–11

September 14, defeated Western Michigan in Tallahassee 58–0

September 28, defeated Michigan in Ann Arbor 51–31

October 5, defeated Syracuse in Tallahassee 46–14

October 12, defeated Virginia Tech in Orlando 33–20

October 19, defeated Middle Tennessee State in Tallahassee 39–10

October 26, defeated LSU in Baton Rouge 27–16

November 2, defeated Louisville in Louisville 40–15

November 9, defeated South Carolina in Tallahassee 38–10

November 16, lost to Miami in Tallahassee 16–17

November 30, lost to Florida in Gainesville 9–14

January 1, 1992, defeated Texas A&M in the Cotton Bowl 10–2

Seminoles and
the Conference Mentality

The first Atlantic Coast Conference schedule was still a full year away, but Seminoles were anxious to learn what to expect as members of a major college athletic conference. Was the perception so different when you were a member of a league? Could Seminole fans adjust their thinking to embrace the conference mentality?

A young Ohio State Buckeye player was quoted as saying, "We'll beat Florida State because no team has ever beaten us twice in a row at home, not since 1904." And then he added, "Besides, even if we do lose, it's not a conference game."

I put down the newspaper, filled with the pleasant conviction that we were going to win a football game against the Buckeyes. It was 1982, a few days before we went back to Columbus to play, and to beat, Ohio State for the second year in a row. The Buckeye player who was quoted in the paper had exhibited a classic example of a "conference mentality." The OSU players were thinking Rose Bowl, not Florida State.

FSU would play a full complement of ACC games in all sports, and be eligible for the conference titles in 1992. How would a "conference mentality" affect our thinking? Could we use it to our benefit? Could we learn to avoid its pitfalls?

A "conference mentality" defines a way of viewing ourselves and our goals from within the context of our particular conference. The old and more established conferences are as much social and political alliances as they are athletic. It's powerful stuff. I noticed earlier in the fall of '91 that FSU fans were already beginning to pull for fellow ACC teams against schools from other leagues. Our folks celebrated when Georgia Tech won.

Seminole fans never really developed a "conference mentality" in the Metro Conference. The Metro seemed somehow less fraternal than the other leagues. Maybe it was because we didn't play football, or because we weren't a dominating force in basketball. Or it could have been because we *were* the dominating force in just about every other sport. Unless one followed closely, it was difficult to appreciate the extent to which Florida State overwhelmed other Metro schools. The Seminoles won just about every track and golf title the Metro offered. We had won more volleyball titles than all the other schools combined, and twice as many baseball titles as all the other schools combined. Not only that, but Florida State also won the Metro All-Sports Trophy more times than all the other schools combined.

It was wonderful, and most appropriate, that as we bowed out of the Metro, both our men's and women's basketball teams won their tournament championships. Coach Marynell Meadors and Coach Pat Kennedy were the Norman Schwarzkopf/Colin Powell of the hoops campaign. After fourteen years in the Metro, we finally earned our basketball diplomas. The following year, in the ACC, we began our graduate school.

In football, I had always suspected that the Seminoles held an advantage over conference teams. Conference teams played each other every year and generally had no secrets. They knew who was hurt, who was healthy, how the other coaches thought, and they remembered which plays were run against them in 1958.

A second advantage sprang from the fact that a "conference

mentality" deemphasized the importance in the minds of players, coaches, and fans of nonconference games. For many years, and certainly when the athletic directors played, nonconference games were considered to be warm-ups for the conference season, and appropriate teams were scheduled. That thinking remained pronounced in the conferences. If you were going to lose or have problems, then best to get them out of the way before the conference schedule began.

The real plum was the conference championship, however. With that came a shot at the national title. It wasn't so very long ago that the national title was determined *before* the bowls were even played. SEC football fans knew that, for them, the road to the national title ran through New Orleans. The Sugar Bowl was the most coveted prize. Big Ten and Pac-10 coaching successes was measured by how often your team got into the Rose Bowl.

But times have changed, and the mentality that once embraced tie-ins with certain bowls actually worked against some conferences. Since the 1940s, the Pac-10 and Big Ten had been under contract to the Rose Bowl, and the Southwest Conference to the Cotton Bowl. The Big 8 had an on-again off-again contact with the Orange Bowl since 1953. In 1977, the Southeastern Conference started sending its champion to the Sugar Bowl.

But consider this: Since 1980, no Pac-10 team, no Big Ten team, no SWC team, and no SEC team had won a national football championship. From 1980–1990, nearly every national title has been won by Independents or by conference teams (BYU, Clemson, Georgia Tech) that did *not* have major bowl tie-ins.

Here is the point of all this: The sort of conference mentality that may have been helpful in the '70s would not be so much of an advantage in the '90s. But old habits of thinking are hard to break, especially when all your friends think the same way. Now that we were in the ACC, we had to learn how to use the conference mentality to our advantage, and be smart enough to avoid the negatives.

There was every indication that FSU's athletic leadership would do precisely what was best for Florida State. And what was best for us may not have been what was best for someone in another conference. For instance, there had been a lot of talk about Florida being afraid to play Miami. I didn't buy it. Florida was a proud, powerful old school, and was not impressed as being much afraid of anyone or anything (the cynic here might add "getting caught" to the list of things Florida did not fear).

With a nod to conference mentality, it appeared that Florida dropped Miami not from fear but from a sense of prudence. Florida and Miami last played in 1987, a 31–4 Hurricane win. Only the most ardent Gator fan would suggest that the Canes would not have continued to run up dramatic wins. That's important because Florida was walking on NCAA eggshells, and rogue alumni—not easily corralled under the best of circumstances—might have been pushed beyond endurance by Hurricane playing-field antics and lopsided scores.

At the Seminole Booster Monday luncheon after our 52–17 win in 1988, fans demanded to know why Bobby Bowden had shut the offense down in the fourth quarter, why he didn't turn them loose to score more points. Bowden shrugged and said, "Well, I figured we had enough to win." Miami coach Jimmy Johnson wouldn't have stopped there, however. He would have scored 100 if he could have.

Florida would probably drop us too if they could. They were not afraid of us—playing us simply didn't help them meet their goals. Florida State and Florida were both trying to get to the same place, but by different routes. The Gators looked at a map and decided that the best roads for them ran through Starkville, Lexington, and Nashville—not Dade County.

The fact is that we went into the ACC with our eyes wide open.

We knew that an ACC schedule wouldn't fill our stadium—at least, not right away. We *needed* Florida and Miami on our schedule. Florida didn't need either of us. That's just the way it was.

But we would be fine. There would be no shortage of good teams coming to Tallahassee. I fully expected Florida to become one of the SEC's dominant teams, and as long as Miami could recruit South Florida, they were going to be trouble for everybody. Couple that with the fact that *no* conference had more than one team in the 1990's final top 10, *except* the ACC (which had three), and it was evident that Florida State's plate was going to be full.

Finally, there was a dark side to the conference mentality, and we needed to be weary of it. We could not underestimate the depth of animosity among some SEC folk over our decision to join the Atlantic Coast Conference. The previous summer there was serious talk about Texas, Texas A&M, Florida State, and Miami all joining the Southeastern Conference. With that league, the SEC would have controlled big-time college athletics—and lucrative television contracts—from Coral Gables to the Rio Grande. The reasons it did not happen are many and complicated, but the fact remains that it did come a whole lot closer to a conclusion than most people can imagine.

The SEC went after four major, high-profile national pro-grams and ended up with Arkansas and South Carolina. In another day, perhaps, Arkansas and South Carolina would fit the profile. But in 1991, the 3–8 Hogs and the 6–5 Gamecocks were just two more mouths to feed. It was like inviting the Corleone family to your home for the social event of the year. You antici-pated that Sonny and Michael would be there, but in the end only Fredo showed up.

At Florida State, we prided ourselves on conducting our ath-letic affairs with integrity. One could be certain that our integrity would be challenged, questioned, tested, and probed. Any mis-takes, any weakness, any shortcomings would be subjected to an adversary's microscope. We stood at the threshold of possibly the greatest era in our university's history. We were well prepared, well led, and well supported.

We would no doubt develop our own conference mentality as we settled into the ACC. Our task, however, was to ensure that it was a mentality that continued to reflect all the best things about our university, all the things that had brought us to where we stood in that moment.*

---

* Much of this chapter's material was initially published in the *Report to Boosters* (March/April 1991).

On Fan Behavior:
Who Do We Want to Be?

One of the arguments in favor of joining the ACC was that it would allow Florida State to establish our own distinct identity. Instead of patterning our fan psychology after the schools closest to us, the ones with which we were most familiar, the ACC experience would encourage us to create an atmosphere similar to the University of Nebraska. Our Seminole leaders and fans were profoundly influenced by the experience of playing the Huskers in Lincoln in 1980.

Newsweek magazine reported about a Minneapolis, Minnesota, construction worker named Lance Gangaruth who was accidentally struck in the head by a nail gun. "I heard the gun go off," he told *Newsweek*, "but I didn't know it got me until I tried to take off my hat and I couldn't." No doubt Gangaruth had been warned about the dangers of nail guns. Like all of us, perhaps he just grew careless.

Our Booster club leaders got a warning in February 1991. It came during our Annual Leadership Conference here in Tallahassee, attended by a hundred or so Booster club presidents and about an equal number of volunteer fundraisers from as far away as Houston and Washington, DC. One of our guest speakers was a sportswriter from a major newspaper in the central part of the state. He said, "You know, I've always liked FSU people. It's a classy school with a classy reputation. But I'll tell you something I've noticed lately that's pretty disturbing, and you need to be aware of it."

He was talking about trashy behavior, especially at the games. It wasn't the fans who had been around for a while, he explained, but the newer ones—the students, the young alumni, maybe the fans who had come around since we started winning big. We were starting to act, he said, just like the fans and alumni of the school from which he graduated, the same one from which a great many of this state's sportswriters graduated.

He didn't mince words: mouthy, provocative, belligerent, and arrogant. Indeed, these were all the attributes we routinely ascribed to the supporters of his school. "Maybe you just aren't aware of what's been going on," he said. "Or maybe you just haven't been effective in getting the right message across to the people who need to hear it." He spoke like a stern uncle; he had been a good friend to Florida State. I listened to him—we all did—and then went on about my job and didn't think much about it.

Then we went to Pensacola in the spring for the Bobby Bowden Banquet. Pensacola's banquet was as first-class of an affair as you could imagine. It was held at the Naval Air Museum, a colossal structure at the heart of the Naval Air Station. There were some special surprises, including a visit from the Navy Choir.

Even the base commander was on hand to welcome the Seminole crowd. He was especially pleased to learn that we had joined the Atlantic Coast Conference, he said, because he was himself a graduate of the University of North Carolina. At that point, some fellow in the crowd let loose a loud boo. The base commander ignored it, but our crowd did not. Many were obviously embarrassed and angry. They glanced around, looking for the culprit. It passed quickly and was gone, but I understood that moment what the sportswriter had been trying to tell us.

We had been extremely fortunate the previous fifteen years that Bobby Bowden and Bernie Sliger had been the two most highly visible people associated with our school. Their public personalities had been the ones most closely identified with Florida State.

The gracious and hospitable behavior of Nebraska's fans in 1980 so affected Coach Bowden and our Booster leaders that they determined to set up a model for our own fans to follow. Jim King organized a university-wide program to aggressively welcome opponents' fans to Doak Campbell Stadium. The athletic department set up similar programs to welcome and entertain visiting officials. Many Seminole fans and alumni began to consciously reflect a vision of the university that embraced good sportsmanship, integrity, enthusiasm, and congeniality.

It is true, of course, that it is much easier to maintain those virtues when you are winning. The irony is that we were winning recognition as a classy program during the years when we were losing to Auburn, Florida, and Miami on the field. But we had finished among the nation's top 4 from 1981–1990 (only three other schools in the history of college football could match that), and now it seemed we may be letting our off-the-field reputation slip.

Some who supported FSU joining the ACC felt the move would help us in better establishing our own identity, compatible with the new league, and distinct from either of our two major rivals. And they were not being sanctimonious, like the fellow in the Bible who gave thanks that he was so much better than other men (see Luke 18:9–14).

Florida State, like Notre Dame and Penn State, enjoyed a national reputation for its clean, winning program. These were model programs, classy programs. But it was sure not due to any inherent moral or ethical superiority on our part. I knew that our players, coaches, fans, and alumni had the potential to be as sorry as anybody, or as good as anybody. If we enjoyed a good reputation, it was because we had worked awfully hard at doing the right things, and because our Boosters had a healthy, nearly paranoid fear of doing the wrong things.

Maybe winning big on the field had caused us to work a little less hard elsewhere. I didn't want us to be one of those outfits that answered every criticism by saying, "We won it on the field, where it counts." The truth is that it counts off the field too.

On September 5, 1991, the Duke Blue Devils came to Tallahassee for our first conference football game. It was my hope that every one of us would go out of our way to single out Blue Devil fans and welcome them to Doak Campbell Stadium. And after we beat the tar out of them on the field, I hoped we would invite their alumni to have dinner with us after the game and toast the most prestigious academic and athletic Division I conference in America.

The alternative was to ignore everything the sportswriter said. "I didn't know it got me until I tried to take off my hat and I couldn't," the man told *Newsweek*. We couldn't say that we hadn't been warned.*

---

* Much of this chapter's material was initially published in the *Report to Boosters* (September 1991).

In Praise of
Unreasonable Fans

Anxiety very often accompanies success. Anxiety is often born of fear that the success will be taken away. The most frequent cause of decline in college athletic programs is forgetting to do the things that made the program great in the first place. Where fans and donors insist on a high level of performance, those programs are likely to stay strong. But where fans and donors are willing to accept mediocrity, the results are likewise predictable.

This is a true story: One of our alumni who donates a lot of money (and I mean a *lot* of money) to FSU's athletic and academic programs was so distraught over the losses to Miami and Florida in 1991 that he did these three things in this sequence: He wrestled the metal Booster plate off the front of his car and tossed it into Biscayne Bay; he cancelled his subscription to the *Osceola*; and he put his Tallahassee condo up for sale. I love that guy. If it weren't for unreasonable people and their passions, virtually nothing would ever improve in this world.

Much like you, I don't have a lot of use for the fence-sitters. There are always those who will support us when we are winning and then fade when we're not winning. Their loyalty to the greater vision of the university is only minimal. But the guy who tossed his tag in the bay isn't like that. There's a world of difference between him and some halfway fan whose passion fluctuates with our standing in the polls. Our man in Miami knows he does not have the option to retreat, and maybe that's what makes him so animated in his frustration.

There are those who are basically along for the ride, and then there are those whose love and loyalty toward their university is so deep that when it gets set back, well, a fellow's got to do something to blow off steam. There are some things in life you can just walk away from when they hurt you. But sometimes your family lets you down, or your friends disappoint you, or maybe your church or your school falls short of great expectations. You can't walk away then, because those are the people and institutions that mean the most to you.

College football games pale in importance compared to a sick child or a failing business. But when those who loved Florida State contemplated the vision of our university as a first-class academic institution with a premier, nationally-renown athletic program, we knew that winning and losing made a difference. Winning mattered.

We had done a good job of raising money to build competitive facilities, and winning had made that possible. Such would not be the case in a more perfect world, but the fact was that years of winning under Bobby Bowden enabled us to marshal strength in the halls of power, which is where the money is. In 1991 we had a hundred-million-dollar academic and athletic center under construction at Doak Campbell Stadium. Politics—above the table, under the table, and all around—loomed large in the struggle to get where we were, and Florida State's reputation as a clean, winning national power played no small role in that political mix. That was the real world.

Some—mostly those who pooh-pooh college athletics generally—sniff that at Harvard they don't care whether the team wins or loses; they say it makes no difference in giving to the institution.

True enough. Harvard is 350 years old, and it has a thirteen-billion-dollar endowment. The truth is that we are not Harvard, nor are we going to become like them. But we could become another Michigan or Penn State or Notre Dame. And if the populations of the country keep moving South, we might even become better.

I had a couple of houseguests the weekend of the Miami game in 1991. He was an FSU grad, while she went to the University of South Florida. One thing that struck me was how mystified she was at how hard all of us took the loss. To her it was just another good game, like we would watch a boxing match. I realized how incomprehensible big-time college athletics was to people who didn't grow up with it, people who didn't go to school with it.

South Florida, by the way, was considering starting a football program during that time. In the December 4 *St. Pete Times*, a former mayor of St. Pete was quoted as saying that USF could never achieve its goal of becoming one of the nation's top twenty-five public institutions without "an emotional infrastructure." He said, "A football program does much to create that."

And even among college football programs generally, it seemed there was a real lack of understanding about what goes on at the level Florida State had occupied the last few years leading up to 1991. We were in a different league at the time. Back in 1977, we had only two regular season losses and the newspapers said that was a wondrous thing. The world was our oyster. In 1991, however, we dropped two at the end of the season, and the same newspapers wrote about bitter heartbreak and the death of dreams.

In 1979, we went 8–3 and couldn't pull enough strings to get into the Peach Bowl. In 1991, our concession prize was one of the great traditional New Year's Day bowls. We were the Cinderella team in 1979: undefeated and headed for the Orange Bowl, our first New Year's Day bowl.

At the hotel in Miami, however, I found myself on a long, slow elevator ride with a passel of Oklahoma fans who seemed to be not very enthusiastic, certainly not when compared to our ecstatic Seminoles. I asked if they were happy to be there, and they said—choosing the words so as not to offend me—that while they were honored to be playing Florida State, this was not a game for the national title and so the season had been something of a disappointment for them. I thought, *Wow! If we could ever get to that point, our program would be on top of the world.*

We were no longer a Cinderella program; in fact, we hadn't been for a long time. We had become a fixed star around the top of the college football pyramid, where every loss was more devastating and every win was more significant. Only two schools in the history of college football had finished among the nation's top 4 five years in a row. We were one of them. It wasn't very crowded where we were, but it was wrong to dwell on the look-how-far-we've-come theme. The tide that brought us up raised up the other boats in this state too.

Back in the 1970s, Miami had yet to win much of anything, and Florida was pretty much the definition of an average SEC program. Whatever the distance FSU had traveled since that time, the others had too. As of 1991, Miami had four national titles and played to full Orange Bowl crowds. Florida was the flagship team of the SEC, and they played in a fabulous new stadium. Let's not be too reasonable when it comes to FSU.

We had gotten to where we were by pushing ourselves to do our best, and sometimes more than our best. We had placed unreasonable demands on our coaches, our players, and on the loyalty and generosity of our fans, and they had all risen to meet those higher goals.

There was always an alternative to us continuing do our best—our best at raising money, our best at running the athletic program, our best at coaching, and our best at recruiting the right players. The alternative to doing our best was to *not* do our best, and thus to fall out of that tiny fraternity at the top of the pyramid. Other schools had fallen out, and most of us know their names. Their fans and alumni have felt frustrations, but wouldn't they have liked to trade places with us? Instead, they had to say, "Well, remember when we were in the hunt every year?"

We dreamt big because we were in Florida, a state where anything seemed possible. The vision of what we could become loomed larger here than if we were located in some other place, some place without a magic kingdom, some place where the opportunities weren't so dramatic. What other university began intercollegiate sports after World War II and accomplished what FSU had in forty-five years? What other university, no matter how old, had cumulative winning records in every men's and women's sport they had ever played?

It was a good thing that our fans were spoiled, and that we weren't willing to settle for the considerable laurels we had already won. Once losing was accepted at all, then it was easier to keep on losing. If we ever accepted the role of second best, then second was the best we could have ever hoped to be.

The frustration that made our man fling his Booster license plate out across the gentle waves of Biscayne Bay wasn't unhealthy at all. It was healthy precisely because we compared ourselves to our rivals and to older, better schools. It was okay to vent some short-term frustration as long as we kept a firm grip on the knowledge that the future really did belong to FSU, provided that we took advantage of the opportunities. We couldn't allow anything to spoil the long view of our place in the scheme of things.

The truth is that all of us have to choose our own priorities. For those who love Florida State, FSU is a priority. That may not be so reasonable in tough times, but we Seminoles had never been a very reasonable people, had we?*

---

* Much of this chapter's material was initially published in the *Report to Boosters* (February 1992).

False Controversy
at the Cotton Bowl

Unlike the old-line schools of the SEC, the fans and media culture following Florida State were still adjusting to the trappings and traditions of big-time college football. When Florida State journeyed to Dallas on January 1, 1992, to play Texas A&M in the Cotton Bowl, our hometown newspaper editorialized that spending so much money on a bowl trip was scandalous. It was an unfair charge, of course, and not unexpected given the attitude and personalities running the local paper at the time.

I like the Salvation Army. I admire the way they go about their business with humility and without any hint of extravagance. In fact, my father beat the drum for them on the street corner when he was just a boy, partly to thumb his nose at an aristocratic sister, but it also gave him a lifelong appreciation for the Army and their good works. He told me that the Salvation Army bought a lot of automobiles, but they insisted on black ones only. He explained: "A red car doesn't cost any more than a black car, but a red car just seems flashy and extravagant to some people." They didn't want anyone to complain and say, "I'm giving my money to the Salvation Army and they're buying flashy cars with it."

Our hometown Tallahassee newspaper published a big, splashy piece criticizing FSU's expenditures at the Cotton Bowl

119

as "extravagant." I'm dwelling on it here because my business was in raising funds for FSU. Anything that diminished that purpose, or that might have caused our loyal supporters to question their contributions, had my immediate attention.

The hometown paper published facts provided to it by the athletic department. But there can be great distance between what is factual and what is accurate. For instance, if you say Florida State spent $750,000 going to the Cotton Bowl, then you are telling the truth. But if you say it with a smirk and a raised eyebrow, then you are still telling the truth, but you are also suggesting something else that is not accurate.

Athletic director Bob Goin and Coach Bowden got the raised-eyebrow treatment during that time. There was even a special feature on Bowden written in the gossipy, breathless style of "… and you know what else? Bobby Bowden took his whole family with him to the Cotton Bowl!" Well, yes. College football's all-time winningest bowl coach took his whole family with him so they could be together for the holidays.

I am not a journalist, but I do know something about writing. I know a writer can frame facts to influence the picture he or she presents. Our hometown newspaper focused on the $750,000 spent on FSU's Cotton Bowl trip. It ran photos of influential people who were guests, members of the president's official party, and they waggled their finger at the "extravagance." Some readers were left with the impression that the official party was made up of pals of the president and wealthy Golden Chiefs who elbowed their way onto the plane. That's the way it sounded because that was the way it was written.

But here's what was accurate.

Let's start with a million dollars. That's what the Atlantic Coast Conference allocated to Bob Goin for the trip, which is what they estimated it would cost for a big-time Division I program to travel a thousand miles away for a major New Year's Day bowl. That figure was based on what other schools at our level expected to spend as well.

Knock a $250,000 off the top of that—chalk it up to the prudence and frugality of the athletic director. Goin spent about $650,000 on his end; the president's official party added just under a hundred thousand more to the total. Then take Goin's $650,000 and deduct the cost of taking 450 members of the Marching Chiefs.

Yes, FSU enjoyed the honor of having the largest collegiate band in America, and we were expected to take them to Dallas. Also you can deduct the cost of flying out the entire football team, along with equipment, trainers, coaches, key department administrators, and some families. No, families do not go on team trips during the regular season, but regular season games are not bowl games, and they are not played over Christmas and New Year's holidays.

The number of days the team was expected to stay, and even the specific hotel where the team was housed, was determined by the bowl. We had no choice, and we were required to pay for it. But make no mistake about it—this was and continues to be routine practice among major bowls. FSU stayed the minimum number of days. Many schools stay longer—some, much longer.

The accusation of "extravagance" was probably the most galling to Goin. He ran a lean program during the year; I would suggest that some might complain that it was too lean. His sixteen-million-dollar annual budget was between five million and ten million (depending on how you figure it) less than that of our biggest rivals. And I think we stacked up pretty well by comparison.

Let's also take a look at the president's official party. Many and probably most of the donors to Seminole athletics are also major donors to the school's academic programs. All, certainly, are prospects for the Capital Campaign. The hometown newspaper ran photos of some of these guests and identified them as "Golden

Chiefs." They were that, but it was like identifying someone as "a New Yorker" or "a Presbyterian"—it doesn't tell you why they're on the plane.

It was accurate to say that some big-money prospects were invited along on every team trip. And a small amount of money spent on someone who can and will give literally millions back to the university was not badly spent (trust me—this will not come as a surprise to any of these people if they are reading it here for the first time). Others invited along included those who had been especially helpful to the university, either as outstanding leaders or exceptional fundraisers.

There is something else you need to know, which is necessary to give you an accurate picture of the whole ordeal. Goin balanced his athletic department budget with ticket revenue and conference income. The fall of 1991, president Dale Lick asked the athletic department to transfer eight hundred thousand dollars to the university for academic purposes—the request was unexpected and unplanned for.

FSU was hurting during that time, as were many schools, because of state budget cutbacks. Goin was glad to do it, but the eight hundred thousand would have to be made up somehow. It would come through a combination of belt-tightening and Seminole Booster funds. Goin said, "We are ready to do anything that will help Florida State. I just considered the hundred thousand we spent on the president's official party as an addition to the eight hundred thousand we had already transferred. If we can spend a hundred thousand and raise several million down the road, that's a pretty good deal."

Florida State athletics was a great source of pride for our alumni and fans. Any person has every right to expect everyone involved to adhere to the highest standards of ethics and financial responsibilities. We had asked our friends and supporters to give more, and they did. It was important that everyone knows that the money that comes out of their pockets was spent wisely and to the benefit of the university.

Ours was not the most expensive or most luxurious car on the lot, but it reflected well on us and we were proud to drive it. It was clean and polished, it ran efficiently, and we didn't steal gasoline from anyone else. It was as fast as any other on the road. And we could make the payments. When people who are your friends want an explanation, then they will respond to the truth. People who are your enemies will throw rocks at your car no matter what.[*]

---

[*] Much of this chapter's material was initially published in the *Report to Boosters* (March/April 1992).

1992 Season

During the dynasty years of the 1990s, we won two national championships while Miami and Florida got one each. What's more amazing is that each of us played two additional times in the national championship game during that span. In other words, FSU or Miami or Florida played in the national championship game every year from 1991 to 1996, and then again from 1998 to 2000.

In 1987, 1988, and 1992, FSU went 11–1 each year, our only blemish being a loss to Miami. Miami went on to play for the national championship each of those years, winning two of them. We also had 11–1 seasons in 1996 and 1997, our only loss coming at the hands of Florida. They won the national championship in '96 and played for the championship again in '97. It was fair to say in those days that any team hoping to contend for the national title had to go through the state of Florida to get there.

I had to play both of those teams every year during the regular season. I don't know that anyone played two tougher teams year in and year out than we did during that stretch of years. From 1987 to 2000, we split the series 7–7 with Miami and won eleven of fourteen against Florida, not counting the tie game in 1994. Looking back, it amazes me that we won as many as we did. Those were great days to be a fan of college football in the state of Florida … or anywhere else, for that matter.

—Bobby Bowden

1992 Season

Began the season ranked No. 4
Ended the season ranked No. 2
Record 11–1
ACC Champions
Orange Bowl Champions

September 5, defeated Duke in Tallahassee 48–21

September 12, defeated Clemson in Clemson 24–20

September 19, defeated NC State in Raleigh 34–13

September 26, defeated Wake Forest in Tallahassee 35–7

October 3, lost to Miami in Miami 16–19

October 10, defeated North Carolina in Tallahassee 36–13

October 17, defeated Georgia Tech in Atlanta 29–24

October 31, defeated Virginia in Charlottesville 13–2

November 7, defeated Maryland in Tallahassee 69–21

November 14, defeated Tulane in Tallahassee 70–7

November 28, defeated Florida in Tallahassee 45–24

January 1, 1993, defeated Nebraska in the Orange Bowl 27–14

Sportsmanship:
Shake Hands with a Blue Devil

J ust before beginning our first full season of ACC competition, I published an essay in August of 1992. Our relationship with our rivals, Florida and Miami, had never been a tale of grace and good sportsmanship. Seminole Booster leaders were determined to establish comradely relations with their new ACC partners. We had been accepted into the family in principle, but now we wanted to ensure we would be in fact welcome.

When Duke football came to town on the weekend of September 5, I encouraged our people to go out of their way to welcome their fans. I encouraged them to tell them how proud we were to be in the ACC with them. I encouraged FSU to congratulate them on their national basketball championship, praise their academic standards, and tell them how much it meant to us to be associated with a university of their caliber. And when they told us that they were sure the Seminoles would win, I encouraged our fans to just smile and say that we hoped so, and to acknowledge that we had been blessed with a great coach and a successful program.

I knew there wouldn't be many Duke people at the game, and some of the ones we would see would be from Tallahassee. Professors, probably, who are Seminole fans except for the few days each year they don the blue-and-white of their alma mater. But they would all be paying attention. We would have about sixty thousand Seminoles at the game. If only 1 percent of those—six hundred people—went to the trouble to seek out a Blue Devil or two, and offer a genuine welcome, then the letters of our university president's office would be coming for years.

Our people still talked about the classy Nebraska fans at that 1980 game in Lincoln. Years ago, Jacksonville's Jim King put together something called Project Image, which was an attempt to capture some of that Nebraska sportsmanship for ourselves. Volunteers, mostly from the Jacksonville Seminole Boosters Club, handed out complimentary bags of boiled peanuts to opposing fans and welcomed them to Doak Campbell Stadium.

King had been asked by the Seminole Boosters' board of directors to resurrect Project Image in some form in 1992. In addition, a second group led by local businessman and Booster board member Mel Pope III made contact with ACC school representatives in Tallahassee and helped arrange accommodations, pep rallies, and receptions for their visiting fans during the previous basketball season.

All that was good, but the most widely felt impression that Florida State would make on our fellow ACC universities would come via the direct contact between our fans and theirs. We traveled to their stadium; they traveled to ours.

It was unfortunate but true that major college football fans in the state of Florida did not enjoy a reputation for hospitality. Both Steve Spurrier and Dennis Erickson, fine men themselves, felt the need the previous year to apologize publicly for the behavior of their home crowds. And we had the potential to be just as bad. Our fans could get rowdy with the best of them, and I was afraid it had gotten worse over the previous years.

We could be just as bad, but we didn't *have* to be. One of the reasons we had joined the ACC was to establish our own identity, which was separate and apart from our in-state rivals. We may never have been able to affect an amiable and fraternal athletic competition with our two biggest rivals; it may be that feelings had already run too deep among the armies of alumni. But the ACC was a whole new game.

With the ACC, we had the most wonderful opportunity. We had the chance to orchestrate someone else's first impression of us. That chance didn't really come in basketball. Florida State only got about fifty tickets for each ACC away game. Only rarely could we get more, and so our fans were not present in great numbers at the away games we played. Football was where we would be more visible, both at home and away.

There was a feeling in the ACC that a few schools do affect superior or condescending attitudes. If they acted that way to our fans, then we were encouraged to ignore it. If we did see fans who acted badly because they viewed Florida State as a threat to their position within the conference, or if we found some who were hostile because they feel intimidated, we were encouraged to ignore those too.

The truth was that our opponents would never like us when we beat them. But if we were going to be disliked, then we wanted it to be because we were so gracious in victory. And on those rare occasions when we lost, we needed to win their admiration in spite of whether or not they wanted to give it.

Word got around fast, and we were certain that all eyes would be on us in the fall of 1992. Whatever impression we made during the season, on and off the field, we knew it would establish our identity within the conference family. We were not bound by old rivalries; ours was a first-class, clean, winning athletic program, and we carried no unsavory baggage into the new league. The shape of our future in the ACC was solely and completely in our own hands.

In 1980, Nebraska stood among college football power pretty much where we stood that day. Nebraska was a giant. Routine losses at the hands of lighter, faster opponents were still unthinkable. But on that bright fall day, thousands of Cornhusker fans stood at the end of the game and applauded. They applauded a worthy opponent who had just handed them a shocking upset defeat on their home field. There was a feeling among some in Florida that as long as we won, sportsmanship didn't matter. No class in victory, and no grace in defeat.

Things had changed at Nebraska, and I didn't know if they'd stand and applaud us again. Surely it was easier to be gracious when you almost always win. And I didn't think we'd ever do something like that at Doak Campbell Stadium, but I knew that we could shake a few hands. We could move among the Blue Devils and Demon Deacons and Tar Heels and Terrapins as they strolled into our stadium and treated them like the new in-laws. We could tell them how happy and proud we were to be a part of their family.

One percent. One out of every hundred fans. That's all it would take. We had been talking about Nebraska for the previous twelve years. Wouldn't it be great if the ACC talked about us that way for the next twelve?*

---

* Much of this chapter's material was initially published in the *Report to Boosters* (July/ August 1992).

Real Seminole Spirit

In 1992, fans of the University of South Florida in Tampa were lobbying to start a football program in order to create a new well-spring of school spirit. Seminole spirit runs deep among the hills of Tallahassee. More than a hundred years ago our Florida State College football team won the State of Florida Championship. And more than three hundred years ago, the Apalachee Indians played a game with a ball and goal posts in Tallahassee, possibly on the very site that Doak Campbell Stadium occupies today.

Seminole Spirit. The "war chant," legions of loyal alumni, University Center, Osceola, and Renegade. Florida State's college spirit was one of its most prized and valuable assets. The University of South Florida was searching its collective soul trying to decide whether or not to start a football program.

Why was school spirit an issue there and at similar non-football-playing public institutions? It was because smart educational leaders and fundraisers knew that a clean, winning, high-profile football program was about the best way to energize great numbers of undergraduates and alumni. Successful football creates an emotional infrastructure, a long-term identity with the university that translates into increased enrollment and alumni giving.

Kansas State was a first-rate academic institution, but had been a Division I football bottom dweller for decades. K-State's gridiron fortunes were up, according to *Sports Illustrated*, because the university president observed that the public perception of Kansas State was along the lines of "if the football program is dreadful, then the whole university must be in disarray too."

The president ordered an improvement in football because he recognized that college athletics was a window through which the public could view the other, more important work of a university. That realization was powerful stuff. We only needed to consider how winning football had enhanced the public perception of Notre Dame, Alabama, Southern Cal, and Penn State.

Desire, on the part of students and alumni, for lifelong identity with their schools has always been strong. Small colleges address the issue in one way, while the Ivy Leagues do it in another. Public Division I universities like Florida State used athletics as a tool to nurture relationships with large numbers of faithful supporters and potential supporters.

Americans are an optimistic people. Combined with the desire to "be true to your school," that optimism is a source of great strength for the nation's universities. It seems, in fact, to have always been that way.

Jim Melton allowed me to rummage through his library of old yearbooks at FSU's Alumni Office. Florida State's yearbook at the turn of the century was called the *Argo*, and this was the editorial outlook in 1903: "The prediction last year that Florida State College would soon be at the head of intercollegiate athletics is rapidly coming true. The stand she took in football last autumn assures even the rankest pessimist that she is forging to the front."

And forge to the front she did. In 1904, Florida State College's 23–0 victory over Florida, then located in Lake City, was its third shutout in a row of their pre-Gator rivals. Florida fans were bitterly disappointed, and a local newspaper urged that "the university should be made stronger before it attempts to play again." That 1904 team, "undefeated by any State team," was crowned State Champions. In their formal team photo, these fresh, clean-faced lads of "Ought-Four" look at us with confident eyes from the faded pages of the *Argo*. They are good-looking kids, probably not much different from our players.

Perhaps they had a quiet and unassuming team leader like Charlie Ward. No doubt some of them were tough-as-nails blue collar guys like Matt Frier and Robbie Baker. Maybe they even had a Deion. The talent of 1992 didn't compare with the state champions of 1904, but their hearts beat with the same spirit.

The 1904 team appeared again—six of them anyway—in another faded photo from the 1948 *Tally Ho*. The occasion was a reunion celebrating Florida State's return to football. It had been forty-three years since Florida State College became FSCW in 1905. This time, however, Florida State University was taking the field to begin a new era. They looked happy, these boys of '04, now men in their sixties. If our undefeated Seminoles of 1950 had a reunion in the fall of 1993, they would have traveled the same distance in time. But whatever the distance, all Florida State hearts beat with the same spirit.

Football is a uniquely American sport, and perhaps more than any other indicator of our true character as a nation. I had always assumed that football had evolved from English rugby, but it looks as if that may not be completely true. In fact, documents sent to us by alumnus Joel Padgett, plus some help from our friends at the Florida Governor's Council on Indian Affairs, suggests that football may owe more to our Indian namesakes than we ever dreamed.

Padgett, long a key volunteer leader in Palm Beach, pointed to a work detailing the culture and customs of the Apalachee tribe. The book was written by John Hann in 1988, entitled *Apalachee: The Land Between the Rivers*. In it, he writes:

> Three hundred years ago, the Apalachee occupied the ground where FSU stands today. Remnants of the tribe eventually joined with the Creek Confederacy and migrated

to Central Florida where the Seminoles also became part of that Confederacy.

Documents provided by the Governor's Council describe the Apalachee as "very tall, very valiant, and full of spirit." When the Apalachee lived where Tallahassee is now, the best-known feature of their culture was sports, "particularly one of their ball games." In fact, "considerable information on this game survived" because of two literate natives and Friar Juan de Paiva, pastor of San Louis mission, who developed a strong animosity toward the game itself.

The Leturiondo Visitation Record of 1677–1678 contains their compiled writings and descriptions of "the Game." Consider these excerpts from the translation, and see if any of it sounds familiar:

> The ball game was a village affair. Its pregame ceremonies and preparation involved the entire community. ... The basic components of the game were a tall goal post ... a small hard buckskin ball ... and two teams of varying size. No instruments but the human hand were used to propel the ball. ... They painted their bodies in colors associated with the dominant clans.

The book recounts that 1 point was awarded each time the goal post was struck with the ball, which was propelled by the foot. If the ball struck an eagle's nest positioned on the top of the post, then 2 points were awarded. Victory went to the first team to achieve 11 points.

"Violence often was not confined to the game itself," wrote a disapproving Friar Paiva, noting frequent fights among spectators. He also mentioned that those who defended the game argued that this was merely healthy competition between villages:

> In preparation for the game, an elaborate series of rituals was observed. ... Players assembled in the main council house, or around the goal post to maintain a vigil during

the night before the game, talking very quietly, and occasionally howling like wolves.

Players sat on low, flat benches during the game. Bill McGrotha might note that the exact positioning of these seats was determined by "interpreting the dreams of several elderly men who would be awakened early in the morning to be questioned on the nature of their dreams." Forerunners of today's sportswriters?

A new fire would be lit. "Before the game, this fire was carried out onto the playing field." Then, "the Chief was to advise the players during the night, exhorting them to risk their very lives in the quest for victory."

The book also contains this wonderful passage:

> If Friar Paiva is to be believed, not all the prospective players were eager to participate. They often had to be cajoled into playing by entreaties or by a gift of something with which to wager. Skilled players were especially pampered. To keep them in the village, they were given a house, their fields were planted for them, and their misdeeds were winked at by the village authorities.

It is not unreasonable to speculate that "the Game" was played very near where Doak Campbell Stadium now stands. The FSU players of this generation may be in many ways different from the lads of Ought-Four, and they in turn may have been different from the young Apalachee men of 1678. But their hearts all beat with the same spirit. In their final commentary at the end of the 1903 *Argo*, the editors offered their toast to their beloved Florida State: "College spirit is on the rise; may it continue to grow."

Oh, yes. Yes, indeed. May it continue to grow.[*]

---

[*] Much of this chapter's material was initially published in the *Report to Boosters* (December 1992).

1993 Season

An old dog trainer once remarked that if you can't teach a dog to do what you want him to do, then teach him to do what he can do. Think about that for a minute. We best help others when we build upon their strengths rather than condemn their flaws. Our '93 championship season bears witness to this truth.

The revelation occurred in 1992. On two occasions in midseason, we were forced into a hurry-up offense after falling behind in the score. Out of desperation we put Charlie Ward into a shotgun formation to take the snap. Such a formation put the game on his shoulders, or more specifically, on his instincts as a runner, passer, and decision-maker. Charlie proved to be much more productive in the shotgun than under center. From that formation, he led us to a near victory over Miami and an incredible comeback victory over Georgia Tech. So I asked, "Why don't we work from the shotgun every down?" We decided to do just that for the rest of the 1992 season. We won all our remaining games. And Charlie's performance at quarterback was spectacular. When 1993 rolled around, we practiced almost exclusively from the shotgun that spring and summer. We called it our fast-break offense. And we used it for all of the 1993 season.

By building on Charlie's strengths rather than forcing him into an exclusively I formation or option scheme, he flourished and helped make the team much better. We went 11–1 in 1993 and beat Nebraska for our first national championship. Charlie won the Heisman Trophy. He did so by doing what he did best. And we all were the better for it.

—Bobby Bowden

1993 Season

Began the season ranked No. 1
Ended the season ranked No. 1
Record 12–1
ACC Champions
National Champions

August 28, defeated Kansas at the Meadowlands 42–0

September 4, defeated Duke in Durham 45–7

September 11, defeated Clemson in Tallahassee 57–0

September 18, defeated North Carolina in Chapel Hill 33–7

October 2, defeated Georgia Tech in Tallahassee 51–0

October 9, defeated Miami in Tallahassee 28–10

October 16, defeated Virginia in Tallahassee 40–14

October 31, defeated Wake Forest in Tallahassee 54–0

November 6, defeated Maryland in College Park 49–20

November 13, lost to Notre Dame in South Bend 24–31

November 20, defeated NC State in Tallahassee 62–3

November 27, defeated Florida in Gainesville 33–21

January 1, 1994, defeated Nebraska in the Orange Bowl 18–16

Attack on the Seminole Name

Seminole fans of recent vintage may not know that the controversy over the use of the Seminole name was an issue on fire during the 1990s. Protests and threats were routine. The university set up a circular corral of sorts outside the stadium on game days to isolate the protestors and to "protect" them from fans who might respond to their inflammatory insults. The Seminole Boosters organization stood strong against the shrill chorus of critics.

National Signing Day for football was February 3, 1993, and some said that FSU had a chance to assemble its most impressive class ever. That would be some accomplishment considering the platoons of exceptional talent that had come our way the previous few years. The young men who would form the 1993 freshman class were just babies in their mothers' arms when Bobby Bowden enjoyed his first big year with the Seminoles. He became head coach in 1976, a losing season like the previous three before it, but a 5–6 mark that included a run of late season wins was evidence that the corner had turned.

No one really expected what was waiting around that corner in 1977. It was the first 10-win season for any Division I football team in the state, which included the first win ever against Auburn. We had gotten spoiled early at Florida State. Head coaches Don Veller, Tom Nugent, and Bill Peterson made it all look so easy. That's why our 3–30 record from 1973 through 1975 was such a rude shock and such a humbling experience for the Seminole faithful.

The athletic department produced a big wall poster after the 1977 Tangerine Bowl win over Texas Tech. A collage of photos included Bobby Bowden hoisted on the shoulders of his players, and a reproduction of the entire Associated Press' top-20 list for 1977. In 1993, as we were getting ready to enjoy our sixth consecutive finish in the top 4, it was sobering to recall that even at 10–2 we would have only finished No. 14 in 1977. And we were thrilled to have that.

The polls' view of Florida State didn't change overnight. When we played Nebraska for the first time in 1980, the Huskers were ranked No. 3 and we were in the bottom half of the top 20. After our upset win, however, Nebraska dropped some and we rose a bit, but Nebraska remained ahead of us in the rankings.

Another thing on that poster from 1977 was a Bobby Bowden quote, prominently displayed. It said: "We're not second-rate anymore!" At a distance, that quote sounds quaint, almost endearingly humble. But it was the expression of a program that had just clawed its way out of a dark basement and broken into the bright sunlight.

That year really was the beginning of the modern era of Florida State football, and the first step on the road to a permanent position of national prominence. The following year, 1978, Chief Osceola and Renegade made their first appearance. In 1985, the "war chant" rocked Doak Campbell Stadium for the first time. Now those are two of the most familiar, envied, and respected traditions in all of college athletics.

It is important to understand that Florida State's successes and traditions were arrived at honestly, and with concern at every step for the proper mission of the university. Our coaches, administrators, and alumni did it the right way, which means the hard way. Fortunately, we had leaders who knew FSU's value of a clean, winning, nationally respected athletic program. More than most schools, we had enjoyed a positive and mutually beneficial cooperation between our athletic programs and the university's academic authorities.

There was a man from Oklahoma, flanked by lawyers and funded by activist groups, who wanted—no, he demanded—an end to all of Florida State's honored and honorable traditions regarding the Seminole Indians. There had been sporadic protests against the use of Indian nicknames for college and pro athletic teams. But there was a close relationship between FSU and the Seminole Tribe of Florida, thanks to the extreme care and sensitivity the university employed in nurturing that relationship.

For example, alumnus Bill Durham, owner of the horse and overseer of the Osceola and Renegade tradition, had maintained his own close ties with the tribe, consulting with them to ensure that the associated costumes and rituals were authentic. Two key executives with the Florida Governor's Council on Indian Affairs were FSU alumni (though neither were native Seminoles). And FSU had enjoyed a long and beneficial relationship with James Billie, chairman of the Seminole Tribe of Florida. Billie was adamant about FSU's standing with the tribe: "We are very proud of the Florida State University Seminoles." Period.

None of this cut any ice with Michael Haney, however, an official of the Seminole Nation in Oklahoma, and a member of the board of directors of the National Coalition Against Racism in Sports and the Media. Haney threatened us with lawsuits and was loudly denouncing FSU as a racist institution.

FSU officials met with Haney before Christmas of 1993, and FSU president Dr. Dale Lick invited him to be his guest at the basketball game on December 22. There, surrounded by reporters, Haney compared FSU fans to the Ku Klux Klan, claiming that our traditions "humiliated and angered" him. Lick remained gracious but firm, saying, "[Haney] can file any suit he wants. At this juncture, we will not give up our tradition."

Others within the local community rallied to FSU's support, especially two prominent local celebrities: syndicated columnist Mary Ann Lindley and Charles Billings, who was an author, columnist, and professor of political science at FSU. In her January 10 column, Lindley wrote: "Variations of this protest are going on all over the country where old symbols meet the new supersensitivity. ... Florida State could [change its mascot] but it shouldn't. It ought not to get wrapped up in a clichéd and winless contest: political correctness guilt facing victimization fever. ... [FSU] should make sure real grievances are addressed, but stand up to paper tigers."

Lindley made some suggestions that were on the mark, like beefing up a summer program for Native American young people, encouraging them to seek higher education, and perhaps providing scholarships for, and recruiting, true Seminoles to attend FSU. She also pointed out that our religion department was considering an idea that would lead to a center for Native American studies.

She ended her column with a profile of FSU student Shayne Osceola, "the only true Seminole the Noles can claim." Osceola, a twenty-two-year-old senior in social sciences, was on his way to Navy flight school after graduation, and "is an utterly enthusiastic Seminole sports fan." His father was a full-blooded Seminole; his mother was Scandinavian. "We feel a lot of pride in the FSU Seminoles," Shayne said. "Our mascot here is a portrayal of a Seminole Indian who is noble, strong, and full of integrity. All I know is when I go to South Florida to visit my family, there's nobody who doesn't wear an FSU shirt."

In his column, Charles Billings recognized that as Florida State's reputation grew through its high-profile athletic program, it would become a larger target for those who wished to attack the Indian symbolism: "Those critics obviously do not understand what it means to be a Seminole," he wrote. "Technically speaking, Seminoles do not comprise what would ordinarily be termed

a Native American tribe. They are the descendants of indepen-
dent-minded Americans who left their tribal governments [black,
white, and red] to govern themselves."

Billings is right. In the 1830s, many Seminoles surrendered
and were forcibly removed to Oklahoma by federal troops. Many
of those died along the way because of the brutality they endured.
Those Seminoles who refused to surrender fought on under the
leadership of Osceola. When they were ordered to give up, get in
line, and move out, Osceola's answer was no. There was much for
us to admire in this courageous tribe of Indians, runaway slaves,
and renegade whites (Osceola, some contend, had some white
ancestry) who never gave up and were never defeated.

Billings ended his column with this most eloquent observation:

> We are not all of one race, or class or gender. We are
> defined by what we do, not by what our forbearers once
> were. We are the descendants of slaves and slave-owners,
> of warriors and soldiers, of strong men and strong women.
> Our spirit is the spirit of the undefeated Seminoles. Like
> the old Seminoles, we speak many languages but when we
> gather to celebrate our achievements or to support our
> team we speak as one. Go Noles!

Why then was there such a concern about the threats and ravings of Michael Haney? Lindley and Billings were educated people,
skilled in the reasoned discourse of a university community, but
Haney was no such thing. His was not reasoned discourse at all,
but a shrill and relentless tirade of hatred and visceral accusations
designed to gain publicity and to embarrass the university in order
to advance his own agenda.

When this sort of thing began to take off, it quickly moved
from a reasoned academic discussion into the political arena,
where it took on a life of its own. Pressure built up, and universities never really comfortable with political hardball, and especially

vulnerable to these outside pressures, sometimes found themselves being used as a pawn by unsavory elements.

To even suggest that FSU was a racist university was to engage in the vilest sort of demagoguery. Yet listen to Michael Haney: "They [FSU] started the tomahawk chop. We thought we'd come right there in the belly of the beast and confront their racist conduct." There's no room for compromise here: "Florida State must drop its name and find another mascot. In four months, if I'm satisfied ... then I won't file suit." No compromise would suffice, except to move him closer to his goal. The *Florida Flambeau* reported, "Haney said he's determined to see that FSU drops its Seminole mascot altogether within the next couple of years. In the meantime, he's looking to see whether the university is willing to meet him half-way."

It is dangerous to meet anyone halfway who equates a caring and noble university with the Ku Klux Klan. Would you be willing to stand still while decent people suffered these accusations from the likes of Michael Haney? Would *you* be willing to bow and scrape to avoid him falsely branding you as a racist, or to pay tribute to or change any of our honored traditions just to make him go away and stop calling you names in the national media?

We must give the same answer that Osceola gave 150 years ago: No.*

---

* Much of this chapter's material was initially published in the *Report to Boosters* (January/February 1993).

University Center Symbolizes the Seminoles' Rise

Florida State's University Center is one of the most magnificent venues in all of college football. It contains five colleges of the university, as well as the athletic department, the University Center Club, almost the entire student services operation, the offices of Seminole Boosters, Inc., and nearly a hundred private skyboxes. Upon its completion in 2006, it was the largest contiguous brick construction in the United States. The struggle to win approval and funding for the massive project stoked passions on all sides. Opposition to the project was intense and partisan, but Seminole leaders prevailed.

In 279 BC, the daring Greek general Pyrrhus defeated a Roman army at the battle of Asculum. However, the engagement cost him the lives of many of his men, most of his senior officers, and all of his baggage. One of the Greek officials congratulated Pyrrhus on his victory, to which he replied, "Another such victory and we are surely ruined."

FSU won a Pyrrhic victory over LSU in Baton Rouge on a stormy late October night in 1991. Coaches later suggested it might have been the most courageous game they had ever seen their Seminoles play. As our men came off the field—some of them were carried off the field—soaked with mud and rain, matted with blood, they likely didn't comprehend the full significance of the game. The injuries at LSU probably cost us the Miami game, and that loss in turn surely contributed to the season-ending loss at Florida. But the '91 LSU game also marked the end of Florida State's "Road Years," a spectacular run of thirteen seasons that saw FSU burst into the national spotlight as a giant killer, and, finally, as one of the giants.

Bobby Bowden—"King of the Road," they called him. And FSU played this role to the hilt, season after season, to millions upon millions of television sets. Six out of seven victories over LSU in Baton Rouge, plus one more in Tallahassee. Three over Arizona State, which were away games. Two over Ohio State, which were also away games. The big one over Notre Dame in 1981 and the bigger one over Michigan in 1991. Also the multiple wins over Nebraska. Remember that question the writers asked? "Who are the only teams with winning records in Lincoln? The answer: FSU and Nebraska!" And toward the end of that thirteen-year passage, Auburn and Florida began to fall once again.

Whatever the motive of the original schedule maker long before the arrival of Bobby Bowden, the end result was more favorable than anyone could have imagined. By playing, and beating, the big names on the road, FSU made a dramatic and relatively quick leap into the public eye. That leap helped build our athletic program to prominence, and it contributed greatly to the positive image of the entire university. During those days, attacks on college athletics were coming from a variety of directions, but we could look at FSU and almost see a model of the ways a major university benefited from being identified with a clean, winning, high-profile athletic program.

Probably the purest and most complete expression of that model was the eighty-million-dollar University Center that was under construction at and around Doak Campbell Stadium. University Center was the most massive and ambitious construction project ever undertaken by the university. It would shift the focus of the entire campus by providing a half-million square feet of office and classroom space. Five complete colleges would be housed there—the film school was scheduled to begin classes in their new building in the spring of 1994. All student services would be consolidated under one roof, and there would be restaurants, bookstores, and a host of other operations that catered to the bustle of a growing university community.

The athletic portion of the center involved increasing the stadium seating capacity to seventy-two thousand, plus the construction of new skyboxes could be used as seminar meeting rooms during school hours. It would also house a state-of-the-art academic counseling center for all Seminole athletes in all sports.

The architect's concept model of University Center in 1988. In the early planning stages, the initiative to cloak Doak Campbell Stadium in massive walls of brick was code-named Project SBI (Seminole Boosters, Inc.).

Land purchased early on by the Boosters helped us stay a step ahead of construction and still provided parking for a growing number of football fans. The university finally closed on a huge parcel of land south of the stadium, which would provide storm water retention. This was a major step toward covering those dangerous and unsightly ditches that crisscrossed the stadium grounds. It would also enable us to solve the severe flooding problems that plagued the campus for years.

We also needed to consider the architecture. Collegiate gothic was expensive, even at the time, but it was also emotionally powerful and it endured. The massive towers, the graceful arches, the elegant gothic detailing recalled the grandeur, integrity, and sense of permanence of our original campus. When Florida State wanted to put on its best face, it showed the Westcott Building, not any of those regrettable 1960s and '70s constructions that stretched west from Woodward Avenue along Tennessee Street.

University Center was built for the ages, and on a breathtaking scale, I might add. When University Center was finally finished, it would rank among the finest and most impressive collegiate facilities in America. But it was important to note that without Seminole athletics, there would be no University Center. Of that we could be certain. And without the forty-million-dollars' worth of academic construction and enhancements, Doak Campbell Stadium would still be sitting there to this day, ugly and unchanged.

The "Road Years" began on a brilliant sunlit afternoon in LSU's Tiger Stadium in 1979, and they ended in a drenching rainstorm on the same field twelve seasons later. Seminole alumni, especially Seminole Boosters' president Andy Miller, had taken more than a passing interest in the stadium. LSU had constructed a dormitory and classrooms underneath their stadium and walled up the outside, giving the entire structure a massive and appealing look.

Miller, in 1993, in his eighteenth year as Booster CEO, was rightly credited with originating the University Center concept. In fact, for several years there was an elaborate architect's model of a combination academic and athletic wraparound building at Doak Campbell Stadium that Miller used to promote the concept. "Actually, several people in different areas of the university started coming up independently with ideas about locating nonathletic facilities at the stadium," said Miller. "We in athletics were looking for a way to expand the stadium and to improve its appearance. We played on the road in some tremendously impressive facilities, and our own erector set stadium was an embarrassment and did not properly reflect the image of the university."

At the same time, the university's top academic and administrative minds were trying to solve a long list of problems, almost all of which boiled down to the fact that there was not enough room on the state's smallest campus to accommodate nearly thirty thousand students plus all the faculty and staff and support apparatus they required. And so it became clear that there was a solution—a grand solution tailored to promote the best interests of Florida State as no single project ever had—which would require the complete cooperation of the athletic and academic sides to make happen.

If Miller was the head cheerleader and chief fundraiser for University Center, then Jim Pitts was the master traffic manager. As vice president for advancement, Dr. Pitts guided the project through complex thickets of subcommittees, boards, and governmental bodies. Having returned to the faculty, Pitts was the chairman of the University Center Building Committee. There were others too—many others within the faulty, the administration, and within the legislative staffs. At each step of this exceedingly difficult, frustrating, and demanding process, key individuals stepped forward to provide what was needed in the moment.

But without T. K. Wetherell, it would all have been for nothing. T. K. learned his football from Bill Peterson and his hardball in the Florida legislature. As speaker of the house, he saw to it that funds were appropriated to pay for the academic phase of the construction. Seminole Boosters, Inc. was responsible for the forty-million-dollar bond being used to finance the athletic portion.

Wetherell was the key when the politics got interesting. All sorts of mischief can be done in the legislature by folks who are so inclined. T. K. was there to see that FSU was treated properly. And the project was never really controversial until it was made so by a particularly bitter partisan.

Perhaps you remember hearing about the fellow, an outspoken graduate and supporter of a rival institution who squandered his own money as well as untold under-the-table contributions from like-minded followers, in a frantic and desperate campaign to discredit Florida State University and to destroy the University Center project. At one point, he jetted up and down the Eastern Seaboard meeting with editors from the *New York Times* and *Washington Post*, hawking his anti-FSU propaganda. But he failed. Perhaps a clue to the transformative significance of University Center can be seen in the extreme measures that partisan opponents were willing to adopt in order to stop it.

Tiger Stadium, and other splendid stadiums we visited during the road years, may have planted the seeds of inspiration. But University Center was a distinctly unique concept: clusters of buildings attached to the stadium and surrounding the stadium like a massive gothic fortress. Beautifully landscaped and magnificently designed, University Center would fire the imagination and pride of all those who called Florida State University their own. It would serve to sustain one enduring identity for our *entire* community.*

---

* Much of this chapter's material was initially published in the Report to Boosters (March/April 1993).

"We're Going to Assault
This University!"

Florida State's preseason No. 1 ranking brought wider national attention and continued assaults on our use of the Seminole as our honored symbol. It would be another decade before activists could influence the NCAA to consider their political agenda, but 1993 saw threats and inflammatory rhetoric directed at FSU to force immediate change.

Perhaps you took notice of the two Big Ten schools that announced in 1993 that, while they do not actually play Florida State in any sports, they did not intend to do so in the future either. This was to punish FSU for our use of the Seminoles as a team symbol. This was the sort of politically correct silliness that richly deserved all the ridicule it was receiving.

The *Florida Times-Union* led off its report in this way: "Two universities with mascots of weasels and rodents said they want to limit games against Florida State University because of its mascot." But the University of Minnesota Gophers and the University of Wisconsin Badgers would continue to play the University of Illinois Fighting Illini (named after a regional Indian tribe) because they were all members of the same conference. I couldn't imagine how they were dealing with that in the radical activist coffeehouses.

Since the conference had expanded to include eleven schools, but kept the Big Ten name, maybe they were just not counting Illinois at all. Besides Illinois, exceptions were also made for post-season games, and certain regional rivals like the North Dakota Fighting Sioux and the Central Michigan Chippewas. Still, they had to find someone *not* to play, so why not a team a thousand miles away that they had never met in football or basketball and had no plans to play in the future. Take *that*, Florida State.

The Wisconsin sport's information director sounded a bit sheepish. "In politically correct Madison, we're trying to take as good a stand as we can," he said. FSU athletic director Bob Goin reiterated how proud we were to be associated with the real Seminoles, adding wryly, "And we have an awful lot of people who are interested in playing us."

Goin was too classy to point out that Wisconsin's 4–7 record the previous year was punctuated with a season-ending loss to Northwestern, and that Minnesota (2–9) was so dreadful that it was slated to become the first team in history to finish No. 11 in the Big Ten. Neither of those programs needed to be anywhere near Tallahassee on a hot early-September afternoon. In fact, if I were them, while I was at it I would have refused to play Miami too. The Hurricanes didn't show up on any future Gopher/Badger schedules either, but why take any chances? Besides, tropical hurricanes are violent destroyers of both lives and hope. That was reason enough for the compulsively politically correct to eschew them as a collegiate symbol.

Just a few weeks before this news came, the Cleveland Indians announced that the team symbol, known as Chief Wahoo, would be retained. "Our ball club exists for our fans, and it's very clear they love the Chief," said Indians owner Richard E. Jacobs. "While many things will change when we move into our new ballpark next year, the Chief will remain." Likewise, most college and professional teams were refusing to buckle under the pressure.

But it was an issue that would not go away. Michael Haney, the activist from Oklahoma, had threatened an all-out attack on Florida State earlier in the fall of 1993. We, as Seminole fans, needed to be prepared for their tactics. As we approached our magnificent new stadium that September, we weren't surprised to see the various of society's loose threads parading up and down loudly demanding that we change our lives to suit their politics. And we couldn't be drawn in by whatever other disruptions they had planned either. Causes of barely marginal worth had been able to generate sympathy for themselves by deliberately provoking the overreaction of mainstream bystanders.

Haney and his kind were professional rabble-rousers. *Racism* was the red-hot word during that time, just as it is in our time. Racism was the electrifying sword Haney wielded to carve out chunks of media for himself and with which he flashed in the face of opponents to silence and intimidate them. Florida State is "a racist institution," Seminole fans remind him "of the Ku Klux Klan," and the university president "is a racist."

Haney had no desire to compromise. His stated goal was the total and complete elimination of our Seminole symbol. It was so important for our university not to appease Haney and his followers in any way. If history shows us anything, it is that if you appease people whose goal is to destroy you, then you will suffer all the more terribly for it in the long run.

After being rebuffed by President Lick on the general issue, Haney turned his tactics to aim at individual traditions. First on his hit list, according to media reports, was our use of the name "Scalp Hunters" for two men's and women's student organizations oriented around athletics. "Scalping," of course, was the latest lightning rod of political correctness.

The Scalp Hunter name was an inconsequential issue really, and one we could easily let go. But then what would be next? And what would be next after that? The fact was that the wars against the whites were especially bitter for the Seminoles, and as author Kenneth W. Mulder points out in his book *Pirates: Days of Long Ago,* the Seminoles delighted in scalping enemy soldiers. He wrote, "Scalping was one of the rewards to the early Seminoles in resisting the United States Army."

Osceola himself seems to have particularly relished the practice too. Mulder tells of an Army general named Wiley Thompson who threw Osceola into irons for defying him and refusing to sign a punitive treaty. Several years later, Osceola laid an ambush for Thompson and one of his lieutenants just outside Ft. King: "[They] had eaten their noonday meal, lit their cigars and were taking a walk outside the stockade. They had not gone far when Osceola and his party of warriors shot General Thompson fourteen times. The lieutenant was also killed. Both were scalped within earshot of the fort; Osceola personally scalped Thompson as revenge."

Thompson was only one of many Army leaders who failed to subdue the Seminole. Two of them—Andrew Jackson and Zachary Taylor—went on to become presidents of the United States. "But not one of these military leaders ever bragged in his memoirs about defeating the Seminoles," Mulder wrote. "No peace treaty was ever signed."

A second and just as important reason for refusing to accede to Haney's demands was that it would undermine the position of our friends, the Seminole tribe of Florida. These real Seminoles had been steadfast in their support of Florida State and of FSU's position on this matter. Listen to the words of James Billie, who was chairman of the Seminole tribe:

> Nothing has been broken. Nothing needs fixing. We Seminoles have no objection to Florida State University using the Seminole symbol. In fact, as long as the Seminoles keep winning, we're happy. We do not want to participate in this ridiculous debate just to fan the flames of news hype for those few … instigators who have assigned themselves the lofty job of telling us Seminoles how we are supposed to feel.

Billie said that his tribe refused to be included in the games "these egotists" were playing with the students, officials, and alumni of Florida State. As for waffling, or negotiation, or compromise on our part, Billie had even stronger words:

> I am surprised and disappointed that the sophisticated Florida State University is allowing itself to be sucked into the tornado of this issue. I have more important things to do than to worry about a mascot or the uniforms of a football player or a cheerleader. ... A dashing character on a horse with a flaming spear has nothing to do whatsoever with educating our children of the economic development of our Tribal resources. Those who try to connect the FSU mascot with problems in Indian Country are playing a cruel, self-serving joke on anyone who takes them seriously.

This was the calm before the storm. But September was just around the corner. All we needed to do was witness the rantings of Michael Haney, who was looking forward to football season as much as we were: "We're going to target [Florida State] University as the most racist school in America today. ... We're going to make sure that every state in the Union knows FSU is the most offensive school in the nation. ... We're going to have an Indian attack here. ... We're going to assault this university!"

There was no doubt that Haney had the ability to whip up a lot of dust around the issue. Could our university administration withstand the political and media pressure that would be brought to bear? The answer was yes, but they needed to know that our loyal Seminole alumni and fans were fully supportive of the no appeasement, no compromise position. Michael Haney and his henchmen were no match for the spirit of Osceola. There wouldn't be any treaty *this* time either.*

---

* Much of this chapter's material was initially published in the *Report to Boosters* (July/ August 1993).

Building on Tradition:
The Loss of Bill Peterson
and Bill McGrotha

Bobby Bowden's dramatic turnabout of Seminole football naturally brought stark comparisons with the record that preceded him. But as dreadful as the bad seasons were, there were only three in a row (1973–1975). Seminole football enjoyed a solid tradition from its beginning in 1947, and Coach Bill Peterson brought the Seminoles into the national spotlight in the 1960s. In this 1993 season that brought our first national championship, we lost two stalwarts who helped construct the foundation for our success.

Some fraternity brothers of mine attended Coach Bill Peterson's funeral. One of them brought along a twenty-five-year-old alumni newsletter published in 1968. It bragged about a big rally—banners, placards, boys shouting while perched on each other's shoulders—staged to convince Coach Pete to stay in Tallahassee. "Don't Go, Coach Pete," and "Don't Leave Us" the signs and banners pleaded.

The newsletter grandly reported that the rally had been a success. Pete ended up staying three more seasons as Seminole head coach, and the conceit of young fellows was such that we thought we had had something to do with that. The boys in those old pictures were in 1993 graying men in their late forties, who were then very close to Bill's age in 1968. They mourned together on this football-perfect Saturday afternoon in Tallahassee. A couple of the men stared at the faded photograph of the banners and again whispered its plea: "Don't go, Coach Pete." But this time he was already gone.

Bill Peterson was a great coach, but he wasn't the first great coach at Florida State. Don Veller's teams lost a total of only four games in the first four years he led them. They were the first major college program in Florida to win a conference championship (1948), the first to go to a bowl game (1949), and the first to go undefeated (1950). That undefeated record included a 20–6 win in Doak Campbell Stadium over Howard College and their All-American quarterback, Bobby Bowden.

Coach Tom Nugent took the Seminoles through most of the 1950s. This energetic and innovative coach invented football's I formation while at FSU, and his teams waded into a heavily upgraded schedule, which was designed to lift FSU into the mainstream of big-time college football. Nugent's teams squared off against the big SEC powerhouses, including the first games against Florida. In 1958, FSU whipped Tennessee 10–0 in Knoxville, a win much more shocking in its day even than our upset win over Nebraska in 1980.

Don Yeller and Tom Nugent, and Coach Pete until his death, had all remained loyal and active members of the Seminole Boosters. When Nugent left FSU, a committee was drawn up to pick the new coach. Bill McGrotha and Dean Coyle Moore told about the meeting where everyone seemed to panic because time was short and no one could agree on a candidate.

Ray Graves, then assistant at Georgia Tech, was interviewed but turned it down. Bill Peterson, an LSU assistant, was to be interviewed but was off on a recruiting trip. A third assistant, this one at West Point, was highly recommended by Army's head coach.

But the committee did not grant him an interview, and so Vince Lombardi had to look elsewhere for a team to lead. They finally settled on Perry Moss. In that brief, unhappy 1959 season, Moss negotiated secretly with a Canadian league pro team, and signed a contract after only seven games as Seminole head coach.

Bill Peterson coached the Seminoles from 1960 through the 1970 season. The bedrock foundation of a first-rate program had already been put in place by Veller and Nugent. Pete arrived with a clear vision of the greatness that FSU could and should achieve, and he believed that his own destiny was interwoven with the success of the university.

To fully appreciate what Peterson did, one has to get a feel for what he was up against. Finances limited the number of scholarships he could offer, but those were the days before the NCAA placed limits on team size. Large, wealthy programs could offer as many as they wished, and frequently they signed boys just to keep them from playing for opposing teams. In the last year before the NCAA restricted the size of recruiting classes, Alabama signed a hundred incoming freshmen to full scholarships.

We faced a killer schedule in 1993, but we also had the No. 1-ranked team in the country going in. We enjoyed the advantage of five years of great recruiting classes, and the assurance that no team had more or better players than FSU. Many of the opponents Coach Pete's teams faced were armed with overwhelming numbers and resources. And the schedule in 1962 was no less foreboding than it was in 1993.

Think not? Consider that the list of opponents in 1962 included Georgia, Georgia Tech, Miami, Auburn, Florida, Kentucky, and Houston. And yet, incredible as it was, only one opponent (Miami) scored any points at all against FSU in the first five games of the season! It was the eighth game before any opponent scored more than a touchdown, and no opponent scored as many as three touchdowns all year long.

Also of incalculable importance to Pete's success were the writings of *Tallahassee Democrat* sports editor Bill McGrotha, who covered the Seminoles from 1952 until his death in January 1993. It was his skill that again and again articulated the grand vision of a program straining to join the ranks of college football's elite. McGrotha was enormously talented; his words flowed with the effortless ease of Lawrence Dawsey gliding across the field beneath a long ball. His words inspired, they educated, and they explained and encouraged both fans and players alike. Bill's writing was imaginative, gracious, polished, and entertaining without being hurtful to anyone.

McGrotha didn't recruit football players, but he mightily helped to create a campus and community atmosphere that was for decades one of the most positive attractions of Florida State athletics. In an unprecedented move, the board of directors of Seminole Boosters, Inc. gave a memorial gift of five thousand dollars to the Bill McGrotha Scholarship. No, it wasn't an athletic scholarship. It was in the college of communication, for the encouragement of fine writing.

What Bill McGrotha envisioned in print, Bill Peterson envisioned on the field, installing the pro-set passing game—and recruiting the players to exploit it—ahead of any other major college program. When No. 4-ranked Kentucky was hammered 48–6 in Campbell Stadium in 1964, some wire services reversed the score, assuming it was a mistake. Fred Biletnikoff and his fleet friends scored six touchdowns against a befuddled, run-oriented Oklahoma team in the 1965 Gator Bowl. The 1968 Peach Bowl was such a burner that LSU immortalized their 31–27 win as one of the "Five Most Exciting Tiger Victories of All Time."

Coach Pete's record against Florida was 2–8–1 (or 3–7–1 depending on your view of the Lane Fenner catch), a mark that brought more smiles to Seminole faces, and more frowns to Gator ones than the raw numbers would suggest to a nonpartisan. And

Pete had Miami's number. He went 5–2 against the Hurricanes, winning four straight in the Orange Bowl. Georgia was 0–4 against Peterson's Seminoles. In fact, the Bulldogs didn't even score until the third game, and recorded only 17 total points in all four outings.

But the University of Houston was Bill's nemesis. Then an Independent like Florida State, Houston had built a powerful football program on the anything-goes, oil-rich flatlands of South Texas. We went 1–7–2 against Houston. Bill's final game as Seminole head coach was a 53–21 loss to the Cougars.

Coach Pete left Florida State in 1970 for the city of Houston, to become the head coach and athletic director at Rice University. A year later, he became the head coach of the Houston Oilers. One of those old NFL films specials you see on late-night ESPN features head coaches, and you can watch Bill Peterson rant and rave along the Houston sidelines.

Coach Pete had been close to and in Tallahassee since the early '70s. His longtime friendship with Bernie Sliger, which went back to their Louisiana State University days together, was a strong magnet. He raised money for the FSU Foundation for a while, and he did so very successfully.

There were some rough years in between the tenures of Bill Peterson and Bobby Bowden, but not enough to ruin the tradition and the following that Peterson and others built. Bobby Bowden was the right man at the right time. He was the latest great coach in a sequence of great coaches at Florida State. They labored for forty years to build a winning tradition inside Doak Campbell Stadium, a tradition enclosed in Gothic brick and stone in 1993.

Much had been made in the media of Coach Steve Spurrier's lament: "Florida State must have the best recruiters in the country. How they can convince guys to come up there and beat out All-Americans who are already there is beyond me." How? Let's take a look. Tradition, to you and me, was Florida State football over the previous ten, twenty, or even forty years. What was tradition for an eighteen-year-old? Consider that Bobby Bowden had been Seminole head coach for that youngster's whole life.

Most eighteen-year-olds began playing serious football within the previous six years, and maybe they started really following college teams for the previous several years. In the previous six years leading up to 1993, Bobby Bowden had won at least ten games per season, the only coach ever to do so. In the previous six years, Florida State players had won two Butkus Awards, one Lombardi Award, two Thorpe Awards, and one Unitas Award. Four different FSU players finished in the top 10 for the Heisman Trophy in the previous two years, and in 1993 our team boasted two leading Heisman candidates, as well as a leading candidate for the Butkus, and the leading candidate for the Thorpe. The preseason issue of *Sports Illustrated* featured FSU on the cover, as well as an unprecedented twelve pages of coverage inside. That's how.

Plainly stated, our job as Seminole Boosters was to build against the day when we no longer had Bobby Bowden. And we built, as Coach Bowden built, on the foundations and traditions established by the likes of Coach Pete and Bill McGrotha. Two hundred years ago, the English philosopher Robert Burton suggested that all of us, even the least of us, could see more clearly when we stand on the shoulders of giants. Coach Pete and Bill were giants who had departed, but the strong shoulders remained.[*]

---

[*] Much of this chapter's material was initially published in the *Report to Boosters* (September/October 1993).

"We Would Be Lesser Men ..."

It probably couldn't have happened at a better time. The goal-line stand against Kansas in the 1993 Kickoff Classic at the Meadowlands was destined to become a headline, and maybe a whole chapter, in the already storied history of Seminole football. It was the stuff of Seminole legend.

Kansas, riding an 8–4 season and a bowl victory from 1992, personified the hard-running, bull-necked Big 8 style of offense. Florida State offered a potent offense, but the defense was, some felt, too untested, too undersized, and too crippled with injuries to shoulder its load of the Seminoles' No. 1 ranking.

One magnificent series became the signature of this defense. The Jayhawks were given a dozen tries from inside the 10 and still couldn't crack the fragile goal-line plane. Three offside penalties pushed the Seminoles seemingly to the breaking point. Kansas ran ten plays from inside the 8. Defensive players, stiff with exhaustion, slowly picked themselves up after each down, clasped each other's hands, and then lined up to face the next assault. Defensive coordinator Mickey Andrews screamed, "One more time!" through cupped hands. Offensive players leaped and jabbed helmets into the air, and shouted encouragement to their teammates.

Kansas ran six plays from the 1-yard line. Yes, *six* plays from the 1-yard line. Each time was a hammer blow. And each time sparks showered the ground and the hammer shook, but the anvil remained solid and unmoved. In the end, it was Florida State's ball on the 1.

The Seminole offense—that splendid, flashy, movie-star Florida State offense—was in awe of the defense. When the offense once again took the field, fullback William Floyd stepped into the huddle and said, "We would be lesser men if we don't go on and take this ball 99 yards and score." And that's exactly what they did.

Victory over Kansas wasn't on the line; FSU had the game under control. Had Kansas scored a touchdown after a half dozen tries from inside the 10, our defense would have been congratulated for their tenacity. Had the Jayhawks kicked a field goal, the defense would have been counted successful for allowing 3 points instead of 6. But even when it meant winning or losing, one can't expect a defense to turn back a Division I running offense eight times from inside the 2—six of those times from the 1. In fact, one can't even *ask* it of them.

No, the defense wasn't doing it to win the game. They were doing it for themselves. That heroic series at the goal line may have far-reaching effects that are yet to be realized. Once in a while, a great sacrifice is made or a great adversity is overcome, and suddenly the rest of us are able to see what is truly possible. William Floyd caught a glimpse of it on that day. He saw not just what was possible at the goal line, but what was possible for a year.

Attitude is extremely important, but it is not the most important element in success—a gerbil spinning in its cage may have a wonderful attitude. Nor is talent the determining factor in success—unfulfilled and unrealized talent is more common than not. But on those occasions when attitude, talent, and vision clasped hands, oh my! History's creaking wheels have been forced to shudder and jump.

Before the Kansas game, FSU was already being touted as the preseason No. 1. After Kansas and "the stand," sportswriters began examining the possibilities that these Seminoles were a team of destiny. Some even asked if this was the greatest college football team of all time. At that point we didn't know the answer. The Seminoles played the nation's toughest schedule in 1993. Nearly every opponent was, or would be, ranked during the season. And given our ranking and reputation, we knew that all opponents would play their best games against us. No one could expect any team to go 13–0 under those circumstances. No one could even ask it of them.

But what if that team asked it of themselves? What if a team imbued with a rare combination of attitude and talent discovered its own inspired vision along the goal line in the first game of the season? "We would be lesser men," said Floyd, if we did not rise to match the sacrifice and achievement of this stunning defensive stand. And, if we could hold Kansas out for twelve plays from the 10, could we not also hold Clemson out for a full series from the 4? Could we not dominate Miami? What else could we accomplish?

After our victory over No. 3-ranked Kentucky in 1964, many in the Seminole locker room were sullen. A few players wept, while others slammed their helmets into the lockers. They had defeated the Wildcats—destroyed them actually, 48–6. But Kentucky had scored a meaningless touchdown late in the game because of a careless error by one of our players.

Kentucky had been our fourth game of the year. Seminole defenders had shut out the first three opponents, including Miami, and they had been determined to do the same to UK. That attitude, that vision of what was truly possible, set the tone for what was up to that time and for years beyond the greatest team in Seminole football history.

When Bobby Bowden returned to become Seminole head coach in 1976, he found a proud program that had fallen on hard times. It was a myth, and not a useful one, that Florida State seriously considered dropping football in 1974. Dr. Stan Marshall, then FSU president, had no intention of really dropping the sport at all, but he used the threat to generate a quick-fix infusion of community support and cash.

In a more ideal world, Dr. Marshall might have been able to assure Coach Bowden that FSU would build a splendid new stadium, and actually fill it. And that money would be lavished on new weight facilities and locker rooms, and it would be used to hire the finest assistants. And that all this would attract the most talented and committed players so that Bowden would have a chance to win. Instead, Dr. Marshall probably told his new coach that the facilities were not good and that attendance and support and enthusiasm were low. Bowden needed to find a way to win, and winning would build the program.

In the real world, support follows success. That fact is the key to the mechanics of motivation. In the heat of the contest, however, it is not the coach's locker room talk that spark the surge of one team over another. It happens when one man makes the most spectacular tackle he has ever made. It is when one receiver makes the catch that no one thought possible. It is the goal-line stand that no one thought could be successful.

Remember the 1988 game against Clemson in Death Valley? It wasn't the Puntrooskie that inspired the Seminoles to win; it was Deion Sanders, standing on his own 24-yard line to receive a punt and signaling to the Clemson bench and crowd that he intended to run it back for a score. Deion cut through the middle of the field past Clemson defenders, finally hurdling the Tiger punter on his way to the end zone. It was that glimpse of what was truly possible that inspired men to be more than others supposed them to be.

The genius of Bobby Bowden, and really of all great coaches for that matter, was in his ability to take players with ambition and talent and focus them on a vision of what was possible. "I don't know much about football," said Bear Bryant, "but I know a lot about winning."

Bobby Bowden provided the national image of a clean, winning program at a first-class university. Others, including Andy Miller, Jim Pitts, Bernie Sliger, and T. K. Wetherell, supplied the inspiring vision of University Center, and they raised the money to pay for it. Raising money was what we did at Seminole Boosters, Inc. We took advantage of every opportunity. We encouraged the generosity of all alumni and supporters. We worked hard to make Seminole athletics a source of strength and pride for Florida State. To do less would dishonor the vision of what our university could achieve.

In December of 1991, basketball coach Pat Kennedy prepared for Florida State's inaugural game in the ACC: North Carolina in the Dean Dome. Everyone expected the Seminoles' initiation to be a painful one. Kennedy would be without starting forward Doug Edwards and reserve guard Ray Donald when he faced the No. 3-ranked Tar Heels.

Assistant Coach Tom Carlson remembers those four days of preparation leading up to the game: "Kennedy never stopped talking, and he never stopped talking about winning. He made it clear that the game was not up for grabs, that we were not going to try to stay close, and that we were not going to play to keep from being embarrassed. We were going to win."

Kennedy and his assistants composed an excruciatingly detailed game plan that called on the players to assume a discipline far beyond what they were used to. Starters would have to play the entire game. Individual players would sacrifice their scoring and their stats for the sake of the team. Carlson said, "With Edwards out, Charlie Ward had to completely change his role for us to win. Sam Cassell made a tremendous sacrifice for the team; so did Andre Reid."

North Carolina officials made a show of welcoming FSU to the conference. They presented Kennedy with a game ball, then they sat back to enjoy the anticipated Tar Heel feast. It was to be the signature game for Florida State's Atlantic Coast Conference basketball ambitions. Untested, unproven, and playing without their best player, the Seminoles stunned North Carolina 86–74.

In the postgame locker room, the players collapsed. "I've never seen an entire team so exhausted," said Carlson. "If we had to go into overtime, I'm not sure we could have answered the bell." Kennedy, his assistants, and his players had gambled to be great. They spent every last measure of physical and emotional strength in pursuit of victory. They would have considered themselves lesser men had they not done so.[*]

---

[*] Much of this chapter's material was initially published in the *Report to Boosters* (October/November 1993).

Seminole Ambush in the Swamp, the Trap at Notre Dame, and the Speech No Cornhusker Gave

Seminole dreams of a national championship berth were renewed after Notre Dame lost to unranked Boston College the week after beating FSU in South Bend. The Ward-to-Dunn touchdown in the Swamp, along with the final 1:18 in the Orange Bowl, were among the most emotionally charged moments in Seminole football history. All the following spring, the scoreboard in Nebraska's own stadium showed Nebraska 16, Florida State 15, with 1:18 left.

A few days before the Florida game, some of us were speculating about our chances of being the first team to beat Steve Spurrier in the Swamp. On his way out the door, one fellow laughed and said, "Ask Major Dade what's going to happen. Ask Major Dade about the swamp." We asked who Major Dade was, and he told us to look it up. And so we did.

Major Francis L. Dade, a career soldier, became familiar with Central and South Florida when he was stationed in the Tampa Bay area for a few years in the early 1830s. Dade was proud of his forward-thinking ideas about military hygiene and tactics, and bragged that he had never lost a man to the terrors of the Florida swamps. Indeed, his command suffered no losses to fever, snakes, or other pestilences, including the creature considered most dangerous in the swamp, the alligator.

On December 28, 1835, Dade and his regiment were marching along the edge of the Wahoo Swamp, near present-day Bushnell. The soldiers wore blue uniforms with red piping, which the hot Florida sun had faded orange. The men were in good spirits, having just been told that Major Dade was planning a late Christmas party for them at the end of their march.

They did not know that 180 Seminole warriors were waiting quietly for them to walk into a trap. It was a brilliantly constructed ambush. In the first salvo of musket fire, Major Dade and half his command fell dead. The survivors retreated to a spot two hundred yards away where they set up their cannon and dug in. Relentless assaults by the Seminoles overwhelmed them. By late afternoon, all but three of Dade's 109 remaining men were dead. Those three managed to escape.

The moral of the story? Never forget that the most dangerous item in the swamp is the Seminole. Seminoles 33, Gators 21.

The Trap at Notre Dame

On New Year's Day we had the chance to play one more game, winner take all. This 1993 Seminole team certainly deserved a title bout. How many ranked teams had we beaten? Six? Seven? This was a team that laid waste to their Atlantic Coast Conference schedule, defeating all eight league teams by an average score of 48–6. This was the team with the leading Heisman candidate and the leading Butkus candidate under the same banner. This was the defense that outscored five opponents and gave us the legend of "the stand" vs. Kansas. This was the offense that had mastered the shotgun as perhaps no other college team before.

The night before the Notre Dame game, our team stayed in an isolated little town about thirty miles from South Bend. The players seemed calm and confident. I felt confident too. That is, I felt confident right up until I sat down to breakfast Saturday morning and opened up the *Chicago Tribune*. The splashy headline read, "Bold Seminoles Mock Irish Lore ... Holtz Fires Back as Drama Builds."

There was a color photo of our men working out in the Notre Dame stadium, wearing the green baseball caps with shamrocks on the side. The *Tribune* sportswriter called it "an extraordinary scene." He went on to write that the Seminoles "swaggered into the stadium as if they had come not only to bury the Irish, but to boast of it ahead of time and heap a little dirt on Notre Dame's storied tradition."

He quoted Kevin Knox (whom, they noted, showed up with his personal video camera to tape practice): "Mystique? There is no mystique. They should be scared of our mystique. We're a dominating team. This could be the best college football team ever." Knox wasn't the lone gunman either. There were quotes from other Seminole players as well: "I hope the defense gets another shutout. By getting a good shutout here, that really kind of simplifies that we're the best team ever," and, "Rock Knootne?—whatever his name is."

Then the sportswriter started drawing comparisons with Miami. If you want to raise the hair on the back of an Irish fan's neck, then talk about Miami. Notre Dame wasn't playing Miami that day, but Lou Holtz and the faithful needed a demon, and the demon had to be given a name. Florida State was portrayed as Miami, but with different colored hats.

Coach Bowden said all the right things and made all the right gestures, but his words drowned in a sea of Irish indignation. It was like watching the light brigade trot toward the guns at Balaclava. You felt you should shout out a warning, but they were too far away to hear and too far gone to turn back.

Lou Holtz had put his extra week of preparation to good use.

He booked the X's and O's, but he also created a powerful psychological landscape, with Notre Dame Stadium as a fortress where the true believers would turn back this latest wave of demons conjured up from the lower regions. Part of Holtz's landscape included a minefield for Seminole players. Midwestern sportswriters put their arms around our boys' shoulders and smiled, telling us what it was like to be on the greatest team of all time. And our players smiled and stepped forward to tell them.

Jerry Kutz, publisher of the *Osceola*, went to the Irish pep rally on that Friday night. More than twelve thousand had jammed into the Joyce Athletic Center an hour ahead of tipoff for the upcoming basketball game. Thousands more were turned away. Irish players ran into the arena jabbing their fists in the air, and the noise seemed like it would bring down the walls.

Haley Scott, the Notre Dame swimmer who had made a remarkable recovery after being paralyzed in a team bus crash, addressed the audience on overcoming great odds. "There comes a time to prove the experts wrong," she told them, "and that time is tomorrow." Old men wept. Young men shouted. And when they cranked up the Notre Dame fight song, even Seminoles in the audience sang along with enthusiasm. Kutz said, "I thought to myself: We're in real trouble, and our people don't even realize it."

But still we nearly won. The Seminoles' remarkable talent and leadership came within one play of defeating what was surely one of the most motivated Irish teams in history, on their own turf. Kutz thought we may have fallen prey to what he called "the Miami syndrome." That's the ingrained feeling that the Seminoles and the Hurricanes were consistently the two best teams in the country. If we could beat Miami, then no other team would be difficult to beat. It has to do with perspective and attitude.

I would have bet the previous season that Alabama might not even score on Miami in the Sugar Bowl. I was in a mall in Miami on New Year's Day and saw a display in the window of a sporting goods store that featured shirts, sweaters, and hats all proclaiming Miami had already become national champions for 1992. The Sugar Bowl game, of course, had yet to be played, but I had no doubt that the Miami players and fans shared the sentiment that victory was a given. After all, they had already beaten Florida State. But Miami lost to Alabama, and they lost badly.

The Speech No Cornhusker Gave

Here we were, headed toward a bowl in our own state, capping a movie-script season to play for our first national title. We faced Nebraska, a team the Seminoles handled with increasing ease over the last dozen years up until this point. Some of our partisan entrepreneurs jumped the gun and started selling hats and shirts and anything else that could be printed, announcing FSU's yet-to-be-won championship. And no doubt a lot of us would go along with the idea that it was a done deal.

We would be favored; Charlie would win the Heisman. Seminole stars would be in great demand for interviews, and our fans would flood the Orange Bowl with a good deal of celebrating already under their belts. If you were underneath the stadium, down in the locker rooms before the game, you would have heard the Marching Chiefs belt out their theme songs. You'd hear the foot stamping and the relentless wail of the "war chant."

Maybe our locker room would be rowdy, the players congratulating each other on a fabulous season. The twin demons, Miami and Florida, would be defeated. A wake-up call at Notre Dame that refocused our team at just the right juncture. And the good fortune to draw Nebraska for the title game. Maybe the Nebraska locker room would be subdued, their players quietly going about the business of suiting up and girding themselves for what waited outside.

Perhaps Coach Tom Osborne would ask for everyone's attention, and the Cornhuskers would turn toward the front as their coach introduced a man. But I didn't know if Coach Osborne could find such a man. If so, he would be in his early thirties; maybe he would be a little heavy with close-cropped hair flashing a touch of gray. He would have a Nebraska pin in his coat lapel, and he would be wearing a red Nebraska tie:

Men, he would say, *for me it is an indescribable honor to stand before you tonight. I believe that you are special; special in a way that even you do not realize. You see, in 1983 I played on the greatest college team in history. That's what they called us in the newspapers and on television. We were preseason No. 1. We were No. 1 all season long. We beat Colorado. We beat Oklahoma. We beat everybody. We had Heisman Trophy winner Mike Rozier on our team. And we had Dean Steinkuhler, who won the Outland Trophy and the Lombardi Award that year.*

Best of all, he would continue, *when it came time to go to the Orange Bowl, we drew an opponent that most people felt had little chance to beat us. They had a mixed record in big bowls, and it appeared that they hadn't played a really demanding schedule. We were so excited. We spent time on the team plane designing our national championship rings. The Orange Bowl game was difficult. The lead changed hands five or six times. In the end, however, we failed to convert on one play, and we lost to the University of Miami Hurricanes on New Year's Day 1984.*

You probably didn't know that we were the greatest team in history. In fact, you probably haven't heard much about our team at all. In 1993, however, I saw that Florida State was called the greatest team in history, but I was a little confused. Florida State wasn't undefeated—you are. Florida State wasn't ranked No. 1 in the final Coalition Poll; you are. Florida State isn't going to win this game; you are.

My team was one play short. One play. And it's true that an opportunity lost is gone forever, it is also true that once in a while—on only the rarest occasion—life's time machine reverses. Tonight is one of those times.

This is January 1, 1994. But for me and for my teammates, when the Big Red takes the field it will be January 1, 1984. Same time, on the same field, exactly ten years ago. We will play beside you tonight. Our dreams will drift across your sidelines like an unseen vapor, like the clean, soft air of summer in a Nebraska cornfield. You will feel us; you'll know we're with you.

We have been given the opportunity that they say never comes to any person. You can play our game over again, for us. You can be the greatest team in history. For the rest of your lives, that is what you'll be after you win tonight. Every play is the one play you'll need for victory. Don't let up, no matter what. Remember that this is your time. You have played all your lives for this moment. God bless you. Go, Big Red!

But I hoped Tom Osborne couldn't find anyone to deliver that speech. And I hoped our Seminoles approached the game knowing that we would have to play as well as—maybe even better than—we had played all year. We Seminoles were at our best when we were quiet, prepared, and didn't give our opponents any warning. You can ask Major Dade all about that.[*]

---

[*] Much of this chapter's material was initially published in the *Report to Boosters* (December 1993).

Charlie Ward: The X-Factor

The 1993 national championship game in the Orange Bowl was the matchup of No. 1 vs. No. 2 orchestrated by the BCS. Florida State was 10–1 and ranked No. 1, while Nebraska was 11–0 and ranked No. 2, and there were those who felt that the rankings should have been reversed based on the winning record. However, Florida State was the 17-point favorite to win their first national title.

Mike Bristol christened it the X-factor, and it caught on big among Seminole fans. Bristol, the popular assistant director of Seminole Boosters, knew that talent alone couldn't explain the near metaphysical advantage Charlie Ward seemed to bring to the national championship–contender Seminoles. "Charlie Ward equals talent plus X," quipped professor Bristol.

Charlie was extraordinarily talented, to be sure, but talent by itself didn't account for the whole range and substance of his accomplishments over the previous two years. We had heard it a lot in 1993, but could we finally beat the Miami jinx? "Well, Charlie is the X-factor." Could we break Steve Spurrier's winning streak in the Swamp? "Charlie Ward is your X-factor." Only one quarterback, Texas Christian's Davey O'Brien, had ever won the Heisman and then led his team to a national title in their bowl game. That was in 1938, and O'Brien's achievement was so outstanding that they named a trophy after him to recognize the nation's best QB.

Could Charlie Ward overcome the Heisman hype in the Orange Bowl? "The X-factor."

It was not enough to have talent. One has to be able to do it when it counts.

In the spring of 1993, on the Bobby Bowden Tour, someone asked if it was true that new signee Scott Bentley had kicked a 60-yard field goal in practice. "I don't need somebody to kick it 60 yards in practice," Coach Bowden said. "I need somebody to kick it 30 yards straight ahead in a game." That's the theme that makes college football so fascinating: the games aren't played out on paper and they aren't played out in practice. They are played out in terrible, stress-filled cauldrons of physical and emotional pressure. Talent alone does not rule. The cool hand, the unselfish leader, the noble heart that will not be defeated, the willingness not just to play but to *prepare*—all of these define the champion when the game is on the line.

If you see a replay of the Orange Bowl, watch the body language of the opposing kickers at the end. With twenty-three seconds left, freshman Scott Bentley strode onto the field with a poise that read "tee it up; let's put this one away." The Nebraska kicker trotted out shaking his head, as if he felt the whole weight of the world was on his shoulders.

Imagine the pressure on these young men and their coaches. Fifty million people watched the FSU-Notre Dame "game of the century." It was the largest television audience since the NCAA television rules were changed in 1985. A record fifty-five million viewers saw the Seminoles win on New Year's night. Heck, there were only 250 million people in the country. Better than one out of five Americans watched this college football classic: FSU, ranked No. 1 in one poll, vs. Nebraska, ranked No. 1 in the other poll— winner take all. Imagine the pressure. And pressure is what draws out that quality that lurks beyond talent.

Trev Alberts, Nebraska's great linebacker, playing with a busted elbow, stepped up and said, "Fire your shotgun!" Even healthy, he should never have been able to get into the Seminole backfield play after play. But there he was, sitting on Charlie. Then there was Clifton Abraham. On the last play of the game, a jump offsides would have brought Nebraska 5 yards closer, greatly increasing kicker Byron Bennet's chance of making the field goal. But Abraham made a phenomenal leap with the snap and shot straight at Bennet. He said he felt the ball burn the back of his hand as it grazed off and hooked wide left.

Charlie Ward had made it look easy for two years. As we had gotten used to Charlie, we had come to accept his achievements as routine. But they were not routine. Consider this: quarterback Thad Busby, drafted out of high school by Toronto, tried FSU baseball but had to back out citing the strain of academics and football, even though he was projected as a solid performer on the mound. Receiver Andre Cooper, runner-up as Florida's "mister basketball" the previous season, dropped off the Seminole basketball team citing academic pressures. And Scott Bentley, who said one of the reasons he decided to become a Florida State football player was the opportunity to also play baseball, wouldn't play baseball that spring so he could concentrate on his grades.

It was not as easy as Charlie made it look. Charlie had already graduated with a 3.2 GPA in his major, and was taking courses toward a second degree. The area beyond talent. The X-factor. *St. Pete Times* columnist Hubert Mizell wrote, "I swear, I think Charlie Ward could pick the hubcaps off a passing car." As remarkable as Ward's talents were, it was doubtful even he could snatch the hubcaps. But there once was a fellow who might actually have been able to do it. His name was Ed McGivern.

McGivern was a sort of lumpy, middle-aged man "built close to the ground," as he described himself. He was from Montana, and he flourished in the early part of the twentieth century. His appearance notwithstanding, he was a physical phenomenon. He was simply the most remarkable pistol marksman who had ever lived. He was a magician with a revolver. McGivern's signature stunt was so breathtaking that all other feats paled beside it.

If you try, you can blink your eyes five times within the space of one second. Holding a standard manufacture .38 caliber Smith & Wesson double-action revolver in one hand, McGivern could fire five rounds in two-fifths of a second—as fast as you can blink twice—into a target twenty feet away, and group the shots within an area that could be covered by a playing card.

If you know anything about pistol shooting, then you know that such a feat is not possible. It's in the same league as snatching the hubcaps. Yet credible witnesses and electronic timing devices confirmed what he could, in fact, do it. He did something else too, and here's where the story of Charlie Ward's performance on the field intersects with Ed McGivern's staged show.

McGivern was a great fan of the Old West, and so he set up a re-creation of the famous O.K. Corral gunfight that took place in Tombstone in 1881. The real Earp-Clanton shootout had Wyatt Earp, his two brothers, and Doc Holliday on one side, and five bad guys led by Ike Clanton on the other. Shooting started with the two groups of men standing about five or six feet apart. Each side fired seventeen shots in perhaps a minute and a half, longer than the time Charlie Ward took to bring his team down the field against Nebraska at the end. Three men on the Earp side were wounded; three on the Clanton side were killed.

In McGivern's version of the O.K. Corral, *one* man faced six life-sized paper targets, set up in a row, at a distance of thirty-five feet. The shooter drew and fired six shots from a double-action revolver within three to six seconds. Six hits, no misses. In six trials, only three bullets missed. McGivern's book says, "The results of our experiment are herewith offered for the benefit and interest of those who may enjoy making comparisons and studying probabilities."*

The suggestion, of course, was that had Ed McGivern been at the O.K. Corral, the bad guys would have been dispatched quickly and really without much chance to protest the result. And had the Orange Bowl been played only on paper, the Seminoles would have won by the 17.5-point spread.

Wyatt Earp lived to the age of eighty-one. He and his wife were something of a fixture on the social scene in Los Angeles in the 1920s. I don't know if Wyatt Earp ever heard of Ed McGivern, or if he was aware of McGivern's marvelous skills. But Earp did know that firing at paper targets thirty-five feet away was a lifetime removed from standing close enough to a man to read his watch and calmly shooting at him while he was trying to shoot you.

My guess is that Earp's response to McGivern's O.K. Corral setup would be similar to Charlie Ward's thoughts about people who told him that he should have seen a wide-open Matt Frier in the end zone on the last play at Notre Dame. Doing it while someone else was shooting at you, or while the blitzing linebacker was trying to run you down, required a steady hand and clarity of focus that few can claim.

Florida State was the prime target in college football during the 1993 season, standing toe-to-toe against desperate opponents every week. Every opponent, every week of the season. We were no Cinderella program. FSU's Wayne Hogan said, "Bobby Bowden's team has been no lower than fourth in the final rankings for the last seven years. ... We've been so highly visible, it's not like we came from out of nowhere and won it."

It takes more than talent to stay top gun week after week, month after month. Notre Dame played their greatest game

---

* Ed McGivern, *Ed McGivern's Book of Fast and Fancy Revolver Shooting* (New York: Skyhorse Publishing, 2007), 119.

against us and had nothing left with which to stop three-touchdown underdog Boston College the following Saturday.

Our magnificent defense played for beyond what could reasonably be expected. A team can practice all they want, but practice alone doesn't enable them to stop a Big 8 running offense eleven plays in a row at the goal line. And practice alone doesn't begin to explain all the big plays in the Orange Bowl.

Even the marvelously talented Charlie Ward had to draw from time to time on his secret reserves; he had to draw on that quality that makes him greater than the sum of his talents. The X-factor is hard to pin down. But we know with certainty of at least one thing that lies out there in that elusive, mysterious terrain beyond talent: the 1993 national championship.[*]

---

[*] Much of this chapter's material was initially published in the *Report to Boosters* (February/March 1994).

1994 Season

I can't tell you how many times I've stood at what I thought was a dead end only to discover that a door was opening up to a new path. No matter how impossible or desperate things look, life and my faith have taught me to never give up. Something new and rewarding can be wrestled from the jaws of a bad situation.

I'm reminded of this when I think of our season-ending game against Florida. By all rights they had us beaten. With twelve minutes left in the game, we were down 31–3. FSU fans were flooding out of the stadium. Some who remained were yelling for the quarterback to be replaced. Meanwhile, I was working on my concession speech. Then something extraordinary occurred.

Our quarterback and receivers caught on fire. Our running game joined in. We scored a touchdown. And then another. And that got the defense fired up. Long story short, we scored four touchdowns in the fourth quarter and kept them from scoring another point. This against a team—Florida—that weeks earlier had been ranked No. 1 and had but a single loss all season. I think we tied an NCAA record that year for the greatest fourth-quarter comeback. Given the quality of our opponent, it certainly is the greatest comeback I've ever been party to.

As fate would have it, we got matched up again with Florida in the Sugar Bowl. This time we won. No one would have imagined it back when we were down 31–3.

—Bobby Bowden

1994 Season

Began the season ranked No. 4
Ended the season ranked No. 4
Record 10–1–1
ACC Champions
Sugar Bowl Champions

September 3, defeated Virginia in Tallahassee 41–17

September 10, defeated Maryland in College Park 52–20

September 17, defeated Wake Forest in Durham 56–14

September 24, defeated North Carolina in Tallahassee 31–18

October 8, lost to Miami in Miami 20–34

October 22, defeated Clemson in Tallahassee 17–0

October 29, defeated Duke in Tallahassee 59–20

November 5, defeated Georgia Tech in Atlanta 41–10

November 12, defeated Notre Dame in Orlando 23–16

November 19, defeated NC State in Raleigh 34–2

November 26, tied Florida in Tallahassee 31–31

January 2, 1995, defeated Florida in the Sugar Bowl 23–17

Foot Locker
and the Media Storm

Only a few months after winning our first national championship, a writer for *Sports Illustrated* accused Seminole players of a variety of sins, including participation in a Foot Locker shopping spree paid for by a sports agent. The media's response was both fast and furious. Unhappy that an "outside" source had broken the story, reporters from the state news outlets flooded every Seminole Booster event that spring where Coach Bowden appeared.

They're called "Maggot Rooms." The Smithsonian Institution has one, as well as do a number of universities. Anthropologists at FSU use the one located at the Florida Museum of Natural History. And they aren't, technically, maggots, but rather "dermestid beetles."

Dr. Rochelle Marrinan, FSU Associate Professor of Anthropology, explains that fragile bones are extremely hard to clean to the extent necessary for proper examination. So scientists simply place the objects in the Maggot Room and, within a reasonable mealtime period, these tiny ravenous creatures have stripped away all organic matter with far more delicacy and precision than any clumsy human could manage. "They're messy," said Dr. Marrinan, making a face. "And they have their likes and dislikes. For instance, they seem to be more fond of attacking mammals than, say, reptiles." Interesting. "Personally, we may find them repulsive and their methods unappetizing," she continued, "but these little guys are really necessary to our work, and they help advance the greater good."

In the days of 1994 Seminole Booster–types may have been eager to draw comparisons between Dr. Marrinan's messy little friends and the practice of journalism. The truth, however, was that Florida State owed much of her prosperity to television, newspapers, radio, and magazines, and to the journalists who propelled those engines of the media. Yes, their methods could be less than appetizing, even comical at times (as we shall see), but our ultimate goal was the integrity of our athletic program and the university, and toward that end journalists served an important function.

Notre Dame and the University of Southern California were perhaps the only schools ever to have gained more from national media exposure than Florida State. Just as winning football teams promoted the small Catholic college in the heartland and the West Coast school in the shadow of Hollywood, so had Bobby Bowden's Seminoles launched FSU into the happy circumstance of unprecedented national popularity and respect.

An extraordinarily fortunate marriage in 1976 brought Bobby Bowden together with a school that was hungry for success, in a state that was rich with talent, explosive growth, and enthusiasm. Florida was the nation's fourth largest state, and anything that happened there seemed to be of interest to everyone.

Bowden the Giant Killer worked his magic on Goliaths all across the map of America. In time, David himself became Goliath, albeit a lighter, faster, stronger, quicker, smarter, and more dangerous version of the original. And all of this was done with integrity, humor, and good grace. And it was always done with an eye toward the benefits of positive national publicity for the school.

If we did have one advantage over the powerful University of Florida, it was our schedule. Bobby Bowden took his troops into America's major media centers and whipped their hometown teams and their bowl opponents. New York, Chicago, Phoenix, Columbus, Pittsburgh, Boston, Atlanta, Dallas, New Orleans, Omaha, Miami, and Los Angeles—how many "games of the century" had there been in just the previous four years?

Seminole football's popularity had translated into enormous benefits for the entire university. Much of the momentum for FSU's two-hundred-million-dollar Capital Campaign was provided by donors and volunteers who were also major contributors to the athletic program.

That spring's Bobby Bowden Championship Tour, hosted by Seminole clubs in thirty cities, was everything one may have imagined it to be: magnificent golf tournaments, superb banquets, and record attendance at all events. On May 7, 1994, midway through the tour, Coach Bowden went back to Tallahassee for the press conference to address *Sports Illustrated*'s charges. From that point forward, the tour became a decidedly different sort of adventure.

Please understand—this is important—Coach Bowden continued to hold a press conference at every tour stop. Any media representative was welcome, and they could ask him whatever they wanted. But with the *Sports Illustrated* piece, a new competition blossomed among journalists. Each reporter seemed to have his or her own secret question that no one else could possibly know about, a question only he or she could ask Coach Bowden when no other reporters were around.

I realized that the landscape had changed about the time the reporters began hiding behind potted plants in the hotel lobby and staking out our rooms. We left a hugely successful Booster banquet in Sarasota, and drove around for about an hour to give the crowd a chance to clear before returning to the hotel. We got back about midnight, and I took Coach Bowden to his room on the deserted (we thought) tenth floor. Coach was staying in the Karl Wallenda Suite (a bad omen, I thought, to have him in a room named for the sire of the famous circus high-wire family, which, unfortunately, is most widely known for their tragic falls from great heights).

Coach entered his room and took two steps before the knock at his door came. Always gracious, Coach sat with the fellow for a half hour or so and answered his secret questions. I have no idea where he sprang from, but I suspect—and I'm not making this up—that he was hiding up above the hallway ceiling tiles.

Another day and another city: the press conference had been concluded and 144 golfers spread out across the course. Most of the journalists left, but a couple hung around the clubhouse. Two high school girls driving the beverage cart came back to take a break. The reporters smiled, watched the girls head into the lady's room, and then flew like bats for the cart. They were last seen scooting merrily across the rolling hills in search of the Bowden foursome.

Then we were in a friendly but isolated rural community, and all the golfers had just gotten out on the course. I was in the pro shop chatting with some local Booster volunteers when the club manager walked in, dazed, and handed me a phone. We were the target of an airstrike. A news helicopter from a metropolitan daily paper three hundred miles away was asking for permission to land on the course. They too had some questions for Coach Bowden.

Hotels in different towns over the course of several days had been taking urgent phone messages from Ann Bowden. Coach Bowden's wife was insistently and repeatedly trying to get in touch with him they said, but there was never a return phone number. Our calls to the family home in Tallahassee went unanswered, and Coach Bowden began to get concerned. He asked his assistant to try and find Ann, and, after another day or so Ann was located safe and sound at their condo in Panama City. Ann placed no calls to Coach Bowden. Reporters were simply trying to get through the hotel switchboard by claiming to be the coach's wife.

Later, in another city, another news helicopter attempted to land in the middle of a metropolitan golf course where Coach Bowden was playing. It was waved off by angry golf club–wielding Seminoles. They never did get to ask their secret questions.

It should be said that at no time were any of these reporters rude or disrespectful to Coach Bowden. I knew many of the FSU beat reporters, and they were pretty good guys. But I had seen the same look on the faces of hunting dogs as they spilled out into the smoky morning air. Nothing personal against the quail, mind you. They were just deliriously happy to be out and about, and on with the business for which they have been trained.

FSU had never been in serious trouble since Coach Bowden arrived in 1976. And I believed there was a good chance, despite all the thunder and lightning, that good record would remain intact. Having a clean program doesn't mean you never do anything wrong; it only means you monitor activities and watch for wrongdoing. In the Seminole Booster organization, if we found out that a Booster had violated NCAA rules, we reported it immediately and moved to correct the problem. We educated constantly. Our club leaders and donors were used to calling us for direction on NCAA issues. That was the essence of institutional control, the centerpiece of the NCAA enforcement structure.

Of course, we preferred to deal with problems privately and without publicity. That was not always possible, however, and every once in a while, a journalist would uncover a problem before we did. Regardless, our commitment to a clean program had been strong and would remain that way into the future. When we had done wrong, we would take our punishment, correct the problem, and move forward. It was a fact that our kids had their hands out. Journalists didn't create those things; they actually happened.

Ronald Reagan's ability to deliver his message clearly through the national media was one of the reasons he was so enormously popular among the people, despite the fact that he was so hated and vilified by many mainstream journalists. The public loved his optimism and good humor, and maybe there's a lesson there for all of us. Once, when asked to comment on reports that communist guerrillas in El Salvador had fired on a plane carrying American journalists, Reagan smiled and said, "Well, there's some good in everyone."*

---

* Much of this chapter's material was initially published in the *Report to Boosters* (July 1994).

Bobby Bowden
and Sandy D'Alemberte

Foot Locker turned what should have been an exuberant spring into a cauldron of stress for Bobby Bowden and new university president Sandy D'Alemberte. Fortunately, both men were tough enough to meet the challenge. When Sandy D'Alemberte took office in January of 1994, Seminole Skies were unclouded. His first official act was to ask Bernie Sliger to ride in the presidential seat of honor in the national championship parade. D'Alemberte even drove the car. But the clear, cool day of the parade passed quickly and the clouds scudded in. And when the storm came, it hit with violence.

Like Napoleon, who quizzed himself several times each day as to what he would do if the enemy was suddenly to appear at his front, or to his sides or behind, D'Alemberte was one of those leaders who was never unprepared for the surprise attack. Florida State had always seemed to be a lucky institution, and our luck seemed to be holding true with D'Alemberte. Given his charisma and national stature as past president of the American Bar Association, plus his lawyerly inclination toward fierce advocacy, he was nearly the perfect choice to be president, especially if Florida State had known what was coming.

Florida politics being what they were in 1994, the pairing of

D'Alemberte and Florida State was not a shotgun wedding exactly, but something like an arranged marriage. Crises of the previous months had given Florida State the chance to get to know their new president on intimate terms. His powerful intellect, courage, and strength under fire had won over an astonishing array of converts.

D'Alemberte's handling of the Foot Locker affair, and our complicated relationship with the NCAA, had been masterful. He also had a genuine appreciation for Bob Goin's contributions as athletic director, and he gave Bob a fair opportunity to answer the charges against him. D'Alemberte's relationship with Seminole Boosters, Inc. was exceptionally positive. And, after undergoing a painful metamorphosis, the FSU Foundation emerged as a first-class academic fundraising institution. The Capital Campaign was in good shape, and it went on to gain considerable strength over the next eighteen months.

D'Alemberte was solidly in charge, and we were better for it. There was a toughness that underlied his easy charm and good humor. When D'Alemberte was asked about quotes widely attributed to the University of Florida's head football coach, he quickly shot back: "It just makes me that much more proud to have Bobby Bowden as the head coach of Florida State."

Bobby Bowden was another remarkable piece of good luck for Florida State. Such was the nature of fans that we had come to assume Bowden's obvious virtues to be the natural order of things. We knew Coach Bowden was glib and charming and brilliant and popular with the media. We knew that the course of his life had been guided by an unshakable strength of character and his faith. But, truth was, he made it look easy because he worked at it so hard. And sometimes circumstances are such that he had to work just a little harder.

Steve Spurrier had spent most of the summer cruising around the various Gator booster congregations, spreading merriment at the prospect of Seminole misfortune. Free Shoes University. That's what he said FSU stood for. Not everything Spurrier said that summer was funny, however. He had pointedly accused Bobby Bowden of cheating: "I'm starting to understand why they're getting so many of those blue chip players now. ... There's a perception out there about Florida State. Good things seem to happen to their players with regards to material things once they get there. When [the blue chips] would get called and asked why they didn't come to Florida, they said they were more comfortable with Florida State. I always suspected what 'comfortable' meant, and now I think everybody is realizing what it means."

Pressed by reporters for specifics, Spurrier turned demure. "Well, they've beaten us four out of five years in recruiting [since Spurrier came to Florida in 1990]," he said, "so we've always suspected. We've always heard rumors about them."

Many of the sports columnists writing about Spurrier's summer commentary agreed that it had more than a little to do with recruiting. In any discussion of Florida's Heisman Trophy winner, the word *genius* slipped in as easily and naturally as Spurrier's fingers wrapping around the grip of a four-iron. But word in the coaching fraternity had long been that Spurrier's undeniable genius as a field commander was not matched by corresponding enthusiasm for recruiting. All things being equal, however, his record against Miami and Florida State would seem to bear this out. Perhaps he sensed an opportunity, while FSU was under fire, and he had decided to pile it on.

Spurrier was not paid to be gracious to opponents; he was paid to win within the rules and he had done so, and done so brilliantly. Florida had never won ten games in a season; Spurrier did it and then won eleven the following year. Florida had never won the Sugar Bowl; Spurrier's team destroyed an undefeated West Virginia squad. He did not lose at home for nearly four years, and it only seemed as if the SEC was not allowed to hold a championship game without the Gators. If he remained at Florida, it was a near mathematical certainty that Spurrier would win a national championship.

So why the bitter edge? Why the personal invective against Coach Bowden? Perhaps the answer was no more complicated than this: We took Bobby Bowden for granted. He was forty-seven when he took over the Seminoles, and he would be sixty-five when the Gators played us on November 26, 1994. An entire generation of Seminoles had grown up under his eye. In fact, 1994's freshman class was born in 1976, which was the year Bobby Bowden became head coach at FSU.

Steve Spurrier, one of the most extraordinary coaches of the game, did not take Bobby Bowden for granted. He was not lulled by his own stellar record. He knew that he was 1–3 against our coach, and that he would come to us in November. Could there be a more profound acknowledgement of Bowden's greatness than Steve Spurrier's angst?

We arrived in Houston in the late afternoon on May 26, which was the last stop on the Bobby Bowden Tour. It had been a long plane ride from Philadelphia, and his back was causing him great pain, although he wouldn't admit it. The weeks of the Foot Locker controversy had worn him down; he chafed at the challenges to his integrity. He was hungry, and the private dinner wasn't scheduled to begin until eight in the evening. Not only that, but he'd lost his wallet and $1,700 cash during our layover in Atlanta.

The two of us got on the hotel elevator and began the long ride up. He grimaced as he shifted his weight. He could see that I had my head down. "Hey!" he elbowed me in the ribs. "You okay?" I told him I was fine—I was just worried about him. He laughed that easy laugh of his, and grinned wide. Then he said, "Don't you waste any time worrying about me. I've got so many things to be thankful for I nearly can't stand it."

Right, Coach. Don't we all.*

---

* Much of this chapter's material was initially published in the *Report to Boosters* (August/September 1994).

The Emergence of the Dynasty

The 1990s was a time when the state of Florida was center of the college football universe. The Seminoles, Gators, and Hurricanes each regularly won our respective conference championships, often all three in the same year. Bobby Bowden suggested that these three could be their own super-conference—"Big Florida." The Seminoles kept winning and winning, and the realization of the dynasty decade began to emerge.

In 1994, someone stole O. J. Simpson's Heisman Trophy from its pedestal at the University of Southern California. Even though it was a loss, it really didn't matter because they had plenty more. Tradition Hall, the impressive entry to USC's athletic complex, features an array of all four Heismans won by Trojan running backs between 1965 and 1981. One staple of 1980s late night television sports fare was an hour-long documentary titled *The Tailbacks of Southern Cal.*

So long, the glamour team of the West—Southern Cal's star eventually faded. In September 1994 the Trojans lost at home to lowly Oregon, and posted a total of only 35 rushing yards. It was announced on Sunday, the day after the game, that USC was under investigation for possibly falsifying recruit's test scores.

Notre Dame's star, of course, remained undiminished. While touring the Irish athletic facilities in 1993, *Osceola* publisher Jerry Kutz did a double take at the tarnished piece of iron being used to prop open a main door. It was an ancient Cotton Bowl trophy. Notre Dame wasn't being disrespectful, you understand; it was just that, well, with eight national championship displays to look after, the occasional Cotton Bowl hardware tends to get lost underfoot. All those trophies clutter up the place.

All dynasties have a spiritual beginning, and Notre Dame's probably sprang from their journey out of the Midwest in the fall of 1913 to take on the eastern giant, Army. Notre Dame had five hundred students, while the football team had eighteen players but only fourteen pairs of cleats. To save money, the team took along sandwiches and fruit so they wouldn't have to buy food while traveling. Team captain and end Knute Rockne shocked Army 35–13 primarily through adroit and unexpected use of the forward pass, and college football strategists raced to follow the Irish lead.

While Notre Dame's star still shined bright, other, newer dynasties were beginning to emerge as well during that time. It is worth noting that, except for their national title in 1988, Notre Dame had finished behind the Seminoles in the final season polls in each of the previous eleven years leading up to 1994.

Tradition tends to sort of creep up on us, doesn't it? We sometimes forgot that FSU had been to a dozen bowls in as many years, and had not lost a bowl game since 1980. Bobby Bowden was the winningest bowl coach of all time.

A remarkable transformation was taking place in the state of Florida. It began a decade before with Miami's 1983 national title. The Canes staked out a spot on top of the college football pyramid and bullied anyone who tried to push them aside. Florida State staked its own claim on a spot near the top in 1987, and it flourished in that rarified atmosphere ever since. Since '86, Bobby Bowden had become the only coach in NCAA history to string together seven consecutive 10-win seasons.

The University of Florida in 1994 made it a triumvirate. Just ponder the significance of Terry Dean as the frontrunner for the

Heisman Trophy that year. Miami quarterback Gino Torretta was 1992's winner, while Charlie Ward won in 1993. With Dean, the quarterbacks of all three major state teams could win in consecutive years.

There were only a few states wherein more than one major conference was represented. South Carolina comes to mind with Clemson in the ACC and South Carolina in the SEC. Iowa has the Big Ten Hawkeye and Big 8 member Iowa State. There's Georgia, of course, with UGA and Georgia Tech, and Virginia, with UVA and Virginia Tech. But I don't know if any state, other than Florida, has been able to boast of two major conference champions in the same year. Had it not been for Miami's upset loss to West Virginia in 1993, the champions of the SEC, the ACC, and the Big East would all have resided in the Sunshine State in 1993. And, unless there were major realignments of the conferences, it was unlikely that any state other than Florida would have even the *opportunity* to crown three champions in a single year.

Coach Bowden called this triumvirate the "Big Florida," and he likened it to a separate league. Sports dynasties only seem to spring into full flower overnight. The Big Florida took a while to develop and, like Notre Dame, our origins were humble. In November of 1974, the Seminoles snapped a twenty-game losing streak by beating Miami in the Orange Bowl, 21–14. At the time, the Hurricane program was mired in circumstances nearly as unhappy as our own.

By 1979, the Seminoles sported an undefeated regular season and high national ranking. We envisioned a dynasty of our own, but reality met us in the Orange Bowl on New Year's night. A disinterested Oklahoma team, in a slump between their fifth and sixth national titles, dispensed with the Seminoles 24–7. It wasn't until our signature win over Nebraska in Lincoln in 1980 that the national press began to see FSU as a consistent national power, and not until 1987 that a true Seminole dynasty began to emerge.

Charley Pell's Gators went 0-10-1 in 1979. That year so scarred Pell's tender psyche that he felt driven to orchestrate one of the most massive and comprehensive cheating scandals in NCAA history. It was only Spurrier who was able to pull the disarrayed program back together again and fix the Gators on the true course to national prominence.

The Canes didn't fare much better than the Gators in 1979. I watched from the press box at Doak Campbell Stadium as the Hurricanes lost to Florida A&M on a last-second field goal. No, you did not misread that sentence. Florida A&M's Bragg Stadium was undergoing repairs in 1979, and they played Miami in Tallahassee in Doak Campbell. The game was tight. Miami drove the length the field in the last moments to set up a game-winning field goal from the 15-yard line. And yes, Miami's kick sailed wide right as time ran out. Florida A&M 16, Miami 14.

But Miami's 1983 upset of Nebraska in the Orange Bowl for the national title changed everything. The Hurricanes would win four national titles in nine years under three different head coaches. Dade County was suddenly regarded as the hottest high school talent pool in the country. Assistant coaches from schools out of state genuflected every time they crossed the Florida border.

Florida State began to assemble top-ranked recruiting classes, and then the University of Florida followed suit. It was a myth— told and retold, for what reason I do not understand—that Miami never signed heralded recruiting classes. The truth was that Miami's stars were well known and highly recruited. There had never been any magic to Miami's success, unless you counted their speed as magic (and surely such a case could be made).

Why the dominating strength of the Big Florida in 1994? Why were players from this state seemingly swifter and more skilled than others? Coaching was likely a part of it. Howard Schnellenberger and Jimmy Johnson were among the all-time best. Dennis Erickson had his critics, but he was one of only thirteen men who had won two or more national titles. Bobby Bowden and Steve Spurrier had earned their seats at the table of legends too.

The weather also had something to do with it. Boys could run and jump outdoors year-round.

Spring football in high schools was another key. If there was one secret, it could well have been the outstanding high school football programs we enjoyed. And too, almost unnoticed were the small changes in recruiting rules, passed in the 1980s ostensibly as cost-cutting measures. The practical effect had been to make it more difficult for out-of-state schools to identify and evaluate Florida talent, and easier for state schools to keep the top players at home.

The Big Florida's dominance of conference play was a frightening prospect for opponents. Miami was undefeated its first year in the Big East, lost one game in 1993, and was projected to sail through the Big East undefeated again in 1994.

The University of Florida had sobered many in the SEC who were looking for the Gators to fold. There was a bumper sticker circulating around Jacksonville, a crossroads city loaded with Seminoles, Bulldogs, Yellow Jackets, Hurricanes, and Clemson Tigers. The sticker said: Honk If You've Never Won a National Championship. The Gators were not amused, and conference opponents were learning to walk softly around the orange and blue, lest Steve Spurrier decided to put his first-string back in at the start of the second half.

As for Florida State, a win at homecoming, October 22, 1994, would tie the ACC record for consecutive conference victories. Maryland had a string of 21 back in the 1970s. If we could get past dangerous road games at Georgia Tech and North Carolina State, the Seminoles would likely complete three straight years of conference play without losing a game.

We would lose one eventually, of course, but our record of consecutive victories would probably outlast anyone who was around.

There was one record the Seminoles would set, however, which may never be broken: the record for consecutive conference games as the favored team. When we lost, it would be an upset. Since 1986, Florida State had been favored in every game except two, both against Miami. No matter which bowl, no matter our rank versus the opponent, no matter at home or away—we had always been the oddsmaker's favorite. And one of those times when we were the underdog to Miami, which was in 1989, we won!

It was as if we were in the midst of a grand parade, a wonderful and endlessly enjoyable pageant. But among those who have seen the bottom as well as the top, there was a vague uneasiness lurking around the edges. There was a fleeting fear that perhaps FSU had struck some sort of Faustian bargain, and that someday the Devil would show up and demand his due.

How much of what we had was Bobby Bowden, and how much was Florida State? Would it all turn back into mice and pumpkins when he retired? The answer could be that dynasties do not necessarily, inevitably fall. The Seminole Booster organization had been working feverishly for years to take advantage of on-the-field successes. Our new University Center was part of the payoff.

The truth about preserving the dynasty was that leadership and character were what counts. In the dozen or so years it had taken Florida State to emerge, the University of Southern California, with three national championships and four Heisman Trophy winners to their credit, may have made the wrong choices. But Notre Dame continued to make the right ones. We could always replace stolen hardware. However, it is the heart one can't do without.[*]

---

[*] Much of this chapter's material was initially published in the *Report to Boosters* (October/November 1994).

Life at the Top of
the Pyramid

Life at the top of the college football pyramid is intoxicating, but it brings with it a unique set of problems. While the Seminoles were winning on the field, the Seminole Boosters organization strove to raise money to build University Center and to secure a permanent financial foundation for the athletic program.

The Ring, Richard Wagner's sweeping nineteenth-century masterwork, consumes four complete operas and tackles no less a theme than the end of the world and the fiery destruction of the gods and their mountaintop home, Valhalla. It all begins innocently enough with the gods displaying a mortal quality: they contract to build a magnificent castle for themselves, but the cost is greater than they can afford. Through the length of this formidable German epic, gods and mortals alike struggle over possession of a magic golden ring that has the power to set everything right. But the ring is cursed, and pursuit of it is what finally brings all to such an unhappy end.

It is far too great a distance to leap directly from this tragic tale of the castle in Valhalla and lust for a gold ring into a consideration of our University Center and our newly-minted national championship. The Germans can be a fatalistic sort. Toward the end of *The Ring*, the gods understand their fate and come to accept it. But we Americans are an optimistic people, not given much to brooding about inevitabilities; we believe in our abilities to overcome, to triumph. It is a useful belief for people who wish to build grand stadiums and wear championship rings.

It is also useful to understand the dangers, and not be blind to them.

By any measure, Florida State dwelt among the elite of college football. We owned the nation's longest streak of bowl wins. Seminole players had won almost every postseason award available. Bobby Bowden's eighth consecutive ten-win season was a record, as was FSU's seven top-4 finishes in the polls.

John Nogowski, sports columnist for the hometown newspaper, asked Coach Bowden to recall his last bad season. "The last bad season?" Bowden said. "I guess I'd have to say 1986." In 1986, we went 6–4–1 and then won an All-American Bowl victory over Indiana in the snow and sleet of a freezing December Birmingham night. That's what it had come down to for the Seminoles: the definition of a bad season was 6–4–1 and a small bowl in bad weather.

In Wagner's opera, the gods at one point complain bitterly that mortals have no understanding or appreciation for the unique problems of being deity. And they are correct. The mortals, who had little choice but to struggle under the whims and caprice of the gods, had no appreciation for their "problems," and no sympathy for them either. Lou Holtz knew. He said he never complained in public about his problems, "because 80 percent of people don't care at all, and the other 20 percent are glad to hear about 'em."

That was the way it was in the ACC for us. Florida State's three-year 24–0 romp through the league was unprecedented. Survivors were gasping in the wake. The average margin of victory had been about 30 points, and we would probably have an even better team the next year.

And don't think it was lost on our ACC brethren that FSU was the only school in the country that considered its nonconference schedule to be the "real" season. Florida, Miami, and Notre Dame: those are the big games, and would be so until FSU fell to an ACC team. When that day came, we couldn't be surprised or disappointed (as Wagner's gods of antiquity were) at the intensity of the reaction around the league. They had little sympathy for FSU's unique problems. Our best course was to continue to welcome our fellow ACC fans with good grace, hospitality, and sportsmanship. And to keep on winning.

Did you ever think you'd see the day when the Gators were jealous of us? If you were at the Notre Dame game in Orlando, then you likely saw the airplane pulling a Blockbuster Video banner that read: "FSU vs. Notre Dame. Who Cares? Go Gators." It turns out some pinhead in Gainesville who owns a Blockbuster franchise paid for the flight. (The use of Blockbuster's logo was an accident; Blockbuster's corporate hierarchy had done some fast dancing on that one.)

Florida played a regional schedule with no Notre Dame, no Miami, and no real showcase game except the Seminoles. Mike Bianchi, the excellent *Gainesville Sun* columnist, wrote a late summer piece in 1993 before our national championship season focusing a green eye on the Seminoles' great expectations:

> The success, the phenomenal success, is shackled to them like a ball and chain. It hovers over them. ... In a few days, the AP's preseason poll will come out and you will see the Noles ranked No. 1 again. It will be the third time under Bowden that FSU goes into the season ranked No. 1. ... Back in 1991 FSU won ten games before losing to Miami on a missed field goal in the final seconds. FSU then lost two weeks later to Florida before beating Texas A&M in the Cotton Bowl. ... The Seminoles finished the '91 season 11–2 and fans cussed their cursed luck. ... It's hard being good.

Yes, well such was life in the gardens of Valhalla. And you should have overheard the Gators' comments when they saw University Center for the first time on November 26, 1994.

Florida State, and the few programs much like our own, really had problems unique to the class. Florida State, Miami, Notre Dame, Florida, Michigan, Penn State, Alabama, and maybe a few others found hovering around the top of the college football pyramid were able to confine their recruiting to the nation's best student-athletes.

The problem was that even though players are good students, how did one maintain high graduation rates when numbers of them are lured out of school early by the pros? It was a problem that mortal teams with mortal talent did not have. Unscrupulous sports agents, impossibly high expectations, and the relentless demands of the media were all problems that the top-tier programs dealt with routinely. And the expertise and poise with which university leaders handled these problems determined in each case whether the program would continue strong or fall into mediocrity.

Foot Locker could have been worse—much worse—but we got lucky. The spree took place Sunday before the Notre Dame game in 1993. Had it been discovered right away, as many as eleven players could have been suspended for that game. The loss likely wouldn't have been close, and Florida State's title hopes would have ended there. Imagine the fallout, the finger-pointing, the outrage that would have followed that team for the rest of the season, and into the '94 season.

We certainly took our hits as it turned out, but Sandy D'Alemberte's genius for crisis management, combined with our coaching staff's deserved reputation for honesty, played to FSU's advantage. The cost to the university for the law firm investigation reached $250 million. When the final report to this most thorough of investigations was released, we were all able to take justifiable pride in a program that consistently operated at the highest levels of success and with the highest standards of integrity.

Would Foot Locker have been the focus of so much national attention if FSU had not been the No. 1 team? Probably not. Would Bob Goin's roof have been a career-ending issue, but for the publicity surrounding Foot Locker? Possibly not. If our defense and our offensive line had been complete from the beginning of the season, we may have done better against Miami in the fall.

From about March of 1994 to December of the same year, Booster contributors wanted to know more about the composition of the Seminole Booster board of directors, and more about how decisions were made in matters of Booster policy. It was a large board, about sixty people. A few of the spots were predetermined (the athletic director, the president's representative, the BOR representative, one each from the alumni and foundation boards), but the rest of the directors were elected to three-year terms, the names chosen from a slate proposed by the board's nominating committee.

The board met four times a year; there was an executive committee where most of the detailed proposals were hammered out. The bylaws specified some geographic diversity so the members didn't get too bunched up, but no director represented a specific city or group of donors. The purpose of the board was quite simply to raise money in support of Seminole athletics and everything else that was subordinate to that.

The criteria for selection was simple: we wanted people who could give money, raise money, or open doors to money that we could not open ourselves. Most of the directors, though not all, were large donors of the Golden Chief/Silver Chief stripe. The required minimum annual contribution from a board member was only $250 per year, but each director was expected to raise a minimum of five thousand in new money every year.

These were some of the state's most prominent business, professional, and political leaders. Former House Speaker Bo Johnson was a director, as was state representative Jim King. Here were a few more.

Yvonne Brown called from Miami and asked what she had to do to join the board. Give money and raise money was the answer; show us what you can do. Giving was no problem. Yvonne owned her own accounting firm, and she and her husband were already Golden Chiefs and had established a fifty-thousand-dollar endowed scholarship. Installed as the new area chairman for Dade County, Yvonne and her team of volunteers raised more than sixty-five thousand in new money in 1993.

Lawton Langford, 1994 chairman of the Booster board, and CEO of the Municipal Code Corporation, was a relentless fundraiser whose skill rivals even that of his father, George Langford, who was also a past chairman of the board. Carl Domino, the quiet and thoughtful financial wizard from Palm Beach who endowed a fifty-thousand-dollar scholarship for basketball, was the incoming board chairman for 1995.

Former Seminole defensive standout Joe Camps raised major gifts among his fellow physicians and the Tallahassee medical community. Prominent lobbyist Barbara Palmer also exceled in the major gift category. North Carolina businessman Bill Burkhardt had brought in eight new Golden Chiefs from among his business associates in the Carolinas, while banker Michael Grantham specialized in raising scholarship endowments for women's athletics.

Jim Kirk of Ocala asked a fellow to join the Boosters, and ended up bringing in the largest academic gift ever received in the history of Florida State University. Jim's new task was to solicit his fellow members of the board. By the end of 1994, his nine-million-dollar goal had been met and exceeded. The truth is that I do a disservice by singling out only these few. Our board has an extraordinary membership, and each of their stories bears telling.

The board determines all policies of Seminole Boosters, and is willing to tackle any problems that affect Booster contributors or Booster fundraising. Seminole Boosters, Inc. is now America's largest collegiate booster organization, and keeping nineteen thousand donors happy is a daunting task. In 1976, there were sixteen Golden Chiefs in the charter group. It seems impossible, but in 1994 there were nearly one thousand Golden and Silver Chiefs! There are 1,500 donors in the Tomahawk Club (a thousand dollars per year), and more than two thousand Warriors (five hundred dollars per year). Seminole Boosters, Inc. provides parking for more than eight thousand vehicles every football game.

We were running short of parking, and we were short of seats. We suffered from an embarrassment of riches, but Florida State's prosperity was tied directly to the success of Seminole Boosters. If anyone wanted the board to consider a particular issue, or if anyone wanted to be considered for membership on the board, then all they needed to do was to contact the Booster office directly.

In the end, Wagner's ancient gods were destroyed because, though they possessed all the power in the world, they lacked strength of character. Our Booster board of directors was dedicated to making certain we could pay for our Valhalla while fully supporting the integrity of the athletic program.*

---

* Much of this chapter's material was initially published in the *Report to Boosters* (November/December 1994).

Clemson's Lost Generation:
The Seminoles Prosper

Florida State's rise to national prominence was a fast and dizzying ride. Each year brought more enhanced recognition and another championship season. With steady expansion of the massive brick edifice, University Center grew to become the signature symbol of Seminole athletics.

Wind-driven rain whacked and rattled the pane-glass windows at a Denny's on 1-40 through Greensboro where George Bennett and I sat stirring cups of muddy coffee and swapping Booster stories. That's where I first heard about Clemson's "Lost Generation."

Still athletic-looking and clean-jawed, Bennett was very much what you'd expect the head of Clemson's legendary IPTAY booster organization to be. If you had a roomful of choices and you had to guess which fellow had been head cheerleader for the Tigers, class of '55, your gaze would most likely come to settle on George. He was the inheritor of IPTAY's glories, as well as their problems. The challenge of the "Lost Generation" fell to him.

To those of us who were in the business of raising money for college athletics, Clemson's IPTAY Club was nearly what Bear Bryant's Alabama football program was to a generation of coaches. They were the eternal standard. Even though our Seminole Boosters,

Inc. had surpassed Clemson in both number of donors and annual fundraising, Clemson remained the original mold from which the success of so many other schools had been cast.

IPTAY, which meant "I Pay Ten a Year," was founded in 1934. Clemson athletics had flourished for six decades under the attentions and innovations of this organization that was most appropriately characterized by its marketing genius. It was IPTAY that directed its members to pay for all their bowl game lodging and food with two-dollar bills, a dramatic illustration of Tiger spending power that left local merchants clamoring for Clemson's return. It was also IPTAY that developed the ubiquitous Tiger Paw logos that directed the faithful along the highways to Memorial Stadium, and which ranked with the shamrock and the mounted Seminole as the most instantly recognizable collegiate symbols. And it was IPTAY that introduced the concept of luxury skyboxes to college football. One hundred skyboxes lined Memorial Stadium, and the income was a dependable and substantial source of IPTAY funding. "Until not too long ago—maybe five years—Clemson had one-third of all the skyboxes in college football," said Bennett.

The challenge of recovering the "Lost Generation" probably best illustrates IPTAY's—and Bennett's—brilliance. Clemson had always been a school that commanded loyalty, and that loyalty had been expressed in the form of generations of sold-out football seasons at Death Valley, their storied football stadium. "We've always had great enthusiasm," George mused, warming his hands around the thick white ceramic mug. "But when we won the national championship in 1981, it really went through the roof. We hold eighty-one thousand officially, but I think the record for a game is about eighty-four thousand, and you literally couldn't find an empty seat. Those were great days for Clemson and for IPTAY … but we paid a price."

The price was the loss of a generation of potential contributors and Tiger fanatics. During the gridiron rapture of the late 1970s, and on through the 1980s, Clemson students could get into a game simply by presenting a valid ID card. Once out of college, however, they had to buy season tickets. And the problem, of course, was that there were no season tickets to be had. "Those kids came up through school with Clemson football at its peak. They became passionate and devoted fans. Then when they graduated, we had to tell them they couldn't come to the games anymore because we didn't have any tickets to sell."

That situation persisted for maybe fifteen years, and slowly these thousands and thousands of loyal Tiger alumni drifted away to other passions. "We lost them," said George. "We lost them and we couldn't get them back. Not a thing worked. Nothing." Well, not exactly nothing. In fact, IPTAY's magic dwelt in its creative genius, and so the magician created the Tiger Cubs.

Bennett smiled and said, "We lost the parents but we're getting their children." For thirty dollars, a child could be a Tiger Cub and receive a certificate, puzzles, pins, a cheap watch, and maybe a bib, depending on the child's age. Kids ten to fourteen years old got a fanny pack and Tiger Paw stickers ("Kids are real big on stickers," George said). Older teens got a subscription to the *Orange & White* thirty-two times per year. How old did they have to be to participate? "Before birth to twenty-two years old. ... We've got a bunch of 'Unnamed Baby Smith' and 'Unnamed Baby Jones,' that sort of thing." A bunch is right. As of 1994, there were between two thousand and twenty-five hundred Tiger Cubs, and the ranks were growing.

There was a lesson in all this for Florida State, which was this: Success brings growth, and growth brings problems. But creativity and innovation can be employed to overcome those problems. Surely, not all the geniuses in fundraising and in the marketing of college athletics lived in Clemson, South Carolina.

Stated as succinctly as possible, our job at Seminole Boosters was to take advantage of Bobby Bowden. University Center was, quite literally, a house that Bobby Bowden built. Jim Melton, president of

FSU's National Alumni Association, chuckled about taking some visitors on a tour of the stadium. This particular group was made up mostly of alumni of "rival institutions," as they say. "Some of them gasped, one of them cried when they first saw it," he said. "Isn't it amazing the effect three million bricks can have on people?"

Nineteen ninety-four would be Coach Bowden's twentieth anniversary season as Seminole head coach, and it hardly seemed necessary to recount the success and prosperity that had flowed into our athletic program, and indeed the entire university, because of his accomplishments. But recount is what we need to do.

Clemson's IPTAY occupied the top ring of the college booster ladder for decades. In 1993, Seminole Boosters moved ahead of them for the first time. They had just over eighteen thousand members, and we had just slightly less than nineteen thousand. They raised $6.1 million in annual contributions, while we raised $7.6 million in annual contributions, and had total revenues of more than sixteen-million dollars for the year.

In 1993, with an average attendance of 76,535, Florida State finished in the nation's top 10 (No. 9, actually) for the first time ever. And we passed both Nebraska and Alabama to do so. We didn't ever think we'd see the day when FSU would be in the top 10, and finish ahead of schools like Nebraska, Alabama, Clemson, and LSU. When we joined the ACC at the end of 1990, our stadium held 60,519. In the fall of 1994, when our fans crowded into Doak Campbell for the home opener against NC State, about eighty thousand Seminole fans surrounded them. By September of the same year, the wedges connecting the north end zone to the main stands were completed, and our stadium was a complete bowl, up to forty-one rows in the end zone.

Florida State had become popular and prosperous because of winning, but we could not discount the value of winning and of being located in the state of Florida. The impact of FSU football on the ACC was massive and overwhelming. There were more newspapers in Florida with a circulation of two hundred thousand or better than in the other five ACC states combined! And televised "games of the century" were routine. As *Charlotte Observer* sports columnist Tom Sorenson lamented after his first visit to Doak Campbell, "The ACC as we know it, this is not."

Though there were some who would argue that it was not so, the power of winning and national prominence flowed freely over to the academic side of the university as well. In the fall of 1994, we anticipated that a hundred Merit Scholars would enter FSU. There were only thirteen schools, public or private, in the country with that many or more. One hundred was better than Duke and better than North Carolina. In fact, it was No. 2 in the ACC, just behind Georgia Tech (most Merit Scholars go into engineering).

Jim Melton, who had worked closely with Merit Scholar recruitment, credited the Seminole Club Network as primarily responsible for this huge increase. The clubs were administered jointly by the Boosters and the Alumni Association, and Seminole athletics had been a driving force behind the popularity and enthusiasm of these clubs.

Money from sales of the state of Florida FSU license plates went into the university's academic programs. (Most states offer some sort of affinity license plate for their various colleges.) The latest figures showed that in 1993 Florida State Seminole fans and alumni led the country in purchase of these tags. More than Florida—more than anybody else. In fact, the University of Florida and Florida State people together purchased more of this type of tag than all of the alumni of all the schools in all the other forty-nine states combined!

But as Clemson knew, with all the sterling success comes problems. Oh my, yes there were problems. Parking was a huge problem. Longtime Tallahassean Lewie Moats gave a thousand dollars to the Seminole Boosters when we first came into being in 1951. "That gave me two personalized parking places in the shadow of the stadium," he remembered. "I kept giving a thousand dollars, and as the years went by those two personalized spots became one place in a lot if it wasn't full by the time I got there. "Now," he laughed, "now I still give a thousand dollars and about all they give me is directions to the field." It wasn't really that bad, but stadium construction had the Seminole Boosters board of directors juggling and making interim recommendations to keep pace with the demand during the building phase.

Seats in Doak Campbell were another problem. There was pressing demand for prime seats, but prime seats were always largely spoken for. Like Clemson, we had invested heavily in sky-boxes. By 1996, we would have sixty-three in place, with more to be built in the end zone. And while eighty-thousand seats should hold us for some time, and even give us some room to grow, the fact was that that Florida State graduates between seven and eight thousand new alumni every year. We didn't want them to become "lost."

Money was also a continuing problem, and we strived to meet our obligations every year with the assistance of hundreds and hundreds of loyal, committed volunteer Booster fundraisers. The Booster (athletics) portion of University Center costed fifty-two million. And it was Seminole Boosters, Inc. that made those annual payments.

Much was raised every year for athletic scholarships, but that money could not be touched for any other purpose. Issues of gender equality required massive new facilities construction for softball and women's soccer, and all of it had to be done quickly. More money was needed for making up any deficit in the athletic department's budget. We also tried to put a little aside for a rainy day and, well, you know, Tallahassee weather.

The challenge of all this fell to us, but it was a challenge welcomed by those who loved the university and its traditions. And, after all, the problems of winning were far more preferable than the alternative.[*]

---

[*] Much of this chapter's material was initially published in the *Report to Boosters* (April/May 1995).

Fifth Quarter in the French Quarter: Gators Consider Dropping the Seminoles

After the Seminoles' fabulous comeback from a fourth quarter 31–3 deficit, Nole fans delighted in christening the game "the choke at Doak." A month later, the Sugar Bowl staged a dramatic rematch in which the Seminoles won to settle the issue. Frustrated by playing a tough SEC schedule, plus the Seminoles, Florida made noises about dropping the FSU series when the contract ended in 1996. They had already dropped Miami after the 1987 season.

Unofficially, it was called the "Bear Bryant Rule." You may not have heard of it, but it was the reason orange-and-blue warm-up suits and Gator hats streaming through the French Quarter in New Orleans outnumbered our own garnet-and-gold-clad fans by a factor of ten to one. In the 1970s, the Sugar Bowl yearned to be the official bowl of the Southeastern Conference. Such was the power of Bear that nothing could be done without his blessing, and Bryant was not inclined to approve any arrangement that did not greatly favor the host SEC team.

Actually, the popular and prestigious Sugar Bowl had been the SEC's neighborhood clubhouse for more than six decades. Only five times since 1935 (and only twice since World War II) had the Sugar Bowl hosted a pair of non-SEC teams. The Southeastern Conference and the Sugar Bowl were living together long before they finally married in 1976. The "Bryant Rule" had become a ubiquitous term used freely to describe any number of advantages and privileges that accrue exclusively to the SEC host team—not just the perks envisioned by Bryant, but all those that are the natural products of more than a half-century of cozy cohabitation.

Both parties were absolutely giddy over the arrangement. Former Sugar Bowl director Mickey Holmes called it "a longtime love affair," and in January 1995 SEC commissioner Roy Kramer gushed, "It was almost too good to be true."

Among the delights that kept the romance alive was the distribution of tickets. By contract, the Sugar Bowl gave the two opposing teams an equal number of tickets—that means that Florida State and Florida each received 12,500. FSU had to take 2,500 off the top to accommodate the Marching Chiefs, the football team, coaches, players' families, athletic department personnel, the university president's party, and sales to FSU students. We mailed ticket order forms to 4,500 Seminole Boosters—those who gave at least five hundred dollars in 1994—and hoped that we could adequately fill those orders with only ten thousand tickets.

Gator fans, however, found it considerably easier to obtain tickets. A large allocation of tickets—the number kept secret by contract (the Bryant Rule, don't you know)—went to the SEC office in Birmingham. Roughly 2,500 additional tickets from this allocation were sent to Florida.

The major Sugar Bowl season ticket holders were hotels, restaurants, ticket brokers, tour companies, bus companies, and a variety of speculators and profiteers. Because of the familiar and ongoing relationship between the SEC and these sources for so many years, great numbers of these tickets naturally found their way into the hands of the SEC host school and their fans.

FSU fans not able to get tickets through the university had to purchase travel packages, which often carried exorbitantly inflated room rates. Several large wholesalers, regional travel agencies, handled SEC *host* teams almost exclusively. Surplus tickets from this source are resold to "guest team" local travel agencies at greatly increased prices. An SEC fan might pay, say $95.00 for the same room that costs you $150. Travel industry sources told me that if Alabama had gone to New Orleans instead of Florida, FSU fans would have found it even more difficult to get tickets and rooms. Alabamans, it seemed, traveled in greater numbers than did Gators.

All this ensured that the overwhelming majority of fans in the Superdome were going to be wearing the colors of the SEC host team: and there seemed to be no end to the perks and privileges afforded the conference representative. Florida was the "home team," but was allowed to wear their road white jerseys—a matter of superstition, according to the New Orleans papers (it was suggested that this edition of the Gators was an unusually superstitious lot).

The Sugar Bowl determined each team's headquarters hotel, where the team and athletic staff, as well as where the president's party, stayed. The university had no choice in this selection, but all major bowls had the same policy. And so an unusually superstitious opponent might conceivably exercise their conference leverage to influence hotel assignments. Florida State was assigned to Le Meridien Hotel, which, coincidentally, had hosted the last five Sugar Bowl losers. In 1988, FSU stayed at the Hilton and beat Auburn. In 1995, however, Florida's assigned hotel was—golly!— the Hilton.

But New Orleans wasn't all SEC. In fact, the Seminoles took an aggressive approach to promoting Florida State in the Big Easy. University communications director Frank Murphy and his staff churned out a slick daily newspaper called the *FSU Overtime*

Times, and handed them out in most of the hotels, as well as the more popular French Quarter watering holes.

The tabloid was designed to make Nole fans feel more at home. Seminole football got front-page coverage, of course, and fans were also treated to information on pep rallies, Marching Chief concerts, a Lady Noles basketball game against UNO, advances in the Capital Campaign, and important developments in academic research at FSU. There were even restaurant reviews by various Boosters.

Murphy's team also put together something called "Seminole Vision," which was featured in the downtown hotels. One channel in each selected hotel was devoted to round-the-clock play of a rich jambalaya of Seminole football highlights, academic features, and promotion of FSU's two-hundred-million-dollar Capital Campaign.

Apparently, there was an upheaval in the Hilton when it was discovered early on that the Gator team hotel featured "Seminole Vision" twenty-four hours a day. There was simply no escape from the fourth quarter comeback, segments on the coaching genius of Bobby Bowden (his faith and his family), and exhortations about what a fabulous institution Florida State was and why you should give them your support and money.

Murphy was a quiet, self-effacing sort. You might not have noticed him, but he left his mark, like a guerrilla who loves to slip behind enemy lines and blow up bridges. I asked Frank how in the world he ever got "Seminole Vision" into the Hilton. "Oh, we bought the channel outright." He smiled. "In advance."

The Sugar Bowl and the SEC have parted company. The Orange Bowl has dropped its affiliation with the Big 8 too. Both bowls, along with the Fiesta, are part of the new Bowl Alliance that was set up to ensure a national championship match at one of those three sites, which began in 1996.

Probably the best story to come out of this Sugar Bowl, other than the outcome of the game, was the stadium scoreboard.

When the teams took the field for pregame warm-ups, the Super-dome scoreboard read: FSU 31, Florida 31, Quarter 5. Fans were delighted, cameras flashed—the bowl made the best of this unique promotional opportunity to enhance the rematch.

The scoreboard display was negotiated by two FSU students who did it to win a bet with their professor. Dr. Jay Rayburn was one of those robust, happy souls who loved being a college professor. It was right after the game against Florida in Tallahassee that Rayburn was lecturing his public relations class on the value of publicity: "Can you imagine the value of the publicity if you could get the scoreboard to start the rematch with a 31–31 score?" He said, "It would be good for the schools, and good for USF&G Insurance. People would take pictures: it would be replayed on every television sports show." Rayburn was enthusiastic. "Only once in a while does something this good come along. You get it for free, and it has no shelf life; something like this lasts forever."

Rayburn was prowling the aisles of his class of 150 students. He glanced down at one young woman. "Really, I just picked someone at random," he explained. "If you can get this done, I'll give you an A in the course."

After class, the student and a friend approached Rayburn. "Are you serious? Will you give us the grade if we pull this off?" Rayburn was delighted at their initiative. He offered to give them an incomplete for the semester, until after the rematch game. They decided that a letter in advance from the Sugar Bowl would suffice as proof.

The two students, Marci Sandberg and Barbette Someillan, started networking at the bottom and made their way slowly up through the Sugar Bowl and USF&G hierarchy. Rayburn laughed as he retold the story: "They kept me informed, and it sounded like they were getting the big-time runaround. I had already decided I was going to give them extra credit anyway, just because of their persistence and initiative."

The students finally got on the phone with Jeff Hunley, a vice presidential poohbah with USF&G. Hunley was the decision maker. "Yes, we have kicked it around," Hunley told them. "We've been sort of laughing about the idea. But tell me why we should really go through with it."

Marci and Barbette made their pitch. They talked about how it was a rare and unique opportunity, and about all the timeless goodwill and publicity that would attend the bowl, the insurance company, and both schools. "And there is one more reason," they said at the end. "If you'll do this, we both get an A in our public relations class."

Hunley let out a whoop that must have cleared the room. "You can consider it done!" He laughed. Rayburn got the letter before the end of final exams.

"They got it done," he said, swelling with pride in his students. "They took the initiative, they persisted, and they'll never forget this."

Florida Making Noises

Just as the SEC and the Sugar Bowl officially divorced, there was a better-than-ever chance that the next FSU-Florida football matchup in Doak Campbell Stadium would be the last one. Florida was already making noises about dropping FSU, and it was building the case before the contract expired in 1996.

The heart of the dispute had to do with the timing of the game. Florida wanted to move it to the beginning of the season; FSU wouldn't budge from playing it at the end. Florida assumed that they would play in the SEC championship game every year (probably a solid assumption as long as Spurrier was there), and so they didn't want to play against a heart's blood rival one week prior. It was too much, they said. Florida can hardly be slighted for wanting what was in their best interest.

FSU's position was that *any* compromise put the Seminoles at a disadvantage. We played Miami at midseason, and so a front-end loss to Florida would put even more pressure on a Miami game that was already at world-class stress levels.

Florida dropped Miami after the 1987 season, which was a controversial move at the time, but a smart and practical one nonetheless. Florida's probation-weakened program faced a brutal SEC schedule, plus Miami and Florida State. The Gators were handling FSU pretty easily at the time—Miami had won a national title in '83 and looked like a killer, so Miami was the logical one to drop. In 1995, however, the excuse for not playing Miami was an enforced eight-game SEC schedule. There was no such rule in 1987; Florida simply exercised the better part of valor.

It is important to try and see the landscape of 1994 on Florida's terms. Florida State was the killer, and the Sugar Bowl only served to reinforce that bitter reality. The evidence seemed to suggest that Miami could face major NCAA sanctions. The largest Pell Grant scandal in federal history ($173,744, involving fifty-seven football players) had one athletic department employee already in prison, and the NCAA hadn't even begun their investigation. Add to that the *Miami Herald's* scalding series on the cash incentive big-play program supposedly put in place by rap artist Luther Campbell, and allegedly administered by an assistant football coach, and Miami could be "headed for what Florida experienced a decade ago."

I don't want you to think that Florida had forgotten what that was like. They knew if they dropped FSU, they could pick up Miami on whatever terms they cared to dictate. And they were betting they could handle Miami a lot easier than they could endure the Seminoles. Because we had played Florida for nearly forty years, some long-ago myths were in place about how that series got underway. There was a popular misconception that the two schools were *required* to play. But they were not.

FSU's great football coach of the late 1950s, Tom Nugent, made constant overtures to Florida about a game, but the Gators would have none of it. The Gators even offered in 1954 to play FSU in baseball and other sports if the Seminoles would drop their demands to play them in football. FSU turned the deal down.

Early in 1955, the legislature started making noises about requiring the two to play. "Study committees" were set up at each school, with predictable results. In April of the same year, the legislature actually voted on a bill that would require the two to begin playing each other in 1956. The bill failed in the Senate by a 19–15 vote. It seemed inevitable that the two would have to play some day. Pressure was building, perhaps from a sense of sympathy for FSU's role as an underdog or as a victim of Gator arrogance.

Politics eventually carried the day, as it usually does. Governor Leroy Collins, an Alabama graduate, got in a room with the State Board of Control (forerunners of the Board of Regents) and the two university presidents. No one knows exactly what happened in that room—there are no written records and no reporters were allowed in—but when everyone emerged it was announced that FSU and Florida would begin playing each other in 1958.

In 1995, the legislature and the Board of Regents had more pressing business than who plays whom in football. FSU was no longer the underdog, nor were we a victim. Some might have said, however, that humility still tended to elude the Gators.

Their plan was simple: drop FSU and replace us with Miami. For public consumption, Florida needed an issue—something on which to hang their decision. The "issue" was going to be the timing of the game. Listen to Florida athletic director Jeremy Foley, quoted in the *Gainesville Sun*: "At some point the FSU game will have to be adjusted. We might have to tolerate the situation for several years, but we will not tolerate it forever." And listen to Steve Spurrier: "It takes two signatures to make a contract," and the contract with FSU ran out in 1996.

But Florida fans may not have found the switch as much to their liking as they once thought. Miami was facing possible probation, but their new coach, Butch Davis, was a Jimmy John-son clone (indeed, he was Johnson's defensive coordinator at Miami). They made a tremendous last-minute surge in recruiting in February 1995. All Miami had to do to stay strong was continue to recruit Dade County athletes—"Keep it in the family," as the Canes said.

Also, Gator fans who felt mistreated and unloved when they came to Tallahassee for a game were in for a shock when they showed up at the Orange Bowl. Gators were advised that the Hur-ricane fans of 1995, who crowded the stadium, were somewhat less *collegiate* than one may remember from ten years previously.

Perhaps Florida should have taken to heart an admonishment from their own SEC legend Bear Bryant, especially when it came to things like pushing for a rematch against Florida State, or drop-ping the Seminoles for Miami: Be careful what you ask for because you might just get it.[*]

---

[*] Much of this chapter's material was initially published in the *Report to Boosters* (Janu-ary/February 1995).

For Your Amusement:
A Reprise of the 1994
College Football Season

These were golden days for the Seminoles. Following the national championship in 1993, the Seminoles entered, and finished, the 1994 season ranked No. 4. FSU entered the 1995 season ranked No. 1 and would enter four of the following five seasons ranked No. 1, No. 2, or No. 3.

All the drowsy little bees and grasshoppers that inhabited Doak Campbell Stadium would probably drop dead of heatstroke before summer finished broiling its way through Tallahassee. How the construction workers survived I could not say, but there they were, along with the masochistic stadium-step runners and the awestruck pilgrims, fans who had come to stand and stare wordlessly at the grand sweep of University Center.

The football magazines coming out at the time had already tagged the Seminoles No. 1 in the preseason for the fourth time in eight years. Well, I suppose if you wanted to be No. 1, then you had to embrace No. 1 whenever it came courting. And here it was, standing on our porch in midsummer like an overeager prom date. Before we accepted the bouquet and drove off to the dance, however, perhaps we could treat ourselves to one more glance back at the 1994 season. Here is a quick and random reprise of 1994, a season that left many of our Seminole fans as happy and satisfied as they were after winning the national championship in 1993.

Week One: Virginia

Labor Day weekend saw the Seminoles run up a big score on Virginia on national television. In their bid to be the first ACC team to upset FSU, the Cavs brought their own lucky totems: nifty new navy-blue helmets with crossed orange swords. The charms had limited effect, however; Virginia scored only a field goal more than the previous year's total before being buried under an avalanche of Seminole touchdowns.

Florida, the preseason No. 1, destroyed New Mexico State 70–21, and was subsequently bumped from No. 1 to No. 2 in the polls. *Orlando Sentinel* columnist Brian Schmitz suggested that if 70 points weren't enough, then maybe the Gators "should make a human sacrifice at midfield" to impress the voters. In California, the Stanford University marching band was reported to be preparing a "Tribute to O. J. Simpson" for the Southern Cal game.

Week Two: Maryland

Seminole fans, already anxious about life in a post-Charlie world, were aghast to see Maryland leading 20–17 at halftime. The Tribe bucked up and shut out the Terrapins in the second half, winning 55–20, but the fans were not appeased. On Monday after the game, our office received an overnighted copy of the *Weekly World News*, which featured a story announcing that the moon was turning to blood (right next to a story about a pet cockatoo that pecked out his abusive owner's eyes—the cockatoo was in a good home and was happy).

The moon-to-blood development was seen as a sign that the

world was coming to an end. Other signs of the apocalypse were listed as well: your boiling seas, your plague of frogs, etc. At the bottom of the list someone had written in, "Florida State trails at the half to an ACC opponent for the first time in history."

In Gainesville, Coach Spurrier had taken Brian Schmitz's suggestion about a human sacrifice to heart. Kentucky's Bill Curry, no pal of Spurrier's, was to be the designated victim. After Florida's 73–7 slaughter of the Wildcats, reporters asked Spurrier what he said to Curry after the game. "The same thing I say to him every time," Spurrier said. "'Nice game.'"

Week Three: Wake Forest

The Wake Forest game went about as expected: 56–14. Florida State's offense scored six touchdowns the first seven times the Seminoles touched the ball. This was Alan Schmadtke's lead in the *Orlando Sentinel*: "Given the number of Atlantic Coast Conference coaches who devoted the offseason to discussing how their gap behind Florida State has narrowed, it becomes clear now that more research is necessary."

Florida continued its reign of terror in the SEC, shutting out Tennessee 31–0. *Knoxville News-Sentinel* columnist John Adams mourned, "Maybe natural grass is prettier and safer, but no grass looks pretty when you're buried beneath it." And Larry Guest added, "The score was misleading; it wasn't that close. The United States vs. Haiti figures to be more competitive than last night's feature in Neyland's Nursery."

Week Four: North Carolina

Our 31–18 victory over North Carolina was the closest any ACC team had come to beating us since we beat Virginia back in 1992. The late-game Tar Heel surge had some Seminole faithful hemorrhaging internally before the gun sounded. One fellow in the stands wore a T-shirt that pretty much summed up the attitude of most of our fans. It had a big Seminole head on the front, and on the back was written: "It's not whether you win or lose … it's whether I win or lose!"

Week four saw a miracle victory by Auburn over LSU. Leading Auburn in the fourth quarter 23–9, LSU's offensive coordinator, Lynn Amadee, elected to keep throwing … and Auburn picked off five consecutive LSU passes, running three back for touchdowns. Auburn won, and Amadee blamed the LSU quarterback for the loss. For his play-calling and for his loyalty to his players, the *Tampa Tribune's* John Romano named Amadee the "Southeastern Conference Twit of the Month."

Miami was upset by Washington in the Orange Bowl to end the Hurricanes' long win streak. Miami athletic director Paul Dee was a model of sportsmanship, telling the *Miami Herald*, "If it had to end, at least it was a class team playing a great game." FSU fans hoped he would have something equally noble to say after the Seminoles beat the Canes in week five.

Week Five: Miami

Oh, well. Like so many games against Miami, we had them on the ropes then let them roll the momentum back the other way. We had them down by 7, until three Cane interceptions turned into 21 Miami points and a two-touchdown margin in the final score.

It was a bad week all around for the ACC. Clemson was destroyed by Georgia, and Georgia Tech was in the midst of an awful series: Tech had already lost to the Blue Devils, the Wolf-pack, and the Tar Heels—three schools within walking distance of each other. The lead paragraph in the *Atlanta Constitution* followed that theme: "The terrible Trifecta is now complete: Duke, North Carolina State and North Carolina. For Georgia Tech, the Research Triangle has become the Bermuda Triangle."

Week Six: Clemson

Seminole defense shut out Clemson 17–0 before a homecoming crowd of nearly eighty thousand at Doak Campbell. The *Orlando Sentinel*'s Larry Guest wrote:

> While 17 points is considered offensive calamity at FSU, it was more than enough to turn back a Clemson team. This is, uniquely, the only team in the country with two offensive coordinators but no offense. … Clemson's "attack" gives new meaning to the old saw about football being a game of inches.

Later, commenting on Bowden's decision to go for fourth and 1 at our own 41-yard line, Guest wrote, "Presumably, Bowden assumed that even if they had failed to convert, Clemson might have needed three days and a blowtorch to cover 41 yards."

The Clemson game was routine. The fun game was Terry Bowden's Auburn Tigers' victory over Florida in Gainesville. John Romano, writing in the *Tampa Tribune*, led with a tale of frustration: "When sleep does not come and the mind falls prey to midnight wanderings, it must be the image that comes forth to haunt Steve Spurrier's thoughts: The round, cherubic face, the Southern twang. The pudgy body stuffed into droopy drawers. Good heavens! It's a Bowden!"

Week Seven: Duke

It was rumored, some said, that basketball coach Pat Kennedy was on the sidelines trying to get Coach Bowden to hold the score down. Columnist Gene Frenette of the (Jacksonville) *Florida Times-Union* wrote of Duke University's preeminence in medicine, law, and engineering: "You can't be the best at everything," he said. "An esteemed institution of higher learning such as Duke needs to be mediocre at something. History tells us that football is its humiliation of choice." The final score was 59–20.

Georgia lost at home, badly, to Vanderbilt in week seven. The *Tampa Tribune* surveyed, "Vanderbilt? Forty-three points? At Sanford Stadium? At Georgia's homecoming? ... If there is a Bulldog hell, this is the game playing nonstop on ESPN. "

Week Eight: Georgia Tech

No one seems to know what happened to the Yellow Jackets. National champions in 1990, Georgia Tech was a program that faded in and out like the reception on a bad antenna. Scatback Warrick Dunn split the seat of his pants and had to leave the game for a play or two. Bob Harig of the *St. Petersburg Times* wrote that that turned out to be Tech's best defense against him. FSU's 41–10 win at Bobby Dodd Stadium insured the Tribe of at least a share of its third consecutive ACC title.

In California, twenty-three members of the Stanford University band were suspended for showing up at the Los Angeles County Courthouse and playing the USC fight song during the O. J. Simpson jury selection proceedings inside.

Week Nine: Notre Dame

Greg Dawson, who was not a sportswriter, but who wrote for the news sections of the *Orlando Sentinel*, had this observation about week nine:

> I grew up in the hometown of Indiana University where football season ranks just ahead of allergy season in popularity. ... So the Florida State-Notre Dame game was my first in-person exposure to big-time college football, and let me tell you, it was awesome. I've never seen that much alcohol consumed before 11 o'clock in the morning!

Father Terry Morgan, an FSU alum who was stationed, if that is the proper word, at the Vatican, dispatched this telegram to the FSU alumni office:

Regards to all the "Bravi" (that's Italian for good ole boys). Tell the coaches and players that perhaps the sweetest part of beating Notre Dame is the sound you cannot hear from over there: the moaning and groaning and explaining and taking-back-of-huffing-and-puffing that is going on all over the Vatican amongst my colleagues. ... Please thank Coach Bowden for the kind words and the photograph which will be mounted in my room. I'm still looking for one of the Pope, but for now Coach Bowden will be enough. ... Besides, the Pope never autographs his photo handouts.

Week Ten: North Carolina State

The Seminoles beat the Wolfpack by eight touchdowns in 1993. In 1994, the Pack managed to hold the Seminoles down to half that total in a 34–3 FSU victory that anointed them undisputed conference champs. Larry Guest opened his column with this: "The proverbial 500-pound gorilla completed its third lap of the Atlantic Coach Conference, unbeaten and apparently unlikely to drop an ACC game until well into the next century."

Osceola correspondent Rob Meadows wrote that Florida State's domination of the ACC wasn't good for Florida State: "It forces the normally candid Bobby Bowden to pretend that other teams in this league have a chance. ... Right now, teams are tickled pink, when they can stay with the Seminoles for a quarter. So far, no one in the ACC has torn down the goal posts because they were close at the half but hey, that might be next."

In a Sunday afternoon press conference, Florida coach Steve Spurrier spoke of the upcoming game against FSU in Tallahassee: "Let me say it one more time. We are playing Free Shoes University this week, okay? You can all quote me on that."

Week Eleven: Florida

All week before the game, the talk around town was that if quarterback Danny Kanell showed up for the game, figuratively speaking, then we would win. However, if he didn't show up, then we'd lose. But nobody thought much about what would happen if he showed up late.

It was a 31–31 tie, but make no mistake about it—it felt like a win to us and a loss to them. The game story in the *Gainesville Sun* began, "Florida fell to Florida State Saturday, 31–31." Another headline in the *Sun* bellowed, "Choke at Doak Leaves Gators Bewildered." And the story: "Nobody could explain it. … The Gators had just pulled a 1990's version of the Great Florida Flop, falling completely apart in the fourth quarter, turning glorious victory into the most hideous tie since that wide, psychedelic job your children got you last Father's Day." The *St. Pete Times'* Hubert Mizell wrote, "If there's been a better comeback than Saturday's it was by Lazarus, a biblical figure who was even deader than Bowden's team."

The Sugar Bowl

The *Orlando Sentinel's* Brian Schmitz pushed the FSU-Florida rematch: "New Orleans is a city that tends to make you drop your defenses, so what more appropriate place for FSU-UF again? Defense was just a rumor in last Saturday's wacky 31–31 tie. … Imagine how laid back they'll be after a week on Bourbon Street. If the Gators' secondary lays back anymore, they'll be whistled for too few men on the field."

The scoreboard read "FSU 31, Florida 31, Quarter 5" before the game even started. The Sugar Bowl's sponsor, USF&G Insurance, was thrilled almost beyond endurance. "The fifth quarter in the French Quarter" was a constant theme within both schools and throughout the media.

The game lived up to the hype. As soon as Warrick Dunn bounced a ball off a Gator defender's helmet into the hands of 'OMar Ellison for a Bowl-record 73-yard touchdown strike on a trick-play halfback pass, Florida came charging right back with a third-and-12 Wuerffel-to-Hillard 82-yard touchdown pass that set the record again.

The Seminoles' 23–17 win marked an NCAA-record thirteen bowls in a row without a loss. Bobby Bowden became the only coach in NCAA history to lead his team to eight consecutive ten-win seasons.

Senior receiver and team captain Matt Frier celebrates the Seminoles' first national championship in the Orange Bowl, January 1, 1994. His brother, safety Todd Frier, was also senior team captain of the 1999 national championship team. Both were four-year lettermen (*Sports Illustrated*, January 10, 1994).

Churning Ahead into 1995

The year 1995 would be Coach Bowden's twentieth anniversary season as the Seminole head coach. The talk shows would start to buzz, bewildered freshmen would show up and join the veterans in the brutal late-summer heat, and vast numbers of our loyal and generous fans would be assailed by the fact that we could actually lose a game. It was shaping up to be another wonderful year.[*]

---

[*] Much of this chapter's material was initially published in the *Report to Boosters* (July/August 1995).

1995 Season

In our Orange Bowl game against Notre Dame, we led 14–10 at half-time. Lou Holtz was their head coach. We were longtime friends. He spent one night of his honeymoon at our house when I was an FSU assistant coach in the mid-1960s. He and his new wife happened to be traveling through Tallahassee on their way to Miami. None of us young coaches made much money in those days, so you stayed with friends when you could. And Ann and I asked them to stay with us. Looking back, it probably saved him twenty or thirty dollars.

Anyway, our game in the Orange Bowl went south in the second half. Lou's boys jumped up 26–14 in the fourth. Then we came back, scoring a touchdown and then converting on fourth and 5 when E. G. Green made a near-impossible catch across the middle, which led to another score. The defense bowed up, recovering a fumble and causing a safety on Notre Dame's next two possessions. We held on for a 31–26 win.

Lou owed me. But after this game, I called us even.

—Bobby Bowden

1995 Season

Began the season ranked No. 1
Ended the season ranked No. 4
Record 10–2
ACC Champions
Orange Bowl Champions

September 2, defeated Duke in Orlando 70–26

September 9, defeated Clemson in Clemson 45–26

September 16, defeated NC State in Tallahassee 77–17

September 23, defeated Central Florida in Tallahassee 46–14

October 7, defeated Miami in Tallahassee 41–17

October 14, defeated Wake Forest in Tallahassee 72–13

October 21, defeated Georgia Tech in Tallahassee 42–10

November 2, lost to Virginia in Charlottesville 28–33

November 11, defeated North Carolina in Chapel Hill 28–12

November 18, defeated Maryland in Tallahassee 59–17

November 25, lost to Florida in Gainesville 24–35

January 1, 1996, defeated Notre Dame in the Orange Bowl 31–26

Life after Bowden:
FSU vs. the ACC

Until the questionable call on the goal line at Virginia on November 2, 1995, FSU had not lost an ACC game since joining the league. It was whispered in some quarters north of Tallahassee that FSU winning so often and by so much was "bad for the conference." There had been a sidebar item in one of the state newspapers a few years previous to this noting that the university was going to name the football field for Bobby Bowden, but the process was derailed at Coach Bowden's request.

The process of naming something after someone at a state institution is a long and convoluted procedure. The legislature gets involved; various faculty and administrative committees have to sign off on it. It was supposed to be a surprise to be announced on the field before the Central Florida game, but Coach Bowden caught a wisp of a rumor and asked us not to carry through with the plans.

Seminole Booster president Andy Miller and I went to see him to make one last pitch for the naming. Coach was gracious and in good spirits, but we couldn't change his mind. "Look," he laughed, "I just don't think you need to name things after people until they're gone ... and I'm not going. In fact, I don't want anyone to even *think* I'm going!" He went on to say: "I'm really flattered, and maybe someday after I'm retired you'll still want to do it."

That was probably not the whole story, however. Bowden was a genuinely humble man, and even after four decades of coaching success he still took the losses personally, and he was still sensitive to the sting of even casual criticism. He knew that there were some fans and some writers and other several of society's gadflies who lived to talk down the high and mighty, especially one, let's say, after whom a playing field was named and who then proceeded to lose a game or two on that field.

As an amateur historian, Bowden may have been familiar with the life of Cato (the Elder), the Roman statesman who flourished in the second century BC, and who was surely a philosophical forerunner of our coach. Romans looked upon him as embodying the integrity, discipline, and incorruptible independence that were the chief virtues of the Roman Republic. Because Cato had served the Republic so well, someone had once asked him why no statue had been erected to him, to which Cato replied, "I'd rather have people ask why I have no monument than why I do have one."

At some point Bobby Bowden would retire. With luck, that wouldn't be until he had been our head coach for at least twenty-five years. By that time, the hope was that the Seminole Booster organization would have spent a quarter century or more preparing for what Andy Miller called "life after Bowden."

Miller became CEO of the Boosters in 1975, the year before Bowden came to be our coach. Since then, he said, "We've been taking advantage of all the success and recognition he's brought to us." It was true that we had been building toward the day when we would have all the toys necessary to make sure our athletic program was secure for the long term. "Twenty years ago," said Miller, "the big names in college football were interested in us only as homecoming fodder. We had no money, no facilities, and no conference affiliation. Our players gave it everything they had, but we just didn't have the horses to compete in the big leagues."

But in 1995, he pointed out, we were the marquis team on

everyone's schedule. We were the game that packed even the most reluctant stadiums. And when Bobby Bowden *did* retire, FSU would have both the facilities and the scholarship endowment that would ensure future Seminole success. "Whoever does follow Coach Bowden will have no excuses," said Miller. "Everything will be in place."

Seminole Boosters, Inc., was and is a large and complex organization, but our primary focus was on fundraising. Of course, we wanted to take care of our fans; we wanted to keep them happy and make their trips to Doak Campbell as enjoyable as possible. However, when we were accused of being mainly interested in raising money, we had to plead guilty as charged. The truth was that we had to strive to be one of the nation's best collegiate booster groups; in fact, we probably *were* the best. We needed to do this if we were to achieve our goal of having the athletic program self-sufficient and ready for life after Bowden.

We had about ten million in cash in the bank in an irrevocable, untouchable scholarship endowment in 1995. That was about one-third of what we actually needed. It would take an endowment of around thirty million to fully fund annual scholarship costs for all eighteen men's and women's sports.

The second reason we needed to be relentless in fundraising was the University Center. The graceful gothic fortress with eighty thousand seats was the largest contiguous brick construction project in the history of the southern United States. It was being built with about thirty-five million in state funds, and another fifty-two million in private money raised by the Seminole Boosters. The Boosters needed to ensure the annual payments of $3.6 million against a thirty-year bond.

Our goal was to pay off the bond in half the time—in just fifteen years! Doing so would save a staggering fifty million dollars! We believed that money could be used to further strengthen the university's hand. There were many thousands of FSU alumni and friends who also wanted these goals to be realized. That was why we asked for money so relentlessly, and it was why their money was given with such generosity.

It was the nature of things that there would be changes in life after Bowden. We wanted those changes, whatever they were, to be for better, and we did not want any unexpected or unpleasant surprises. Preparation was key. Having the financial means and stability to meet any challenge was our goal.

One change that was likely to follow in Bowden's wake was a realization on the part of our fans of the significance of the Atlantic Coast Conference as a football league. Trust me, Florida State fans were not even remotely possessed of what was called a "conference mentality." It was not bad that we were the way we were. It was just that we found ourselves in the unique position of being in a conference that wanted to play big-time football yet seemed to have not the slightest understanding of what that meant.

We had a good bit of fun in the spring of 1995 on the Bobby Bowden Tour with a letter the *Tallahassee Democrat* published in January after the Sugar Bowl. It was written by a disgruntled Gator who sniffed, "I can assure you that three Southeastern Conference Championships in four years are far sweeter than any victory over FSU." Our response, of course, was that it was not three championships in four years—Florida had won three championships in sixty-two years.

Florida had beaten FSU only one time in the last nine tries. Oh, how we hooted and whooped and made raspberry sounds when our Gator friends told us we were not the biggest game on their schedule. When a Gator fan looked a Seminole fan in the eye and said winning the SEC title was more important than beating FSU, the Nole found it difficult—no, impossible—to believe such a thing was true.

But it was true, and the reality of that was a complete mystery to FSU fans. The fact was that the alumni of most old-line schools in the SEC or Big Ten or Pac-10 or Big 8, or our own ACC, had a conference mentality that was deeply woven into the fabric of their genes. We Seminoles just didn't get it, and the reason had to do with Florida State having achieved one of the most remarkable feats in the history of college football.

FSU had been a member of two football conferences in our forty-nine-year collegiate athletic history: the Dixie Conference (1948–1950) and the ACC (beginning in 1991). In those six-going-on-seven seasons, the Seminoles had been conference champions every year and had never even lost a game!

In only our second year of football, the Seminoles joined the Dixie Conference and proceeded to roll unimpeded over the likes of Millsaps, Mississippi College, Tampa, Stetson, and Howard College. Howard, by the way, was led during that era by a Little All-America quarterback named Bobby Bowden. After three years the other conference teams got bored, or went broke shipping all the hardware down to Tallahassee, and voted to disband.

In 1995, which was more than four decades later, FSU found itself again blessed with an embarrassment of riches and success. As of 1995, FSU led the nation in scoring offense with a frightening 60-points-per-game average. Our *average* margin of victory in ACC contests was about five touchdowns. At least one ACC coach had called the Tribe's fast-break offense unfair and called for unspecified "new rules" to bring it to heel.

Stung by partisan criticism from some up-country sportswriters, Coach Bowden penned a letter of apology to Duke for appearing to run up the score. The hapless Blue Devils were subsequently blown out by several more ACC teams. Maybe some sort of conference pro-forma would emerge: anything above 70 points would require a full-blown letter of apology, but less than 70 but more than 40 required only a Care Bear balloon and a personal note.

Teams who had been members of a conference—any major conference—for a long time had won and lost enough to have

LIFE AFTER BOWDEN: FSU VS. THE ACC • 235

developed deep-rooted rivalries. Old grudges were reborn when the teams, and fans, met every fall. Ole Miss alumni still felt cheated out of a decades-old win at LSU when the officials let LSU run one more play, the winning one, after time ran out. Florida fans will never forgive Tennessee for soaking the playing field with water the night before the 1928 game—a game that cost Florida the SEC title by 1 point.

Simply put, we had no rivals in the ACC at the time. We had not yet lost, even once. Our "conference" was Miami, Florida, and the occasional Notre Dame. We all knew that we had lost and won enough within that circle to make the heart's blood pound on game day. Say "Lane Fenner" to any Seminole, and the crystal-clear memory of the touchdown play that beat Florida in 1966 appears. Then we mouth the name "Doug Mosley," the SEC official who called that touchdown out of bounds. See? You know the names.

As of 1995, the ACC had been little more than a distraction, a scrimmage to prepare us for the regular season. It looked much different going into the ACC in 1991, however. Clemson had clobbered us on our own field in 1989, the year after we nipped them with the Puntrooskie in Death Valley. And prior to 1992, we had failed to defeat Georgia Tech in thirteen tries. With Tech as the 1990 national champs, and Clemson as a perennial powerhouse, the Jackets and Tigers looked like natural rivals for us. The schedules were even arranged so we would never play both of them away in the same year.

What happened then? What happened was nothing more complicated than a coaching change. Bobby Ross, who led Tech back into national prominence and a national title, left for the pros. Danny Ford, who had led Clemson to the 1981 national title, simply left town. Both programs plunged into a dark and difficult terrain, an instructive image for Seminoles who wished to contemplate the eventual onset of life after Bowden.

It was being whispered in some anterooms of the ACC that Florida State's domination was "bad for the conference." Let me tell you what would have been bad for the conference. What would have been bad for the ACC was for FSU to begin regularly losing games to Miami and Florida and to fade from the national scene. It was FSU's clout that helped include the ACC in the Bowl Coalition. FSU gave the ACC entry into the Florida market, rich in high school talent and television sets. There were more major media outlets in Florida than in all the other ACC states combined.

The ACC was definitely good for FSU. ACC schools included some of America's most prestigious universities with sterling academic credentials. Our association with them gave us our own distinct identity; we no longer needed to define ourselves by how we compared to Florida. ACC schools could play baseball—we had learned that. And almost every ACC institution boasted a richer basketball tradition than our own. But we were in good company; our own basketball program was flourishing.

We did not need to worry that we were winning too much in football, or that we were winning by too great a margin. We needed only to worry if we were not taking advantage of every opportunity to be as successful as possible, and that we conducted our affairs honorably and with good grace. But during that time, all we needed to do was to relax and enjoy the margin. Those were great days.*

---

* Much of this chapter's material was initially published in the *Report to Boosters* (October/November 1995).

Seminoles vs. Notre Dame in the Orange Bowl

Following the 1995 season, this series of four essays appeared in the *FSU Overtime Times*, one in each of the four days leading up to the Orange Bowl vs. Notre Dame. The *Overtime Times* was a creation of university communications director Frank Murphy. It was published onsite at each major bowl game and distributed free to thousands of Seminole fans in the bowl city. Florida State vs. Notre Dame matched Coach Bowden with his longtime friend Lou Holtz.

Fighting the Irish: 1981

If you had a key to the secret chambers in Bobby Bowden's heart, you might find out which game, of all games, gave him the most satisfaction in winning. I'm certain it was Notre Dame in 1981.

Coach was in his sixth year as FSU's headman in 1981, and the Seminoles' battle flag was already decorated with bright victory streamers. There were four consecutive wins over Florida, and more important to a program battling for national respect, his team had defeated No. 4 Nebraska and No. 3 Pittsburgh on back-to-back weekends just one year prior.

In fact, the first five years of the Bowden era were a deluxe Carnival Cruise for victory-starved FSU fans. But 1981 had been waiting for the Seminoles like an ominous dark bruise on the horizon that came a little closer and closer even as we splashed in the sun.

The killer defense that ranked No. 1 in the nation in 1980, graduated en masse and the backups had had little play. And the schedule, contracted a decade before by a long-departed athletic director, wrapped around the infamous "Oktoberfest": five consecutive road games against Nebraska, Ohio State, Notre Dame, Pittsburgh, and LSU. As it was, we whipped Ohio State, Notre Dame, and LSU, and lost to Nebraska and Pitt. And that short series of games, compacted as they were over just five weeks and all away from home, propelled FSU onto the national stage as a featured player. That one brief run through a gauntlet of Goliaths made our Seminoles one of the most familiar names and faces of college football.

Why was the Notre Dame win so special to Coach Bowden? Notre Dame's winning tradition had churned along for generations before Seminole football even existed. To a boy growing up in football-rich Birmingham in the 1940s, Notre Dame's national championships of the 1920s were already ancient lore. "Those gold hats," Bowden mused, "I remember seeing pictures of those gold helmets and hearing talk about how great Notre Dame was."

Florida State's program was much different in 1981 than it was in 1995. In 1981, just the idea of playing Notre Dame inspired awe among the Seminole faithful. It was widely believed by program insiders that FSU would probably have only one chance at beating the Irish. No future games were on the schedule, nor were any pending for discussion.

Our alumni body was younger then, all filled with the wonder and passion of young graduates, and achingly impatient for national recognition for their Seminoles. One Seminole bride had the misfortune to choose game day for her wedding. It was a big Catholic church in Palm Beach, and the groom was late to the altar because he'd been in the back listening to the broadcast. When he was finally dragged to the front, he left his radio with one of the altar boys, who reappeared occasionally holding up fingers to indicate the score.

At the end of the ceremony, the groomsmen "beat people down to get to their cars." Upon arrival at the reception in North Palm, guests found the groom and his friends standing in the parking lot catching the final minutes of the game.

There was a group of about a dozen young professionals from Atlanta who made a week-long trip of the back-to-back Ohio State and Notre Dame games on October 3 and October 10. They watched FSU beat OSU in Columbus, then kicked around the Midwest for a week watching the autumn colors wash the landscape. On Saturday, they went to South Bend to see the Tribe beat Notre Dame. "We nearly wept, we were so happy," said one of them. "We just sat there after the game, not wanting to leave. Ever. Not wanting the magical trip to end."

They sat there in a group until everyone else had left, and the sun began to fade, when finally, a groundskeeper approached them. "We thought he was going to throw us out, but he sat and talked to us and gave us the whole history of the stadium."

If you love Florida State, the 1981 Notre Dame win was one of a series of dramatic wins along our journey to national prominence. If you were the coach who loved college football, looking at it in 1995, you might not pick that game as the most satisfying in a long career that included conference and national championships. But in 1981, it was the win of a lifetime.

Team Symbols: Saturday, December 30, 1995

The politically correct crowd that lapsed into a deep swoon over the Cleveland Indians-Atlanta Braves World Series would probably implode with angst over the Orange Bowl clash between Notre Dame and Florida State. To the PC disciples, "Fighting Irish" is a stereotype of loutish, drunken, brawling Celtic-Americans. As for our Seminoles … well, you already know the drill.

Ties between the Seminole Indians and FSU were strong. Seminole Tribal Chairman James E. Billie had been under attack by those who columnist George Will identified as "the sensitivity police and thought vigilantes." They tagged Billie as "Uncle Tom-Tom" for his steadfast support of FSU's use of Osceola as an honored symbol. But they would have probably not said this to his face, as Chief Billie is a man who wrestles alligators—and wins.

"This whole issue is so trivial," Billie told the *Fort Lauderdale Sun-Sentinel*. "I get tickled when I watch on television, and the announcer says, 'Here come the Florida State Seminoles,' and fifty black guys come running out onto the field. That's pretty neat. … To me, it's kind of flattering, as long as they win."

It was a little more than flattering, actually. Tampa attorney Howard Hunter told us that there were running radio commercials for the Seminole Indians' gaming palace that featured the FSU "war chant" as background music. When one voiceover asked if that was the FSU chant, the second voice responded, "Where do you think they got it?"

Had you been lucky enough to be among the seven hundred faithful in Orlando on a balmy evening in the spring of 1995, you would have witnessed the most electrifying moment in the twenty-year history of the Bobby Bowden Tour. It had been the custom for the Seminole Club of Greater Orlando to invite several dozen Seminole Indians to attend the annual banquet, to sell their crafts and participate in the evening. Carla Gopher, dressed in the traditional raiment of a Seminole princess, signed the Lord's Prayer in the Creek language.

During Coach Bowden's address, the talk naturally turned to the 31–31 tie in our last home game. He spoke of the courage and resolve of our boys, and the poise it took to come charging back from a 31–3 deficit in the fourth quarter. Then Coach Bowden stopped and turned to face the several tables of Seminole Indians clustered together.

"I'm so glad you are here tonight," he said to them. "I want to tell you how honored I feel to have our team bear your name. There could not have been a greater inspiration for this game than Osceola and the other Seminole leaders so long ago. They never gave up; refused to give in even against hopeless odds. But they won in the end because they refused to quit. They refused to be defeated. And I believe that some of that Seminole spirit lives in our program today, or else we would never have been able to fight back to win. ... Thank you, for what you mean to us."

At that, the hundreds of FSU Seminoles leaped to their feet. Chairs were knocked aside; cheers exploded in the air above the crowd. Our people turned as they applauded and faced the real Seminoles. The sentiment was deep, and it was real.

I had wondered what Osceola might have thought had he known about our re-creation of his image riding Renegade. What would he have thought of our gold helmets with the arrow symbol; of our eighty thousand fans joining in the "war chant"? It might have confirmed most of his suspicions about whites, or perhaps a wry grin might have creased his face as he contemplated the extent of his ultimate victory, and that of his people.

In the rich fabric of American history, the virtues we admire as being American—courage, individualism, resolve, and resistance in the face of tyranny—were all present among the Seminole Indians who survived in Florida and refused to surrender. And Osceola remains worthy of emulations as one of our own—a truly great, unhyphenated American.

Great Expectations: Sunday, December 31, 1995

Two small vignettes serve to illustrate the distance that FSU traveled since 1981 game against Notre Dame. The first of these occurred as the affable Jerry Kutz was being given a VIP tour of the athletic facilities in South Bend the day before our 1993 game. Kutz tripped over a piece of iron, dark stained with time, being used to prop open a door. It was a Cotton Bowl trophy. In 1981, Notre Dame had already won more national championships than FSU had won bowl games.

The second scene was Matt Frier's passionate despair as he left the field after the 1993 game. In 1981, we went to South Bend as the underdog and upset mighty Notre Dame. By 1993, however, Notre Dame was the underdog in their house to the mighty Seminoles. We lost, but we were the favored team even in South Bend.

During the last half of Bobby Bowden's first twenty years as our head coach, the expectations of our fans had lurched into a place where reason was not always a welcome companion. I was sitting in the hot Orlando stadium watching us play Duke in September 1995, and we were leading 41–10 with a few minutes to play in the second quarter. Our offense was driving the field again. I turned to my friend Joel Padgett, who was a serious, *serious* fan, and said, "Well, 48–10 at the half wouldn't be shabby, would it?"

He chewed on that for a moment, and then said, "The 10 bothers me …"

We expected to win 10 games every year. We expected to finish in the top 5 every year. We *expected* to beat Florida. We *expected* to run the table in the ACC. We *expected* to win our bowl game, and it goes without saying that a major bowl was on menu. Gator fans expected to win the SEC. Every year. The Canes expected to win the Big East, and both those teams expected to beat us just as we expected to beat them.

And why shouldn't we have expected that? In just a little more than a decade, Florida's Big 3 had become the center of the college football universe. In 1981, FSU and Florida battled at the end of the season with a Peach Bowl bid on the line. The loser went home alone. In 1995, the FSU-UF winner was guaranteed a spot in the national title game. And we expected it, before the season even began.

The perspective of Florida's Big 3 was markedly different from that of their respective conference fellows. Perhaps no one had summed it up so clearly as *Tampa Tribune* columnist David Whitley did in just one sentence: "Virginia's players will proudly wear the ACC co-championship rings the Seminoles probably will never even try on."

After our undefeated 11–0 season in 1979, the Seminoles were rewarded with a bid to the Orange Bowl, our first-ever major New Year's Day bowl. It was difficult to grasp just how emotionally overpowering this was for our fans. After inheriting a program that won only three games in four years, Bobby Bowden took only four seasons to achieve the highest mark in FSU football history.

We flooded into Miami. Thousands couldn't get tickets but went anyway. We were as yet unschooled in the nuances of big-time bowls. There was a meeting of the Seminole Booster board of directors at the top of the tall Marriott down on Biscayne. Afterward, I found myself taking the long, slow elevator ride down in the company of a group of Oklahoma fans who were staying at the hotel.

They were very nice, and as we had time to talk I commented about the difference I'd noticed between the FSU fans and the Sooner fans walking the same streets. The Seminoles, I said, looked exuberant, as if they might begin to dance at any moment. In contrast, the Sooners strolled along sober-faced, almost bored. The Oklahoma people in the elevator were every kind, and I could tell that they chose their words carefully so that I would not be offended.

"The Orange Bowl is very nice, and, of course, we're honored to be here," they said. "But we had expected to play for another national championship this year and things didn't work out the way we had hoped. The Orange Bowl is an enjoyable trip, but we've been here quite a few times, and it may be that a lot of our fans just don't feel the incentive to come this year."

I didn't say anything, but I was struck by how far the Seminoles had to go. I thought, *If we could ever get our program, somehow, to the point where our expectations were so high that anything less than a national championship game was disappointing … well, if we could ever get to that point, we'd be on top of the world.*

Preparing for Battle: Monday, January 1, 1996

The young coach had a family and little money. His pal in the coaching fraternity had just gotten married and was even more strapped financially. So much so in fact, that as he and his bride meandered south on their wedding trip, they were grateful to stay a night or two as guests of their friends. That is how Lou Holtz and his wife came to spend part of their honeymoon with Bobby and Ann Bowden.

Florida State Bowl Media Guide from the January 1, 1996, Orange Bowl: No. 7 FSU vs. No. 6 Notre Dame. A 31–26 victory assured FSU of a ten-win season and No. 4 final ranking in the ninth year of the dynasty. Lou Holtz was in his tenth year as head coach of the Irish. After Holtz and his wife, Beth, were married in the summer of 1961, they spent two nights of their honeymoon at the home of Bobby and Ann Bowden in Birmingham to save money.

More than thirty years later, Bowden and Holtz had pressed their respective careers to the top of the pyramid. Both men stood among the most successful, most heralded, most renowned college coaches of the twentieth century. They led the two most nationally televised college football programs of the previous ten years.

Bobby Bowden was an earnest student of World War II, and

his preparations for each season were not unlike those of a military campaign. In the summer of 1981, prior to the season of the "Oktoberfest," the Bobby Bowden Tour stopped in Bradenton. They put us up in a condo, and as I puttered around the place, I noticed a thick book lying open on the coffee table where Coach had fallen asleep studying it the night before. It was the compiled notes of presentations made at a recent coaches' conference. Each head coach's remarks were reproduced in about five pages of text.

The book was open to a talk by Earle Bruce on "Ohio State's Winning Offense." The margin was crowded and bright red with Bowden's scribbling. What caught my eye was one phrase Bowden had underlined not once, but three times in red, and was followed by a red exclamation point. It was Bruce's best advice to other head coaches on how to build and maintain a great tradition: "Never … *never* lose at home."

A few days later I went to Coach's office to pick him up for the drive over to Lake City, and I noticed a biography of Notre Dame's Gerry Gaust stuck under some papers on his desk. I remembered the passage in the movie *Patton*, where General Patton studied a manual on tactics written by German Field Marshall Erwin Rommel, and used the information to set up an ambush of Rommel's armored columns. As shown in the movie, American artillery pounded the Nazi tanks while Patton strode back and forth on the battlements, shaking his fist in triumph and shouting, "I read your book … ! I read your book!"

I wondered how Earle Bruce and Gerry Faust would react to the ambush by Bowden's Seminole artillery. Ohio State fell on October 3 and Notre Dame fell on October 10.

Coming into this game, Lou Holtz had lost his phenomenal quarterback Ron Powlus for the season, and had suspended his stud running back Randy Kinder, who was the core of the offense. Do not weep for the Irish; Holtz is the master magician in just such conditions. In fact, Notre Dame insiders knew that the suspended-players-before-the-big-game ploy had become something of a Holtz signature. It was a battlefield tactic to lull the opponent, and there are some who would say that our 1995 Seminoles were a team especially susceptible to lulling.

How would we fare against Notre Dame in the Orange Bowl? A headline in the December 8 Jacksonville paper suggested that the Seminoles lacked enthusiasm and motivation. "FSU's rock is shaken," they wrote. Shaken by an unexpected loss to Virginia and a stinging rebuke by Florida. The season that began in Orlando with such promise seemed to have faded somehow toward the end.

But let's take one more look at that rock, and a handsome one it was. One thing that had been lost in the commentary was that our nineteen seniors constituted the only class in the history of the program never to have lost at home. We were 22–0–1 in our own house, the best four-year record ever. Those boys were on the team that won the national title. They had never allowed Miami or Florida to break our hearts in Doak Campbell. They had never failed to win ten games in a year, never failed to finish in the top 4. And they would not fail in this last and most important contest of their Florida State careers. The character and toughness and determination of the true Seminoles surrounded them with an aura unseen but real.

As for which of the two coaches would prove to be the shrewdest and savvy in his preparations—which would have the most deceptively slick plan—my bet was with our own Seminole chief. After all, this wasn't the first time Lou Holtz had been taken in by Bobby Bowden.

The Grand Parade:
Reprise of the 1995
College Football Season

We seemed to be at a crossroads of anniversaries at the end of 1995. Bobby Bowden's twentieth year at the helm concluded with a victory over Notre Dame in the Orange Bowl, and in the fall of 1996 we would celebrate our fiftieth season as Seminoles. In 1997, we would ceremoniously recognize completion of our beautifully constructed hundred-million-dollar gothic fortress which gave us, if not the largest, surely the most handsome college football stadium in America.

This was a grand parade we were riding in; these were the days to be remembered for all our lives. So before we opened the 1996 season with the traditional sacrifice of Duke, I want us to savor the ins and outs of 1995, a year that saw the Noles ranked No. 1 in the preseason for the fourth time in eight years.

Week One: Duke

It was hot in Orlando, almost as hot as the Southern Mississippi game in Jacksonville in 1989. And when the Dukies showed up in dark blue uniforms and hats, you figured they'd last about twenty minutes before fainting. Actually, twenty minutes turned out to be optimistic.

"Pooh Bear" Williams rushed for three touchdowns and amassed about 1.5 total yards. It was entirely possible that Pooh Bear would break the all-time scoring record, and not break 100 yards for his career. The *Orlando Sentinel's* Larry Guest wrote: "Williams, the Seminoles' jocular 280-pound fullback/Winnebago, oozed in for three pointblank touchdowns, and fortunately geared down to a stop before bumping into any nearby buildings or the East/West Expressway. ... Duke retreated to North Carolina with a $850,000 check to rub on their wounds. ... Most of the FSU team flew back to Tallahassee Saturday; Pooh Bear is expected to arrive back there early today by flatbed truck."

While the offense was busy scoring 70 points, the defense allowed only 26, which was the most ever scored to that date by an ACC opponent.

Week Two: Clemson

The defense again allowed 26 points and 321 yards on the ground, the most allowed since Miami gained 334 in 1990. But the hero on offense was Warrick Dunn who registered his fifth consecutive 100-yard game against ACC competition, and was named the ABC Player of the Game. Martin Fennelly wrote this in the *Tampa Tribune*: "We're not saying Warrick Dunn is hot, but after Saturday's game he took off his cleats in the locker room, and *they* proceeded to run for another 11 yards."

As Duke's season continued to free-fall into despair, Northwestern began to emerge as the Cinderella darling of the Big Ten. Turns out the biggest upset of the season may have been Miami University of Ohio's win over the Wildcats.

Looking for some clue, Duke Coach Fred Goldsmith called Northwestern to see how a school that shared Duke's lofty academic ambition could take on the big boys and win. The news was not good; it seemed that Northwestern had managed to recruit some legitimate big-time talent. "I found out they're running the same defense as we are," a gloomy Goldsmith told reporters. The problem wasn't a poor technique; rather, it was a lack of talent. "If I sleep in a garage, it doesn't make me a car."

Week Three: NC State

Coach Bowden was late for the Monday luncheon as he was busy Xeroxing more letters of apology. After the 77–17 destruction of the Wolfpack, and in light of the Fred Goldsmith swoon following the Duke massacre, the consensus of state sportswriters seemed to be that Coach Bowden ought to send form letters at the beginning of the season to any coach not located in Miami or Gainesville.

This from the *Tampa Tribune*: "Winning big these days means having to say you're sorry. Bowden mailed a letter to Duke Coach Fred Goldsmith apologizing for beating the Blue Devils 70–26. North Carolina State Coach Mike O'Cain can expect a box of chocolates sometime this week." And from the *St. Pete Times*: "It is highly likely that even if FSU's top 24 players were quarantined for the next three months, the Seminoles would still win the ACC. As a league, the ACC is basically the Southwest Conference, only with acceptable SAT scores." And here's the *Jacksonville Times-Union*: "Give it up, ACC. The Serbian Air Force has a better chance of knocking off NATO than you have of ever gunning down the Seminoles."

David Whitely piled it on in his *Tampa Tribune* column:

The Seminoles settled for 77, though it could have been worse had FSU not finished with Gene Deckerhoff at tailback. ... The Seminoles' offensive Death Star is redefining reality. A 42–14 score used to constitute a blowout worthy of a Goldsmith pout. ... There's no hope for the rest of the ACC: as for Central Florida, the apology is in the mail. Only Miami stands in FSU's way before the game in Gainesville that might decide the entire future of Mankind. ... Until then, it will primarily be a matter of staying awake and keeping Pooh Bear away from fried foods.

Week Four: Central Florida

Former FSU All-American Gene McDowell gave the Tribe all they wanted as his Central Florida team employed a new scheme against us that our opponents adopted for the rest of the season. Early in the game the scoreboard read 7–7. Later, the Knights Boosters sold T-shirts with a photo of the score and a banner proclaiming, "I Was There!" The No. 1-ranked Seminoles held off the Knights 46–14.

That same weekend Maryland routed Fred Goldsmith's Duke team 41–28. It was not a margin that would require a full-blown apology, but maybe just a gift basket with a nice card. Miami lost to Big East rival Virginia Tech, and the *Miami Herald* reported a screaming match between the team chaplain, Father Leo Armbrust, and a player who had suggested the father had an attitude problem. "*You* think I have an attitude problem?" the good father shrieked, lacing his outburst with obscenities in the locker room after the Tech game.

Week Five: Open Date

Miami beat Rutgers 56–21. Despite early season losses to UCLA and Virginia Tech, and reports that college football's most talkative bullies were on the decline, the *Ft. Lauderdale Sun-Sentinel* warned: "The meek have not yet inherited the earth." On top of that, South Carolina destroyed Kent State 77–14. A bewildered Kent coach, Jim Corrigal, struggled to understand exactly what had happened. "Every time we went out on the field, they scored," he told reporters. "That's not good."

Week Six: Miami

It was just fine. David Whitley in the *Tampa Tribune* wrote, "Miami's fallen and it can't get up. We have come to expect the unexpected series, but we have not come to expect the game being so one-sided that FSU fans can laugh about their kicking game. … The series that once defined college football—that gave ESPN their highest rated game ever (1994)—may be quickly slipping into Jefferson Pilot territory."

Larry Guest in the *Orlando Sentinel* wrote, "Though Miami appears unarmed this season, Bowden says the memories of Miami nightmares past were too humbling and too recent to relax. 'If a guy breaks into your house and robs you and comes back three weeks later without a gun, you're still scared of him,' said Bowden. Interesting that he would use an analogy featuring lawbreakers."

From the *Times-Union* in Jacksonville: "Dingdong, the witch is dead. … That Hurricane hell hag who has hovered over and haunted Florida State for so very long died a sudden, merciless death last night. … With Prime Time in the house, and a sellout crowd chanting 'Run up the score,' the top-ranked Seminoles dismantled the sad sack Hurricanes."

St. Pete Times columnist Gary Shelton drafted a mock letter of apology from Coach Bowden to Miami coach Butch Davis: "Dear Butch … Good seeing you again Saturday night. … My heart did a drum solo when I saw your players run out in those same old Miami uniforms. Thank goodness the guys inside them play a lot like Rutgers. Hey, you said you wanted to fit in with the Big East. Well, now you do. … Your offense played so badly I understand Luther Campbell is asking for refunds." Just in case you have forgotten, the final was 41–17.

Week Seven: Wake Forest

It got ugly early. Wake scored on two long, scary touchdowns in the second quarter, but it was still 41–13 at the half—and 72–13 at the merciful end. Among the several suggestions for the latest apology letter: "Dear Wake, I'm sorry. I'm sorry I let the game get out of hand early. I was watching the Auburn-Florida game on the sidelines television monitor and I got distracted. ... By the time I started paying attention, Ann had grabbed the headphones and was calling plays. She really wants to see Jeffrey's receivers do well."

This was from the *Tampa Tribune*: "Will the last fifth-string walk-on to score a touchdown for FSU, please turn off the lights. ... On Saturday, the Seminoles played an Abdullah, a Librizzi, and two guys wearing #35. By the fourth quarter, walk-on QB Librizzi was handing off to a variety of running backs known only to their families."

And here's the *Jacksonville Times-Union* weighing in: "A season of nonstop mercy killings proceeded without a hitch yesterday. ... Nothing new to report. Just another ACC football opponent against which FSU scored more points than its basketball team did last year against the same school."

Week Eight: Georgia Tech

It was another rout on paper (42–10), but somehow it didn't feel quite right. The Tribe trailed for the first time in the season, and the third quarter was our first scoreless quarter. Warrick Dunn was held to just 60 rushing yards. The *Times-Union* had this to say about the game: "Say what you will about the state of ACC football, but at least Tech tried to show some spunk. The Jackets could have easily slinked into Tallahassee with a sign taped to their backs that said 'Rout Us.' OK, they still got routed, but you had to treasure the way the Ramblin' Wreck actually swaggered in."

The *St. Pete Times* noted: "After so many lopsided ACC games, at least this time (FSU) had reason to stay interested in the game." It was an ominous comment in light of the fact that the next game was Virginia. "Staying interested in the game" was a virtue that tended to elude us as we got deeper into the ACC schedule.

All that week, Southern Cal coach John Robinson had been complaining about No. 1-ranked Florida State, and how it would be inconvenient for his team to go to the Rose Bowl and have to be concerned about the title claims of an undefeated, but undeserving, Seminole team. Robinson even continued to bellyache about it on the long plane ride to South Bend. Notre Dame 38, Southern Cal 10 was the way the game ended, after which Robinson didn't seem to have as much to say. He had even less to offer after the following week's tie with Washington and the season-ending loss to crosstown rival UCLA.

Week Nine: Open Date

In light of Florida's remarkable and sustained success, a national theme seemed to be emerging around Steve Spurrier. Mark Bradley, writing about the Falcons in the *Atlanta Constitution*, said: "Here's my star of the year: The Falcons have scored eight offensive touchdowns in six games; the Gators scored nine touchdowns against Tennessee. Could it be that it's better to have an evil genius as head coach than a nice, unassuming guy named June?"

The October 30 edition of *Newsweek* reviewed the personalities of several major coaches. "Florida," it said, "is brilliantly led by Steve Spurrier ... often described as an offensive genius." *Newsweek* recounted this story: "You called me arrogant? I thought you'd be the last man to say that," Spurrier once said to a columnist. Replied the scribe, "Coach, I think I *am* the last."

Week Ten: Virginia

Thursday night on ESPN, the No. 1-ranked team in America went into Charlottesville looking glamorous—as glamorous as one of those fabulous ocean-side homes perched high on the cliffs along

California's coast. The living is so grand, and the view so spectacular, that after a while we tend to forget what just one little hiccup along the fault line can do to our wonderful little world.

After Thursday's 28–33 mudslide, credit the quality of construction—and the builder himself—for the fact that we didn't slide any further down the cliffs than we did. It was a great game for television. That's about all one could say.

Week Eleven: North Carolina

It was cold, miserable, and it rained. We defeated the Tar Heels 28–12 in Chapel Hill to win a share of the conference title. On the way back to Tallahassee, the team equipment bus caught fire and all the uniforms and pads were destroyed. Many felt the bus should have been burned after the Virginia game a week before. Obviously the equipment was cursed, and *should* have been destroyed.

When Connie and I arrived in Raleigh Friday night, we found that longtime Seminole trainer Don Fauls had died at Joe McGee's home the night before. Don was there for the annual reunion of Nugent's boys, the rollicking crew of 1950s players who gathered each season in Raleigh for golf and general excess of all kinds. Bill Childers, Joe McGee, Tom Feamster, Bo Davis, Bill Burkhardt, Vic Prinzi, and Don were all among the regulars.

The whole Florida State traveling party gathered for a social at McGee's that Friday night, as planned, but the mood was subdued. Nugent's boys had stayed up late Thursday night, telling stories and looking through the old game programs that were still lying about. There was one on the pool table from the 1958 contest against Tennessee, the first great shutout victory by the Tribe over an SEC opponent. "Assistant football coach Lee Corso" looked very young, while "athletic trainer Donald Fauls" beamed a smile that was full of life.

Don's beloved wife Marg had died in June, and his already-weakened heart had been stressed even more. I saw him Thursday on the flight to Atlanta. He looked frail, but he was excited and enthusiastic about being with all his friends once again. They were to all play golf together the following morning, but sometime after the frost settled in among the clean-limbed Carolina pines, Marg slipped into his room and brushed her fingers against that fragile cheek. "Come, Don," she whispered. "It's time." And they were gone.

When our time comes, if we are lucky enough to slip away in the small hours between staying up too late enjoying the company of our pals and getting up to play golf in North Carolina, then we may count ourselves among the truly blessed.

Week Twelve: Maryland

The newspapers didn't have much to say about our 59–17 rout of Maryland, or Florida's 38–7 destruction of Vanderbilt, except to advise both the Terrapins and Commodores to get out of the state as fast as they possibly could. All media eyes were focused on the clash of Titans just one week away.

Burt Reynolds' comments made just about every paper. He had been explaining why he wasn't going to Gainesville, now or ever again: "I don't go to Gainesville for the game anymore. ... I've been in four fights. I'm 4–0, but my team lost two of those games."

The *Tampa Tribune's* David Whitley canvassed his fellow scribes: "In my halftime survey, 13 of 14 sportswriters who regularly cover FSU predicted that Florida would win. ... But you can question the collective wisdom of a group that didn't have one matching pair of socks." *Tribune* columnist Tom McEwen took a meant-to-inspire jab at his Gators: "But there remains that haunt of the northwest. When somebody asks, 'How close is Florida to a national championship,' FSU fans answer: '149 miles'—the distance from Gainesville to Tallahassee. Unfortunately, they're right."

Week Thirteen: Florida

For only the second time in nine years, the Seminoles fell to the Gators. This team ended the season as it had begun: a mystery. Who are these guys? This is the same team that lost badly to Miami in '94 and then came back and pounded them in 1995, and had fun doing it. This team beat Notre Dame in '94 and then lost to Virginia in '95. These were the same guys who broke Florida's hearts—twice the previous season—and made Florida's fortune at the end of this one. Sometimes it just happens. Florida played inspired ball; we sacked Wuerffel seven times, and he still kept coming. Florida prevailed 35–24 and won the honor of facing Nebraska.

The Bowl Game

It was the last Orange Bowl in the old house, and even then the writers wouldn't let it retire with grace. Sportswriter Andy Reid compared Miami to New Orleans in light of the running controversy over whether the Seminoles should go to the Orange Bowl or the Sugar Bowl: "Sure, a matchup with Notre Dame in the Orange Bowl might make a top-5 finish more realistic, but that will require a major sacrifice on the part of FSU fans traveling to Miami," Reid explained. He continued:

> It begins with the search for parking. You'd better be bilingual if you hope to negotiate for a parking space in the front yard of one of the ever-so-friendly Orange Bowl neighbors. For $20, Carlos will let you squeeze your car between his palm tree and the cement Jesus. … If FSU returned to the Sugar Bowl, Seminole fans could watch their team beat up on Texas and then ring in the New Year on Bourbon Street. In Miami, FSU fans will dodge drug dealers and pray they make it back to their hotels.

1996 Season

There's an old saying that the Lord gives us what we need but not necessarily what we want. I certainly didn't want a rematch with Florida in the Sugar Bowl following our '96 season. We had just beaten them in our last game of the season. They came in ranked No. 1 at the time, and we were ranked No. 2. It was billed as yet another "game of the century." The contest was a slugfest between two great teams. We won, 24–21, and moved into the No. 1 spot.

Next up came the Sugar Bowl. We were playing yet again for the national championship. Naturally, I prayed for an easy opponent. Unfortunately for us, we got matched up again with Florida. One never wants to play the same team twice in one year, especially when they are one of the best teams in the country, and even more so if they are your biggest rival and you just beat them a few weeks earlier. Incentive and motivation would now be in their favor.

The 1994 rematch against Florida was different because that game ended in a tie, and both teams were eager to butt heads again and prove which one was the best. This time the tables were turned against us. And it translated onto the field. They beat us handily.

—Bobby Bowden

1996 Season

Began the season ranked No. 3
Ended the season ranked No. 3
Record 11–1
ACC Champions
Played for the National Championship

September 7, defeated Duke in Tallahassee 44–7

September 19, defeated NC State in Raleigh 51–17

September 28, defeated North Carolina in Tallahassee 13–0

October 5, defeated Clemson in Tallahassee 34–3

October 12, defeated Miami in Miami 34–16

October 26, defeated Virginia in Tallahassee 31–24

November 2, defeated Georgia Tech in Atlanta 49–3

November 9, defeated Wake Forest 44–7

November 16, defeated Southern Mississippi in Tallahassee 54–14

November 23, defeated Maryland 48–10

November 30, defeated Florida in Tallahassee 24–21

January 2, 1997, lost to Florida in the Sugar Bowl 20–52

The Best Fans

The Seminoles, with all their pomp, glory, and dramatic symbols, and the quotable coach, were a darling of the media. But winning also brought out the critics. Cheap shots were aimed at our fans, and unfair comparisons were made about attendance. The truth was that our fans had to travel further, more often, and spend more money on football travel than fans of any other team in the country. Seminole fans simply are the best, and they proved it every year.

A couple of times in 1996, I had the chance to sit alone in the stadium watching the late afternoon yellow light wash over the long sweep of seats. It should have been serene, but the first time I saw the finished bowl the most compelling emotion I felt was fear. The scope, the scale of the thing, overwhelmed me. I thought, 6–5 won't pay for this; 7–4 won't do it. We can't *afford* not to win ten games a year anymore.

Rod Serling was the creator of *The Twilight Zone*. In the early 1950s, Serling was a young writer of fine television dramas who chaffed against the restrictions of stiff-necked (as he saw them) network executives. Serling's talent was spectacular, as were his clashes with the networks over issues of creative control. In the end, however, he succumbed.

"Here's how they get you," he wrote later. He told how a young writer came to New York filled with fire and idealism and a fresh innocence about the business. After struggling and starving like all the other young writers, the network plucked him up and began paying him a thousand dollars a week. "You still have your idealism, even though that's more money than you've ever seen; more than you've ever imagined you'd make," Serling said.

He then went on to say, "And they keep paying you a thousand a week, but you're determined they won't own you. And they keep paying you a thousand a week, and they keep paying you a thousand a week until you become terrified that they'll stop. That's how they get you."

Serling enjoyed a rich and rewarding career, but he had to leave behind the spontaneous joy of writing only the things he wanted to write, and his naiveté about the realities of his business didn't survive the first power lunch.

There was a parallel here with Florida State. In 1986 we went 6–4–1. No one was very happy about it, but we won our bowl game and people started getting excited about the prospects of a "better" season in 1987. Since those more innocent days of hoping for improvement, we had run off an NCAA record of ten-win seasons and top-4 finishes, and of course the bowl win was always assumed. We had cashed our version of the thousand-dollars-a-week check for so long that anything less than ten wins and a bowl victory in 1996 was unthinkable, unacceptable, and cause for meetings and whispered speculations.

We had built the most beautiful college stadium in America with those ten-win seasons. We depended on the genius of Bobby Bowden to help us make the $3.7-million-per-year payments on the mortgage. We were big time. We stood at the top of the college football pyramid. Along the way, we had given up much of our innocence and maybe even a little of the joy, but that was the standard retail price: we were in the same shopping club with Nebraska, Alabama, Florida, Miami, and whomever else haunted the national championship trail.

It has taken a while to meander around to the subject of this chapter, but here it is: There was not a thing wrong with our FSU fans! Yes, we had taken on some scary responsibilities—our $3.7-million annual mortgage payment came to mind—but taking real risks to achieve one's dreams is always scary. If you were counting reasons to fear, then you could cross fan support off your list. Seminole fans were among the best in the nation, and I'm going to prove it to you.

You may have seen or heard some 1996 commentary about our attendance at home and away games, the implication in some quarters being that perhaps Florida State fans weren't as loyal or as enduring as the fans of some other schools. This all started when our fans noticed how outnumbered they were by Gators at the Sugar Bowl in 1994. In 1995, there were noises about how the FSU ticket office couldn't sell all its Orange Bowl tickets, and there was a string of snotty postgame articles after we were about ten thousand short of filling our new eighty-thousand-seat stadium for the home opener against Duke.

I didn't really blame the sportswriters; Duke was a boring game and they had little else to write about. But what was called "lack of fan support" was a theme that wound its course through all the major state papers. Left unanswered and uncorrected, that's just the sort of propaganda that could be employed again and again by, well, non-FSU types who may have wanted to promote this nonsense for their own advantage.

I want to break it down into its constituent parts and deal with each of them in turn.

The Sugar and Orange Bowls

Conferences, and even individual teams, have close ties with specific bowls. Any SEC team is going to be able to secure many times the number of tickets available to any non-SEC opponent in the Sugar Bowl. This has never been official policy, but it has always been convenient reality. And even though there is no longer any formal affiliation, the unofficial ties still remain.

In Phoenix in 1995, for example, the Gators were stunned to find out that they were badly outnumbered by legions of Nebraska fans. But it was chalked up to Nebraska's longtime coziness with the Fiesta. And don't think it escaped Notre Dame's notice that garnet-and-gold-clad fans in the Orange Bowl overwhelmed the Irish blue by about two to one. Notre Dame didn't like being outnumbered anywhere, and they didn't expect it. But the Orange Bowl was Seminole territory.

It was reported that Florida State couldn't sell all its tickets to the Orange Bowl Classic, but that was not accurate. The Orange Bowl was, in fact, nearly full. Seminole fans bought tons of tickets. They just didn't buy them from the Florida State ticket office. Our fans knew that any schools' ticket office always gets a poor selection of seats; they could get much better tickets for the game in South Florida. Seats were plentiful and easily available to Seminoles who wanted to attend, and we responded in great numbers.

The Duke Game

Jerry Kutz was on target when he said that FSU had a maturing fan base. They were more selective; they had more options. Our fans were more likely to pick out, say, three or four of the six home games and make enjoyable weekends of those trips. Duke, the traditional season-opening human sacrifice, on television and in the afternoon heat of early September, was probably not on the short list for many.

There was a rumor that the students didn't show up, but the truth was that our students picked up fifteen thousand of their eighteen thousand allocation of tickets. Our students were out in force. Who wasn't there was Duke. FSU had to hold out 10,500 tickets each year for either Florida or Miami. Those tickets were also available for each of our ACC opponents. The unfortunate fact was that the ACC's second-best team, North Carolina, sent only 1,500 fans, and that would rank as the most fans sent to Tallahassee by any ACC team in 1996. Duke fans bought, and this is not a misprint, only 150 tickets.

To their credit, our ticket office anticipated these figures, and thus sold the surplus tickets in the spring. But more than ten thousand no-show opponents was and is a big hole to fill up, especially if the game doesn't have star quality.

Fan Enthusiasm

There did seem to be a damper on the crowd morale in 1995, but things were much better all-around in the 1996 season. Program insiders who watch these statistics told me that 1995 was peculiar for several reasons. One of those reasons was the dreadful practice of starting games at noon in the Florida heat. Noon is fine among the cool pine mountains of the Carolinas and Virginia and Maryland. However, noon in Florida in September and October can be near fatal.

The new athletic director, Dave Hart, lobbied the ACC long and mightily, and eventually fashioned a deal allowing us to avoid those noon games. I do believe, and I'm not overstating this, that we would have sold the program's soul if we had agreed to a repeat of that fearful five-home-games-in-a-row-at-noon schedule that we digested in 1995.

Television-driven start times were a pervasive problem that were not easily solved. So many of our fans had asked me why we just didn't say no to the money for one or two games, but it was not that simple. A few years before 1996, Virginia refused to move a game for television—it was parents weekend in Charlottesville and UV felt that changing the schedule would prevent Biff and Muffy from spending quality time with Mum and Dad.

Meetings were held and Florida State was among the most vocal in demanding that no ACC school be allowed to turn down television money that would be split by all. I agreed with that policy then, but the shoe, as it always does, later found its way onto our other foot. We had several night games in 1996, several more in the late afternoon, and only one at noon. But that one was against Florida, which meant we'd all line up for that one if it played at three o'clock in the morning.

We had full houses for North Carolina and Virginia, and a nearly full house for Clemson. And if you thought our fans were not loud and enthusiastic, then just consider these remarkable quotes from Miami players from their game: "I was kind of confused and it was so loud I ran the wrong way" (Hurricane Yatil Green explaining how Troy Saunders intercepted a pass meant for him). And this from Hurricane Danyell Ferguson, despairing in the locker room: "The entire offense was out of sync today. It was the crowd noise." It wasn't the Miami crowd making such noise that befuddled the poor Hurricanes on their home field—it was us!

Florida State vs. Florida

Again, Jerry Kutz gave a succinct picture of the differences. Suppose that you are mowing your lawn on Saturday morning in Tampa. Your pals show up and summon you, "C'mon, let's go watch the Gators play!" You think about it.

"Who are they playing?" you ask.

"Mississippi State."

You tell them that you promised your wife that you'd take her out to dinner Saturday night. They say no problem. Finish the lawn, get dressed, jump in the car, and drive two hours or so to Gainesville, watch the game, and get back to Tampa in plenty of time for a night on the town.

Now suppose you are a Seminole (a much more pleasant contemplation). You select your game, say Virginia. You load the family into the car and make the five-hour trek to Tallahassee on

Friday. You'll pay for two nights in a hotel, but you'll be back home in Tampa by Sunday afternoon, and the weekend cost you north of five hundred dollars.

The truth was that we enjoyed the loyalty of fans who did that much and more every weekend. We couldn't tolerate *any* suggestion that our Seminole fans were not among the nation's best.

Down and Distance: The Myth of the Mighty

We were told by critics how isolated Tallahassee was, and then we were told that Auburn and Clemson and Georgia were also out in the woods but they filled their stadiums every Saturday. But here was the truth: they may be in the woods, but the trees are close to the highway. Auburn and Clemson were each within 150 miles of more than nine million people; Georgia was within the same distance of more than seven million!

Consider this as well: sellout crowds in each of these places were rare on *any* Saturday. The *Osceola*'s research revealed that for 1993 through 1995, Auburn's eighty-five-thousand-seat stadium sold out just five times in twenty-one games, Georgia's eighty-six-thousand-seat stadium sold out just six times in eighteen games, and Clemson's eighty-one-thousand-seat stadium sold out just two times in nineteen games.

In the fall of 1996, Clemson was averaging only sixty-three thousand fans per game, and only sixty-two thousand showed up to see Auburn play Alabama in the fall. And do you remember when we were so in awe of LSU's storied Tiger Stadium? In 1979, when we first played there, it held eighty-thousand—which was the same as ours in 1996. In the fall, however, when LSU played Auburn in Baton Rouge, it was only the first sellout in 75 home games, all the way back to 1983.

Penn State was isolated in "Happy Valley" and they sold out, didn't they? Yes, but let's look again at the *Osceola*'s figures. The Penn State campus was within 150 miles of 7.5 million people!

Nebraska was a fair comparison. They were within 150 miles of only 2.3 million people. But the plain's wind whistles a long distance across the Midwest before it brushes up against a professional franchise of any substance. In Florida, you had to search the local paper for news of the Seminoles sandwiched among features on the Bucs, Dolphins, Heat, Tiger Sharks, Devil Rays, Jaguars, Magic, and so on.

Draw a 150-mile circle around Tallahassee. Much of it is water, but more of it is Georgia and Alabama. And while we had many loyal and enthusiastic fans from roundabout Thomasville, Cairo, Bainbridge, and Dothan, most football fans in those states turned their attention to their own state teams. Within 150 miles of Tallahassee, there were 2.5 million people, only a million of whom were Floridians. The University of Florida was within 150 miles of more than eight million people, almost all of whom were Floridians.

Kutz had uncovered the amazing fact that there were actually 2.6 million more people within 150 miles of Gainesville than there were within 150 miles of Miami. Even if we stretched another fifty miles to take in all of Jacksonville (and we should, for we enjoyed the fanatical support of a mighty contingent of Jacksonvillians), we would add only one million more to the equation.

We had been playing football for fifty years; they had been playing for ninety-five years. We had about a 3.5 million people within reasonable driving range; they had well over eight million. They had eighty-five-thousand seats and filled them; we had about eighty-thousand seats and came pretty close to filling them. Maybe they should have felt a little embarrassed that they weren't further ahead of us than they actually were.

Stadium Capacity

Nowhere amid all the criticism following the Duke game was it mentioned that Florida State ranked among the nation's top 10 in attendance in 1995, in spite of that dreadful five-home-games-in-a-row-at-noon run. And with the addition of a couple thousand more seats over the summer, we would remain among the top 10 in 1996.

A local sportswriter pointed out that plans existed, which allowed the expansion of Doak Campbell to ninety-thousand seats. His suggestion was to throw them away. His sentiment was on track—we didn't need to expand in the foreseeable future. But the stadium was constructed so that if we ever did need more seats, they could be accommodated within the existing architecture.

We knew when we built eighty-thousand seats that we were building for the future. When Bobby Bowden arrived, Florida State had awarded college degrees to a total of sixty-thousand graduates between 1857 and 1975. As of 1996, Florida State University can boast 180,000 graduates. Then consider the significance of the fact that 120,000 Seminoles have graduated from FSU during Bobby Bowden's reign as head football coach. We have seventy-five skyboxes with a price tag of $125,000 each and a large auditorium-style box with 220 seats, which costs about six thousand dollars a pair. All the boxes were sold and all the seats were sold. In fact, there was a waiting list.

Everything was not perfect, and the responsibilities we had taken on in order to achieve our dreams were pretty scary. But we knew that we could count on our fans. As Rod Serling would say: "Submitted for your approval ... the best fans in America."*

---

* Much of this chapter's material was initially published in the *Report to Boosters* (October 1996).

Officiating Becomes an Issue

In 1993 we had to go through Gainesville in order to get to the national championship game. If Florida could come through Tallahassee and win another shot at Nebraska, then they would have defeated maybe the finest defense Florida State had ever fielded. I didn't think they could. Regardless of the outcome of the game, this prototype "game of the century" was the reason great young athletes came to Florida State. It seemed as if we were in the No. 1 vs. No. 2 matchup about every other year, which was watched on television by millions of people around the world. That was powerful stuff.

The defeat of Maryland punctuated our fifth straight ACC championship, and confirmed our tenth consecutive year of 10 wins or more. No other school had ever done that before. The story of the 1990s really was our story. And I encouraged all Seminoles to enjoy it to the fullest possible measure.

The theme that seemed to be a weaving its way around the 1996 season was controversy over the officiating. Florida State fans had always resented what they perceived as unjust treatment by visiting officials. There is one story you won't find recorded in any of the elevated histories of Florida State football. It was the embarrassing epilogue of an unpleasant game from an unhappy time.

Auburn came to Doak Campbell at the end of a gray and chilly

October in 1975. Florida State had already suffered through 0–11 and 1–10 seasons in '73 and '74, and we were churning our way to a 3–8 mark in what would be Coach Darrell Mudra's last year. It was also the final run for Auburn's legendary Coach Ralph "Shug" Jordan, who had earlier announced his retirement. Auburn had already renamed Jordan-Hare Stadium to honor their beloved coach, and their entire season took on the air of a rolling tribute.

Our Seminoles had hit a rough patch. By the seventh game, we had beaten only Utah State. In only a few months, Bobby Bowden would inherit this team that lacked confidence and wins despite a surprisingly strong assemblage of talent. Maybe Auburn took us lightly; maybe our men caught a glimpse of their own abilities. Whatever the reason, the score was tied 7–7 at the half. In the third quarter, both teams scored again, and as time wore away at the end of the game, Auburn held a slim 17–14 lead.

The Seminoles were playing with a confidence that was new to them, but one remembered by our fans from the Peterson days. Our offense drove the field and moved into scoring range. An option sweep powered across the goal line for the touchdown. But an SEC official threw a flag. Holding. Ten yards. There was time only for one last play. Another pitch, another fast sweeping run, and another Seminole touchdown as the clock ran out. This time, it appeared that the SEC referee waited until FSU actually scored before he dropped the flag. Holding. Game over. Auburn won. So sorry.

I didn't know what actually triggered the flood. Maybe it was just the pent-up frustration of FSU fans whose program had fallen into darkness. Maybe it was just the damnable unfairness of having a great upset win stolen away by an adversary's officials.

I could see how wide their eyes got when the SEC officiating crew realized that an avalanche of Seminole fans—hundreds and hundreds of angry, cheated souls—had spilled out of the stands and were charging straight for them. The zebras fled for the northeast corner, for the safety of the field house. But a second mob had closed in from that side too, and the escape gate in the ten-foot-high chain-link fence had been shut.

While I didn't join in with the mob, I did allow a vengeful, approving smile as I watched the SEC officials scurrying like terrified ferrets. Since they couldn't get through the gate, they tried to climb over the fence. One of them fell, or was dragged back into the crowd, and broke his leg. The cops took control of the situation pretty quickly after that, but our side had extracted some small measure of unfortunate satisfaction.

As all of this played out, I yelled at the guy next to me. He was a pal, but an Auburn loyalist. "How can they do that!?" I demanded. "How can the official just drop a flag and throw a game? Is that what the SEC is all about?" At least, that's approximately what I said. That's the shorter, family-hour version of it anyway.

He started to say he didn't know, but instead he smiled and said: "Well, it *is* Shug's last season." I knew he was right. We were the have-nots, the nonconference nobodies who couldn't possibly be allowed to sully "Shug's" triumphal final lap around the course.

Somewhere, swimming around in the deep end of our fans' collective memory pool, was the knowledge of what it felt like to be looked at down the nose, to be dismissed as the sure win at someone else's homecoming. We knew what it was like to suffer the indifferent arrogance of conference referees who weren't about to let nature tip out of balance.

You can probably tell I'm still a little mad about that game, even after all of these years. Any fan who follows with the heart remembers all the slights as well as all the victories. It may have been that all that baggage was what was at the heart of our little tiff with the ACC officials in 1996. Maybe the program that suffered real abuse at the hands of officials when we were barely hanging onto the bottom rung of the ladder still nursed eye-narrowing suspicions even as we sat atop the highest step.

There was grumbling after the Duke game, but the issue really broke open after the Thursday night ESPN game at North Carolina State. To Seminole fans, there was clear evidence that Wolfpack offensive linemen had been given license to sit on Wilson and Boulware. If the officials missed it play after play, the camera's eye surely did not. Dave Hart filed a complaint with the conference office before the next game, and the result was an *increase* in holding calls—against the Seminoles.

And it only got worse. The early out-of-bounds catch by Miami was ruled a touchdown. Fan talk centered on dark rumors of conspiracies. Each game added to the rising chorus of complaints.

Then came Georgia Tech, and the dreadful first quarter. In that game the Seminoles drew over 100 yards in penalties, nearly 20 percent of our total offense for the night. Some blamed the bitter cold for our disheveled start, while others said it was the letdown after our big win over Virginia. But the folks sitting around me were adamant and unanimous. They read first quarter as a pointed message to Florida State from the ACC officials: "You think the officiating has been rough? Well, here's a little demonstration of what it *can* be like—so quit complaining."

Jerry Kutz was a levelheaded fellow who was good at dissecting problems. His post-Georgia Tech column ("Competence, Conspiracy or Coincidence?") tackled the issue with a clinical eye. He gave a good deal of space to the explanations offered by ACC coordinator of officials Bradley Faircloth. In his final analysis, Kutz concluded in part, "While the majority of FSU fans are not so cynical or paranoid as to believe there is a conspiracy, nor are they naïve as to believe it's a coincidence. Which leaves the question of competence ... ."

The competence question was raised to ACC commissioner Gene Corrigan when he visited for the Southern Miss game. Corrigan was a gracious gentleman with sterling credentials. Former athletic director at Virginia and Notre Dame, he was a driving force behind formation of the Football Bowl Coalition. Most importantly for us, Corrigan was the one who sold the ACC on accepting Florida State, and who also sold FSU on joining the ACC.

Corrigan was a popular favorite with the Seminole Booster board of directors, and he visited with them the morning of the game. After a round of pleasantries, director Brian Cunningham asked a question. "I'm not a conspiracy theorist," he said, "but it's obvious that something is going on. If there is no conspiracy, is it possible that the level of football play in the conference has risen so fast that it has overtaken the abilities of the current officials?"

Corrigan stood fast behind his guys, as one expects any good leader to do. He said he thought the officiating was fine overall. "This is an aberration—you guys have had a lot of bad breaks this year." He recalled the year Virginia had a great defensive end (Chris Slade) and they beefed constantly that holding was not being called. "Every year it seems someone feels they're getting the bad calls; every year it's someone different."

Cunningham smiled and asked, "Can we have your assurance then that next year it will be someone else and not us?" There was laughter all around, and it was obvious that the discussion had gone as far as it was going to go. Much had been made of the fact that FSU was the most penalized team in the league. But Florida was the most penalized team in the SEC, and my guess was that any team that dominated with fast, reckless, and aggressive play would draw penalties.

In December of 1996, Miami coach Butch Davis filed complaints with the Big East office about calls in the Temple and West Virginia games. "When you bring something to the attention of the officials and it's repeatedly not corrected during the game, then I have a problem with it." He was especially unhappy with unsportsmanlike conduct penalties against his Canes.

In the same month, SEC commissioner Roy Cramer repri-
manded Auburn coach Terry Bowden for comments he made
about the officiating in their 28–7 win over Arkansas. And West
Virginia defensive coordinator Steve Dunlap went public with
his complaints that Big East officials routinely let Virginia Tech's
offensive line get away with holding. "I've coached twenty-one
years and I've never seen anything like it," Dunlap charged on a
statewide radio show. "It's been a consensus throughout the Big
East, with the Big East coaches."

But probably the most openly critical comments about officiating were made by Florida's Steve Spurrier following their games
against Vanderbilt and South Carolina. "The last two games have
been very irritating to me," Spurrier told the SEC's Kramer. "The
opponents are saying we're whining and crying [but] I'm defending our players."

Spurrier's complaint wasn't so much the large number of
penalties called against the Gators, but rather the failure to call
corresponding calls on his opponents. And he may have had a
point. At Vanderbilt, for example, Vandy tackle Allen DeGraffen-
reid spiked the football at midfield after picking up a fumble to
keep their drive alive. Spiking the ball is usually a 15-yard penalty. "Do you think a Gator player could've done that and not
gotten penalized?" asked Spurrier.

Florida's players were sounding off too. Guard Donnie Young
complained about the same game: "One time I went to the official
and asked him if I was on the line. He said yeah. Then we run the
play and we get a flag because I'm off the line. What is that?"

In the following game against South Carolina, the Gators
were penalized fourteen times for 144 yards. Spurrier told the
press, "I apologize to my players. I made a bad statement after
the game that I thought that was a good [officiating] crew. I was
dead wrong."

Some of the FSU faithful felt that we would get a better deal from the accompanying SEC officials than we would from an ACC crew. I think this was a dangerous and wrong assessment. We had never lost a game because of a bad call by an ACC official; the same surely could not be said for the SEC.

Legions of Seminole fans believed that an SEC referee named Doug Moseley threw the 1966 game against Florida by calling an FSU touchdown catch out of bounds. Photos of the infamous Lane Fenner catch appeared in newspapers nationwide, and still adorn T-shirts today.

Tight end Lane Fenner had gotten to the end zone ahead of two Gator defenders, and was in position for the game-winning score. All three men went up for the ball, and Fenner came down with it, clearly in bounds. Mosely, trailing behind the play at first signaled touchdown. Then he reconsidered and waved the pass incomplete. On that Sunday after the game, Bill McGrotha wrote, "Game photos indicated the official's decision was wrong, but his call was a judgment one and is final."

And later, listen to what Bobby Bowden told the *Tallahassee Democrat* reflecting on the bitter 13–17 loss to Florida in 1986: "FSU was cheated by a SEC referee who negated a 52-yard Sammie Smith touchdown. The official didn't call the penalty until he saw Smith was going to score. That was totally uncalled for, and is why that official hasn't worked one of our games since, and never will."

And don't think there was not a subtle message in Spurrier's remarks to the SEC crew: "The ACC boys didn't do us any good last year, we all know that. We had some very bad calls in that game. I don't know what to do about it." Maybe the SEC boys could make it up to him by laying a few of the same on Florida State.

I suspected that all of them—the Big East, the SEC, and the ACC—just about had a belly full of all of us in the state of Florida. Maybe that was the price Florida State, Miami, and Florida had to pay for the privilege of inhabiting the center of the college football universe. In the ACC, much was made of the fact that it was a collegial league, with a minimum of rules and an expectation of honorable and ethical dealings. I was willing to cast my lot with that philosophy. Maybe Corrigan was right. Maybe in 1997 we would find out that it was someone else's problem. We would see.[*]

---

[*] Much of this chapter's material was initially published in the *Report to Boosters* (December 1996).

Did Steve Make a Deal with the Devil?

"Late hits" was Steve Spurrier's mantra following his team's loss in Tallahassee. The Gators came in ranked No. 1 and lost to the No. 2-ranked Seminoles, 24–21. FSU was headed to the Sugar Bowl for a chance to win another national championship. Only the most bizarre bounces of the football in other late-season games, plus some political intrigue, set the Gators up for a rematch. This is written tongue-in-cheek and is intended only for amusement, but of course not everyone is amused.

Again, let me stress that this is just for fun. Just for fun (and Lord knew we could use some fun after doing hard time in the Big Easy), allow me to suggest an alternative explanation for events unfolding as they did in the Sugar Bowl: Spurrier sold his soul to the Devil.

A Faustian solution would not have occurred to me except that my brother Ed gave me a CD of singer/composer Randy Newman's musical theater treatment of *Faust* for Christmas. It was a remarkable work, retelling in song Goethe's classic dark Germanic tale of a man who traded his soul to Lucifer for worldly delights. The cast, which was as impressive as the music, included James Taylor, Don Henley, Linda Ronstadt, and Bonnie Raitt. And Newman cast himself as the Devil.

Goethe's Faust, an eighteenth-century German doctor, had become in Newman's version a schizophrenic student at 1990s Notre Dame. "Faust has never been in love except for with himself," says the text, and that's probably when I began to think of Spurrier. Please forgive what may appear ungracious on the part of this Seminole, but Spurrier spent all December of 1996 attacking Bobby Bowden as a dirty coach and a bad guy. It never really caught on in the press, and even some Gator fans were embarrassed.

On December 27, 1996, the *Orlando Sentinel* announced the results of a readers' poll that crowned Spurrier "Pinhead of the Year." Closer to the game, on December 30, *USA Today* weighed in with their analysis of Spurrier's "Late Hits" tape. "Game Tape Counters Spurrier's Charges," blared the headline, and the story stated flatly that the tape did not bear out the Florida coach's accusations. The *Ft. Lauderdale Sun-Sentinel* columnist David Hyde wrote two damning indictments of Spurrier's tactics. Under the headline "Spurrier, I've Seen the Enemy and It's You," he wrote, "But the officials (in the FSU game in Tallahassee) were Southeastern Conference officials. You know, Spurrier's guys. They know him. Then again, maybe that was the problem." And this was Hyde's comment on the evil genius' coaching ability: "But with his accomplishments come his personality, and this is the unsavory part. Bowden became much bigger in his big-game losses because of how he handled them. Spurrier became smaller."

Let me make two things very clear. First, I never heard any Gator—not even one—ever chip his teeth over Charlie Ward. The closest thing I ever heard to a negative comment from the orange and blue was along the lines of, "Well, if it wasn't for Charlie you wouldn't have beaten us in the Swamp in 1993 or won a national title." And I can't really argue with that. Likewise, I had never heard even one Seminole impugn the character or ability of Danny Wuerffel. Fans recognized both as the best representatives of all that was good about college athletics.

The second thing I want to make clear is that the Gators won the 1996 national title on the square. Their team played magnificently in the Sugar Bowl and proved themselves to be the best in the country and possibly the greatest Gator team of all time. But this was not about the players or the fans, all of whom I thought were surprisingly well-behaved in the 1996 season, all things considered. This was about Spurrier.

Since his arrival at Florida, and probably before that, Spurrier had been widely described as the "evil genius." And I thought it rankled him and his flock to have the image of "St. Bobby" constantly before them. The championship celebration at Florida Field on January 11 was filled with paeans to God for his intervention in setting up a series of events that led to Florida replaying FSU for the title. I will admit that a curious and highly unlikely set of circumstances unfolded toward the end. The events were so unlikely, in fact, that I could believe otherworldly forces had a hand in making them happen. But the question was this: Did those otherworldly forces come from above, or from below?

Consider what had to happen to put the Gators in the Sugar Bowl. First, North Carolina had to be upset by Virginia, and Tennessee upset by Memphis State (Memphis State!) to keep Florida from dropping too far after they lost to us. Then, a flu-wracked Nebraska team had to be upset by unranked Texas, and Ohio State had to corral Jake "The Snake" Plummer's Arizona State team (interesting name, Sun Devils) in the last-second thriller.

Finally, the 1996 season Alliance Bowl Championship had to be held in the Sugar Bowl. Florida would not have been granted the rematch by either the Orange Bowl or the Fiesta Bowl, but the Sugar was solid with old SEC ties. If you doubted that Florida was given every advantage, including thousands of additional tickets, check out the cover of the official Sugar Bowl game program. There are illustrations of five football players, all in orange and blue. Florida State played an emotional game in Tallahassee, upsetting the favored Gators on a blustery day. Any team in that situation is always at a great disadvantage in a rematch.

Did Spurrier make a deal with the Devil after losing to FSU in November of 1996? I don't know, but if I were the coach and I'd just lost maybe my best chance ever at a national title and faced the prospect of losing Wuerffel and two All-American receivers, I think maybe that would be enough to make me draw a pentagram on the floor and begin chanting, "I summon Thee," over and over again.

There was one curious, striking passage in the Newman musical. Faust's lover, Margaret, delivered her signature song beginning with these lines: "I was born in Gainesville, Florida / and my mother ran a cafe near the university." Sounds suspicious to me. But again, this was all just for fun.[*]

---

[*] Much of this chapter's material was initially published in the *Florida State Times* (February 1997).

The Psychology of Champions

If all you knew about 1996 was the statistic that it began and ended with the Seminoles ranked No. 3 in the nation, then you would be unaware of all the great drama, the wrenching twists and turns, and the political intrigue of this unique season. The Seminoles swept through the season undefeated, including an epic upset of No. 1-ranked Florida in Doak Campbell Stadium. FSU entered the Sugar Bowl ranked No. 1, but events on a series of playing fields and alleged political mischief handed the Florida Gators a rematch. Voters discounted the 32-point bowl loss, and kept the Seminoles in the nation's top 3 in the final poll.

Losing to our bitter rival by 32 points with the national championship as the prize was bad. I mean, really bad. To the Gators, it more than made up for the 31–31 tie and subsequent loss to us in the Sugar Bowl after the 1994 season. After Spurrier's day in the sun, we Seminoles had to pick ourselves up again, along with our team. The stress inherent in a losing program is probably not as great as the constant stress of great expectations when one is favored to win every game and sweep every championship.

Consider the peculiar psychological demands on athletes who compete in the high jump. I thought about the high jump when I received Jay Culley's fax on January 3, the day after the Sugar Bowl. Competition in the high jump (or the pole vault) is structured so that play continues until the champion fails. Each attempt is either successful or unsuccessful. Three unsuccessful attempts in a row and you're out. Succeed, and they raise the bar for the next round.

"Each clearance is a forgiveness clause," explained Dick Roberts, former Seminole track star and track coach. "Succeed, and you advance; but every time you advance, they raise the height you have to clear next time." Any champion in this sport has to deal with *knowing* that he or she will ultimately fail.

Let's say that a jumper in our meet sets a new school record after outlasting the competition. The bar is raised, and our jumper clears it for a new conference record. Even though we have a champion, and two new records, they raise the bar once again. Our jumper has to fail three consecutive times before it's over. It's not an easy psychological trick to balance impulses of elation at winning, setting new marks, and despondency at failing in your last three attempts in a row.

Jay Culley must be an old track-and-field ace because he was so clearly able to peer through the failure in the Sugar Bowl and focus on the real legacy. "Be proud," he wrote. "Be proud of the fact that you can be sad when you go 11–0 during the season and finish No. 3 in the nation."

Our bowl record was unmatched in the NCAA, and may never be equaled. Jimmy Carter was preparing to move out of the White House when FSU had last lost a bowl game, to Oklahoma in the 1981 Orange Bowl. For fourteen years in a row, the automatic bowl win was our "forgiveness clause" that Roberts described. During a six-year stretch at the front of the 1980s, when it seemed we couldn't beat Auburn or Miami or Florida in the regular season, we always won our bowl game to give us an uptick going into the following season.

And later, during the dynasty years, the bowl win was our bridge of optimism, keeping the top 4 national ranking alive and unbroken. Lose a tough one to Miami in '87? No problem. Just beat Nebraska in the Fiesta and finish No. 2. Drop your first two games in '89? Finish strong, crunch the Huskers again, and you're No. 3. Drop a decision to Miami and Florida at the end of 1991? Again, not a problem. You can just bounce back against Texas A&M in the Cotton Bowl and finish No. 4.

In fact, the bowl win was so certain that we began to take it for granted. We lost sight of the fact that someday we would surely lose. The high jumper knew, of course, that even in victory the last attempt will always be a failure, even when he or she wins the meet.

Culley's was the jumper's perspective, focusing on the fact that in 1996 Florida State's Seminoles joined an elite circle of college football programs that had been officially tracked and rated by the NCAA as having achieved a dynasty. There are only eight such programs: Notre Dame, Oklahoma, Alabama, Nebraska, Minnesota, Southern Cal, Miami, and Florida State.

The Seminoles were still the winningest college football team of the 1990s, and my guess was that when the preseason rankings were released later in the summer of 1997, it would be FSU and not the other school that would begin at the top of the pyramid. It did not go unnoticed that even in the wake of a 52–20 loss, Bobby Bowden brought in the nation's No. 1-rated class of recruits, including the national defensive and offensive players of the year.

Our Seminole Booster organization was in the middle of our 1997 annual fundraising campaign. We had forty-five to sixty-five loyal volunteers making telephone contact with Boosters every night during February 1997, asking Seminoles to increase their contribution for 1997. Early returns were encouraging. Seminoles, it appeared to me, were stiffening their backs and digging down deeper to help us build an even stronger and more secure athletic program.

The other schools against whom we competed were in a position to spend vast amounts of money, and money makes a difference. Our magnificent University Center was a pointed example of what was possible when one produced record contributions from generous fans and alumni, and spent the money wisely. We had been able to make up a vast distance of ground to close the gap between our young program and our older and richer competitors.

What exactly did we do with the contributions? The Seminole Boosters met the mortgage payments on the athletic portion of University Center, which was about $3.5 million a year. We also raised millions for our scholarship endowment, so that all the scholarships in all the men's and women's sports would be guaranteed.

The Boosters were also involved in finishing out the grounds and parking fields around the stadium. That included moving the softball field to a new location and constructing a new soccer complex. It meant moving Pensacola Street out of the way. It meant preparing more land near the stadium to accommodate parking, and making those areas grassy and lush.

The Boosters also provided a supplement to the athletic department to make up the difference between their projected budget and real expenses. When, for instance, the department wanted money to send the Marching Chiefs to more games, or to guarantee a valued coach's contract, or to renovate an aging or outgrown facility, then they look to the Boosters. We did not deliver dollars directly into the hands of any coach or student athlete; the athletic director made all of those decisions. The Boosters did not determine season-ticket point priority policy either; the university had an athletic board of alumni, administrators, and faculty types for that. What we did was explain to our fellow Seminoles why we needed their money. Then we spent it on the priorities that would most effectively advance the entire athletic program.

It seemed like the more we built, the more our opponents built.

It seemed that the more records we broke, the more our opponents became obsessed with beating us. It seemed that no matter what we did, the bar was always set a notch higher for the next time. But again, they only do that for the champions.[*]

---

[*] Much of this chapter's material was initially published in the *Report to Boosters* (February 1997).

DIRTY TRICKS?

"Someone" Didn't Want You To Receive Your 1997 Booster Renewal Package!

It was a GREAT mailing piece, celebrating the November 30th victory that marked five consecutive undefeated seasons in Doak Campbell Stadium.

But "SOMEONE" apparently was offended by the picture of FSU's magnificent University Center . . . or by the photo of jubilant students carrying away the goal posts.

IN ANY CASE, SOME OF THE MAIL THAT WENT TO OUR LOYAL SEMINOLE BOOSTERS DISAPPEARED! The Feds are on the case; Postal Inspectors are investigating.

"SOMEONE" may be employing DIRTY TRICKS to sabotage our Florida State University program. BUT OUR BOOSTERS WILL NOT BE BULLIED OR THREATENED OR DENIED!

If you did not receive your 1997 Seminole Booster Membership Package, please take a moment to fill out your pledge card NOW, and return it in the enclosed envelope.
We apologize for asking you to do all this, but we want to get back to our loyal Booster members as quickly as possible.

If you have any questions, please call the Booster office:
904/644-3484

THANK YOU FOR YOUR PATIENCE AND UNDERSTANDING.

Maybe "SOMEONE" just didn't like the idea that Bobby Bowden got the #1 rated recruiting class in the nation . . . AGAIN!

Post Office Box 1353   Tallahassee, FL 32302   904/644-3484   Fax: 904/222-5929

Immediately following the No. 2-ranked Seminoles' victory over No. 1-ranked Florida in Tallahassee on November 30, 1996, the Seminole Boosters mailed out their 1997 Booster membership renewal piece featuring a large photo of FSU students carrying away the goal posts in triumph. Federal postal investigators estimated that as much as half of the mail—ten thousand pieces—simply disappeared as it made its way through postal processing stations down the middle of the state. The Boosters sent a second mailing piece letting Boosters members know about possible "dirty tricks" to suppress Booster fundraising efforts.

1997 Season

If you want to be a good leader, then you are well advised to surround yourself with good people. I always wanted good moral men on my coaching staff, people of character who were hardworking, honest, and dependable. I can coach a guy to be a better coach, if I need to, but I can't coach integrity. Integrity only comes from within a person and is rooted in his value system. I was fortunate to spend so many years with men of high-caliber character.

It also helps to have players who are dependable, coachable, and consistent, which are also traits of good character. That's how I would describe Thad Busby, our quarterback during the 1997 season. He was one of the most underrated quarterbacks we'd had in a while at FSU. We discovered him several years earlier in a football camp run for high school quarterbacks and receivers. What a gem he proved to be. He led us to two 11–1 seasons in a row. In 1997, we ended up yet again in the Sugar Bowl. Thad closed his career there with a victory over Ohio State.

—Bobby Bowden

1997 Season

Began the season ranked No. 5
Ended the season ranked No. 3
Record 11–1
ACC Champions
Sugar Bowl Champions

September 6, defeated Southern California in Los Angeles 14–7

September 13, defeated Maryland in Tallahassee 50–7

September 20, defeated Clemson in Clemson 35–28

October 4, defeated Miami in Tallahassee 47–0

October 11, defeated Duke in Durham 51–27

October 18, defeated Georgia Tech in Tallahassee 38–0

October 25, defeated Virginia in Charlottesville 47–21

November 1, defeated NC State in Tallahassee 48–35

November 8, defeated North Carolina in Chapel Hill 20–3

November 15, defeated Wake Forest in Tallahassee 58–7

November 22, lost to Florida in Gainesville 29–32

January 1, 1998, defeated Ohio State in the Sugar Bowl 31–14

FSU vs. Ohio State in
the Sugar Bowl

In 1997, the Seminoles cruised undefeated to yet another ACC championship and a shutout victory over the Miami Hurricanes. In Gainesville, the Seminoles put their No. 2 national ranking on the line but lost on the game's final series to No. 10 Florida. The Seminoles drew the Ohio State Buckeyes as an opponent in the Sugar Bowl. A thumping 31–14 victory over OSU finished the season 11–1 with a No. 3 national ranking.

North and South Have Always Met in New Orleans

Here we were. We were the Southern Seminoles and Yankee Buckeyes, all camped comfortably in New Orleans, a timeworn and exuberant city where currents of many nations mingled in a rich bouillabaisse for more than 250 years. North and South met again in the Sugar Bowl in a spirit of good grace and sportsmanship. New Orleans' eclectic and hospitable style seemed to encourage that inclination.

In James Longstreet, those currents of reconciliation and history converged like the tendril streams joining the Mississippi River. Confederate General Longstreet, considered the best tactician on either side, settled in New Orleans after the war. He was loyal to the South but joined the Republican Party and supported his old friend and West Point classmate Ulysses S. Grant for president in 1868. He represented to some the personification of the recovery of one nation.

Longstreet, I'm told, loved to stroll down to the Café Du Monde off Jackson Square and partake of the bitter coffee and sugared beignets, just as many of our Seminole fans did on New Year's Day, 1998. He served for a while as a US postmaster, and so was able to read and enjoy a wide range of newspapers from across the country. His biographer noted that he began to take an interest in the increasingly popular sport of college football.

Several events of note took place in 1904. First, Longstreet died at the age of eighty-three, last of the Confederate generals. Also the 1904 Florida State College football team shut out the Lake City–based University of Florida 23–0. It was the last college football game Florida State would play for forty-three years.

Ohio State's football program was already a success by 1904. The Buckeyes were deep into their rivalry with Michigan. But something else happened that season too: Ohio State lost consecutive games to nonconference foes. It would be seventy-nine years before the Buckeyes would again fail to win two straight nonconference games. This time, however, both of those losses would be to the Seminoles of Florida State.

Florida State's wins against Ohio State in Columbus in 1981 and 1982 occurred toward the front end of an eleven-year window through which the Seminoles burst on to the national stage. Between 1980 and 1991, FSU made a pretty good living beating high-profile names on the road. Had we remained a "Southern" team, a conference team with a regional schedule, it was likely we would have stabilized as merely one of many good teams whose names were mentioned from time to time, and who occasionally appeared on television.

But Florida State, nearly always the underdog, took on the giants on their home ground. And more often than not, the giants not only fell, but they fell in front of a nationwide television audience. Look at their names again: Ohio State, Notre Dame, Michigan, Pitt, Syracuse, LSU, Auburn, Michigan State, Nebraska, and, of course, Miami and Florida every year.

The Sugar Bowl of the 1997 season, a friendly combat between North and South, would be played ninety-four years to the day after the death of General James Longstreet. And perhaps after the game we would lift a glass or two with the Buckeyes and make a toast: "Here's to the big games, the hard games; here's to the games that either break our hearts or crown us with glory." The teams that don't understand what that means never got to go and savor New Orleans.*

Another OSU Game, and Another Great Battle

Florida State's series of football exchanges with the Big Ten had been fairly one-sided. Since our first meeting with Penn State in 1967, the Tribe stood 7-1-1 against the Big Ten, and neither of our games against Penn State (one of which was the tie) was played after they joined that league.

Their conference was an imposing collection of institutions known for impressive libraries, rousing fight songs, and massive, traditionalist student bodies. These lumbering Midwestern behemoths are the embodiment of let's-not-rush-into-anything conservatism. Even after Penn State joined the league, the name remained unchanged. Thus to Minnesota fell the distinction of being the first team to finish No. 11 in the Big Ten.

It is safe to say that there was a difference—perhaps even a conflict—between the fundamental cultures of the corn-blanketed Midwest and our own state of Florida with its exotic vices, cosmopolitan distractions, and our cavalier approach to authority. "The rules," as our tourism advertisements say, "are different here."

---

* Much of this section's material was initially published in the *FSU Overtime Times* (December 31, 1997) at the Sugar Bowl.

The first time this was made clear to me was in the 1986 All-American Bowl vs. Indiana. The game was played between two 6–5 teams, in Birmingham, at night, in freezing weather with the precipitation alternating indifferently between snow and sleet. The good people of Birmingham are football fans, but they aren't suicidal, and so the only people crunching and shivering their way into eighty-one-thousand-seat Legion Field were four and five thousand Seminoles and an equal number of Hoosiers.

Bowls being the way they were, the participating schools were given the worst seats. Our section was in the corner of one end zone; Indiana's was at the opposite end. FSU fans immediately assessed the fact that no living soul with a ticket between the 10-yard lines was going to show up, and so they made themselves comfortable wherever they chose. While one side of the stadium was dotted with huddled bundles of garnet-and-gold spread out between the 30s, the corner of the end zone was packed tight with crimson and cream. Not a single one of the Hoosier faithful was out of position, and not another human being was sitting on that side of stadium between the goal line and the 50.

"No, now you stop talking about moving," you could imagine them saying. "These are our assigned seats. Someone else has tickets for those seats at midfield, and they might decide to come to the game, maybe after halftime. Let's not risk embarrassing ourselves by presuming to take something that doesn't belong to us."

Victories over Big Ten powers Michigan and Michigan State came in the previous decade, but the wins in Columbus, Ohio, in 1981 and 1982 were emotional, even inspiring, to a generation of Seminole fans witnessing an early glimpse of what would become one of college football's great dynasties.

One such fan was Ft. Myers' Gary Wilkins, who confided this account after the 36–27 win in 1981: "After the game, a buddy and I just stayed in the stands until all eighty-three-thousand fans cleared out. Then, when we were the only two people left in the stadium, we went down to the field and sat on the players' bench. As darkness descended, one lone groundskeeper came over and had a drink with us. He sat there and recounted all the rich traditions of that historic stadium. I was so overwhelmed by what the Seminoles had done in one of the great football environments in the country I just never wanted it to end."

You got your wish, Gary. Sixteen years later, in 1997, it showed no signs of ending anytime soon.[*]

---

[*] Much of this section's material was initially published in the *FSU Overtime Times* (January 1, 1998) at the Sugar Bowl.

Can Florida State Maintain
Success Indefinitely?

Eleven full seasons of the dynasty had passed by the end of 1997. Each year the team finished ranked among the nation's top 4, and each season we saw at least ten or more victories. There was one national championship and routine appearances in major bowl games. Since FSU began ACC conference play in 1992, they achieved an incredible mark of forty-seven victories vs. just one loss. Including the title they shared with Virginia in 1995, the Seminoles won the conference championship every year since joining. It was an astonishing record of consecutive successes. But how long could it last?

Do you remember the story of Hannibal crossing the Alps, elephants and all? Hannibal's army slaughtered as many as seventy thousand Roman soldiers at the battle of Cannae. After fleeing back to Rome and throwing up defenses, the survivors pretty much turned the countryside over to Hannibal for the next fifteen years. Rome's empire was still massive and powerful, but they feared another crushing military loss to the brilliant Hannibal, so they simply waited him out. Eventually, he overplayed his hand by failing to maintain his strength in the field and neglecting his political interests back home in Carthage.

This is important to the extent that the lessons of history give us advice and caution about our own lives. I have watched upstarts like Florida State interact with the giants of college football long enough to see the parallels with Hannibal, and to understand the dangers.

The Sugar Bowl itself was wonderful, as much fun as the first two wins over the Ohio State Buckeyes in 1981 and 1982. This time, of course, we enjoyed the added drama—and motivational boost to our team—of Buckeye coach John Cooper's announcement to an Ohio State pep rally in New Orleans to wit: "I'll tell you what's going to happen in the game. ... We're going to crush them!" When I first read that in the *New Orleans Times-Picayune*, I thought, Mighty big talk from a bunch of slow, fat guys with two losses. Even that assessment turned out to be charitable, as we watched Wadsworth and company flying around and past the Buckeye offensive linemen like bumblebees buzzing around the heads of drowsy toads.

How enjoyable it was to attend a bowl game in the company of classy fans. The Buckeyes were gracious, friendly, and possessed of all the virtues expected of Big Ten supporters. After the game, Mike Bristol and I walked out with a youngish couple all dressed head to toe in crimson and gray. They had that flat Midwestern "you betcha" twang, and commented that their OSU boys "need to work on their speed just a bit." Mike and I told them how impressed we were with their band, which really was the best college band we had seen or heard, other than the Marching Chiefs of course.

The band comment drew from them the closest thing to a criticism we heard. "You know," he said, "you really ought to consider coming up with something for your band to play other than that Indian thing ... it gets really annoying." She chimed in: "Oh, yeah, *please* tell them not to keep playing that same thing over and over."

The youngish couple was happy to be in New Orleans, lucky

to have tickets to the game. In 1980—the year our freshmen were born—Ohio State *turned down* twelve thousand alumni requests for season tickets. Unless one was a student, faculty member, big donor, or member of the alumni association with fifteen years of consecutive ticket purchases, there was no use in even applying.

You are impressed, I hope, with Florida State's hundred-million-dollar expansion, renovation, and reconfiguration of Doak Campbell Stadium. We spent that money and went into debt to enable us to have a facility that compared with the finest in the country, facilities that compared to historic stadiums like Ohio State's.

In December of 1998, Ohio State would launch a $150-million expansion, renovation, and reconfiguration of their stadium. They projected the work to be completed by 2001, which included a net increase of seven thousand seats, more restrooms, and concession stands, six new elevators, eighty-two private skyboxes, 2,500 new club-level seats, and improved accommodations for four academic units.

More than a hundred years ago, Ohio State was playing football against Michigan, the University of Kentucky, Cincinnati, West Virginia, and more. It is an old school with wealth and staying power. Our victories against them, as glorious as they were to us, were little noticed by them over the broad skein of time.

The ancient empire of Rome simply waited until Hannibal grew weak, and then the Roman legions crushed him. Another Roman legion sailed across the Mediterranean to Carthage where they conquered Hannibal's city, killed all the inhabitants therein, tore down all the buildings, and sowed the ground with salt so that nothing would ever grow there again.

Paybacks are rough.

If I looked hard enough, I might have seen Hannibal's face on the Seminoles. We were flushed with the joy of victories that would come soon and often, but not over a very long period of time. If we wished to have staying power against our ancient rivals, we needed not fail where Hannibal did. We needed to attend to our long-term needs, shore up and secure our base, and we needed to have the patience that taught us how the game was truly won or lost.[*]

---

[*] Much of this chapter's material was initially published in the *Report to Boosters* (February 1998).

1998 Season

You cannot build character, in my opinion, without a willingness to face difficulties head-on. Any life worth dying for must be forged on the anvil of adversity. I might wish it could be otherwise, but it cannot. We must learn to be resilient in the face of difficulty.

The 1998 season puts me in mind of this truth. We opened as the preseason No. 2 team in the country. Chris Weinke was our starting quarterback. I felt he could lead us to a national championship. In his second game as a starter, however, he threw five interceptions and we lost by 17 points to North Carolina State, a team we were favored to beat. Four weeks later, against Virginia, he sustained a neck injury and was sidelined for the rest of the season. His backup came in and led us to a dramatic victory over Florida in the final game of the season.

We completed the season with only one loss and were headed to yet another national championship game. Still, Weinke's absence was felt. We may have won the national championship if he had been able to play. He meant that much to our team. As it turned out, however, we gave up two big plays on defense and ended up losing by a touchdown.

What I witnessed was a team that faced adversity throughout the season and yet fought their way into the national championship game and a final No. 3 national ranking. Their resilience left me feeling confident heading into the '99 season.

—Bobby Bowden

1998 Season

Began the season ranked No. 2
Ended the season ranked No. 3
Record 11–2
ACC Champions
Played for the National Championship

August 31, defeated Texas A&M in the Kickoff Classic 23–14

September 12, lost to NC State in Raleigh 7–24

September 19, defeated Duke in Tallahassee 62–13

September 26, defeated Southern California in Tallahassee 30–10

October 3, defeated Maryland in College Park 24–10

October 10, defeated Miami in Miami 26–14

October 17, defeated Clemson in Tallahassee 48–0

October 24, defeated Georgia Tech in Atlanta 34–7

October 31, defeated North Carolina in Tallahassee 39–13

November 7, defeated Virginia in Tallahassee 45–14

November 14, defeated Wake Forest in Durham 24–7

November 21, defeated Florida in Tallahassee 23–12

January 4, 1999, lost to Tennessee in the Fiesta Bowl 16–23

Dan Kendra and the Emergence
of Chris Weinke

Quarterback Dan Kendra was a popular, if eccentric, figure among the Seminole faithful. The 1998 season held high promise in Seminole hearts, but Kendra went down in spring practice with a wounded knee. Though he was inexperienced, former professional baseball player Chris Weinke was promoted to starting quarterback and the backup was a walk-on known as "Rooster."

Whenever I heard stories about yet another Dan Kendra adventure, I thought to myself, *Somewhere, Kelly Lowrey must be smiling.* Lowrey was the Dan Kendra of his era, a muscular 240-pound bull-necked quarterback out of Lake City who could have started at linebacker—and I think he actually *did* try defensive end—before finally being tapped to command the Seminole offense in 1982.

The public's perception of Kendra as a football phenomenon was based on quirky images of relentless weight training, exotic pets, religiously structured diets, and a random dalliance with explosives. Kelly Lowrey's eccentricities tended toward those of the Joe Namath variety. In those days, we found ourselves in New Orleans every year to play either LSU or Tulane, and it seemed as if no two entities were ever more deliriously happy to see each other than Bourbon Street and Kelly Lowery.

Lowrey's natural ease as a leader and his versatility and love of raw hitting power made him arguably the most dangerous college quarterback of the time. And, like Kendra, his was an independent spirit. Coach Bowden was only half kidding when he complained, "I ain't used to sending in the play and then having the quarterback wave me off!"

Lowrey's signature game came against Ohio State, in Columbus in 1982. He scored three touchdowns, one passing, one running, and a third where he caught a halfback pass and crushed overmatched Buckeye defenders at the goal line. An AP photo showing Lowrey looking up at the official for the TD signal went nationwide. *Sports Illustrated* had nice things to say and named him Player of the Week.

Unfortunately for those Seminoles, FSU's proud defense was enduring a long, extremely painful rebuilding process. The glorious defense that had led the nation in 1980 was not rated among the top-100 Division I defensive teams by 1983. In the summer of '83, *Street & Smith's* wrote, "The bad news for the Seminoles is their defense probably can't stop anyone; the good news is their offense is so good it may not matter."

Street & Smith's called it about right. Seminole victories in 1982 took on the appearance of road races: FSU 47, East Carolina 46; FSU 40, LSU 35; FSU 29, Arizona State 26; FSU 45, South Carolina 30. But even with a hobbled defense, the 1983 team went 9–3, including a shootout vs. LSU in the tenth game with the winner assured of an Orange Bowl bid. And the 1983 edition went 8–4, including a thumping bowl victory over North Carolina on a frozen day in Atlanta.

Don't think Dan Kendra didn't dream the same dreams Kelly Lowrey did. And don't think he didn't see himself passing and running for glory, puny defenders bouncing off him like lances off a tank. That's why Kendra's unexpected decision to sit out during the 1998 season was so courageous. There was probably no more compelling ambition in that young life than to command the Seminole offense. Finally, after all the study, the training, the endless grueling practices, and the standing by with clipboard in hand, and the repetitious hours and hours of weight room isolation—finally, after all that, this would be Dan Kendra's team to lead.

There was an exceptional toughness of mind and body about Kendra. He believed his passion would inspire his teammates and that his strength would give them confidence. And he believed that when the big game was on the line, and the ball was just a yard from the goal, there would be no coaches' consultation about whether or not a Kendra-led offense should go for the touchdown. Like Kelly Lowrey, Kendra would welcome the crash of helmets.

The news came suddenly. Coach Bowden was surprised, as was Mark Richt. I had spoken to head trainer Randy Oravetz in June and gotten an encouraging report. So positive, in fact, that we published a letter to our nonrenewed Boosters to the effect that "you can count on Kendra in 1998, can he count on you?"

The rehabilitation was going splendidly. He was jogging six miles per hour, and the scars had not only healed, but they had almost disappeared. Only Dan Kendra knew that he couldn't rely on that knee. He knew that in order to have the thing he wanted the most, to achieve the position toward which he had worked so hard for so long, he would have to betray his teammates by pretending to have the full strength that he knew he did not possess.

Dan Kendra had already proven his ability to lead; he did it by making an unselfish and courageous decision that only he could make. I hoped we could keep him, and I hoped he came back full bore. If he did, then we'd have a proven leader and winner we knew we could count on.

The media greeted the surprising news with sympathy for a great player, but no prediction of doom for the Seminoles. The preseason magazines that had predicted FSU variously between No. 1 and No. 4 to start the season were nearly all written with the assumption that Chris Weinke would start in place of the recovering Kendra.

In a lengthy July 6 analysis in the *Jacksonville Times-Union*, sportswriter Gene Frenette pointed out that every starting FSU quarterback had won First Team All-ACC QB honors since the Seminoles joined the league six years before. Frenette's view was that Bowden's system was designed to produce great quarterbacks in sequence, and that if the next All-ACC QB wasn't to be Kendra, it might as well be Weinke. Frenette wrote:

> No Seminole fan should go into a state of panic because Kendra is out and Chris Weinke looms as Thad Busby's replacement. Kendra's injury is certainly not a good thing, but this contingency plan may work just as well or better. … [Kendra] might have been number one on the depth chart before tearing up his right knee during the Spring game, but any separation between him and Weinke always seemed about as thin as a play sheet.

With a smile he added, "Other than spending 16 more months in the FSU system, and throwing 113 more game passes, what does Kendra really have over Weinke? I mean, besides a less receding hair line and less fear of chemical experimentation."

The news about Kendra's decision broke while a group of us were having lunch at the stadium. The talk around the table had been all about the preseason magazines, most of which held the top 4 to be, in various orders, Ohio State, Kansas State, Florida State, and Florida. There was some less-than-objective questioning as to whether Ohio State's offensive line could possibly get fast enough over the summer to challenge defenders as quick as the Seminoles. "Did you see their faces when Andre disappeared right in front of them and nobody saw him 'til he was sitting on their quarterback?"

Ohio State's pretensions to greatness were hooted down, and

the assessment of Kansas State was even more uncharitable. "They ain't even been kissed yet" was the approximate comment, the suggestion being that K-State had achieved a great deal with the exception of having never actually beaten another really good, top-rated Division I team, something that would have to take place before the Wildcats were taken seriously as national contenders. Or taken seriously at least by our lunch crowd, experts that we were.

When word arrived about Kendra, our first reaction was shocked silence. There were expressions of sympathy all around, and of admiration for his courage in doing right by the team. This soon gave way to concerns about how the Seminoles would do without an experienced quarterback.

When Ken Cashin joined us and was told of the news, he nearly jumped out of his chair with excitement. Understand, Cashin was a big Kendra fan, but he was positively rabid about the abilities of Chris Weinke. "What we've got now is a twenty-six-year-old NFL prototype (six foot five, 250 pounds) who is tall enough to see over the linebackers and can put the ball down field with authority. And we've got a receiver corps now that is fast enough to let him air it out. The long ball threat is back!"

When it was mentioned that the Seminoles might face Ohio State or Kansas State in Phoenix for the national title, Cashin was emboldened. "Tell ya what," he volunteered, "if Weinke comes through like I think he will, and if the spring garnet-and-gold game is a pretty good indicator of what we can expect from the defense, then we could play Ohio State and Kansas State on the same day and beat both of them!"

"Ah, yes, a doubleheader," said all of us approvingly. "What a great idea."

When I mentioned that I might put his prediction down on paper, Cashin's smile disappeared. "Well," he said, "if you write it, please make sure you cover me by adding this caveat: For us to win *both* games, we'd have to play K-State in the *afternoon* half of the doubleheader ... and there'd have to be a minimum of three hours between games." Heads nodded in agreement. Yes, that would do it. We also agreed that if, in fact, Florida State did meet either Ohio State or Kansas State (or both on the same day) in any bowl at the end of the season, we would recover all copies of that issue of *Report to Boosters* and burn the evidence, and swear all Boosters to secrecy.*

---

* Much of this chapter's material was initially published in the *Report to Boosters* (July 1998).

Big Brawl, Big Win

If Florida State vs. Miami was the rivalry of the 1980s, then Florida State vs. Florida was the great college football rivalry of the 1990s. Twelve games in a row, both FSU and the Gators were ranked in the nation's top 10 when they faced each other.

The Seminole win in Tallahassee in 1998 would rank among the most significant in the program's history. Weinke's absence due to injury and the heroics of Marcus "Rooster" Outzen ensured that Steve Spurrier would never win a game in Doak Campbell Stadium. Faced with starting an inexperienced third-string quarterback against Florida, our coaches crafted a brilliant game plan for the victory.

It has been said that time flies whether you're having fun or not. It wasn't so long before the 1998 season. Just before New Year's Day 1995, tens of thousands of Seminoles cruised down I-10 toward New Orleans, all puffed up with confidence and eager to extend our 31–31 "victory" over Florida with a follow-up pounding in the Sugar Bowl rematch.

Gator fans, already disheartened by the "choke at Doak," and not at all enthusiastic about facing the riled-up Noles once again, were further vexed at being passed by hundreds of automobiles displaying gold signs with this garnet-scripted sentiment referring to the last eight years of the rivalry: "6–1–1 and We Ain't Done!" The "Fifth Quarter in the French Quarter" proceeded gloriously and the 6–1–1 record over our Gator rivals advanced to 7–1–1 with attendant satisfaction and self-congratulations.

THE FIFTH QUARTER IN THE FRENCH QUARTER

Florida State fan Jim McKnight, left, gets some good-natured teasing from Florida fans in New Orleans on Sunday. The Seminoles and the Gators square off today in the Sugar Bowl.

Even the *Gainesville Sun* (above) bought into the "Fifth Quarter in the French Quarter" theme promoted by both schools and the Sugar Bowl. The Sugar Bowl couldn't believe their good fortune when they drew the same rivals who had fought to a 31–31 tie only a month before. The issue was settled on January 2, 1997, with a 23–17 Seminole victory over No. 5 Florida. The game gave FSU ten wins on the year and a No. 4 final ranking in the eighth year of the dynasty.

After that, we dropped one to the Gators at their place in 1995. No problem—we beat them again in Tallahassee in 1996. But the 1997 Sugar Bowl gave the Gator faithful a full measure of revenge. And in the 1997 season, well, you may remember all too well Jacquez Green streaking past Samari Rolle in that nightmare dream sequence at the end of the game.

Suddenly—and *suddenly* is probably not a dramatic enough word—suddenly 7–1–1 was forgotten, and we were faced with the unwelcome reality that Florida had won three of the last four. To make it even worse, after Chris Weinke was lost to injury at Virginia, there was every likelihood that the count would extend to four out of five.

How important was this Seminole win? Many fans felt that the loss in Gainesville in 1997 was the worst loss in the history of our program. If that were true, then a 1998 win in Tallahassee would be one of the most euphoric victories on the same scale. The 1997 loss was so terrible because of the perception that we were out-coached and out-hustled, because we were the undefeated, favored team and supposed to win, and mostly because it was Florida and Spurrier.

The Tuesday following that loss in 1997, I drove over to speak at our Booster club meeting in Jacksonville. The crowd was small and subdued, and in a dark frame of mind. The club officers tried to buck up the faithful with glowing reports of recruiting and a trip to New Orleans to keep our dynasty alive by beating Ohio State. I fielded questions for a while, but the atmosphere wasn't uplifting.

Then an elderly lady, dressed in garnet and gold, raised her hand. She slowly drew herself to her feet, and said, "I would like you to take a message back to Coach Bowden from me, and from all of us." *This will be good*, I thought. This will be a positive conclusion to the meeting. She'll say the right words about how we're all Seminoles no matter what and we'll get 'em next year and we have the best coaches, players, and fans in America.

But she spoke very deliberately. "I'd like you to tell Coach Bowden," she said, "that the next time we're playing Florida, and its fourth down and we're one yard from the goal-line ... tell him to go for the win instead of playing not to lose." The crowd cheered. How bad was it? It was *that* bad.

So how important was this 23–12 Seminole victory in 1998? To upset Florida, to preserve our nation's longest home unbeaten streak, to win with a game plan notable in equal measure for its audacity and its genius, to achieve victory on the leadership of an unlikely red-headed hero, to triumph through the greatest defensive game we could possibly play, to be physically lifted up by the passion and power of our fans, and the sweet harmony of the "war chant" echoing up to the sky. Even beyond all these marvelous things, this victory was important because it validated the strength and legitimacy of the dynasty, and it brought balance back to our most intense rivalry.

It was a tenuous balance at best, as if we were both rolling on the same log. Either one of us could fly into the water with the slightest mistake. Monday, November 30, an Associated Press feature out of Gainesville described the Gators as a program in decline, "no longer great, but just another entry on a substantial list of good teams. ... Florida is left sitting outside the spotlight, with a downgraded set of goals that don't seem quite right."

I wished it were true that Florida was in decline, but I knew it wasn't so. It could have just as easily been us they were writing about. We knew that either team, the Gators or the Seminoles, could have won *both* those games, in 1997 and in 1998. Florida's crime was that they had lost two games in each of the previous two seasons. Such was the unforgiving nature of life and death at the top of the college football food chain.

The Florida State win in 1998 restored order back to nature. Yes, the Gators had won three of the last five, but we won five of the last ten, plus the tie. Yes, they led overall in the forty-year series, but in the last twenty-five games our Seminoles led 13–11–1. Florida owned the nation's longest home winning streak at twenty-seven. FSU owns the nation's longest home unbeaten streak at forty.

There was no doubt that the Florida State-Florida feud had become the premier college football rivalry of the decade. It was the most televised, the most celebrated, the most debated, and the most significant. This was the eleventh contest in a row where both teams were ranked in the top 10 at the time they played. The *Tampa Tribune* said, "Florida-Florida State is America's No. 1 football rivalry. ... On this, the day that civil wars break out all over America, the battle in Tallahassee stands alone. ... It means glory and animosity and drama and cosmic importance."

But I think the hatred was not quite up to Iron Bowl standards. The annual Iron Bowl between Auburn and Alabama was much more purely visceral. There had always been bad blood between FSU and UF, but never quite the dark loathing and abhorrence that we could see between, say, Ole Miss and LSU, or South Carolina and Clemson.

Maybe it was the Florida weather. Maybe it was the distractions. We had three NFL teams—I didn't know how many Arena League football teams, plus professional baseball, hockey, and basketball teams. We had Universal Studios and the Mouse, and great cities as culturally distinct from each other as Jacksonville and Miami. Maybe the Seminoles and the Gators were like two adolescent boys fighting on the beach. We'd keep whacking each other, but, well, the water's warm, and some girls are looking this way, and there's music coming from somewhere. Maybe we could stop for a while and take my dad's convertible to get something to eat.

And speaking of whacking each other: My take on the pregame fight was a little different than the popular view. I was on the sidelines, escorting some major donors who were to be recognized on the field right before the bands came on when I saw the two teams converge.

The pregame show was tightly scheduled; television controlled the time frame. At the twenty-minute mark on the scoreboard clock, the two teams were supposed to finish their warm-ups and leave the field. The clock said twenty minutes, but the Gators weren't leaving. They were spread out from their goal line to midfield, looking away from the Seminoles, smiling, standing around, and waiting. The Seminoles were on their end of the field, waiting to come out to the midfield logo to do our traditional jumping up and down.

It was obvious the Gators were playing a game of chicken with the Noles, seeing who would leave the field first. Our boys were determined to go out and stand on the logo, and their boys were just as determined to stand in their own way. There was no question that Spurrier orchestrated it. Paybacks were very much his style. He was obliged to allow LSU to wear their traditional white jerseys at home, so in 1998 he turned the tables and made them wear dark shirts in Gainesville so the Gators could wear white. Florida had no tradition of white at home, much like LSU did. Spurrier just did it to irritate his opponent.

In 1997, our boys drifted out to the large letter F midfield logo at Florida Field, and jumped up and down. Florida took it as an insult, as surely it was intended to be despite our wide-eyed protests to the contrary. I'm sure he decided that in 1998, his team would engage in a little quid pro quo. Several newspapers reported that Spurrier told his players they could push and shove, but not to throw punches.

Here's where I broke with the popular view: I didn't really have a problem with what Spurrier did, or with what happened between the FSU and Florida players. What I saw was not a fight or a brawl or a riot. Pushing and shoving isn't a fight; pushing and shoving is basketball. In fact, intimidation is part of the game, especially this game. When Renegade gallops to midfield and Osceola plunges a flaming spear into the turf, that has a specific purpose, and it's not to make the opponents feel better about themselves. If the Gators wanted to try and intimidate us with a little clever trick of their own, then we wanted to see what they had.

The state's big-league sportswriters weighed in on the matter on the Sunday after the game. Larry Guest of the *Orlando Sentinel* wrote, "Our state's two finest universities and football programs sadly projected, coast to coast, a single word—thugs." The *St. Pete Times*' Hubert Mizell described what he called a mindless, tasteless Tallahassee melee, "even more stupid and classless than the daily cesspool of guests on *The Jerry Springer Show*." Mizell spoke of a "cellblock mentality," and went so far as to say if the schools couldn't handle it, then the legislature should step in. David Whitley of the *Tampa Tribune* took a less serious tone: "They threw a football game in Tallahassee last Saturday and a World Wrestling Federation match broke out."

I had known these writers for a long time, Mizell and Guest for twenty years. They had always been fair to Florida State and unstinting in their praise of the Seminoles and their coaches when it was deserved. They were intelligent, erudite, clever fellows, and they had a much broader and much more finely instructed view of pro and college sports than I did. In this particular instance, however, let's say that, rather than disagree with them, I just had a different view of the events.

Rather than a fight or a brawl, think of what happened as a ritual. Trust me, when two football players really intend to fight, the first thing they do is take off their helmets. Look at photos of the players at midfield. You'll see smiling faces in the back rows, and helmeted players in the center of the storm. The only fellows who will get hurt under those circumstances are the ones who hit other players' helmets with their fists. In fact, the only ones who got popped were the graduate assistant who got in the middle, and the Seminole trainer whom Doug Johnson beaned with a football. You did not see players wrestling with each other, falling to the ground. What you saw was two tribes ritually pushing and shoving, jumping up and down.

Yes, it was tribal, very ritualistic with no harm intended. It was my tribe versus your tribe, posturing and exaggerating in front of each other before the battle commenced. It was the Zulu warriors rhythmically stamping their feet and chanting and waving their dreaded *assegai* spears before the attack on Rourke's Drift. It was the Scottish clans banging their axes and claymores against their wooden shields in the face of the English cannon at Culloden. It was twenty thousand Confederate infantry brandishing bayonets along a five-mile front, singing to the music of massed regimental bands, girding their courage for their suicidal charge against the Federal defenses at Franklin. It was very primal, very male.

Gator quarterback Doug Johnson's mistake was that he showed disrespect for the ritual. He threw a football at an unprotected head and then slunk away. The *Orlando Sentinel* reported that Gator quarterback Noah Brindise similarly threw a football at FSU players the previous year and then told Gator Boosters and teammates that Spurrier had ordered him to do so. The *Tampa Tribune* also referenced the same story.

If Spurrier really did order the "hits" by Brindise and Johnson, then he was truly despicable. In the absence of proof, I'll choose to believe he did not do it. What he did do was to tell his men to stand their ground, to give our Noles a little of our own medicine. So be it—no harm done. But Spurrier's motivation and instructions, whatever they were, did not change the substance of what I saw.

I saw two teams, both high-spirited but anxious and uncertain, preparing to play a game in which everything was on the line. These two teams knew each other, respected each other, and accepted the reality that only one would win glory while the other tasted bitter defeat. This was no fight. It was an exuberant salute, one tribe to the other, before the real drama began.

I realize that I am in the minority here, so much so that my view would not show up as even a single blip on the radar screen. And the speculation was all academic. The athletic directors of both schools said that it would never happen again. When Dave Hart and Jeremy Foley, both steely-eyed fellows, said that it would never happen again, then you might as well cue Don Meredith to begin singing "Turn out the lights ..."—the party was definitely over.

If 1997 in Gainesville was the most painful loss in the history of our program, then 1998 in Tallahassee must surely rank among the most profoundly satisfying wins. And what makes college football so wonderful for us, especially college football in the state of Florida, was that we got to watch all the great drama play out again the following year.

Time flies when you're having fun. And during those days we Seminoles were most definitely the ones having all the fun.[*]

---

[*] Much of this chapter's material was initially published in the *Report to Boosters* (December 1998).

There's a Special Joy
in Beating Tennessee: Twists and
Turns on the Road to Phoenix

A sportswriter for the Knoxville newspaper picked Tennessee to win the 1998 national championship over Florida State in the Fiesta Bowl. He asked, "Would you expect Tennessee to win a national title with their third-string quarterback?" Well, he speculated, Florida State can't do it either. Despite Seminole heroics in Phoenix, the loss of experienced quarterbacks Dan Kendra and Chris Weinke were too much to overcome.

But Seminole fans understood they were in yet another national championship game, an event becoming routine as the dynasty extended beyond a decade of consecutive ten-win, top 4 seasons.

A Special Joy

The boys were in Phoenix for the game. Nugent's boys, as they enjoyed calling themselves, played for Coach Tom Nugent in the 1950s. The Nugent era, only six seasons long, encompassed one of the most dramatic and ambitious six-year spans in Seminole football history.

Lee Corso was one of the boys. So was Burt Reynolds. So

was Vic Prinzi. Whether the times molded the men, I cannot say. There was no doubt, however, that they and their coach had prospered and embraced life with game-day enthusiasm. If you were out dining in the area, and you heard raucous laughter from a table surrounded by square-jawed, gray-haired men and their beautiful wives, then you were likely in the presence of the fellows who manhandled and embarrassed mighty Tennessee forty years previously.

The 1958 season marked Florida State's inauguration as a Division I football contender after years as a small college power-house. The Seminole season featured games against Georgia Tech, Georgia, and Miami. And for the first time, Florida and Tennessee were on the schedule. Tennessee still reflected the bright aura of its 1951 national championship. The Volunteers had finished No. 2 in the nation as recently as 1956.

It would be hard to find anything in 1998 newspapers to compare with the arrogance of the *Knoxville News-Sentinel* that long-ago October. Florida State had a backup quarterback named Joe Majors, a member of the Majors family that included Tennessee's great tailback, Billy Majors, and his brother, All-American Johnny Majors. Both men were playing for the Vols at the time. On game day, the Knoxville paper sniffed, "The fact is: Billy Majors is a first-class player on a first-class team, and Joe Majors is a second-class player on a second-class team." Prinzi used to smile when he talked about that newspaper article. "The fellows all read it," he had said. "I think we all took a little different attitude after that."

Florida State shut Tennessee out at home, 10–0, a loss so wrenching that for decades Vols athletic directors refused to discuss even the possibility of further games between the two schools. Surely the ghostly spirits of Bobby Renn, Tony Romeo, and Vic Prinzi had found a way to be there with their pals for the forty-year reunion of their greatest triumph. And just to show that history does indeed run in circles, the *Knoxville News-Sentinel* had once again weighed in with a pompous assertion.

The premise of the column was that Tennessee was the last man standing, with a 12–0 perfect record (smugly ignoring 11–0 and No. 9-ranked Tulane, which would play a bowl game in Memphis), and as such was, by elimination, *already* the national champion: "If a team is undefeated in both media polls, and there are no other undefeated teams, there is no need for a mythical national championship game."

Oh sure, the Vols ought to play in some bowl, the article went on, for the fans and for the nine million that the trip to Tempe pays, win or lose: "But a loss in a bowl game really won't mean anything." Accordingly, Tennessee will still be superior to any team that didn't finish the regular season unblemished. "Make no mistake," the author prattles, "FSU hasn't run up against the likes of the Vols yet. Not only will they have to fight the greatest defense in the NCAA, they will have to fight destiny, which always has its way."

Ah yes, destiny. It will always have its way. Maybe destiny had gathered these remaining boys together for a glorious reunion adventure. Perhaps destiny had decided to grant Florida State its second national championship in a game against the team that allowed those Seminoles of so long ago their first significant win in the major leagues.

And just maybe, late that night, as Burt Reynolds was walking down from the broadcast booth, moving down the darkened corridor to some celebration party, just maybe he would catch the slightest scent of smoke from a familiar cigarette. He'll turn and glimpse a ghost half-seen, not quite there. Then he'll smile and whisper to his pal Prinzi: "How about that, Vic. We got 'em again."*

---

* Much of this section's material was initially published in the *FSU Overtime Times* (January 3, 1999).

Left to right: Vic Prinzi, Burt Reynolds,
and Gene Deckerhoff, in the broadcast booth.

Twists and Turns

"What it was, was football." Andy Griffith launched his career as a comedian with that famous 1950's routine about a confused North Carolina backwoods boy trying to explain a strange and wonderful game. How in the world would he explain the unlikely, even bizarre string of events that brought the Seminoles to Phoenix for the national championship game?

Much has been made of the eerie similarities between the turn of events in 1996 and 1998. In 1996, for Florida to get into the title game, several outcomes of doubtful probability had to occur. First, there had to be a huge upset in the Big 12 championship game. In 1996, a bad Texas team upset a sleepwalking Nebraska squad 37–27 in St. Louis. Texas was so bad that a year later the coach was fired.

How did Florida State get to the national championship game in 1998? The Big 12 game, which would also be in St. Louis, featured underdog Texas A&M vs. top-ranked Kansas State. The Aggies came back from 15 points down in the fourth quarter, and at the end of the second overtime, on fourth and 17, a little Aggie back scooted to the 1-yard line before he was pushed out of bounds. I said he was in. Happily, so did the official.

Second, Ohio State had to do something remarkable. In 1996, OSU upset heavily favored Arizona State. In 1998, the Buckeyes lost at home to unranked Michigan State. Thanks.

But the most unlikely hero, by far, of this Florida State story was the Miami Hurricanes team that knocked off No. 3-ranked and undefeated UCLA a week after giving up 66 points to Syracuse. It was supposed to have been the Bruins' defining moment, the game that catapulted them into the Fiesta Bowl for a shot at their first national title since 1954. The *Miami Herald* quoted Rose Bowl representative Mel Cohen saying this was to be "the game of the century for UCLA."

Cohen got it partly right. Maybe it was the "upset of the century." It wasn't just that the Canes had lost so dreadfully to Syracuse; they also came into this fray, having lost seven of their previous eight games against ranked opponents. The euphoria after the game in that rattletrap old Orange Bowl was beyond measure. Miami players described themselves as David and UCLA as Goliath. I thought Miami might of had a chance to win because of the humidity, and because Miami had been getting better, and because the Canes' 66 points given up at Syracuse would mislead the Bruins.

But I knew UCLA was in trouble early in the week when Coach Bob Toledo responded to a press question by blithely saying that, no, he wasn't going to run up the score on Miami even though it would improve his team's BCS standing. These Californians didn't know Miami like I did. Toledo could have been well instructed by the lyrics of Ira Gershwin: "Little David was small, but oh my!"

Actually, Miami was not that little anymore either. Only six players on the two-deep chart were seniors, and Coach Butch Davis had twenty-five scholarships to give out that spring. This win over UCLA was likely the Canes most dramatic and defining victory since beating Nebraska 31–30 in the national championship game in the Orange Bowl in 1983.

Were they officially back, and if so, were they the Miami of old, or a new and more genteel version? Miami trashed an opponent's championship hopes, and then danced on the carcass.

After the game, Coach Butch Davis allowed that the "worst part about the UCLA win [is that it might] end up making some people in Tallahassee happy." And when fifteen thousand fans ran onto the field, the police bludgeoned one celebrant into submission, and turned a dog loose on another, who was bitten in the leg. The *Herald* used the word *mayhem* in the headline. Still, Miami Police Captain Tony Rodriquez merrily announced, "Within the chaos, it really went pretty well."

You've gotta love 'em.

But in spite of all the strange goings-on, we couldn't doubt for a moment that FSU fully deserved to be in the contest vs. Tennessee for the national championship. Our Seminoles played more bowl teams than anyone else in 1998, beating seven of the eight. And four of those seven wins came against teams that finished among the top 15 in the final BCS rankings.

But maybe the quirkiest thing that happened to put us in the Fiesta Bowl happened back in February 1998. Gene Frenette, columnist for the *Jacksonville Times-Union*, wrote, "In the end, FSU was able to sew up a No. 2 ranking because of the gamble Coach Bowden took in scheduling Texas A&M in the Kickoff Classic." Playing that twelfth game and winning it, he said, was the difference between FSU standing at 11–1 vs. 10–1. Had Texas A&M won, it might have been the Aggies in Phoenix instead of us.

Yes, it was hard to explain. One bitter Kansas State player looked into the camera and asked, "How does this happen? How can we be ranked No. 1 and lose in double overtime and end up in the Alamo Bowl? And the ref's call on the 1-yard line that gave a touchdown to Texas A&M ... what was that?"

What it was, son, was football.*

---

* Much of this section's material was initially published in the *FSU Overtime Times* (January 4, 1999).

Seminoles vs. Volunteers
in the Fiesta Bowl

Florida State was a 5-point favorite to win our second national championship by beating Tennessee in the desert. Quarterback Marcs Outzen had only started one game, but it was a triumph over Florida. After we beat Florida in Tallahassee on November 21, and after it was determined that we would play Tennessee for the national championship, I felt pretty good about our chance at victory.

Oh, I gave lip service to the humble gosh-we're-just-lucky-to-be-in-the-title-game litany, but inside I felt this was the best possible matchup for us. We'd get to cart the Sears Trophy around with us on the Bobby Bowden Tour during the spring and then go into 1999 as the preseason No. 1 team. It was a pretty sweet deal. But two doubts kept churning around in the back of my mind. It was like seeing a couple of dark specks in one's coffee: they're probably nothing, but what if the little specks have little legs? Best to take a closer look.

The first speck was the fact that we would not play a football game for forty-four days. Forty-four will get one exactly from New Year's Eve to Valentine's Day, which is a considerable distance to travel and still expect to maintain that game-day edge. Tennessee played another regular season game after we beat Florida, then won the SEC title game as late as December 5.

The second doubt crept out from between the first few lines of a December 31 column in the *Knoxville News-Sentinel*. Sports editor John Adams wrote, "How many teams have won a national championship game with a third-string quarterback? Let me put it another way: do you think Tennessee could beat Florida State with Joey Mathews at quarterback?"

I didn't know who Joey Mathews was, but of course Adams' point was that few Tennessee fans had heard of him either. Adams said he wouldn't quibble with the 5-point spread if second-string quarterback Chris Weinke was playing, but the third guy on the chart was a bit much to swallow: "Now this third-string quarterback, who once thought about transferring, is being asked to do what no QB has done this season: beat Tennessee. And the oddsmakers are saying he'll do it with 4 points to spare."

Adams was effusive in his praise for FSU and its program, calling us the football equivalent of a Final Four team for eleven consecutive seasons. But, he said, "If the Seminoles beat UT, they will have to overcome their quarterback."

Our confidence, and that of the oddsmakers, had been inflated by our win over the Gators. Florida came into Tallahassee overconfident, much as they had done in 1996. And, I might add, much the same as we did going into Gainesville in 1997. This had become a series where it was best to play scared. What Florida didn't realize was that Marcus Outzen enjoyed the emotional support of his teammates and could keep cool under the crushing pressure of what was probably the most widely viewed regular season game of the year. Additionally, Outzen was a running back who could hurt the Gator defense in ways they had not anticipated.

Quarterback coach Mark Richt characterized Outzen as "a mobile back, an accurate passer, and tough as nails." He was right, and Outzen proved it on November 21. But after November 21, of course, Tennessee had the film. In a national championship game against an undefeated top-of-the-line program like Tennessee, *any* weaknesses are magnified. Florida State had enough talent to be able to overcome the occasional heyday. Maybe the offensive line had trouble protecting, or the defensive backs were off, or the passer just couldn't connect. We had seen that happen on numerus occasions, but most days FSU still won anyway.

In the Fiesta Bowl, there was no tolerance for error, no reprieve for an awkward step or a missed block. *Tallahassee Democrat* columnist John Nogowski wrote that Coach Bowden had ordered a review of the bowl film once recruiting was over. "They were wise orders, certainly," said Nogowski. "You can always learn from your mistakes, and there was at least a master's degree worth in that game."

Writers for the *Osceola* echoed the optimism that FSU might benefit in 1999 from the lessons of the Fiesta Bowl. Daniel Mitchell wrote, "Warrick's return cemented FSU as the sure-fire No. 1 team heading into next season. If Chris Weinke's neck makes a full recovery, it's frightening to think how good the Noles offense will be." And if you saw the spring scrimmage, then you would have already known that "frightening" was just the starting point when talking about the Noles' defense.

We all could take advantage of lessons from the Fiesta Bowl. I was an enthusiastic admirer of our Seminole fans. Having traveled for years throughout Florida and Georgia for the Boosters, I knew how difficult and expensive it was to bundle up the family and trek to Tallahassee. The football game takes only three hours, but the trip consumes the entire weekend. There were nine million people within a 150 miles of Gainesville. There were probably not nine million livestock within a 150 miles of Tallahassee. Human beings in that radius number only nine hundred thousand.

You have to really want to be a Seminole fan. It took effort, and it took money, more money than what was required of other schools' fans. Jerry Kutz made the point that no other university's fans had been asked to go to expensive New Year's Day major bowls for a dozen consecutive years.

We've talked about how bad the tickets were at the big bowls. We've talked about how expensive weekends in Tallahassee can be. We knew full well how young our alumni base still was. We knew that our fellow ACC teams' fans did not travel in numbers to North Florida. And yet, Florida State's eighty-thousand-seat stadium averaged *more than* eighty thousand per game in 1998. FSU continued to rank among the nation's top 10 in annual average attendance.

Seminole Boosters, Inc. continued—for twenty years as of 1999—to have more contributors than either Gator Boosters or Hurricane Boosters. In fact, the Seminole Boosters may have been, with the exception of Clemson, the largest collegiate booster organization in America. And as the pregame feature in the *Arizona Republic* said, "It's a lifetime love affair for loyal FSU fans."

I was not just proud; I was nearly euphoric about the loyalty and devotion of our wonderful Seminole fans. I was never pleased to hear Seminole fans being criticized or demeaned. We were still a young school, and our teams and our fans had achieved more than any other schools of similar age and circumstance had ever even attempted. That said, we Seminoles could, and must, learn more about how to advance ourselves as great football fans. In 1980, we experienced a sort of epiphany at Nebraska. Indifferently ranked and generally unknown, the Seminoles handed the Cornhuskers a shocking defeat at home.

The national credibility FSU achieved overnight was important. More important, however, may have been the electric effect that Nebraska fans had on our people. The Huskers stood en masse and applauded our team and fans for their victory. The Boosters, Bobby Bowden, Bernie Sliger, and everyone associated with the program seized on that example. We wanted to be like Nebraska: powerful, accomplished, gracious in defeat, and sportsmanlike in victory.

The University of Tennessee fans had much of the Nebraska

ethic in them. They flooded the Valley of the Sun, with tickets and without, clad in every orange-colored article imaginable. There must have been something different about people from the middle of the country than those of us who dwelt around the edges. I remember in 1995 that my Gator friends were so confounded to see the orange-and-blue travelers overwhelmed by Nebraska fans at the Fiesta Bowl. "There were so many!" they said. "We couldn't figure out where they all came from."

On January 1, the *Arizona Republic* ran articles quoting area merchants who were critical of FSU, fans, and University of Florida fans from two years previous, for not spending up to local expectations. Gator fans were not used to being outnumbered, so it was a shock to hear merchants whine, "We were all counting on Ohio State or Kansas State coming in here. The dreams have been ruined. You need two titans [for a game like this], but neither of them can be from Florida because those schools are the weakest at sending people." The merchants don't bother me ("The dreams have been ruined" because a school from Florida is there? Please.), but there was one course we Seminoles could proceed to embrace right away: We needed to dress differently.

My wife, Connie, and I meandered through the various shops and malls available, and the same little exchange took place over and over again. She was wearing a white warm-up outfit covered with Seminole logos. In several stores, merchants said something along the lines of, "We're sure glad to finally see some Seminoles around here. All we've seen is Tennessee people."

Sure enough, Volunteer fans were in abundant supply. But as I looked around, I saw something else too. In one store where I got the merchant comment, I could see four or five obvious Tennessee fans, covered head to foot in orange, but in the same store I also saw one fellow wearing a baseball cap with a small Seminole head; his wife had on nothing to identify herself as a Seminole. I saw another couple I recognized as Boosters from Pensacola, but he had on a nondescript white shirt with a small Seminole head, and she was wearing a pair of Seminole walking shoes. We Seminoles were there—we were just invisible.

The Vols were remarkable. I had never seen such color. The orange was so bright and loud that you could nearly *hear* their fans before you actually saw them. And there was no wearing of just a hat or a shirt or a pair of orange pants. They draped themselves in entire parachutes of orange.

On the night of the game, the difference was striking. And, I must tell you, I was among the worst offenders. I went to the game dressed the way I usually do for night games. I wore a white golf shirt with a small Seminole head, and a blue jacket with a small tomahawk pin. I thought I looked nice. People began coming up to me and asking for directions to different parts of the stadium. To the world, I looked like some guy who worked for the Fiesta Bowl committee.

All this had a definite effect on me. The Tennessee fans were instantly identifiable. Volunteers who didn't know each other whooped and signaled to other Volunteers, and generally buoyed up all about them who wore the orange. To be surrounded by massive walls of your fellow fans is inspiring and invigorating. The Tennessee Volunteers had that advantage over us Florida State Seminoles.

Our football program, and this particular football team, had to go through a learning process. So also did Seminole fans. We learned how to behave from the Nebraska folks. But now we needed to learn how to overwhelm our opponents from these fine, classy Tennessee fans who were so gracious in victory and so aggressive in their attire.

There's a good story—a true story, which is the best kind— about an exchange that took place in the late second half of the Fiesta Bowl. Quarterback Outzen was having a bad time of it. Protection wasn't all it should be, and he was running out of the pocket only to get hammered again and again by the brutal Volunteer defense. As Marcus picked himself up off the turf, a Tennessee fan behind the FSU bench hollered at Chris Weinke.

"Hey! Weinke!" the Vol yelled at the big quarterback. "You better be glad you aren't playing!"

Weinke didn't miss a beat. He turned and pointed to the orange-clad taunter. "No, friend," he said. "*You'd* better be glad I'm not playing."

There was a fair chance that Tennessee and Florida State would meet again in the national championship game on January 3, 2000, in the Sugar Bowl. If things went our way, then perhaps Chris Weinke would have the chance to add an exclamation point to his reply. In the meantime, however, I was going to go buy some intense Seminole game wear so we could whoop at each other on the streets of New Orleans.*

---

* Much of this chapter's material was initially published in the *Report to Boosters* (April 1999).

Bowl Business
in the Era of the Dynasty

In the first twelve years of the dynasty, our Seminoles played in the Cotton Bowl, four Sugar Bowls, three Orange Bowls, and three Fiesta Bowls. Many Seminole fans actually suffered from "big bowl fatigue." The major bowls are very expensive to get to, and the seats assigned to the participating teams are bad. Still, few would argue that it is better to be toward the bottom of the pyramid than at the top.

Let's talk about bowls, tickets, and real life at the top of the college football food chain. Here are the facts: (1) Many of our most generous fans are angry at the location of their tickets for the Fiesta Bowl, and probably the Sugar Bowl before that, and the Orange Bowl before that; (2) they see or hear about people who give little or no money and who had great seats, and that makes them even more angry; (3) the distribution of tickets, as far as they can tell, seems to make no sense and follows no discernible pattern; (4) they bring people to the games as their guests, and then are embarrassed to be seated dead in the end zone even though they contribute huge pots of money to the Boosters.

While expounding on his unhappiness to Andy Miller, one Booster donor said, "A lot of people are mad and they think you guys, the Boosters, are just getting too big for your britches." Some of our best people were mad as hornets about how they felt they had been treated, and because of that, some of those even felt like the Booster organization itself had a dismissive or uncaring attitude toward the people whose dollars made it possible for our teams to compete at the highest levels.

All this was disheartening to me. Perception is a powerful rival to truth, and so the best course was to deal head-on with the problems as they were, as well as the problems as they were perceived.

Florida State's problem with bowl tickets was a serious one. The first step in solving it was to initiate better communication with our contributors. Beginning in 1999, the *Report to Boosters* was to be published monthly and sent to all donors, from fifty-dollars-per-year Iron Arrow Boosters to ten-thousand-a-year Double Golden Chiefs. Jerry Kutz, popular publisher of the *Osceola*, edited the expanded *Report*. Those who loved the *Osceola* didn't have to worry: Kutz would remain the principal columnist for that important voice of FSU athletics.

For the Fiesta Bowl, Florida State received sixteen thousand tickets. All of them were bad, with the rare exception of odd pairs scattered here and there, and maybe a few sets of four in a decent location. If you and your friends sat dead in the end zone, then you could chat with members of President D'Alemberte's official party. They were right there with everyone else.

I'm told the ticket business was an art. We found out at the last possible minute that we weren't going to New Orleans or Miami. We didn't realize we were going to Phoenix until thousands of Hurricane fans flooded the field, sweeping dejected UCLA Bruin's aside. There was a window of perhaps forty-eight hours for our fans to make their decision about going.

Getting tickets wasn't a problem; getting there with virtually no commercial flights with empty seats to sell was the problem. Tennessee fans had filled them since they beat Florida, and we would have done the same thing. If there were to be chartered flights, they had to be arranged quickly, and speed was not something one readily associates with the charter business.

Every Seminole Booster had the chance to buy Fiesta Bowl (or Orange Bowl or Sugar Bowl) tickets early. The ticket office sent out a "Pre-Bowl" mailing in the early fall with a deadline of November 21. Early purchasers were guaranteed that they would get tickets. In fact, a person could order tickets to any of the bowls likely to see the Seminoles but only paid for tickets to the one bowl in which the Tribe played.

When we suddenly found ourselves headed for the desert, the decision was made to open ticket sales up to all seventeen thousand Seminole Boosters immediately. At that point, any Booster was allowed to purchase up to eight tickets. Athletic director Dave Hart wanted as many Seminoles as possible to be there to support our team. Phone company records confirm that more than three hundred thousand phone calls were made to the ticket office over two days. That means all the tickets were sold out, and sold out quickly.

Most who wanted tickets ordered the maximum number of eight. Very soon after that, a large number of these found that even though they had tickets and hotel rooms, actually getting to Phoenix was another matter entirely. Access was a problem.

Our Seminole Booster office wrote to all those who had received tickets, asking them to sell their extra or unused tickets back to us. We then resold them to the loyal fans who were not able to get through to the ticket office, or who had transportation but needed more tickets than they had ordered. That program worked pretty well. Lots of Seminoles resold their tickets to other Boosters. Some sold them to Internet or Ticket Master brokers who, in turn, sold them to Tennessee fans. More than a few Noles found themselves holding eight hundred dollars' worth of tickets, and hotel reservations, and no way to get to the game.

So why did we get bad seats in the Fiesta Bowl? The nature

of the big bowls had changed dramatically in the 1990s, with the advent of the Bowl Alliance and its successor, the Bowl Championship Series. The Fiesta Bowl guaranteed each of the two teams somewhere between twelve million and thirteen million dollars. Ponder that for a moment. The Fiesta Bowl accepted a financial obligation on the order of twenty-five million dollars just as a payout to the visiting schools. Payouts from the Sugar and Rose and Orange Bowls were also enormous, on the order of eight million per team. And since the Bowl Championship Alliance Bowls had accepted this huge obligation, they had been most creative in coming up with ways to raise the money.

The most universal way of raising these large sums was through sponsors. Sponsors were asked to make massive contributions, and in turn the sponsors were given blocks of the best tickets. *All* the best tickets, in fact. With the exception of a small handful of scattered seats, all of Florida State's sixteen thousand tickets were the worst in the stadium. Tennessee got the same deal.

I thought I saw whole blocks of FSU fans sitting on the 50-yard line. Turned out they were Arizona State fans mixed with Arizona Cardinals supporters. Right colors, wrong teams. No doubt they were local sponsors enjoying their fine, expensive seats. The FSU and Tennessee fans sitting in midfield grandeur did not buy their game tickets from either school's ticket offices. They found other creative ways to conjure up the money.

FSU didn't get to choose its own official team hotel: the Fiesta Bowl chose the hotel and paid the rate they tell us. It used to be, if we didn't sell all our bowl tickets, we could send them back. In this league, the sixteen thousand tickets come out of our budget at a hundred dollars each. You can sell 'em or you can eat 'em, they say.

The Sugar and the Orange Bowls are the same way, and probably the Rose Bowl as well. They determined the team hotel and the rate. They sent us the worst tickets in the house. A few years ago, when we played Notre Dame in the Orange Bowl, tens of thousands of Seminoles bought their game tickets through South Florida ticket brokers. The ticket office had a hard time selling tickets; our Seminole alumni down there knew the school had no good seats to offer, but the brokers had plenty of "sponsor seats."

When we played Notre Dame in Miami, the ticket office ended up returning tickets, and yet the house was packed with Seminoles. In 1999, however, Florida played Syracuse in the Orange Bowl, and the Gator ticket office sold only eighteen thousand tickets from their guarantee of thirty thousand.

Our fans are offended when they spend large amounts of money to follow their team great distances, and they are rewarded with seats on the last row of the upper deck. The bowls, no surprises here, don't see it the same way. They are mystified that we were unhappy, and they became irritated. "We are paying you thirteen million dollars just for being here," they say. "So you just sit down and be quiet."

Dave Hart said there was no doubt that in negotiating these extraordinarily high payoffs to the schools, the big football powers had given up some benefits for the fans. "There is going to have to be some adjustment made, some renegotiation," Hart said. "Even if it means the schools have to accept a lower payout. To have our fans treated this way is intolerable." And you could be certain that Hart was not the only one saying these things.

Here's where FSU's money went. From our twelve- to thirteen-million-dollar take, the Fiesta Bowl budgeted travel expenses for FSU of $1.5 million, a figure recommended by the NCAA. Athletic director Dave Hart added some money from general revenues to that so we could take the entire Marching Chiefs band, and so FSU could make a first-class showing at this historical event. The balance of the millions would be sent to the Atlantic Coast Conference where it would be divided into a pie of nine slices. FSU would then receive one of those slices. Yes, it was true that Duke could actually net more money on the Fiesta Bowl than

FSU. Of course, FSU's share of the conference basketball revenue in that same season would receive a healthy boost from the No. 1-ranked Dukies.

Here was good advice: When the FSU ticket office mailed out their preseason bowl ticket order form in August, I encouraged everyone to order their Sugar Bowl tickets at that time. If we didn't go, then we didn't have to pay for the tickets. We needed to make contacts for hotel rooms in the area well in advance. We were looking square into the face of New Year's Eve 2000 in New Orleans.

It was 1998, twelve seasons since that All-American Bowl. In those dozen years we had been to the Cotton bowl, four Sugars, three Oranges, and three Fiestas. We had played for the national championship three times, and won ten of the twelve bowl games. Only one year, in 1990, could one say we didn't go to a "major" bowl, and that year we beat Penn State in the Blockbuster Bowl and were entertained in one of the most luxurious stadiums in America.

Florida State lived in a world far removed from most of the rest of college football. But what they say about being lonely at the top is true. The reality was that the only people who are going to care for, support, and ensure the success of our programs are Florida State alumni and friends.

I didn't want any of our fans to be angry about their seats, but I understood if they were, and we were trying to get a better deal for our fans. I didn't want them to be mad at the Boosters for any reason. Maybe they were upset at something that happened in New Orleans, and they were thinking about not going back for the bowl. If they were, then I begged them to reconsider and remember that the Seminoles were successful in large part because of the loyalty and generosity of our fans.

In that All-American Bowl in Birmingham, we struggled early, then sophomore Sammie Smith started putting up good numbers and we eventually pulled away. I remember that it was after dark and snowing when we got to the stadium for the game. Hardly any locals braved the weather. In fact, a couple of years later the bowl went out of business. And I remember something else from that night in Birmingham before the onset of the dynasty and the nearly unbroken twelve-year run of major bowls. I remember we had great seats.[*]

---

[*] Much of this chapter's material was initially published in the *Report to Boosters* (March 1999).

1999 Season

During those dynasty years from 1987 to 2000, many people told me how confident they were that our team would win each week. They never really worried, some told me, unless we were playing Florida or Miami, both of whom were rivals with world-class talent. All the other good teams we played were just "interesting for a quarter or two," they said. I never shared their confidence.

It had long since been clear to me that we had talented athletes and a solid coaching staff at FSU. I believed each year that we could compete for a national championship if we could stay healthy and avoid mistakes. Our players had pride in our winning tradition and worked hard to maintain it. They knew success didn't come easy. So did I. But I knew that adversity could derail many a dream. How we handled it would make the difference.

This year we faced adversity once again. In early October, after getting off to a great start, one of our best players was suspended and another was dismissed from the team. We had to scrap hard for wins against Georgia Tech, Miami, Clemson, and Florida. Fortunately, Weinke was back at the helm. And this group of players had learned to fight through challenges. They never quit on themselves or their teammates. They made it through the season without a loss.

The bowl game brought yet more adversity. Leading 28–14 over Virginia Tech at halftime, we fell behind 29–28 in the third quarter. Momentum clearly had shifted in their favor. But my guys refused to buckle under the pressure. They came storming back to score 18 unanswered points in the fourth quarter to win the national championship, 46–29. They turned adversity into opportunity. And they became the first team in NCAA Division I-A history to go wire-to-wire as the nation's No. 1 team.

—Bobby Bowden

1999 Season

Began the season ranked No. 1
Ended the season ranked No. 1
Record 12–0
ACC Champions
Sugar Bowl Champions
Wire-to-Wire National Champions

August 28, defeated Louisiana Tech in Tallahassee 41–7

September 11, defeated Georgia Tech in Tallahassee 41–35

September 18, defeated NC State in Tallahassee 42–11

September 25, defeated North Carolina in Chapel Hill 42–10

October 2, defeated Duke in Jacksonville 51–23

October 9, defeated Miami in Tallahassee 31–21

October 16, defeated Wake Forest in Tallahassee 33–10

October 23, defeated Clemson in Clemson 17–14

October 30, defeated Virginia in Charlottesville 35–10

November 13, defeated Maryland in Tallahassee 49–10

November 20, defeated Florida in Gainesville 30–23

January 4, 2000, defeated Virginia Tech in the Sugar Bowl 46–29

Auburn Cancels Season Opener
vs. the Seminoles

Auburn's Pat Dye dropped the Seminoles in 1991, but Terry Bowden was coaching the Tigers and the first-ever Division I father-son contest was scheduled to be the opener of the Seminoles' championship season. However, dark intrigue pushed Terry Bowden out at midseason in 1998 and speculation was that Bobby Bowden's "Old Testament" instincts would take over on game day in 1999. The Auburn program was down and had no desire to expose themselves upon the altar of Bobby Bowden's vengeance.

Although we had not yet played against each other under the tenure of Terry Bowden, there had been several annual Tiger-Seminole golf tournaments in Tallahassee attended by university officials and both head coaches. The abrupt cancellation made for lively controversy in the off-season.

If there was an upside, it was that the time between the end of football recruiting and the beginning of spring practice was filled with an infinitely entertaining parade of columns, news stories, rantings, and denials. It was not nearly as good as actually playing the game, but it made for absolute theater.

Dropping the game, especially in the craven way it was done, was a no-class, low-rent thing to do, perfectly in keeping with all the rest of the malignant, back-stabbing antics so richly detailed in

Larry Guest's blockbuster investigative report for the *Orlando Sentinel*. By the way, you will be delighted to learn, according to the virulent chat-room ravings published daily in the Alabama press, that the *Orlando Sentinel*—indeed all Florida newspapers—were wholly owned subsidiaries of and propaganda mills for the Atlantic Coast Conference. That was the best news I had heard in years; oh, that it was true.

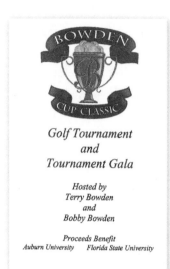

Golf Tournament
and
Tournament Gala

Hosted by
Terry Bowden
and
Bobby Bowden

Proceeds Benefit
Auburn University   *Florida State University*

The Bowden Cup Classic in Tallahassee brought Auburn and FSU coaches and fans together when Terry Bowden was the Tigers' head coach between 1992 and 1998. The Seminoles and Tigers were scheduled to play in 1999, but the game was cancelled after Terry resigned during the 1998 season. Bobby Bowden would have coached against both sons in 1999, Tommy Bowden's first year as head coach at Clemson.

Not much, really, had been seen in the Florida media up until that time, but in Alabama the radio talk shows and daily newspapers were wholly consumed with the subject, so much so that legions of Auburn faithful flooded the Internet bemoaning the fact that even news of the Tigers' No. 3-ranked basketball team, along with any other positive tidings, seemed to be entirely lost in the uproar.

After Terry Bowden resigned as Auburn football coach in the fall of 1998, Larry Guest published a meticulously researched expose of the smarmy conspiracy that led to the most successful coach in Auburn history walking away from his team with five games left to play in the season. As Guest would tell it, former coach Pat Dye, along with trustee/banker Bobby Lowder of Montgomery, and Bowden's defensive coordinator, Bill Oliver, plotted a backstage coup to push Bowden out, even to the point of secretly recording the football coaches' staff meetings. Guest wasn't the only source; everything we had ever wanted to know about the dark inner intrigues of Auburn's athletic operation was speculated upon daily in the Alabama press.

Terry Bowden's and Auburn's business was their own and none of ours. It spilled over into Florida State's lap when Tiger athletic director David Housel, an amiable, recently elevated-up-from-the-mailroom sort of fellow, deliberately waited until after National Signing Day to announce that the big national television date with Florida State was off and that he had already replaced the Seminoles with Appalachian State. Housel had the chance back in October of 1998 to do the right thing. In the wake of his son's resignation, Bobby Bowden said he would just as soon not play Auburn at all, which was an understandable reaction.

But Housel stood pat, and as late as November he looked squarely into the camera and said he expected to be in Tallahassee on September 2, and the game would be played. Evidently Hart received private assurances along the same lines. Hart and ESPN moved ahead; the ACC looked forward to an $850,000 television payout.

Housel told the media that he had been looking for an out since November. The *Atlanta Constitution* wondered, since new coach Tommy Tuberville was hired on November 30, "was Tuberville promised as part of the deal to come to Auburn that the Florida State game would not be played?" Instead of opening with FSU on national television, the Tigers opened with Appalachian State, which was followed by Troy State. A correspondent to the *Mobile Register* pointed out that after Turberville's Ole Miss squad lost two years in a row to Memphis, "Tuberville dropped the 60+

year series with Memphis and rescheduled Northern Illinois and Idaho State. ... Sound familiar?"

Casting his eyes skyward, Housel also begged himself off the hook. "It's not my decision," he told Hart. And to the *Birmingham Post-Herald*, he said, "This was an institutional decision, not just an athletic one." An institutional decision? Institutional control was not an issue on the plains. The Tiger athletic department was under the control of an institution. The problem, many speculated, was that the institution in question was not Auburn University but the owner of the bank in Montgomery. According to Housel, who said this with a straight face, they "did it for the boys."

The tender psyches of the Auburn players were traumatized by an aggressive media. "If we played the game as scheduled, the controversy and turmoil of last season would be rehashed again and again over the next eight months. ... The controversy would become bigger than the game, and that would be unfair to the players." But nobody asked the boys.

Trust me, the boys were fine. Auburn recruits tough kids who are there because they want to be Tigers. If you told them they had a chance to play against a championship contender on national television to start off the season, my guess was that they couldn't get their helmets on fast enough. In fact, the *Birmingham Post-Herald* had been able to determine that in at least one case, Auburn recruiters used the promise of playing against FSU as a selling point to lure a prospect to the Tiger ranks.

Auburn's players had never feared any other team. But there was fear at Auburn in those days. Pushy reporters and columnists in the Alabama media were asking, "Who is running Auburn football?" The answers they were getting reminded me a little of that scene toward the end of *The Wizard of Oz* with the little wizard frantically bellowing orders to "pay no attention to the man behind the curtain!"

The fear was well placed. Had the game been played, ESPN,

national, and Florida media would have stuck their investigative noses behind the curtain and revealed the truth about what went on back there, and who was really pulling the levers of power. Unfortunately, it had come out that the ACC might sue Auburn for lost television revenue and other ACC schools might also drop their own series with the Tigers, and the Auburn faithful had begun closing ranks. For some, it had become an issue of SEC vs. ACC. For others, the feelings toward FSU had hardened: "We'll do what we want, whether FSU likes it or not!"; "Auburn will more than make up the half-million dollars with a home game against Appalachian State. ... It will hurt FSU more than it will hurt Auburn."

Yes, that was the truth. It would hurt FSU more than it would hurt Auburn. We needed to draw big-time football powers to Doak Campbell Stadium. We wanted Auburn to bring their tradition and their thousands of football-passionate fans to Tallahassee. The BCS rankings and playing on national television may not have been as pressing an issue at Auburn in those days, but it was of major concern to the Seminoles. FSU's national reputation as a football power hinged on playing high-stakes television games against teams like Florida and Miami, and, yes, even Auburn. Auburn enjoyed a reputation as a first-class Division I football powerhouse.

Florida State was absolutely the one most hurt by this, which made even more despicable the way in which the game was cancelled. After the contract with Appalachian State was signed, notice was faxed to Dave Hart's office at six thirty in the evening on a Friday in mid-February, with the game scheduled to be played on September 2. This was plenty of time to pick up a Division II replacement, but no time to replace a national television game with an attractive Division I opponent.

We had enjoyed a long and beneficial relationship with Auburn. Auburn, along with Miami, was one of the early big powers willing to schedule the fledgling Seminoles. Burt Reynolds had a 60-yard run against Auburn in 1954. He was tackled at the goal line by a fellow who would become the governor of Alabama, Fob James. They beat us more often than not in the early days, but we had gotten the upper hand in recent years. Pat Dye abruptly dropped the series in 1991. His action was controversial then, and many suspected his fingerprints were visible on this episode too.

For the previous three years, Tallahassee had hosted the Bowden Cup Classic, initiated by the local Auburn Alumni Club to raise money for both schools. Bobby Bowden and Terry Bowden led their respective alumni groups in a golf tournament; half the field of 144 were wearing garnet and gold, while the other half were in navy and burnt orange. There was always much camaraderie and laughter at the post-tournament luncheon. We shared much, including a chip-on-the-shoulder attitude about being the little brother school in our respective states.

Auburn was an excellent and proud institution, supported by tens of thousands and many generations of loyal alumni. These were fine people. Auburn University would be better served by choosing at random several of the loyal Auburn men and Auburn women who revered the integrity of the school and put them in charge of the program that existed, replacing any weaklings and scoundrels who appeared to be hiding behind someone else's money.[*]

---

[*] Much of this chapter's material was initially published in the *Report to Boosters* (February 1999).

The 1999 Bobby Bowden Tour

M uch was expected of the Seminoles going into the 1999 season. Record crowds of excited garnet-and-gold-clad fans packed into every venue as we toured the Seminole clubs in the spring. It was as if the Seminole football program had spent a decade preparing to get to this season. And because all the years since 1986 had been magical, an even more powerful spell of magic was now expected.

More than a thousand Seminoles whooped and pounded and bellowed loud enough to bring the house down as Clearwater welcomed the Bobby Bowden Tour on May 14, 1999. This had been an especially robust spring as Coach Bowden and the rest of the road show meandered through Florida and Georgia, plus a few more exotic points of interest, bringing happiness to the hearts of good Noles everywhere.

On the threshold of his twenty-fourth season, our head coach was lean, tanned, rested, energetic, and about to sign another five-year contract. His seventy-four returning players probably comprised the largest force of veterans among all Division I teams. And the fastest too. The average 40-yard dash time for this team—from scatbacks to interior linemen—was a stunning 4.5 seconds. Chris was back; Mario came back. Corey was back, as was Pete. The kicker and punter were also back. *Fifteen* offensive linemen returned, along with probably the best pair of defensive tackles in

America. A coaching staff composed of mere mortals would be scared to death.

When the vast Spanish Armada set out to conquer England in 1588, it constituted the grandest and most powerful assemblage of ships, guns, and men ever seen to that point in history. Everyone knew the only thing that could possibly save the Britons was an act of God. And, as it turned out, God arrived in the form of a hurricane at sea that sent most of the Spanish fleet to the bottom. We would have to check out the weather forecast between May of 1999 and New Orleans on January 3, 2000. Those ill winds tended to come up in a hurry and without warning.

There was a Miami brand of Hurricane—which was the most unpredictable kind—blowing into Tallahassee on October 9. Also, the action had been pretty stormy in Gainesville since 1993, and I doubted that we could expect clear sailing through the ACC either. In 1998, NC State played the iceberg to our *Titanic*, though our boat did manage to stay afloat after that collision far longer than the original.

No team had ever gone wire-to-wire No. 1 preseason to championship game. Tennessee, by all rights, should have been the first seed. I sort of hoped that they would get that No. 1 spot in the new season's first vote. It was my hope that it would take a little bit of pressure off what surely would be the highest expectations at Florida State in our football history.

Pressure did not appear at all on the face of Bobby Bowden during the spring. He was his usual happy, glib, ornery, and relaxed self. The adoring crowds seemed looser, larger, louder, and more delighted to just be surrounded by all that Seminole energy. Here is an incomplete collection of snapshots from the spring of 1999.

In Panama City, one of the audience members asked Coach about the upcoming game against his son Tommy, who was head coach at Clemson: "What are you going to do about game-plan security when you play Clemson?" After the laughter subsided,

Coach replied, "I'm not concerned. Ann likes spending money too much for me to lose that game."

Orlando had their unique Alumni Band playing for the crowd, and followed the tour's Celebration of Heroes theme by identifying and honoring a dozen Orlando-based "heroes" who had made exceptional contributions of time and leadership to Florida State. Of course, several tables of real Seminole Indians were not only honored guests but also sponsors of the event. The Seminole Tribe of Florida was one of the four major Gold Sponsors during that year.

A rare and valuable game ball, beautifully encased, was presented to the university by the Davis and DeAngelis families through the Seminole Club of Greater Orlando. The 1964 team ball was signed by members of that extraordinary and historically significant team, including then receivers coach, Bobby Bowden.

In Jacksonville, Coach Bowden commented on how pleased he was that Ann was able to attend. "Ann really wanted to come last year too," he said, "and she was all packed and ready to go … but I just couldn't remember everything." It was in Jacksonville that the front desk clerk asked me, "What are you going to do about your name, man? I heard all the Indians were up in arms and everyone like the Kansas City Chiefs were going to have to change." That was a day or so after an unfortunate remark by an FSU faculty member set howls off among the covens of the politically correct.

In Lake City, Coach told the old story about Tennessee coach General Bob Neyland. At a prayer breakfast, Neyland was asked, "If two equal football teams play each other and both teams pray and ask God for victory, who will God grant the victory to?" Neyland replied that he was unqualified to speculate upon the mind of God, but he guessed that God would probably favor the team that had the best pair of defensive tackles.

In Ft. Lauderdale, a Seminole woman in traditional dress escorted by Max Osceola gave the prebanquet blessing in the

Cherokee language, followed by the same message in English. She ended with, "And God bless Coach Bowden so he can win all our games." The following night in Palm Beach, the Reverend "Lucky" Arnold did the honors, saying, "Coach Bowden, I especially enjoying praying for you in the fall and prior to bowl games, but I'll still enjoy praying for you in the spring too."

The schedule was tight in Bradenton, and there was only about forty-five minutes to get showered and drive back to the club for the banquet. When Mike Bristol and I went to Coach's motel room to get him, the door cracked just a bit, and we could see that the star of the show was clad only in a pair of boxer shorts. No one spoke for a moment, and then he said, "You guys said this one is informal, right?"

Orange Park threw a surprise fiftieth wedding anniversary party for Bobby and Ann prior to the banquet. It was wonderfully orchestrated, culminating with the announcement and presentation of a fifty-thousand-dollar endowed scholarship in their names. Coach reminisced, saying that he and Ann had had a formal wedding: "Her daddy carried a white shotgun." By the way, don't get the impression that Ann was a martyr to all these one-liners. She seldom got the microphone, but she could give as good as she got, and maybe even better. Any club that had asked Ann to appear as a speaker knew that she might be the most entertaining one-woman show in the Seminole universe.

Panama City presented each of their four hundred banquet attendees with a gorgeous pair of handmade feathers, fastened with gold clips. Miami held their banquet at Joe Robbie Stadium. Mike Bristol said it was a tremendous show. There was talk during several of the social hours of asking Dave Hart to give Louisiana Tech an extra hundred thousand dollars to have them wear orange-and-blue uniforms and run Auburn's plays.

When Dave Hart, Coach Bowden, and I arrived at New York's LaGuardia Airport, we were to be met by a limo and taken to our function. We came down to the baggage area, and there was a dozen or so limo drivers all holding up signs with the names of the parties they were to pick up. I looked for Bowden, then for Hart, then for Barnes. Nothing. Finally, the last guy with a sign was holding one that said "Koch." He had been told by phone to go and pick up someone named "Koch Bowden." As it turned out, this guy was a great driver. We got into Manhattan about five in the evening, and our driver displayed a masterfully New Yorkesque combination of belligerence and insanity that marked him as a professional. We got where we were supposed to be exactly on time.

A new wrinkle during the 1999 year was the involvement of Gordon Sprague, the Houston financier who became the first individual to make a one-million-dollar gift to FSU's athletic program. One of Gordon's toys was a motor coach, a twenty-five ton, forty-seven-foot long, seven-figure, and custom-built rolling dreadnaught of the highway propelled by a pair of diesel engines that held 225 gallons of fuel. Gordon could drive from Jacksonville to California without stopping, and he had done so. It had an engine room. The main cabin featured marble floors with heat strips underneath, and it could seat ten for dinner. I am not making this up.

Gordon hosted a small band of us on a two-day swing to Ocala, Gainesville, and back to Tallahassee. Besides Coach Bowden, there was Mike Bristol and me, plus varsity club director Brian Wade, facilities director Bernie Waxman, and former FSU kicker Ryals Lee, who took photos.

Mike Bristol drove the regular tour van, which more or less played the role of a lifeboat. Bristol tried to follow right behind us but eventually fell back. "It was like trying to keep up with the Millennium Falcon," he groused. I told Gordon that if he ever got tired of the thing, he could knock the wheels off, subdivide it into condos, and make his money back.

Many things that make civilization worthwhile had improved

since the 1970s, but air travel was not one of them. In the 1970s, air travel meant big planes, decent food, and reasonably comfy accommodations. In 1999, however, coach-class air travel meant smaller planes, surly help, a wholly inadequate beverage service, and perhaps a plastic tray with a slice of raw onion and a tiny spray can of Cheez Whiz if you were lucky. I was not so lucky.

On the commercial flight from Atlanta to New York—a two-hour stretch that should have included lunch but did not—I had a first introduction to what was perkily described to us as "deli snacks." Herding down the long flexible tube into the aircraft like the cattle we so obviously were, we were instructed to pass by a small Dumpster, reach inside, and pick up a paper sack containing our "lunch." It featured a small bottle of warm water, a tiny foil cup of something congealed and alleged to be dip, a small sack of some sort of exotic coconut shell husk chips, and a clear bag of "carrot product," which, I assumed, was powdered carrot parts that were pressed and molded into tiny carrot replicas. All this was accompanied by something that may have been an apple.

Coach Bowden, who was in line in front of me, picked up his bag and started searching inside for a sandwich. I picked up mine and shuffled along, when suddenly some loud voice from behind us in the terminal shouted out, "Coach Bowden! Coach Bowden!" One of the flight attendants ran down the gangway to grab his arm. "Oh, you don't have to take one of those," she cooed. "You're first class—you get full meal service!"

He put back his bag, and then looked at me holding mine. "Well," I said, "it must be nice to be important."

He grinned, leaned forward, and whispered, "Bow down."*

---

* Much of this chapter's material was initially published in the *Report to Boosters* (May 1999).

What Sort of Man
Would Replace Bobby Bowden?

Bobby Bowden was seventy years old in the fall of 1999. After twenty years as head coach of the Seminoles, he was at the peak of his powers as a leader and a legend. The majority of people who had graduated from Florida State received their degrees during Bowden's tenure, and his personality was deeply impressed upon students and alumni alike. Although it was not spoken of publicly, the popular thinking was that Bobby Bowden would retire any day. Few Seminole fans had ever known anyone else at the helm.

As the summer soaked Tallahassee, there was little to report, for which we were all grateful. Weinke was healthy, Bobby was happy, and the press was occupied with other folks. All was well. *Excite Sports* was running their list of the "Top Heisman Hopefuls," of which three of the top 12 were Seminoles: Peter Warrick was No. 1, Chris Weinke was No. 7, and Travis Minor was No. 12. And some thought expectations for the offense weren't unreasonable in the 1999 season.

I was churning through the Associated Press wires when two seemingly unrelated stories appeared side by side. One headline read: "Knight Escapes Charges, But Still Blasts System," and the second was, "A Football Player's Sacrifice Gets Screen Treatment."

The sacrifice story concerned our own Daniel Huffman, the fellow who was honored in 1996 with the inaugural spirit award given by ESPN during their collegiate awards show in Orlando, and was pretty much offered a scholarship on the spot by our coach. Huffman was a promising football prospect from Rossville, Illinois, who gave up his healthy kidney—and any hope of playing college ball—to save his grandmother's life. He announced from the podium that his favorite team had always been the Florida State Seminoles.

They filmed *A Gift of Love: The Daniel Huffman Story* in Toronto in the summer of '99, to be shown on Showtime Cable Network later in the fall. It was released in theaters as well. According to the AP article, Bobby Bowden played himself in the movie. Coach told the AP writer that he almost turned down the role so he could enjoy a vacation with his family, "but decided he owed it to Huffman and to the school to participate."

One of the most endearing of Bowden's traits had been his indifference to ego. How many times had he taken on some burden—additional speaking engagements, carting an extra microphone around, allowing intrusive cameras to follow him, out-of-the-way appearances—just to give an extra publicity boost to Florida State? Surely his willingness to do these things had helped build the program's reputation. And it didn't hurt recruiting when he appeared as a national role model on *Evening Shade*. Folks who knew him could confirm that he did these things because he thought he should do them as the leader of the program.

He had never sought recognition or praise for himself. In fact, given a choice of ways to spend his time, he would likely rather wear his coaching hat and shorts, Oakley shades, a whistle around his neck, and spend the afternoon yelling at large, fast young men. Either that, or driving a tank across some World War II European battlefield. But the day would come when we would have to select the next fellow to wear that hat and whistle.

Which brings me back to that second headline, the story about Indiana basketball coach Bobby Knight. I didn't really follow Knight's career; I picked up some odds and ends here and there. I think it was in the '70s when Knight was arrested in Puerto Rico for punching a cop who had the temerity to question Knight's use of a practice facility for the US Olympic Team. Sometime in the 1990s, I remember seeing pictures in *Sports Illustrated* of Knight flinging courtside chairs across the floor at an Indiana basketball game. In 1998, or maybe it was 1997, apparently there was a flap about Knight's supposed elbowing or slapping of one of his players on the bench during a game.

This latest story had to do with a "restaurant confrontation" that took place on June 7: "[Knight] had been accused of making a racist remark and choking a customer in the parking lot ... but the prosecutor said Knight appeared to have been provoked." Authorities in Ellettsville, just outside IU's Bloomington campus, filed no charges, but Knight held a press conference anyway, blasting all in sight, especially the Monroe County prosecutor's office. "I'd refer to this whole thing as a real Mickey Mouse operation," said Knight, "but that would be an insult to Mickey Mouse."

Knight had been at Indiana about the same length of time Bowden had been at Florida State. The question before us was: What do we really want in a high-profile coach, and what are we willing to tolerate? Players generally do not take on the personality of their coach. The truth is that no two fellows were more dissimilar in their personalities than Bowden and Steve Spurrier, yet for the most part if one put Seminole players and Gator players together in a room, there would be little difference to see.

The fans, though, were different. If a coach was popular enough and was there long enough, the fan base and, by extension, the school would begin to take on that distinctive personality. Bryant at Alabama not only affected Tide fans but a whole generation of coaches who tried to emulate the Bear's style. It was hard to imagine Tom Osborne coaching at Oklahoma, or Barry Switzer at Nebraska. Paterno fit Penn State, but after so many years and so much success one had to ask whether the image of the school reflected the man, or was the man shaped by his experience with the Nittany Lion supporters?

Why did the solid Midwestern folk in Indiana tolerate Bobby Knight? The answer was that he was established, and he won. My guess was that pro-Hoosier partisans who wrote sympathetic pieces about Knight headline them with veiled apologies like, "The Man Behind the Image," or "The Other Side of Bobby Knight," or "The Bobby Knight No One Knows." It's as if they feel Knight needed explaining.

If Bobby Bowden was Michael Jordan, then Bobby Knight was Latrell Sprewell. No question that both Jordan and Sprewell were enormously talented men, but only one was of exemplary character. Just as Sprewell was praised for his physical ability, so Knight was adored by tens of thousands of Hoosier fans for his loyalty to IU. They praised his long and accomplished tenure, and his role in keeping Indiana among the nation's elite basketball programs.

When the time came for us to choose a new coach, what sort of man would we look for, would we accept? Why, another Bobby Bowden, of course. But there would not be another Bobby Bowden. In fact, there could not be another Bear Bryant, or Vince Lombardi, or John Wooden, or Dean Smith. One of the characteristics of great leaders is that each of them is unique. You may be able to replace them with someone just as good, but never with someone who is the same.

We wanted a coach who would win ten or more games a year, and do so with grace, sportsmanship, and good humor. We wanted a man like Bowden, who valued faith and family, as well as football. Would we settle for the football equivalent of a Knight? What if, after being spoiled by the dynasty, we suddenly fell to mere mortal status under a new coach—even though he was the finest, most congenial fellow we had ever seen? How much losing would we tolerate?

It was easy to be noble in the moment, but we were swimming in shark-infested waters, and thus far we hadn't been swallowed. Steve Spurrier and Butch Davis were young men and showed no signs of leaving Florida or Miami in 1999. Against a coach of lesser abilities, and against a weakened program, the vengeance of those two would be terrible to behold, much less to endure.

The coaching profession was full of nice guys who managed to find jobs even after their shortcomings became painfully obvious. There was one, a fellow whom I was told was as fine and decent a human being as walked the earth, who served as head football coach at several great southern universities. He was a role model in every way. He just simply could never produce a winner, or build any program to greatness. He turned out to be a very fine sports broadcaster.

On the other side are those who possessed the talent to lead, to build and to win. But they also had the ability to make one cringe when associated with one's school. Very often they ... well, they need explaining.

Clemson was a fine school with a proud tradition that had been deeply bruised over the previous decade. Before Tommy Bowden was hired, there was a serious movement to bring back Danny Ford. Bowden would prove to be a brilliant choice. Ford had never borne the burden of being a role model, and he had carried the reputation, deserved or not, of being a shady character. But the Clemson faithful knew one thing for certain: Ford was a winner who took the Tigers to a national championship. His teams owned the ACC crown until he left in the early 1990s.

People who are used to winning don't take losing well. And I have to agree with them about Ford's abilities. Tommy Bowden would possibly become the greatest Clemson coach ever, but Ford was a sure thing in the moment. Character aside, when one puts

Jordan or Sprewell in the game, then he or she knows what's going to happen. The great ones, with both the character and ability we want, were out there.

Television had made so much difference over the previous twenty years to our football program. For millions of Americans who were college football fans, Bobby Bowden *was* Florida State. It was ironic that Bowden's greatest legacy would lie in our ability to raise enough money while he was there to secure the future of FSU athletics. Because of him, we would be able to become like Notre Dame, where no one coach has had a larger identity than the university itself.

That would be a legacy befitting of Bowden. For nearly twenty-five years, we had taken some of our collective personality from his good humor, his sportsmanship, and his self-effacing generosity. What we might have become under another coach I cannot say. But I knew that like all fans, we yearned to follow a winner.

I had occasion to sit down with former FSU president Bernie Sliger and the talk turned to 1979—the undefeated season, the year we went to Miami for the magic of our first major bowl. We had no idea there would be a dynasty; we were just excited at the prospect of playing Louisiana State for the first time in legendary Death Valley. Playing LSU meant a step up in status for our young program.

I reminded Dr. Sliger of a conversation he and I had in a popular local restaurant that long-ago fall of 1979. We had both been enjoying our usual refreshments and Bernie became highly agitated over the fact that LSU was aggressively courting Bowden. Sliger had come to Florida State from LSU, so he knew all the political players, and it burned him that his friends in Baton Rouge were not only coming after his coach but they were throwing it in Bernie's face as well. "I made up my mind that I was going to keep Bowden here, whatever I had to do," Bernie reminisced. "But you have to be realistic, and I knew I had to have a backup plan just in case," he said.

He continued: "I started looking around, doing some research on my own, not telling anybody. I finally identified a coach out West, and I sort of lined that up so if the worst case happened I could move quickly to bring the other guy in," said Sliger while covering his sly grin with his drink. "He was at Oklahoma State at the time; the fellow's name was Jimmy Johnson."*

---

* Much of this chapter's material was initially published in the *Report to Boosters* (July 1999).

The Prophet

It is unlikely that your eyebrows will arch with surprise at news of the discovery that Albert Einstein's brain is not like yours and mine. I say *is* because apparently, for four-and-a-half decades since Einstein's death, the thing has been floating around various laboratories as an object of study. What has been discovered is that his brain is physically different from the average brain, not so much in size but in configuration. Einstein's brain has more … well, room to maneuver, more surface space for little electrical impulses to run and play.

It is understood that he was one of the most extraordinary intellects in human history, but it is important to also understand the nature of that intellect. He was no phenomenon with pure numbers. Einstein was fascinated all his life with mathematics, but it was never his great strength. As he developed his theories on the physical nature of the universe, he engaged friends and associates to help him with the skills needed to supply mathematical proofs.

When Einstein set about to produce a special theory of relativity, he isolated himself in a cabin and thought it through. What he did was analogous to laying all the facts out on a large table, staring at it for months until his brain finally came to comprehend the big picture. In fact, Einstein was all about the big picture. His genius was in his vision. He could look at the known facts and see a world unseen by anyone else until he revealed it.

All of this brings us roundabout to another fellow whose brain is still in his possession. He is a lawyer by trade, and a Seminole by his heart's blood. He does not wish me to publish his name, and I have never done so though I have enjoyed his company for at least two of the three decades he has been an active FSU alumnus and Booster. He too has a genius for seeing things that the rest of us do not see. He devours the minutia of college football in prodigious volumes, and then lays it out upon some sort of large-scale mental "table," pondering it until the big picture reveals itself to him.

As Einstein was candid about his shortcomings in mathematics, so the prophet harbors no illusions about his own abilities. He does not think he can coach; he does not try to call plays. He does not gamble. He does not consult. He does not give speeches. He does not have a radio show. He does not write a column. But he does write to me.

About once a month during football season, the mail brought a familiar law firm envelope bulging fat with a mass of lined yellow legal paper. The prophet, my whimsical title for him, scribbles furiously and not always clearly. As I read each letter for the first time, I underline untranslatable words with a red pen, and then go back and block-print what I think the word is based on the context. I suppose it's one of the affectations of genius. Einstein's penmanship never won any trophies either.

He often referred to himself in the third person, as the prophet. He was one of the least egotistical people I had known, so my guess was that he was just not comfortable filling his letters with the pronoun *I*. There was a natural humility behind his desire to be anonymous. He loved to talk football, especially Seminole football, with his friends and fellow Boosters, but if people knew of his power, his uncanny ability, to predict the outcome of specific games and seasons, then the atmosphere surrounding those conversations would change.

His appetite for details was voracious. I have never known or even heard of anyone else who read the ponderous *NCAA News* cover to cover every month. Yet he absorbed it all, and processed it through that unique brain of his. This is from a note sent July 3, 1997:

> Important prophet update just in time for the holiday. The prophet was held hostage by a thunderstorm at Barnes & Noble near my office. As has been documented, the prophet does not use such occasions to read best-sellers; rather, he studies the sports magazine racks for "inside" information from lesser-known publications about football that only show up in giant stores. This helps give the prophet his amazing edge.

He didn't hold gamblers' publications in particularly high regard and was delighted that day to uncover something called the "First Annual Preseason Gambling-On-College-Football Bible," which asserted that FSU would "make up for the Sugar Bowl mess last January because Rock Preston was still mad ... and should carry the Seminoles to the 1997 title." Preston, of course, had long since departed.

That gives you a good sense of all his letters: light-hearted and whimsical with a good measure of engaging self-parody. He has always taken his gift seriously, but never himself.

In a letter dated September 3, 1996, the prophet made these predictions: "FSU will score fewer than 50 points per game in its first six games, part of a new 'friendly offense' that runs more and scores less. FSU will give up a total of fewer than 30 points in its first two games. If FSU scores more than 40 points in each of the first two games, and gives up fewer than 15 points to each, then we will go 11–0. If either Duke or NC State score more than 25 points, then our final record will be 9–2."

The result? Though undefeated, FSU did not score 50 points until the ninth game of the season. The Seminoles gave up a total of only 23 points in the first two games (including fewer than 15 points to each opponent), while scoring 44 and 38 points, respectively. As predicted, the Noles went 11–0, including a spectacular win over the Gators at the season's end.

But wait—there's more. In his September 3 letter, the prophet predicted actual game scores for the '96 season. Our home opener against Duke ended up 44–7; the prophet had predicted 44–10. And his prediction of the final UF score three months later was 30–27. The final, as you may recall, was 24–21. There was a frantic, scribbled update on September 12 with short takes in many directions. "The game that truly holds the crystal ball for FSU's season is North Carolina, not Miami. The handwriting will be on the wall, good or bad, after four quarters with UNC. Winner will have less than 35 points." FSU shut out UNC 13–0.

And of the Florida-Tennessee match, he wrote: "There is too much emotion for the prophet to call the UF-UT winner. The better team appears to be Florida, but Florida is extremely overconfident, which could explode either way. The prophet will guarantee that the winner will have at least 35 points, and the loser at least 25." Florida beat Tennessee, 35–29.

The prophet isn't always right, which seems to cause him no great distress, especially if his beloved Seminoles turn out to be the beneficiary. When he's right, however, he is right to the point of causing goose bumps to chase up your arms. For example, on August 8, 1997, he wrote to predict a 28–20 opener against Southern Cal (the final was 14–7). "FSU wins at North Carolina, guaranteed," he said. "If we lose in the conference, it will be at Clemson (because it's early) or at Virginia (due to injuries)." You may recall the closeness of the Clemson game, saved by the heroics of a young Peter Warrick.

He also predicted FSU would beat the 32-point spread vs. Maryland by the end of the third quarter (final score was 50–7). But here's one he missed: "Guaranteed: the national championship winner or runner-up will have played in and won either the FSU-Miami game or the UF-Tennessee game. All four are excellent, but remember, defense wins championships." Yes, Nebraska remembered it too. Defense was why they won the 1997 national title. Michigan finished No. 2, while FSU finished No. 3.

In 1998, mountains of details indecipherable to the rest of us swirled like galaxies, but the prophet's vision was clear. Prior to the Florida game, he wrote: "[I] feel pretty good about this. Florida is overconfident, and Outzen is unknown to them. Our home-field advantage will be considerable for a team with its back to the wall. Coach Bowden will take a greater-than-usual role in the game plan and play calling. At a critical point in the game, look for a patented Bowden rooskie. It won't be a trick play, just the unexpected play at exactly the right time." His words rang loud as Peter Warrick lofted the loveliest pass to Ron Dugans for a 20–12 Seminole lead in the fourth quarter.

About the Fiesta Bowl he was less sanguine. "Florida didn't know about Outzen," he wrote, "but now Tennessee has the film. We are vulnerable to the long ball, though we do make opponents pay for it. It's a mistake to underestimate Tennessee. They wouldn't be in this game if they weren't good as well as lucky. The prophet sees a close game, with the final score separated by less than a touchdown. Call it 24–17 either way." Call it 23–16.

Here are excerpts from two letters I received from him, the first dated August 9, 1999, and second dated September 2. He began by rambling along for a full page about a dream he had about an FSU-Tennessee rematch, and speculated it was because he fell asleep the night before watching football:

The point of all this is the gross uncertainty of who will play and who will win, which seems to escape the media (and many fans). Yes, on paper we are better than all eleven opponents. However, we have been favored in nearly every game for the last five years and usually lose one or two games despite it. We were favored in all twelve games last year. We lost two and nearly lost to Texas A&M and Florida. The reason? Not complacency, and not lack of togetherness. The reason is those were excellent teams who also wanted to win and gave it an effort. Ask NC State. We couldn't stop Torry Holt and now he's the No. 5 first-round draft pick. Despite that we would still have won at NC State if it had been anything other than Weinke's first away game as a new player—and we still win if he only throws three interceptions instead of six.

Great teams lose to lesser teams every week. When it happens to us (rarely), everyone goes ballistic with finger pointing, which is not smart. We will go 11–0 in 1999 if Chris Weinke is still the starter (healthy) by the end of the season *and* assuming Janikowski is having a good year. At least two games will come down to his kicks.

This is from the letter dated September 2:

The *key game* for us is Georgia Tech. Our offense will set-tle in, good or bad, against Tech. If we can't run the ball (pound it for first downs or to get out of the shadow of our goal line) against Tech we are in trouble. Tech will be the third- or fourth-best defense we play. Particularly with Weinke's lack of mobility [and possible injury] we really need a good running game. Marcus Outzen can run, but is not our best passer.

If we beat Tech by more than 21 points, and are able to rush for 200 yards, then we'll know the Louisiana Tech first half was a fluke and not a good barometer. Georgia Tech is a good team. We will win, and we will know after we play just how great we really are.

The outcome was 41–35 Seminoles, and we ran for only 182 yards.

The first version of Einstein's theory of relativity initially appeared under the title, "On the Electrodynamics of Moving Bodies." The prophet's genius was also expressed through predictions on the dynamics of moving bodies. Colliding bodies, to be more precise. I was anxious to see what was in the next envelope he sent to me.*

---

* Much of this chapter's material was initially published in the *Report to Boosters* (September 1999).

Florida State to Leave the ACC?

A fter eight years of competition, Florida State was not just one of the league's marquis teams; it was the only marquis team in the ACC. The real danger to Florida State was the possibility that the SEC would pick up Miami and cut the Seminoles out of recruiting and media exposure south of the I-10. Our survival as a football school depended on the ACC becoming a more substantial football conference with the attendant leverage over bowls and media contracts. Expansion of the ACC was vital to the continued prosperity of Seminole football.

Did you know that FSU was thinking about leaving the ACC? If you lived in Atlanta or anywhere south of Atlanta, then you likely had no idea what I'm talking about. But if you lived in the Carolinas, or in Virginia or Maryland, then you were reading little else in the sports pages of the summer newspapers of 1999.

The general subject—ACC expansion and all the various real or imagined consequences of the league's decisions—was a visceral issue among the conference faithful north of Atlanta. Conversely, with the exception of the *Miami Herald*, there had been virtually no mention of any conflict or potential departures in the major Florida or Georgia dailies.

While the arguments raged back and forth among dueling sports columnists, and while Florida State had been alternately analyzed, praised, and damned on the sports message boards across the ACC, most of the Seminoles had been strolling naively through the pleasant fields of late summer concerned with little more than whether or not Weinke's neck was sore.

This was most evident in two back-to-back visits to Seminole clubs in August of 1999. I flew from Orlando to speak to the Seminole club in Columbia, South Carolina, at their annual season kickoff meeting. These boisterous, exuberant Seminoles were conversant with the issue. There was no shortage of opinions on whether the ACC should expand by one or two or three teams, and what steps FSU should take if the ACC declined to enhance its roster of "football schools." There was even a corner of enthusiasts lobbying for the inclusion of the universities of Central Florida and South Florida.

Two days later I was back speaking at the season kickoff of the Seminole Club of Greater Orlando. Most of them had heard stray bits of rumors about the possibility of Miami joining the conference, but they were absolutely stunned at news of the many ACC insiders and writers who seemed to believe that Florida State's continued membership would be tied to the league's eventual decision to expand, or to stand pat.

Why we joined the Atlantic Coast Conference in 1991 instead of the Southeastern Conference is a story for another day. It is a good story, possibly even better than what you've heard. There were many factors at play then, and on balance perhaps Florida State made the right decision at the time. In 1991, we said, "We'll know in five years if we made the right decision." The correct number of years appeared to be closer to ten.

Seminole fans in overwhelming numbers had expressed their support and approval for continued membership in the ACC. The Seminole Boosters organization surveyed as many of the seventeen thousand Boosters as possible by mail, and then followed up with a scientific sampling of selected telephone interviews. Opinions were solicited on an extensive list of issues, including favorite sports, parking, game-day amenities, ticket policies, and the general direction of the athletic program. Questions on the issue of membership in the ACC routinely drew approval numbers in the mid-90 percent range.

The ACC was a collegiate league. There were a minimum of rules and an emphasis on cooperation. Analysis of the ACC usually churned up many words that Florida State fans liked to hear. Those words included "class," "integrity," "sophisticated," "gracious," "sportsmanship," "tradition," and "stability." The debate flowed from the fact that "forward-thinking" and "progressive" were not often found emblazoned on the ACC mantle.

The ACC in 1999 was much as it was when it was founded, in the sense that it was a North Carolina–centered collection of schools with similar athletic interests, academic standards, and cultural constants. South Carolina left the league in 1970; Georgia Tech was a very good replacement that was added in 1978. Please understand that this was not a bad thing. The ACC was composed of some of the finest public and private universities in America, and we Seminoles wanted to be accepted in that club.

The problem was in an excruciatingly difficult conundrum: We wanted to be embraced by the ACC, but at the same time we wanted them to be more like us.

I had long suspected that the ACC viewed Florida State in much the same way that the banker, Mr. Drysdale, viewed the Clampett family. He didn't really like having them in the neighborhood, but oh my, they certainly brought a lot to the table. Extraordinary measures were undertaken to keep them happy. Jethro wanted to be a detective? Granny wanted to sell her possum-oil in Beverly Hills? No problem—we'll take care of it.

The critical player seemed to be Miami. Few ACC schools, if any at all, had experience playing Miami, which probably worked in favor of those of us who desperately wanted the Hurricanes in the conference. Those ACC pundits who knew Miami saw them as a sort of psychotic version of the Clampetts. Instead of Buddy Ebsen as Uncle Jed, imagine Jack Palance as Jed and Jack Nicholson as Jethro. That was the Hurricanes. ACC football fans who already didn't relish visits to Tallahassee had no idea what delights awaited them in the Orange Bowl.

Miami was an ideal candidate for expansion. It was a generously endowed, private university in the prime media market of a football-crazed state, and they were consistently one of the nation's leading football powers. Miami also offered the attraction of actually being on the Atlantic Coast.

As the ACC stood in 1999, Florida State was the only consistent national championship contender. Georgia Tech was strong in the hunt, and Clemson was on the verge of a fast-track return to glory, but Miami was there during that time. The addition of Miami would give instant credibility to the ACC as a football league. If the SEC was No. 1 in football and No. 2 in basketball, then the ACC could overnight become No. 1 in basketball and No. 2 in football with no more exertion than the offer of a pledge pin to the Hurricanes.

It was all so clear, but as one journeyed north of Atlanta, the reasoning became more clouded. I had a thick file crammed with articles and columns from that region over the previous four months, July through September 1999, devoted to the passions of this issue. Depending on how much of the analysis you believed, and which side you favored, the thinking seemed to be that Florida State, Georgia Tech, and Clemson were leading the charge for expansion. Duke, Wake Forest, and Maryland, it was speculated, were united in opposing any dilution of the "basketball infrastructure" that would result from the addition of a new member or members. The Tar Heels, Wolfpack, and Cavaliers were fence-sitters.

The elements were complex. As our athletic department derived most of its support and funding from football, so a majority number of ACC programs derived most of their support and funding from basketball. There was a tradition of all-league schools playing each other twice in the regular season. The addition of more schools could reduce the number of valuable seats available at the ACC Tournament, and the regular-season basketball schedule would have to be reconfigured. There was a cultural comfort level ingrained that certain member schools viewed any change with barely concealed horror.

On the other side of the argument was the deep concern about being left behind in the uncertain and unforgiving world of conference realignments and lucrative network television contacts. The ACC could have seen one or two more of its teams improve to the BCS-bowl level. Certainly a staggering amount of money was being spent across the league with that end in mind.

But what if it didn't happen? What if the ACC didn't bring in any proven football powers, and the remaining schools failed to realize their potential? How would Florida State fare in a post-Bobby Bowden arena where our conference was viewed by recruits and television networks as a one-trick pony?

Florida State made no threats to withdraw, though our own Dave Hart said that expansion talks, conducted in private, had been "brutally frank." There had been a great deal of speculation in the press, however, as to the consequences of a conclusive vote on expansion. Scenarios had been floated around, wherein FSU, Clemson, and Georgia Tech would join Syracuse, Miami, and perhaps Boston College and others (East Carolina? Virginia Tech?) in forming a new football-friendly league that would in turn issue invitations to some remaining ACC members. North Carolina, NC State, and Virginia could decide which way they wanted to turn.

It was all speculation, of course, and no knew how much of it was on the mark and how much was wide right. One of the great strengths of the ACC was the fact that the member institutions actually got along with each other quite well, and the conference leadership was intelligent and respectful of the valued traditions of the conference and of the individual schools. There weren't many Seminoles calling for FSU to leave the league. But for each of the few who did, there were corresponding souls in the rest of the ACC who shouted good riddance.

The popular www.ACC.com website offered a fan survey the last week in September 1999, with the question posed: "Should FSU be Kicked Out of the ACC?" It was all good-natured fun, of course. The choices, in addition to simply kicking FSU out, included "No, Keep Them," and "Make Them Play On One Leg." Other entries specified that the Noles play blindfolded, play with only six men, and/or give up a 25-point handicap. The winner, with 36 percent of the nearly thousand votes cast, was to make us play on one leg. A solid 25 percent or so voted to keep FSU under all circumstances. But 11 percent voted to kick us out. And how many of those didn't intend their vote to be taken seriously I cannot say.

Another creation that nearly everyone assumed was not to be taken seriously was sportswriter Ken Burger's September 26 column in the *Charleston Post & Courier*. His column, titled "It's Time for the Seminoles to Leave the ACC," was a release of frustration at FSU's relentless dominance of what probably used to be a fun place to play football.

Burger's premise was that it was wrong to invite FSU into the conference in the first place. "As FSU rolls toward its eighth straight ACC championship, it is painfully obvious that the league pays a big price week in and week out for the privilege. It is clear that eight years into this marriage there is substantial evidence to charge spousal abuse."

Burger said it was embarrassing to endure FSU's routine pummeling of "the more helpless ACC teams," and likened it to watching the clubbing of baby seals. "So the answer for FSU is to move on to a bigger and better league, like the SEC, or the NFC East."

Burger's writing was tongue-in-cheek, I was pretty sure. But the truth was that the ACC leadership valued FSU's contributions, and FSU's fans and leaders valued our association with the ACC. It was also true that there was an undercurrent of unease fueled by the issue of conference expansion. And that issue would have to be dealt with conclusively at some not-too-distant point.

There was a storm out at sea, and most of our fans were completely unaware as they strolled along our own calm and sun-bathed shores. While it would probably play out before it reached us, there was a remote chance it could sweep us away. But at the moment, we were pleased to stand on the beach and enjoy the spectacular garnet-and-gold sunrise.*

---

* Much of this chapter's material was initially published in the *Report to Boosters* (October 1999).

The Peter Warrick Episode

Some predictors ranked Peter Warrick as the No. 1 candidate for the 1999 Heisman Trophy. One publication mentioned only Pete's name among candidates for the 1999 Biletnikoff Award, and listed it three times for emphasis. Then Pete and a teammate were offered an illegal discount on clothing by a store clerk. He was contacted by the authorities and asked to come down to give a statement. But, of course, the clerk was never the target.

When young American infantry soldiers piled off the plane at Tan Son Nut in the summer of 1969, they were given helmets, rifles, and two pieces of advice: "Don't shoot your friends," and "Don't shoot yourself." That seemingly mundane advice turned out to be wisdom that was most profound.

We did such a wonderful job at FSU with our life skills and leadership programs for our student-athletes, but I had begun to believe that when young stars arrived on campus, we should issue them their helmets, footballs, and two pieces of advice: "Get a lawyer," and "Shut up." If Pete Warrick had done those two things—or just either one of them—this sad episode would not have played out as it did.

Pete was much like you and I in that he was young and foolish. But he was decidedly unlike us in that he was arguably the most nationally prominent undergraduate figure in the country's most high-profile college football program. A famous athlete in the country's winningest program is a target. If he behaved badly, then he would make himself more vulnerable to those who would work ferociously to do him harm. They were motivated by a menu of emotions: jealousy, partisanship, boredom, frustration, ego, or sanctimony. And we could throw in racism too.

What Pete did was steal. There is nothing gained by sugar-coating it. It wasn't "poor judgment." Poor judgment is choosing to wear brown shoes with a tuxedo. But neither was it thuggery. Thuggery is when a fellow takes advantage of momentary chaos to identify the location of an opponent's seventy-year-old football coach, turn, and ask a trainer for a football, look back again to identify the target, leap up and fire the ball at the coach's head, then slink back into the background.

The law is pretty routine on petty theft, and if Pete was not who he was, perhaps he would have been treated like anyone else. But being young and foolish, he said it wasn't like he killed the president. Being young and foolish, he didn't even see the need to get a lawyer till after he was charged with a crime. Like Pandora, young Peter Warrick didn't really believe that there were demons in the box, and if you opened the lid they would rush out into your world and wreak havoc.

I was struck with how bewildered Pete seemed by it all. It reminded me of the story from the Old West, supposedly true, about the fellow who was to be hanged for something or other. While he sat on his horse with the rope around his neck, each of the members of the posse took turns preaching and pontificating about the seriousness of the crime and the deleterious effects of such on society, the need for extreme measures to be taken and examples to be made. Duly impressed, when the condemned man was asked to speak his final words, he said, "Well, I don't know what effect this is going to have on others, but it sure is going to be a lesson to me."

This sure was going to be a lesson to Pete. A lesson about fame and celebrity and human nature and right and wrong. I wish it were true that the extraordinarily disproportionate price Pete paid and had to pay for his actions would be enough to bring all of it to an end when he left Florida State. The truth, however, was that FSU was paying a greater price for Pete's foolishness than he ever would, and the unhappy consequences would affect us for a long time to come.

I felt, and a lot of other fans felt the same way, that we owed something to Pete for electing to come back and help our team in a run for the national title. He did it for love of the college game and for his friends.

I was impressed by something else too. When it all blew up, Pete could easily have gone to ground and not come out until NFL draft day. Instead, he was willing to agree to spend days in jail in order to rejoin his team and make amends to his teammates. Pete wrote a letter that appeared in the *Tallahassee Democrat* on November 3, 1999. It was not a smooth, lawyer-drafted state-ment—it appeared to be a sincere apology from a contrite young man, a good kid who did a bad thing and got hammered for it.

As a university we acted honorably in the matter. In some cases, which this was one of them, the dishonorable thing to do would be to bow your head to the howls of the mob. Bobby Bowden was a man of his word, and when he told a young man's mother he would be honest and just with her son, he could be believed. The rules were pretty simple in Bowden's world, and they were fair. Randy Moss could confirm that. So could Laveranues Coles.

As long as we were among the most prominent national programs, there would be a flurry of headlines. There would be headlines about the victories, and headlines about the failures and embarrassments. We couldn't let the good headlines make us think that we were invincible, nor allow the negative to make us lose sight of the proud tradition we were building.

The graduation rate of FSU's football players was astonishingly high. When our average national football rankings were combined with our ranking based on graduation rate, FSU was routinely the national leader. It was almost impossible to have a high number of NFL draft picks and have the players persist to graduation, and yet Florida State accomplished that goal. Yes, both Warrick and Coles were on track for graduation.

Let's talk about President Sandy D'Alemberte's response. Sandy came to Westcott in 1993 unburdened by any illusions about the political landscape. As an institution, Florida State was far from united behind its new president. The Peter Warrick episode had brought all those discussions back into full blossom once again. Unfortunately, much of that discussion had taken place in public.

After six years of paying attention, and after having begun as a skeptic, my observation was that Sandy D'Alemberte was a brilliant man who, at the end of his tenure, would deserve to be confirmed as one of the greatest presidents in the history of our university.

Our athletics program had always been lucky, and we were fortunate to be led and supported by strong-minded, powerful individuals. Begin with Bobby Bowden, and then go to the politicians like T. K. Wetherell, Bo Johnson, Jim King, John Thrasher, and others who made funding possible for great, visionary projects. Add Andy Miller, who ran Seminole Boosters for twenty-five years. Athletics director Dave Hart quickly became the primary leadership force within the ACC, and even nationally.

The very public business over Peter Warrick's plea bargain and his reinstatement to the team may not have been exactly as it was portrayed. I think all parties would have rather that the story not played out in the media as it did. Sometimes events take on a life of their own, and even the most articulate and intelligent leaders are amazed by the ability of a situation to run amok. It is safe to say that some of what you may have read and heard was not as it seemed to be.

Was Sandy a Seminole? Being a Gator or a Seminole is a state of mind. There are Gators in Tallahassee who have degrees from Florida State. There are Seminoles—none finer or more loyal than Gene Deckerhoff—whose degrees are from Florida. Sandy was vintage Old Tallahassee. His mother graduated from FSCW, his grandfather from the West Florida Seminary. Sandy went to Leon, then to college in Tennessee. His law degree was from Florida, taken before FSU had a law school. The unprecedented architectural enhancement and academic advancements during Sandy's service as dean of FSU's Law School were all at his initiation.

When Sandy was a young lawyer and in the legislature in the 1960s, most of the state's movers and shakers had gone to Florida, and those were his pals. With the rise of more recent generations of leaders, the balance had tilted more sharply in FSU's favor. More than any other thing, Sandy was an advocate, an inclination he vigorously pursued at FSU. After he was named president, he could have bunkered in, surrounded himself with cronies, and protected his retirement. Instead, he took chances, caused trouble, bulldozed much-needed changes into place, and breathed life into a vision for our university that was stunning in its scope and imagination.

Was Sandy supportive of athletics? We could all read the scoreboard. As president, Sandy pragmatically understood the value to our university of a winning, first-class, nationally prominent athletic program, well funded, and well led with a great deal of enthusiasm. And Sandy was acutely aware that a great deal of money first entered the university through the locker room doors.

Despite what appeared to be public differences between Dave Hart and Sandy on the Warrick issue, my guess was that Sandy had much to do with keeping Dave at Florida State. Time would prove Sandy's success in keeping the forty-nine-year-old Hart away from Alabama to be in the same range of importance as Bernie Sliger's move to keep the forty-nine-year-old Bobby Bowden from going to LSU twenty before.

We rightly marveled at the accomplishments of Bobby Bowden. Consider Sandy's record as well: In six years, Sandy D'Alemberte directed the raising of hundreds of millions of dollars in private funds to bolster the university's academic strength; he reasserted the preeminence of our traditional architecture and launched a campaign to beautify the campus and return our core buildings to their proper use; he made fundraisers of the deans; he created mechanisms to enable us to take maximum advantage of the fact that we were in the shadow of the state capitol; he fostered a new sense of entrepreneurism on the part of aggressive faculty and staff, all of which served to enhance and increase the university's academic standing; and he embraced the big dreams, including the completion of the University Center complex, and was committed to seeing them become a reality.

He couldn't be strong-armed, and if you asked him a question he would tell you the truth. There were worse things a person could say about a fellow than that. Our university was better than it had ever been, and the goal of every set of leaders should be to make sure that statement remains true in every successive era.[*]

---

[*] Much of this chapter's material was initially published in the *Report to Boosters* (November 1999).

After Florida and
before the Sugar Bowl

The Seminoles' victory over Florida in Gainesville ensured an undefeated regular season and a national championship game in the Sugar Bowl. Fans sensed that this was a team not just of dynasty, but also of destiny. We lived in the best of times for college football. The state of Florida, during that time, was the center of the college football universe.

Our team was at the top of the college football pyramid, possessing the NCAA's longest home winning streak, as well as the longest home unbeaten streak, and winner of more games in a ten-year span than any other team in history. The football team's graduation rate consistently hovered around 70 percent, and we had more alumni on NFL rosters than any other college program. If we were not the team of the '90s, then we were riding in the same car with them, and it was a small car.

Graybeards counseled us to be thankful for our enemies, and in our case that enjoyed an application. If the head coach of our chief rival was a decent guy, possessed of any sense of grace and sportsmanship at all to complement his formidable talent, the distinction between the two opposing leaders would be much more difficult to draw. As it was, however, the other guy's 4–7–1 record against Bobby Bowden provided us with a dangerous enemy who

376 • THE BOWDEN DYNASTY

won often enough to be credible, but who lost in a manner to reassure that good will eventually triumph.

The latest episode the weekend before Thanksgiving was one in which the other guy showed himself to be, once again, as *Orlando Sentinel* columnist Larry Guest described, "more evil than genius." Chalk this win up to St. Bobby restoring order back to nature.

If ever there was a clarion call for all Seminoles to gather in one place at one time, surely the Sugar Bowl in New Orleans was it. If we were fortunate enough to win the Sugar Bowl, then every Seminole with the strength and the means to travel should flood the French Quarter in jubilant celebration of the wire-to-wire national championship, of the inauguration of Bobby Bowden's twenty-fifth season as head coach, and of the magnificent achievements of our Seminole football dynasty.

Tickets to the game were plentiful. We Seminole fans had not quite figured out yet what SEC fans had known for generations: most of the tickets to the game were located in New Orleans and were available through travel agencies and bowl sponsors who had ties to SEC schools. Since we would not be playing an SEC school for the title, those tickets were available to all of us.

Decent tickets were available through travel agents. Tickets bought from any of these sources would likely be better than anything available through official FSU channels. That was not FSU's fault, it was just the nature of the big bowl business during those days. Every time we had played an SEC team in the Sugar Bowl, thousands of our opponent's fans arrived in the Big Easy without tickets. They knew that tickets would be available, and the price dropped as game time approached.

Some came with no intention at all of finding tickets; they just wanted to be part of the atmosphere. They come and stove up in a bar with lots of other fans in the same colors and enjoy the game on television with the good food and refreshments from which

New Orleans was justly famous. Then, after the stadium emptied, everyone joined together in the Quarter to celebrate.

I hadn't yet talked to any Seminole who was having trouble finding rooms. Our game was on the night of January 4, which meant most of the New Year's crowd would be cleared out by then. Some Seminoles were staying over in Biloxi at one of the casino hotels, and then driving in for the game. Some were finding inexpensive rooms in Covington or Mandeville, which was just down the causeway from New Orleans.

Identifying our fellow Noles from all over America was why we encouraged everyone to wear their Seminoles gear. At the Fiesta Bowl, we were amazed at the outlandish extent Tennessee fans undertook to drape themselves in orange. Orange hats, shoes, shirts, pants, jackets, and even orange hair. You had to hand it to Tennessee—they arrived in massive waves, and one knew who exactly they were at any distance.

In Florida, one could find the Seminole logo on just about any color shirt. White was popular, but so was green, blue, and black, in addition to garnet. The same thing went for our hats. Florida was a fashionable, upscale state, and our fans tended to be people who manifested a sense of good taste in their personal sportswear. Unfortunately, this did not work to our advantage. When it was time to be brazen in our support for our Noles—and this was such a time—we found it necessary to allow our good taste in game-day attire to elude us, at least for this game.

In this last game against Florida in Gainesville, both teams put everything on the line. They fought with everything they had and never gave up. The difference was Chris Weinke's maturity and poise, and Corey Simon's awesome personal leadership on defense. To an objective viewer, it was obvious that the Seminoles had the better team, but as we knew all too well from painful experience, the better team was not necessarily the winner in this series of late.

The college football landscape was littered with the wreckage of lost dynasties. The twin dynasties of FSU and Florida were in full swing. Had we not beaten the Gators on their home field, it wouldn't have been much comfort to us to rationalize that our Seminoles were still considered to be among the nation's elite programs. But the truth was, had we lost, the dynasty would still have been intact even if somewhat bruised.

I don't know what the numbers were, but I imagined the national audience for this CBS broadcast was record-breaking, and in line with the numbers for other FSU-UF games in this series, which had become without a question the nation's premier college football rivalry. The numbers for our game vs. Clemson were also perhaps the highest of the year for ESPN, as most of America's college football fans tuned in to see the first father-son match, and Bobby's three-hundredth career victory.

This victory over the Gators, sublimely sweet as it was, didn't do any lasting damage to Florida's program and didn't carry ours to a higher level. We were both beyond that. The expectations on both sides became so elevated that the slightest flaw was cause for despair. Florida would probably beat Alabama for the SEC title, and go on to beat Michigan in the Orange Bowl. There was a time not too long before when either of these accomplishments would cause the Gator faithful to swoon with happiness. But two home losses in 1999 had cast a pall over their season, a fact that did not seem unreasonable to us since we were in the same boat and would feel the same way had something similar happened to us.

The FSU-UF game had become the unofficial semifinal round of the national championship playoff. What sustained us in the face of bitter loss, and what cautioned us in the time of euphoric victory, was the knowledge that we would both go at it all over again the following year, probably for the same stakes.

In the 1970s, the nation's two most glamorous programs played an annual prime time tilt that marked America's premier college football rivalry. Both programs were larger than life, lavishly funded, with famous players, legendary coaches, ten Heisman Trophy winners, and sixteen national championships between them.

It would have been hard in 1979 to imagine any scenario that would result in either of those two programs declining into mediocrity. Mediocre was too strong a word to describe Notre Dame and Southern California, but it needs to be noted that the week following our game against Florida, a 5–6 Southern Cal team played underdog at home to Louisiana Tech. Their signal achievement of 1999 was breaking an eight-year losing streak to crosstown rival UCLA. The same day a few miles up the California coast, Stanford beat Notre Dame, ensuring the Irish of a losing season.

It was not inevitable that FSU or Florida would decline into also-ran status. Michigan and Nebraska, and maybe a few others, were proof that excellence could be sustained. The question was: Were we willing to do what was necessary to provide for future success, and did we have the alumni/Booster strength to do it? The Seminole Boosters' job was to make sure the answer was yes. Our Seminoles were playing in their second straight national championship game, which was our fourth in seven years. We needed to enjoy this to the fullest possible extent.

Finally, it looked as if we would face either Nebraska or Virginia Tech in the title match. All things being equal, I would always rather play a team that didn't have experience playing in that intense of an arena. More than half our team played in the previous year's Fiesta Bowl, the first-ever official national championship game. I was not certain that Virginia Tech ever played in any game that carried the high-stakes nationally televised drama that we routinely faced in our annual clashes with Florida and Miami.

I thought our players would rather face Nebraska. Both the Seminoles and the Cornhuskers had been touted as the "Team of the '90s," and playing against each other in the final game of the decade would be a fun and gentlemanly way to settle the issue.

Nebraska had won against strong competition. Virginia Tech was undefeated, but they had not played any team ranked among the nation's top 15.

There was one difference between the two potential opponents that worried me. Nebraska definitely did not "have our number." I was concerned that Virginia Tech did. I could sense heads nodding who were there when we used to play the Hokies down to the wire in every contest, and we didn't always walk away the winner. We were 6–2 vs. Nebraska since 1980, with the last loss taking place in 1986. On the other hand, we faced Virginia Tech 28 times between 1955 and 1991, and though we held an 18–10 edge in the series, beating them was never easy.

Tech always seemed to have something to prove, and they always played like it. Nebraska had nothing to prove in 1999. Either way, both the Huskers and the Hokies enjoyed legions of classy supporters. We were in the title game, favored to win, and playing a program whose fans placed the same value on gracious good sportsmanship as did we.[*]

---

[*] Much of this chapter's material was initially published in the *Report to Boosters* (December 1999).

Sugar Bowl and
the Seminoles' Casino Cavalry

Virginia Tech alumni and fans began arriving in New Orleans soon after Christmas, most of them via four-day travel packages that would appeal to pilgrims making the long journey from the hills of central Virginia. Early on, the French Quarter was almost exclusively a Hokie arena. Ever looking for Seminoles but seeing few, the Hokies became bolder in their pronouncements, more and more adamant to each other about the victory to come. Fans and players alike predicted—no, they guaranteed—that the Seminoles would fall to the relentless Virginia Tech defense and the prodigious Michael Vick.

It is not uncharitable to note that New Orleans is a city that possesses high culture but is not known for it. New Orleans is a deliciously smarmy city, charmingly unwholesome, whose signature pursuit is the banishment of dull care with a bottomless fount of hedonism, gluttony, occultism, and joyful excess of all descriptions, all served up with guiltless pleasure in the French Quarter.

The Virginia Tech faithful, those clean, good-looking, well-dressed all-American folks with wide eyes and handheld video cameras sometimes seemed as out of place on Bourbon Street as a pair of polished wing tips on a Gulf Coast beach. As the Hokies strolled the French Quarter, the looks on their faces suggested that few of the surveyed delights were ever to be found back home in Pixley and Mount Pilot. Still they remained happy and confident, and increasingly certain that they would outnumber and out-cheer the Seminoles at the moment of truth. And then reality arrived dressed in war paint on the last day.

The night before the game, Hokies began to notice a sudden, marked increase in the number of garnet-and-gold-clad fans mingling with the maroon and orange. And as dawn rose over the Crescent City on the morning of January 4, tens of thousands of our Seminoles began flooding into town, choking Canal Street and Poydras, tipping the scales, looking for tickets, and disrupting what had been the peaceful isolation of Virginia Tech.

Cars sporting Seminole flags poured into town. Private planes landed in squadrons at Moisant International Airport, aircraft filled with Seminoles from Orlando, Palm Beach, Jacksonville, and everywhere.

At four in the afternoon, the casino cavalry arrived. Hokies stared in silence at the caravan of long stretch limousines curling down from I-10 toward the dome. They were gleaming navy blue Lincolns and sleek white ones, each packed with revelers from the gambling casinos and hotels in Biloxi, an hour and a half away. These Seminoles, who after five Sugar Bowls in ten years had elected to sample other diversions before making the game-day trip in to see their beloved Tribe, added an exclamation point to the dynasty.

At five o'clock the room set aside for our Seminole pep rally in the Hyatt Hotel was packed with four thousand rowdy fans. Another two thousand were kept away by the hotel because there was no room, and even larger crowds were jamming access to that floor.

The Sugar Bowl crowd of nearly eighty thousand was the largest ever to see a football game, college or professional, in the Superdome. Organizers and the *New Orleans Times-Picayune* estimated than an unprecedented 120,000 fans had gathered into the city for the game, many of them crowding into the arena next to the Superdome to watch the live broadcast on giant television screens.

Our Seminole fans were absolutely magnificent. A couple of journalists assigned to assess the crowd figured it this way: probably twenty thousand of the eighty thousand people in the dome were not with either team; they were just football fans there to enjoy the championship game. The remaining sixty thousand were split evenly between Tech and FSU. It would be hard to say which school had the advantage in numbers.

But evidently it was not hard to assess which school held the advantage in heartfelt enthusiasm and support for their cause. ABC Sports wrote that the Seminoles were late arrivals to the city, and Hokie fans had owned the Big Easy in the days leading up to the game. "But it was the Seminole faithful who were much more boisterous in the Superdome on Tuesday. From the time the players were introduced—peaking with Warrick's introduction—and culminating in their last Seminole 'war chant' once the game was in hand, Florida State fans registered higher on the crowd-o-meter throughout the night."

Who could ever forget the intoxicating euphoria, the chills up the back, when we were up by 10 at the end and our Seminole crowd began to chant "Pee-ter Waaarick, Pee-ter Waaarick"?

"Do you want me to finish it?" he asked in the huddle. "Yeah, Pete, finish 'em," was Jason Whitaker's response, all heads nodding as one. Weinke smiled. Then he dropped back and threw toward the end zone. The photo of that brilliant, juggling touchdown catch is immortalized on the cover of *Sports Illustrated*, framed by the simple headline: "Dazzling!"

After the game, all the threads of the story seemed to find their ends. The Seminole fans were gracious in victory, the Hokies classy in defeat. Virginia Tech defensive end Corey Moore, who had so many harsh things to say in the days leading up to the game, was seen stopping FSU players one at a time, congratulating them and asking them not to take any of it personally: "I was just trying to fire up my team—you guys are great." A despondent Michael Vick was stopped on his way out and embraced by a couple of our defensive linemen. They were seen speaking closely to him, holding his hand in theirs. Vick wiped his hand across his eyes and nodded his head, then was gone.

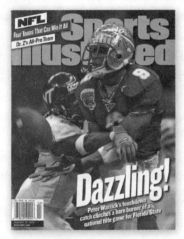

Receiver Peter Warrick makes the sensational touchdown catch to put the Seminoles up for good in the 1999 national championship game vs. Virginia Tech in the Sugar Bowl (*Sports Illustrated*, January 2000). Seminole defenders shut out Virginia Tech in the fourth quarter, and with less than eight minutes left, Peter Warrick entered the huddle and asked, "Do you want me to finish it?" The 43-yard touchdown pass from Chris Weinke put an exclamation point on the 46–29 final score.

Bobby Bowden was less spontaneous than his public image. He was a most genuine fellow, but his public persona was a creation over which he exercised considerable control. That seemed almost to dissolve on the stage where he and Peter Warrick stood behind trophies, surrounded by an adoring mix of players, fans, journalists, and Sugar Bowl officials. You could see the Sears representatives startle and then stop themselves when Bobby grabbed the thirty-thousand-dollar crystal football from its perch atop the trophy and began to toss it about. "Maybe I'll throw it to Pete, maybe I'll pass it behind my back like a basketball. Maybe I'll just stick it in my pocket and take it home."

The casino cavalry clustered happily outside along Poydras

and LaSalle streets. The stretch limousines had been circling around and around the dome like schools of glistening eels. One by one they loaded their cargos and pointed east back toward Biloxi, where the celebrations and the casinos would take no notice of the coming dawn.

By one thirty in the morning, thirty thousand people poured down Bourbon Street like a bright river through the French Quarter. Seminole and Hokies bought drinks for each other; each side wished the other well. It was not possible to walk. Movement was by osmosis—as the crowed flowed, so did you.

Joel Padgett and I fell away and walked down a side street to Jackson Square. It was dark and deserted except for a couple of police cars hidden under a tree. We saw a fellow light a cigarette, and could see his Gator jacket in the glow of the match. He offered us a wordless thumbs-up. Probably one of the locals, and a ghost of Sugar Bowls past, a dimly seen reminder that glory is as fragile as that glass football on the Sears Trophy. We moved back toward the light.

By two thirty, some of the players began to appear on Bourbon Street. Sebastian Janikowski was the first, wearing the black leather Sugar Bowl jacket and his white national champions hat. He stopped for each adoring fan, drinking in the full glory of his last night as a college football player for the best team in the land.

Varsity club president Monk Bonasorte was holding court with his entourage on the second-floor balcony of one of the more popular bars overlooking Bourbon. President Sandy D'Alemberte strolled below arm in arm with his wife, Patsy Palmer, shaking hands, exchanging congratulations. As the newly minted FSU president in 1993, he graciously insisted that Bernie Sliger lead the national championship parade through Tallahassee, sitting atop the flashy convertible while D'Alemberte himself was the unnoticed driver. This time, however, the honor would be his alone to savor.

Around three o'clock in the morning, Jerry Kutz, Mike

Tschirret, and dozens more of Bonasorte's crew on the balcony were feasting on jambalaya, crawfish, and étouffeé, and looking for the faces of friends in the throng below. Some of the faces had to be imagined. Don Fauls would be there somewhere, laughing. Vic Prinzi surely was just out of sight, in a small side shop buying some things. The late Godfrey Smith and Nan Mitchem were over there, where the crowd passed through a shadow. Tallahassee attorney John Miller, one of the original Golden Chiefs, lost his battle with cancer just the day before the game. "He's here with me," said Tschirret, lightly tapping his chest over the heart.

We were all there, all the Seminole souls who ever wanted this victory, for ourselves, for Bobby, for our school. Without a word, all glasses lifted up toward that sparkling diamond of a night in silent toast. And the lights on Bourbon Street leaped up into the stars.*

---

* Much of this chapter's material was initially published in the *Report to Boosters* (January 2000).

The Cool School

Florida State had been officially christened with a new title: We were now "The Cool School." The hip and slick *ESPN Magazine*—December issue, before the Sugar Bowl—featured a long, splashy story effusive in its praise of all things Seminole. "The Hawks, The Chop, The Spear ... Hey, Tallahassee's the Place," trumpeted the cool school sub-headline.

Never mind that most of our fans didn't readily grasp the "Hawk" reference, or that "The Chop" was what the Braves did (we did the chant). The fact was that ESPN had decorated Florida State's claim to the College Football Team of the Decade title with a delicious exclamation point. Weeks before FSU's dynasty was further enhanced with another spectacular, razzle-dazzle national championship, ESPN tagged the Seminoles as college football's reigning glamour program.

The writer, Gene Wojciechowski, had a keen eye and a flair for the colorful turn of phrase. He described the relentless flood of bright lights that recorded and broadcasted every aspect of FSU's program in this way: "The Noles are college football's Truman Show: 44 print, TV and radio outlets enter them with regularity. 'Like I told our kids before the season: If you've got talent, they'll see it,' says Bowden. 'If you don't make All-America, that's your fault. Don't complain.'"

The Seminoles averaged six nationally televised games a

season. "The players understand," he said. "Television exposure, the rings, the championship and the possibility of an NFL future are what draw them to Tallahassee."

Ah yes, the rings. The point was made that Coach Bowden didn't wear any of his championship rings. "He doesn't want his players to think he's satisfied." Being part of the coolest program in college football meant you must accept nothing less than excellence. "The message is always the same: don't bother coming to Florida State unless you're in it for the rings that matter. 'We want the ones that say No. 1,' says Bowden."

ESPN gave all credit to Bowden for FSU's remarkable dynasty run. While almost every other elite program had suffered occasional dips in the previous twenty years, they pointed out that FSU had only grown stronger. Wojciechowski saw the calm and enduring strength beneath Coach's disarming personality. Before assistant head coach Chuck Amato left, six of the nine assistant coaches had been there with Bowden for fourteen years or longer. And his ability to cross generations and identify with the sometimes baffling behavior of younger players was part of his genius. "Name another coach in any sport who could identify with a cast of characters as diverse as Deion Sanders, Dan Kendra, Warrick Dunn, and Chris Weinke."

ESPN pointed out the obvious: FSU was the reigning dynasty of college football.

> Here's what it's like inside. ... This is why Nick Maddox from North Carolina, one of the nation's most heavily recruited running backs, stiffed everyone to sign with Florida State. It's why David Warren, former *USA Today* Defensive Player of the Year, called FSU coaches to ask if they wanted him to visit. It's why former Parade All-American QB Jared Jones chose FSU even though he has to fly from his hometown of Walla Walla, Washington, to

Seattle, Salt Lake, St. Louis, Orlando and then Tallahassee just to get to school.

And it was not just the stars who came; it was also the stars who *wanted* to come. The magazine noted that Travis Minor deliberately wore Warrick Dunn's #28 jersey back in high school in Louisiana, that Tennessee QB Tee Martin used to add the letters "FSU" to his autographs back home as a high school star in Alabama, and that Penn State linebacker LaVar Arrington wore Seminole apparel to his high school workouts in Pittsburgh. "Coolness has its perks," ESPN said. "And no program is cooler than Florida State's."

ESPN's headline reference to "Hawks" was explained in a colorful sidebar called "Hawk Talk." Still confused? Hawks are the tomahawk emblems that covered the players' helmets. Well, they covered the better players' helmets. Each Sunday after a game, it seemed like the coaches evaluated and graded each player's performance, and assigned or deducted a given number of points from that score. The rules for Hawk distribution were complicated and strict. Receivers, for instance, must have 100-yard games and a 60 percent completion rate on at least five catches. Defenders needed 10 points for a hawk. "Nail the quarterback three times, get a Tomahawk plus change."

Peter Warrick had the most, even though he missed a couple of games. "But you don't have to play along with system," said the article. Apparently, freshman walk-on-turned-sensation Atrews Bell didn't wear Hawks at all. "He wants to stand out in his own way."

The dynasty grew slowly, accumulating honors and recognition like sheets of paper, each laid one upon the last, leisurely and carefully. Over the string of years, the stack of papers grew into a substantial pillar of achievement. It used to be that college football movies were only about Notre Dame. But Showtime's *Gift of Love: The Daniel Huffman Story* presented Bobby Bowden's Seminole football program as the wish fulfillment of every young football player in the nation. Even something not so immediately obvious, like star players who came back as seniors while their counterparts at other schools bolted early to the pros, added texture to the richness of this storied program.

We recited the details of the dynasty like a mantra. Thirteen consecutive years of top-4 finishes. Thirteen consecutive years of 10-win-or-more seasons. The nation's longest home winning streak. The nation's longest home unbeaten streak. FSU had not lost in Doak Campbell since 1991. We were crowned the "Team of the Decade" at the ESPY Awards. Two national championships, and one of them a No. 1 wire-to-wire national title that was unprecedented in all the history of college football.

Live broadcasts of ESPN's *GameDay* program had become a fixed icon of college football, and this year former Seminole quarterback Lee Corso capped his 12–0 record of predictions by picking the Tribe to win. The very first college *GameDay* broadcast from a campus was in South Bend for the epic FSU-Notre Dame match in 1993.

Since 1990, there had been only eight games matching the No. 1 team against the No. 2 team, including both regular season and postseason. Six of those eight games involved us, and 4 of the six were for national championships. The Team of the Decade went 3–3 in those No. 1 vs. No. 2 matchups. The great majority of college teams never get the chance to play in even one of those games in the history of their programs.

Like gravity bending a beam of light as it passes by a planet, so FSU shifted the standards by which the successes of college programs are measured. Before the Sugar Bowl, Virginia Tech fans speculated that the Hokies would win because to that point FSU's 1–2 record in national championship games in the 1990s was "not that good." Mercy! How good did you have to be to even *have* a record in national championship games in a single decade?

Every season, like every good story, has a beginning and an ending. It was hard to pin down the appropriate start and stop points for 1999. We could make the case to begin the story on May 29th with the appearance of Gary Shelton's article in the *St. Pete Times* headlined "Auburn Needs to Clean Up Act." You may have forgotten by now all about the way Auburn cancelled their season-opening game with FSU at the eleventh hour, but May of 2000 it was the next roiling, boiling controversy of college football.

Shelton, a Tiger by degree, cut loose with all barrels at once:

> So who is president of Auburn these days? Susan Lucci? Vince McMahon? Every day brings another scandal, another bloodletting where someone betrayed someone else in what has become college football's ugliest garden. The school is being run by a renegade booster named Bobby Lowder, who is not only out of control—he is dangerously close to the salary cap.

It was an important issue to us at the time because Auburn represented quality points in the BCS computer ratings, and our chance of playing for the national title could be lessened if we couldn't sign an opponent on short notice with enough lead in its pencil to impress the computers. As it turned out, Dave Hart pulled off a miracle and signed the Louisiana Tech Bulldogs who held an even higher computer power rating at the time than Auburn.

Where did the story of the season end then? Does a storyteller end it with Pete's flashy spectacle of a catch for the last touchdown? Does it end later that night on Bourbon Street amid the tumultuous shouts of the crowd? Sportswriter John Nogowski suggested in his column that the season might have achieved a neat ending on the way down the stadium elevator as the Sugar Bowl clock ran out. Riding the elevator down, tight ends coach/recruiting coordinator John Lilly said he was pondering the thrill of winning a championship in a way that no one had ever won before. Then another thought intruded, What would it take to come back and win it again?

The story might end with the National Championship Banquet on January 22, 2000. Thousands of Seminoles packed into the Civic Center, fighting for precious tickets, straining to see their FSU heroes accept their trophies from the Atlantic Coast Conference, from the Sugar Bowl, and from the friendly people at Sears. More than thirty-five thousand celebrants had tumbled into Doak Campbell Stadium earlier that afternoon to shout their joy to the world via the magic of the Internet and the Sunshine Network.

After Coach Bowden's address at the end of the banquet, and after the highlight films and the trophy presentations and the wonderfully praise-laden speech by ESPN announcer Mike Gottfried and the players' remarks, the crowd began to drift outward, happy, content, and lingering on every memory of this remarkable championship season.

Two sturdy Capitol officers in their stiff-brimmed trooper hats had stood guarding all the expensive hardware on display during the banquet. A crowd of probably two hundred people were pressing to the front, some to see the trophies, some to pursue the vain hope that they might somehow get Bobby Bowden's signature. I whispered to Coach, "These troopers can whisk you out the back right now. You can go straight to your car and head home."

Coach thought about it for a moment. He looked at the crowd. There seemed to be a lot of older people, lots of young kids, and clusters of young parents with babies. They looked in turn at all the trophies, and then at Bowden as if he were the greatest prize of all. "Maybe I ought to stick around for a little bit and sign a few autographs," he said with a sigh.

"Coach," I said, "if you wade into this crowd, you'll never get away. You'll be here all night."

He turned to me and said, "I know you're probably right,

but"—he glanced back over his shoulder at the lines of adoring fans—"but they've been so good, and they've waited for so long."

I simply shrugged and walked out onto the floor to visit with friends. The police stood by as Bobby Bowden signed autograph after autograph, smiling at every face, laughing at every joke, making each fan feel like they were an old-school chum from Birmingham.

The Civic Center maintenance workers began to turn out the big overhead lights in the ceiling of the great hall. The huge cavern darkened and looked even larger in the shadows. As I walked toward the back door, I turned and saw the crowd, smaller in number, nestled against the head table still bright in the few lights left.

That's where I'd end the story of 1999. The last scene would be that crowd of fans in one end of a huge, darkening room, gathered around a smiling man standing on a low stage, head-high above the people, taking each piece of paper, each football, or hat, or program in turn, writing on it and handing it back with a smile.

No matter where the story began, it always ended with him. "They've been so good, and they've waited for so long," he had said that night. So have you, pal. So have you.*

---

* Much of this chapter's material was initially published in the *Report to Boosters* (February 2000).

2000 Season

At no point during the 1990s did I ever think we might have established a college football dynasty. Coaches don't think that way. You can't afford to look back in this business until you are through. You just do your best to win each game or else go down fighting. History is what you leave in your wake.

The end of the 2000 season found us in yet another national championship game. Our quarterback, Chris Weinke, was a natural-born leader. And a Heisman Trophy winner. And a national championship winner, though not this year. Most folks don't realize it, but Weinke led us to three national championship games in a row. We played in five such games during the 1990s.

As for players and coaches during that era, they are legion and too many to name. But I still see their faces, hear their voices, the crack of shoulder pads, and the thud of footsteps on the field. They were special men, gifted with a tenacity and determination now etched in the record books of college football. I am proud to have led them in battle.

I could never have played that role had it not been for the strength and guidance provided by God. He made me a better man than I ever could have been without him. He helped me meet the challenges of a tough profession. And he made my players better men. You may not believe that, but I know it is true because I lived it and witnessed it.

For this season and those that went before, I give thanks to God. We worked hard, fought hard, and won some games. God made us better people and a better team in the process.

—Bobby Bowden

2000 Season

Began the season ranked No. 2
Ended the season ranked No. 5
Record 11–2
ACC Champions
Played Oklahoma in the Orange Bowl

August 26, defeated BYU in the Pigskin Classic in Jacksonville 29–3

September 9, defeated Georgia Tech in Atlanta 26–21

September 16, defeated North Carolina in Tallahassee 63–14

September 23, defeated Louisville in Tallahassee 31–0

September 28, defeated Maryland in College Park 59–7

October 7, lost to Miami in Miami 24–27

October 14, defeated Duke in Tallahassee 64–14

October 21, defeated Virginia in Tallahassee 37–3

October 28, defeated NC State in Raleigh 58–14

November 4, defeated Clemson in Tallahassee 54–7

November 11, defeated Wake Forest in Winston-Salem 35–3

November 18, defeated Florida in Tallahassee 30–7

January 3, 2001, lost to Oklahoma in the Orange Bowl 2–13

Imagining Coach Bowden's Home Visit with a Recruit

NCAA rules limit the number of new recruits any school may sign in a given year. Championship programs require a steady flow of top talent to be honed and developed by the staff. Coaches looked at three areas in evaluating potential Seminoles. "First is speed," said Coach Bowden. "You can't make somebody fast; they either are or they're not." Next was athletic ability. The final evaluation was character: "Character is number three, but it's the most important," he said, "because a player who lacks character will quit on you when things get tough."

Everything was new once again. After dry weeks of choking on dust, we had a passage of brief but spectacular storms. The air was washed clean. Long dried yellow rivulets of pollen tinted the gutters. All the balmy, fragrant greens of spring were melding to seduce us with another April.

One of the many wonderful things about college football was that each season starts fresh, all hope was new each fall. All of the Gator angst about a 9–4 season was behind them, and if you needed further evidence of the exalted level of football played in Florida, consider that nine wins and making it to the SEC championship game but not winning it were causes of near suicidal unhappiness among the orange-and-blue ranks.

The FSU freshmen students of 2000 who would cheer for the Seminoles were not yet enrolled in kindergarten when their team last failed to win ten games in a given year. However, how would we survive the day when our win total dropped into single digits? The Gators had a new hero to wash their air clean, a freshman quarterback with the Hollywood name Brock Berlin. The Seminoles had an old quarterback, a fellow of such imposing physical gifts that one opposing ACC coach complained the previous year, "[FSU's] kicker is bigger than any of my linemen, and their quarterback is bigger than anybody on my team!" We were spoiled. But we knew what the cure was, and we didn't want to take it.

We weren't always spoiled, of course. Not too many years before this all three members of what Bobby called "The Big Florida" struggled. A good year for Florida was to finish in the top half of the SEC. Miami counted a winning season as a blessing. In the previous two decades, all of us had come of age, with championships and trophies and big-win seasons. FSU and Florida built spectacular new facilities.

Spring practice was underway across the country. The previous year was finished. The Hokies of Virginia Tech were not spoiled. I had neglected to delete a path on my computer that automatically brought up the Virginia Tech fan websites and message boards. Reading their fans' relentless optimism as they chattered to each other about the prospects for the 2000 season was like peering into a time machine and seeing how Florida State must have appeared twenty years before.

Their venerable old Lane Stadium looked strikingly like our old Doak Campbell Stadium of 1980, and their graphic portrayals of future grandeur seemed inspired by Doak as it was in March of 2000. Theirs was an institution with sterling academic credentials, yet it was still looked down upon by the state's "first" school, the University of Virginia. Their coach, Frank Beamer, was a Bobby Bowden–looking sort of fellow in his forties who was building a solid record and reputation. Their fans were restless, relentlessly exuberant like ours. And their burnt orange and maroon colors could be mistaken at a distance for our own.

But distance did exist between us. It was a distance not only of years but also of the experience of fans and the achievement of teams. The Hokies didn't want to wait; they wanted to be at the top of the pyramid. Frank Beamer understood what his fans did not: that a one-time appearance in the national championship game was only the ante that Tech must chip in to sit at the table where the real game was played.

After the Sugar Bowl, and during weeks of recruiting as January played out, there was some traffic about Florida State on the Tech message boards that one might have thought carried a hostile edge had one been inclined to think that way. Some couldn't understand how FSU was able to lure great players to join an already full roster of other great players, while Virginia Tech, whose well-earned spot in the Sugar Bowl could not be faulted, was having trouble getting visits from some of the brighter lights among the nation's high school prospects.

The question was asked rather pointedly, and with just a shadow of suggestion that prospects making their official visits to Tallahassee were perhaps receiving something more than just a handshake and a tour of the facilities. "Both teams played for the national title and Beamer should benefit from that," was the complaint. "Why aren't we getting the interest? We've got lots of holes to fill and FSU doesn't. What does Coach Bowden say to get the great players to join other great players at Florida State?"

I don't know what Coach Bowden actually said when he visited a prospect's home, but if I had to write the script here is what I imagine it would be:

Son, the first thing I want to say is to your Mama. Mama, I know you are considering a lot of first-class programs, but here is why your precious boy should be a Seminole. First, he'll graduate from one of the most popular schools in America. We are the second most applied-to undergraduate institution of higher learning in this decade, in the entire country. That includes all technical universities, all community colleges, all large and all small colleges and universities, public and private. Period. His degree will carry the reputation of a first-class academic institution, and it's pretty obvious that everyone knows it's a great place to go to school.

Mama, you know boys can be a handful. I've raised four of my own. We can't be with your son all the time, but Sunday morning he will be in church. Every Sunday we all go together and we go to a different church every week. Protestant, Catholic, Jewish, we do each in turn. Whether it's High Episcopal organ music or a Gospel Choir, he'll see and hear all different ways to glorify God.

Now, son, let me tell you how it is at Florida State. We play on television every game. Not some games, but *every* game. Mostly it's national or network regional broadcasts. True, you may not get the ball more than a few times each week, but when you do millions and millions of people will be watching your every move.

And we play a national schedule. In addition to our conference, we play Miami and Florida and schools like Notre Dame and BYU and Southern California every year. Not just some years, but *every* year. No one else in America plays Miami and Florida in the same year. Heck, they don't even play each other.

And we play in the big games, the nationally televised games watched by every fan in America. In all the 1990s there were only eight games that matched the No. 1- and No. 2-ranked teams against each other. We played in six of those and won three. We play in somebody's "game of the century" every year. There are Division I schools that play football for a hundred years and never come close to being in even one game like we play every year.

And we win. We won more games in the 1990s than in any other team in the history of college football has ever won in any decade. We win at least ten games every year. *Every* year. And we win against the big boys, the big names.

So, son, if you're looking for the possible exposure, the most glamorous program, and the most popular school; if you want to win big games and play on a national stage in front of millions and millions of fans who know this program and expect you to be a champion; and if you feel you're good enough to come in here and compete against great players who have the same drive, the same ambition, and the same fire that has given FSU more current NFL pro players than any other school, and the discipline to give us a 70 percent player graduation rate, a rate that ranks us among the top 10 of all Division I programs, then this is where you need to be.

Will I still be here when you finish at FSU? Well, how do I look to you? I'm seventy years old, and I've been a head coach since the 1950s. I coached championship college teams when there were only forty-eight states and Dwight Eisenhower was president, and I coached championship players who are older than your grandfather. I'm driven by a passion to win.

There's nothing else I want to do in life, except maybe drive a tank across Europe one summer, but that's another story. During the August heat of preseason practice, I'll be out on that field before you get there, and I'll still be writing notes to my assistant coaches after you hit the showers. And do you know what I'm writing down? I'm making notes on everything you do or fail to do in practice. My teams have won more than three hundred games, and that's because I make certain that I know not just what every player can do, I also know what he's willing to do.

Tell you what—I'll promise that I'll hang it up the day I feel that I can't coach longer than five years more, if you'll commit to being the best man and the best player and the best student and the best team leader you can be for the next four. Is it a deal, son?

Heck yeah, Coach. Sign me up!

Florida State finished somewhere between No. 1 and No. 4 nationally in recruiting again in 2000, depending on who was doing the ranking. Virginia Tech finished on the outskirts of the top 20, definitely among the top 30. I don't remember where our FSU recruiting class was ranked twenty seasons ago in 1980, but that sounds about right.

Time and distance. Twenty years from now, some Hokie may dredge this up and write his own column: "You may not remember," he'll write, "but decades ago Florida State was once where Virginia Tech is today."*

---

* Much of this chapter's material was initially published in the *Report to Boosters* (March 2000).

The Exuberant 2000 Bobby Bowden Spring Tour

The year 2000 was Bobby Bowden's twenty-fifth season as head coach, and the Silver Anniversary Bobby Bowden Tour in April and May was the grandest parade of Seminole glory and fan exuberance since Bowden arrived in 1976. Never before had the tour seen such displays of manic zeal in town after town. Bobby Bowden was the nation's most admired and most honored active coach. That spring, such disparate entities as radio talk-show icon Rush Limbaugh and a camera crew from *60 Minutes* all rushed to stand at Bowden's side. Here is a glimpse of the sights and sounds that energized tens of thousands of Seminole fans that spring.

The 2000 tour opened in grand style on April 17 at Jim Dahl's River Ridge Plantation north of Tallahassee. Following a golf outing at Golden Eagle with special guests Brad Johnson, Casey Weldon, Kevin Long, and Edgar Bennett, couples gathered at the Tallahassee home of longtime Seminole Booster Jim Dahl, who generously offered his property or an evening of BBQ, closest-to-the-pin chipping contests, free-throw shooting contests, and casino games (not with real money, which was probably a good thing since the casino attraction far outdrew all the others).

April 18, Marianna: The Seminole club put together their largest Bowden day dinner in Marianna history with four hundred

FSU faithful in attendance. They served smoked steaks and got all four hundred through the serving line in less than thirty minutes. The moment before the golf tournament was captured with a panoramic photo of all golfers and Coach Bowden in one shot. After dinner, club officers, Coach Bowden, and Mike Bristol made their way with a ceremonial police escort out to I-10.

April 19, Monticello: The club president began the evening's program by presenting a five-thousand-dollar check from the club to Seminole Boosters. The decorations were unique: a strand of wire ran the length of the ceiling ("wire-to-wire") and all in sequence hung the score placards from each game of the undefeated season, capped by the front page of the *Tallahassee Democrat* the day after the Sugar Bowl. The club also presented Coach Bowden with an engraved brick, which some unknown Seminole had "removed" from the structure of the Superdome following our victory. The presenter said to Coach Bowden, "I can assure you that the manhunt for whoever carved this brick out of the stadium has long been abandoned, and certainly no one here is talking."

April 20, Pensacola: The banquet was held at the fabulous Naval Air Museum, which appeared to be a construction about the size of Doak Campbell Stadium, but with a roof. The particular arena where our banquet was held was just a portion, and a minor portion at that, of the vast and fascinating facility. More than 650 Seminoles piled uncrowded into the rotunda. Suspended from the ceiling high above the banquet tables, and arranged as if flying in diamond formation, were four actual Navy Blue Angels jets.

A high school band dressed in brilliant garnet FSU shirts marched in playing the "war chant." A presentation by the Marine Color Guard followed. Coach Bowden was presented with a signed lithograph of the Blue Angels, and a Navy flight helmet that had been creatively (and expensively) converted to the colors and markings of a Seminole football helmet. Jim Miller, the "Old

Nole," announced that the club had completed their fifty-thousand-dollar endowed athletic scholarship.

Gordon Sprague picked Coach up at the airport and later that night drove him over to Panama City. Sprague and his wife, Bette, were the first individuals to contribute a million dollars to the Capital Campaign in 1989. Marty Stanovitch recapped the results of the day's events, announcing, "One competition ended in a dead heat. Coach Bowden completed eighteen holes in four and a half hours. Ann Bowden visited eighteen stores in $45,000."

April 21, Panama City: Club president Shirley Jackson meant business and looked the part as she and her club officers went about their Bowden day work wearing headsets with microphones. The crowd of around five hundred Seminoles converged on the Sheraton Hotel to honor Coach Bowden.

Behind the head table, the club had built or somehow assembled a full-size highway billboard and suspended it from the ceiling inside the cavernous meeting hall. The left section, about ten or twelve feet high and as wide, was a photograph of Coach Bowden holding up the trophy. The right segment, same dimensions as the left, displayed a giant reproduction of the twenty-fifth anniversary crest. The center section, the largest of the three, with a width probably in excess of fifteen feet, proclaimed for all to see: "Panama City Seminole Club Welcomes Bobby Bowden 1999 National Championship Coach. Two National Championships in the '90s | 1993 & 1999 | Only Team in History of Associated Press to Go Wire-to-Wire No. 1."

The podium was flanked by stylized models of the Sears national championship trophies, with large glass eggs that looked exactly like copies of the real thing. Each trophy was nestled in a large glass bowl of pure sugar. Similar trophies were the centerpieces on each of the fifty tables. They took their championships seriously in Panama City.

April 24, Jacksonville: Over six hundred fanatic Seminoles crowded the Morocco Temple in Jacksonville, celebrating in a carnival atmosphere festooned with balloons and flanked by rows and rows of merchandise tables piled high by the vendors. Susie Brown acted as capable escort for Coach, and gave him a haircut as she always did when he visited.

On stage, they had constructed a Greek temple-like structure through which Coach Bowden and I were marched through and presented to the crowd. Coach was presented with a huge anniversary cake, three tiers, and he cut the first ceremonial piece. During the program, fans came up to side tables and got pieces of the cake for dessert.

During questions, one little boy asked, "What do you think of Steve Spurrier?" After the laughter died down, Coach said, "Excellent coach. Great offensive mind. Done things down there that no one else has ever done. Done more in the conference than anybody except Bear Bryant." Then as the little boy turned away, Bowden muttered sotto voce into the microphone, "It don't hurt to lie once in a while."

April 25, Lake City: This was the site of Bobby Bowden's first visit to a Booster club twenty-five years previously. A camera crew from Sunshine Network was there to film the evening's program. During the question period, a small boy asked, "How many players do you have back next year?" Coach said about sixty. "How many are good?" the little guy piped up. Coach waited for the laughter to subside, then said, "It's coaching, son. It's all coaching."

Tanya Edenfield had called us to ask if there was something special that Coach Bowden really liked that the club could put in his room. I told her he loves something called Goo Goo Clusters, but his real passion, an echo of his days as a good ole boy growing up in Alabama, was to take a bottle of Orange Nehi soda into which an entire sleeve of salted peanuts would be carefully sifted before drinking/eating it all at once. Tanya made sure those items were on the bedside table.

April 26, Gainesville: All events took place at the staid and elegant Gainesville Country Club. Of all the places we had visited, the hotel in Gainesville (the Baymont Inn) exhibited possibly the most gracious and helpful staff.

Gainesville was also where we ran into the year's first crop of stalkers. Mike Bristol and I called them stalkers because they haunted the hotels and the secluded holes on the golf courses, trying to snatch a moment of Coach Bowden's time to sign as many balls, mini-helmets, or photographs as they could convince him to sign. Then they sold the items to the "Black Bag Mafia" out of Miami.

The "mafia" is a consortium of guys who resell celebrity sports signatures. The "black bag" refers to their habit of sneaking into golf tournaments with black plastic bags filled with stuff to be autographed. These are not FSU fans; they are businesspeople who take advantage of Bowden's good nature and of our loyal Seminole supporters. When we spot them, we have the police run them off, but they keep returning like a persistent infection.

Two young men had been sitting at a table in the hotel lobby since at least two o'clock when I began making phone calls from an alcove near the front desk. When Coach Bowden and I walked off the elevator and out into the parking lot at a quarter after six, the two men stood straight up and followed us closely, within a step, outside to the parking lot. Halfway between the hotel and the van I stopped, turned, and braced to face them. They both extended stacks of probably twenty-five photographs each to Bowden, and asked him to sign them. He signed one each, and said he wouldn't do anymore. They turned away disappointed.

"Why do you sign them at all?" I asked him.

"Aw, they're usually college kids who need the money," he said. "I needed money too when I was in school at Howard. Sometimes if I'm in a good mood, I'll sign some for them. I ain't in that great a mood right now."

The Gainesville banquet was exceptional, as was the golf. It was hard to be a good, visible Seminole in Gainesville, but these nearly two hundred Nole fans took loud delight in celebrating their latest victory in the Swamp. The national championship was mentioned too, albeit briefly.

April 28, Atlanta: For someone who raises money to help the Seminoles, this was a dream. During the cocktail party at Atlanta's elegant Renaissance Waverly Hotel, a good-looking couple approached me with a question. The man had founded a company that had recently gone public. "I have been very fortunate," he told me. "I understand that if we make a gift of six hundred thousand, the state of Florida will match it. Is that something you can help us with?" Of course I could.

Bob Stuke retired as longtime area chairman for Seminole Boosters and so, of course, we piled on the insults. Coach Bowden spoke to the delighted crowd of three hundred, saying, "Bob Stuke's always sending me plays he says are guaranteed to work. I saved them up and tried to use them all in the first half of the Clemson game."

During question time, a young woman stood up and identified herself as a district manager for the clothing store chain, the Gap. She relayed news that all Gap stores would be painted in colors of orange and blue. But she reported proudly, "The two Tallahassee stores boycotted and refused, so their walls will be white, with no colors at all." Our crowd cheered.

Special guests flying to Atlanta for the events included athletic director Dave Hart, and both Don and Fran Veller. Everyone knows Coach Veller was FSU's golf coach for decades, but not all were aware that he was FSU's head football coach from 1949–1954, during which we won every Dixie Conference championship trophy and never lost a conference game.

May 1, Tampa: Mike Bristol accompanied Coach Bowden on the flight down and back, along with guests athletic director Dave

Hart and head basketball coach Steve Robinson. The Vic Prinzi Memorial Golf Tournament was played at Temple Terrace, chaired by former football player Billy MacPhillips. In 1976, MacPhillips was one of the few college players in the country to play both ways, seeing service as a Seminole defensive end, and then switching to tight end when the ball changed hands. Four hundred and fifty Seminoles crowded the ballroom of the beautiful new Marriott Waterside Hotel in downtown Tampa.

Security was always an issue when we traveled with Coach Bowden, especially in larger metropolitan areas. Mike Bristol worked with the two private security guards assigned for the evening. "These were probably the two largest human beings I've ever seen," Bristol laughed. He said, "After a while, the security guys came up missing. When I finally found them, they were eating, not surprisingly."

May 4, Ocala: Ocala was always a special visit. The Seminoles turned out in great numbers, and their leaders always went out of their way to make Coach Bowden and the rest of our traveling party feel welcome. A contingent from Tallahassee included FSU facilities director Bernie Waxman, varsity club director Brian Wade, Seminole Booster event coordinator Bonnie Doyle, as well as Judge Jimmy and Betty Lou Joanos, both past national presidents of the FSU Alumni Association.

At exactly 6:45, Coach Bowden rode through the entrance to Silver Springs on the back of a custom-built Corvette, dark deep garnet with brushed gold wheels and appointments, all this to the triumphant cheers of four hundred enthusiastic Seminole fans. The car's owner, Jerry Lee Taylor, had Coach autograph the dashboard with a metallic gold paint pen.

During the program, the club presented a ten-thousand-dollar check to Seminole Boosters and a garnet-colored "Master's Jacket" with gold buttons to Coach Bowden. The club presented him with an official green Master's Jacket the previous year, which he was wearing, so he slipped off the old one and put on the new one, this one in Seminole colors.

Judge Joanos was gracious enough to introduce Coach Bowden, pointing out that the last time he introduced an FSU head coach was 1973 when he presented a 0–11 Larry Jones. "Now I've completed the full circle," he said. "Now I've got a 12–0 Bobby Bowden."

During his remarks, Coach referred to his bandaged hand and announced that he had placed himself on "injured reserve." Just the morning prior he had minor surgery that required about a dozen stitches across the top of his hand, between the wrist and fingers. After he had returned to the football office around mid-morning, Mike Bristol and I decided to go see him and discuss whether or not he should even try to make an appearance at the Ocala golf tournament the following day. He waved us in with his gauze-covered hand.

He was scheduled to play golf with some Booster campaign prospects, but swinging a club could break the stitches. There had been talk about him just riding a cart around the course with the guys, of being social without playing. "Coach, be straight with me," I said. "Is this something you want to do? These are good guys and they'll understand if you don't want to roam around in a golf cart all day."

"Nah," he said, smiling. "As long as I can get a pouch of Levi Garrett, I'm good to go."

I asked if the doctor had given him something for pain. "Oh yeah," he replied. "They gave me some prescription pills—they're in a bottle over there on the table." I looked at the dark plastic pill bottle, still full to the top. One of the things I found out about him over the years was that he didn't take medication for pain unless he felt he couldn't stand it. It was generational, I suppose. It was toughness, or orneriness, but probably both.

"You haven't taken even one of those pills, have you?" I asked.

He grinned. "Nah, I don't imagine I will."

At that point Bristol, a fellow known to have had a good time at parties in his younger days, perked up and said with mock seriousness, "Coach, if you're not going to use those pain pills ... can I have them?"

It was the loudest and longest I've heard Bobby Bowden laugh in a long time.

May 5, Polk County: This was one of the largest and loudest Bowden days ever in Polk County, a venue traditionally host to some of the most boisterous FSU activities. Their post-golf luncheon may have taken the prize; they made more than $1,100 just selling mulligans.

The dinner was held at a civic arena in downtown Winter Haven. Giant video screens on stage promoted Seminole Booster programs on a continuous reel, as Coach Bowden signed autographs at a table beneath the show. The podium was festooned with bright gold-and-silver foil footballs.

Presenting Coach Bowden with the keys to the city of Winter Haven, and an official proclamation of Bobby Bowden Day was Vice-Mayor Charles Richardson, former star linebacker for Maryland (and looked every inch of it). When Richardson rose to address the record crowd of 450 Polk County Seminoles, he thundered, "How are you tonight?" The crowd managed a pretty lame, tepid response. Richardson said, "You sound like a bunch of Gators! How are you tonight?" That brought the house down and made Richardson an immediate favorite with the Noles.

May 6, Orlando: Orlando's functions were always elaborately theatrical, fitting for the realm of the mouse. Five hundred dinner-goers each received a copy of *The Event Book*, a fabulous phonebook-sized creation unique to Orlando by Rob and Kim Sahlin. Full-sized silver footballs decorated each table, capping the production's Hollywood look. The main event sponsor, AT&T, made sure that a full-size chocolate cell phone was beside every place setting.

Orlando was long on leadership for the Seminoles. Incoming Seminole Booster national chairman Raymond Cottrell was there with Stella, and son Keith, who punted for the Tribe and who, on this night, gave an inspired introduction of Coach Bowden. To begin the program, the current Seminole princess sang an inspirational song in the Creek language. Then the club presented Coach Bowden with a large framed display of the front pages of the *Tallahassee Democrat, The Times-Picayune,* and the *Orlando Sentinel* trumpeting our national championship victory. Representing the Seminole Tribe of Florida, Louise Gopher presented Coach with a beautiful ceremonial sweet grass basket, embroidered on the sides with the FSU Seminole head.

Longtime beloved (by Seminoles) principal sports columnist for the *Orlando Sentinel* Larry Guest announced his retirement, and the evening's gathered Seminoles asked him to come to the podium so they could have the chance to say good-bye. It was an emotional moment. For as many years as Coach Bowden had been at Florida State, Seminole fans could open the *Sentinel* sports pages and always be assured of three things from Larry Guest: he would analyze with integrity, he would speak with good humor, and he would tell the truth.

May 8, Orange Park: What Orange Park lacked in size it more than made up for in enthusiasm and tangible support for the Seminoles. Club president Charlie Fields presented Coach Bowden with a huge, beautifully framed photograph of the field in New Orleans taken during the championship game. Coach was also presented with a similarly framed photograph of the "Bowden Bowl," Coach's three-hundredth career win over his son Tommy at Clemson. The University Center Club was so impressed with the photographs that Coach Bowden generously allowed them to be displayed in the lobby of the club where all Seminoles could enjoy them.

One of the club's four founders, longtime loyal Seminole Leonard Voyles, spoke to the crowd about his love for FSU and his respect for Coach Bowden, and then presented Coach with a fifty-thousand-dollar check to endow a football scholarship.

May 11, Miami: We knew it was going to get interesting when it was announced that a crew from the *60 Minutes II* television show would be traveling with the Bowden Tour caravan for two days and nights. The *60 Minutes* guys were already there when I nosed the travel van up to the Miami aviation hangar in Opa-Locka at eight o'clock Thursday morning. Seminole Jorge Azor, owner of Zuni Limousine, was there as he always was with one of his elegant stretch cars when Coach arrived in Miami.

Producer John Hamlin has three Emmys on his mantle. He walked around the site, the flat asphalt of the landing strip warming quickly even at this early hour, checking angles, asking questions, setting shots for the cameras. When the orange-and-garnet (okay, brown) state of Florida plane rolled up to the hangar, employees ran out the red carpet, and the leader of the only college football dynasty that still existed unfolded himself from the confines of the tight cabin and stepped down the stepladder to the ground. In a moment we were off to the golf tournament at Don Shula's just a few miles away.

Bob Kilian ran the tournament that was now bearing up under the weight of a full field of 144 golfers. Dinner at the elegant Hotel Sofitel drew more than four hundred people, and not one more person could have been spooned into that banquet room. Security for Coach Bowden was superbly managed by former Marching Chief Joey Cecio.

Coach Bowden usually signed autographs for thirty minutes before dinner, but this time the production crew had a microphone on him so they could pick up bits and snippets of conversation from adoring fans.

The decorations were fabulous. Giant banners draped from ceiling to floor behind the podium. Huge photos framed the banners: Coach Bowden holding the crystal Sears trophy aloft, and the national championship celebration logo. Pilasters lining the walls of the ballroom were decorated with silver wreathes, each overlaid with a silver "25."

Past national Booster chairman Andy Haggard was recognized appropriately. Then there was one more special announcement. Yvonne Brown and her husband, Judge Stephen Brown, made an estate gift to Seminole Boosters, Inc., of $7,125,000.

The Sofitel ballroom was on an upper floor, so when Coach Bowden and our traveling crew walked out behind the curtain after the program, we had to maneuver down long corridors and to and from freight elevators to reach the back lot. This presented special challenges for the *60 Minutes II* crew as they chased ahead of us to get the "escape" footage.

It had come up in conversations with John Hamlin that Coach Bowden from time to time enjoyed stopping at a convenience store after the evening program. We stopped and stretched our legs, and to maybe buy a soda. Coach liked to stock up on Levi Garrett, and will occasionally revert to his Birmingham roots by buying an orange drink and pouring a packet of peanuts into it so he could consume the two together. It turned out that Hamlin's father had been known to do the same thing, so we told John we'd try to find a place along the drive north to Ft. Lauderdale where his crew could film Coach strolling through a Quik Stop.

Miami is a city of many charms and mysteries, a true international metropolis, this country's gateway to Central and South America. Be that as it may, finding the right kind of convenience store along I-95 after midnight between Coral Gables to the south and Aventura to the north could be a daunting task. We had three vehicles. Mike Bristol, Coach, and I were in an unmarked purple van, the television crew was in an unmarked white van, and the producers were driving in a black limo sedan. We looked like a sinister caravan straight out *X-Files*.

I pulled down an exit ramp to a cross street where two well-lighted quick-stops faced each other across the road. There were no cars in either parking lot, but there were about twenty to thirty young men exchanging what appeared to be somewhat less than friendly gestures with each other, and none of them were wearing shirts. We blew through the intersection and back up onto I-95.

Another off-ramp led nowhere, but the third try was a charm. Just before the Broward County line, we pulled off onto a quiet road and there, like a movie set, was a clean, brightly lit 7-Eleven. We could see there was no one inside except the clerk who smiled nervously as our *X-Files* caravan pulled up to his door all at once. The smile gave way to near panic when a television crew burst through the double glass doors but Bristol calmed the fellow; he was a very nice guy who was relieved that we had come only to shop.

As Coach walked up and down the aisles, a customer came in. He was a young guy with a round face and long black hair, wearing jeans and a T-shirt. He recognized Coach, and his face brightened up with a huge grin. "Are you Bobby Bowden?" the young guy asked.

"Yeah, glad to meet you, buddy," Coach said. "Are you a Seminole?"

"Nah, I'm Korean, man. But listen—hey Coach, good luck next year, but take it easy on my Canes, okay?"

"You bet, buddy," Coach Bowden replied.

May 12, Ft. Lauderdale: Broward County Seminoles always have one of the best organized and most elaborately produced tour stops. More than 350 Seminoles crowded into the Airport Hilton to enjoy great food and fellowship, fabulous decorations, and to celebrate the national championship and the onset of Coach Bowden's twenty-fifth season.

Bristol had security run a stalker out of the lobby of the hotel, and Mike wasn't in the mood to be pleasant or understanding. The day before in Miami, stalkers had hidden in the hotel lobby. As Bristol waited at the front desk for room keys, the stalkers descended on Bowden outside. Fortunately, the Broward Club had without a doubt the best security of any tour stop during that year. There were six big, uniformed guys on the case, and they made sure Coach was in and out and where he was supposed to be on time.

There were many wonderful things about that day in Ft. Lauderdale, not the least of which was Marvin Jones' spontaneous, inspiring tribute to Coach Bowden at the dinner that brought the thundering crowd to its feet and made it on *60 Minutes II*. The dinner had lots and lots of varsity club members in attendance, including Mike Fuentes, college baseball's first Golden Spike Award winner.

President Steve Masterson-Smith addressed the crowd on the subject of the dinner invocation: "Last year, Max Osceola's mother gave the invocation in Creek, and prayed that Bobby Bowden would win all his games, which he did. Keeping it in the family, and hoping for the same result, we have Dan Osceola, Max's uncle, to deliver the message tonight."

Dennis Newman presented Coach with a set of experimental golf clubs. They were prototypes that were not yet available. Then Dennis got carried away by the moment and told everyone how excited he was about the season opener. "FSU-BYU! Everybody will be so starved for football, even my grandmother will watch. And she's dead! It'll be that popular."

But always, the unique thing about Ft. Lauderdale was golf with the Indians. Golf and Indians are words some people don't expect to see in the same sentence, but one of the secrets of the Seminoles is that they are a people who carefully craft their image so that the general public sees exactly, and only, what the Seminoles want them to see. Then the Tribe goes about its business as it wishes.

The *60 Minutes* film crew set up their cameras at the golf tournament, and I explained to them that Coach Bowden's foursome was composed all of Seminole Indians because the Seminole Tribe of Florida was the major sponsor of the golf tournament and the dinner. I also told them that they had made a Capital Campaign donation of a hundred thousand to the FSU golf program.

I could tell by the look in their eyes that I was not describing a picture they could clearly imagine. At that moment, a golf cart screamed by, driven by a giant, laughing man with a large round dark face and a long black mane of hair streaming behind. He was wearing a bright multicolored ceremonial Seminole jacket. "There's one of their chiefs now," I said. "That's Max Osceola."

"You mean ... the guy with the aqua and white, custom Don Shula Edition Miami Dolphins golf bag strapped to the back of his cart?" they asked.

"Yeah, Max is a big Dolphins fan too," I told them.

"Oh. Okay. I guess these guys really aren't kidding about golf, are they?"

"Nope," I assured them. "You want to get some good shots for your show?"

"Absolutely!"

May 13, West Palm Beach: The beautiful garnet club banner hung behind the head table. This banner was a continual work in progress, displayed at all meetings, adding each new ACC and national championships in every sport since 1993. It was a gorgeous display, and unique to Palm Beach. The most popular auction item was a full-size Pepsi machine, but instead of Pepsi logos, the white plastic front was decorated with a beautifully painted Seminole head, the Three Torches, spears, and the words "Go Noles." As additional incentive, Coach Bowden signed the front with a huge, thick Magic Marker.

Without question, Palm Beach won the award for best dessert. Each dessert was a large, intricately sculpted chocolate football helmet filled with goodies, garnished with raspberries and blueberries. The helmet logos were exquisite Seminole heads colored in garnet on white.

FSU punter Keith Cottrell introduced Coach Bowden. Cottrell told a few stories about his roommate, Sebastian Janikowski, before getting to the business at hand. He spoke eloquently about how "Coach Bowden impacts the lives of his players athletically, but because of who he is and the way he lives his life, he has a further impact on the spiritual lives of all his players."

When Coach took the podium, he told a story about Keith. He talked about a young man of exceptional promise who came to FSU and would be called upon to be the Tribe's starting punter as a freshman. Coach said he used to stay after practice and just stand alone in his tower and watch Keith punt. Keith started out well, Coach said, but then he began to shank a few. Then he began to shank all of them. Finally, Coach Bowden climbed down out of his tower and approached Keith.

"Son, why are you shanking all those balls so bad?" he asked.

"Well, Coach, I just get so nervous with you watching me. If you weren't watching me I'd do a whole lot better."

Coach Bowden put his arm around the young man and said, "Son, I think you should know that I plan to be at nearly all the games next year."

May 18, Sarasota: Sarasota and Bradenton took turns hosting the tour in alternate years. A full boat of 144 golfers was normal fare for the Sarasota golf tournament. The celebration dinner at the Sahib Shrine Temple drew a record crowd of more than four hundred fired-up Seminoles. They sent up a roar when Coach Bowden entered to the sound of trumpets playing the FSU fight song.

If there was an ultimate Seminole, Gene Gainer was in the running for the prize. His Florida license plate was: 12-0-99. Senator John McKay and his wife were present, as was Marlow Cook, chairman of the board of the Ringling Museum. The first lady of college football, Ann Bowden, was there as well, and Ann had the best line of the night. Maybe it was the best line of the whole tour.

As Coach Bowden concluded his remarks, he responded to a question about his retirement by saying that it was up to Ann. "I'll coach until Ann tells me to quit," he said. When he turned to leave the stage, a voice from the audience rang out: "Ann, how long is he going to coach?" Ann Bowden smiled sweetly and leaned into the microphone: "As long as the paychecks keep coming."

Ann Bowden helped foster a family atmosphere with the coaches' wives and other people involved in the football program.

May 19, Pinellas County: It was hard to describe what transcribed in Clearwater in 2000. I didn't believe in the twenty-five years of the Bobby Bowden Tour there had ever been an event filled with the electricity, the passion, and the noise of this year's magic night in Pinellas County.

The Long Center is a sprawling athletic complex in the northern part of the county. Their main arena has high ceilings, and hard walls and floors, which rendered an echo-chamber effect. Its vast size could swallow a dozen basketball courts. Into this cavern poured more than one thousand Seminoles and their families, eager to party and dressed in game-day attire. Add a professional rock-band grade sound system. Stir in a national championship and the presence of St. Bobby, and you have an emotional earthquake that would put the old tent revivals to shame.

It began with an overwhelming, thundering Seminole "war chant" and fight song as club president Shirley Donovan stepped to the podium to take command of this army of fanatics. I had been in Doak Campbell when the crowd of eighty thousand wasn't as loud as or as boisterous as that thousand-fan army in Pinellas.

Club president Barry Scarr might have had his proudest moment when his beautiful daughter Kelly, a music student at FSU, stood and sang both the "National Anthem" and the hymn to the garnet and gold. It was electrifying.

In his remarks, Coach Bowden made the point that FSU played fifty-four men in the first quarter against Virginia Tech. During questions, he was asked, "How many videotapes do you get on individual players in a year?" Bowden answered, "About seven hundred in a year, and then we have to pare that down to the twenty we're going to offer and try to sign."

Regarding the national championship team's strength of schedule, he pointed out that Florida was at No. 3 and Miami was at No. 8 when we played them, and Virginia Tech was at No. 2. The highest-ranked team Tech faced during the regular season was one at No. 15. There were lots of teams that never played a top-10 team, said Bowden. "You know, there ain't but ten of 'em."

May 20, Ft. Myers: Radio talk-show icon Rush Limbaugh's attendance had been a closely held secret. Club leaders, not wishing to attract a crowd more interested in politics than football, kept Limbaugh's commitment quiet. Seminole excitement was already frantic enough to ensure a record 152 golfers plus more than four hundred at the dinner.

Limbaugh's security team flew in days early to examine the golf course and the banquet facility. He and Coach played golf in the same foursome. Limbaugh spoke at the dinner and posed for photos with Seminole fans. As it was discovered, Rush Limbaugh wanted to come to a Florida State function not just to meet Bobby Bowden, but because Rush and Marta Limbaugh were Florida State parents! Their son was a sophomore civil engineering major at FSU. Limbaugh said he was a great young man, but joked, "We don't know how good an engineer he's going to be. We broke the window blinds in our house and he can't fix them."

When Limbaugh's turn came to speak, he said: "I've had the opportunity to meet people who are the best at what they do. When I was offered the opportunity to meet Bobby Bowden, I had to take advantage of that. He gets the best out of people every day. Bobby Bowden is an amazing man."

Yes, he was (and is) amazing. After twenty-five glorious years, *amazing* was just the right word.*

---

* Much of this chapter's material was initially published as two lengthier columns in *Report to Boosters* (May and July 2000).

The Seventy-Million-Dollar Dynasty Campaign

Seminole Boosters president Andy Miller said, "Our job is to take advantage of Coach Bowden's success for the betterment of the overall athletic program." In 1988, the second year of the dynasty, Seminole Boosters began quietly planning "Project SBI," which was a code name for the grand expansion of Doak Campbell Stadium with adjoining academic buildings. Nearly ten years later, the "quiet phase" of a massive capital campaign was initiated, and in 2000 the seventy-million-dollar Dynasty Campaign was publicly announced with great fanfare.

Some think Bobby Bowden was a sorcerer. Among some rival tribes, he was even rumored to be a demon. Surely, even though the gift he had conjured up for us was no illusion, he must have at least been a magician. Bowden's gift to us was this dynasty.

When it arrived in a package in 1987, there was no picture on the box that told us what was to come. We relied on our imaginations as the years progressed. We used Florida State's success on the field to drive the revolutionary construction of University Center. National championships, 10-win seasons, and top-4 finishes all fired our passions and led us to see a destiny that could be ours. And thirteen years in a row, the dynasty flourished. We understood not just how to win victories but also how to use them.

We knew exactly what the nation's leading college football program should look like, how it should perform, and what it took to maintain the standard of superiority. And we also understood what constituted an iconic, comprehensive collegiate athletic program on the national stage. It expected to contend for championships in every sport. It featured first-class facilities and modern playing fields, along with superb training and sports medicine accommodations. Such a program provided intense and personal guidance in life skills for its student athletes, and for its professional and ethical administration. Such a program was well funded and well led with a generous abundance of enthusiasm.

Such a program, if it could be brought into being, would be a magnificent picture window through which America could view the greater work of our university. Indeed, the lofty profiles enjoyed by Notre Dame, Penn State, Texas, Southern Cal, Ohio State, Michigan, and the like all stood upon original foundations of athletic excellence. Those impressive profiles brought the universities' stories to the nation. In turn, if the universities knew how to use that attention, they benefited in far greater proportion than those whose needs and ambitions were not so clearly heard.

Florida State had not yet achieved that kind of collegiate athletic program. Ours was very good to be sure, superior to many, and it was well led. But we could not yet provide all our student athletes with competitive, championship-caliber playing facilities, or with the training and rehabilitation and treatment machinery and capacity that was needed to sustain excellence indefinitely. We knew, however, exactly what needed to be done in order to achieve that ambition. And, most especially, we knew what it would cost.

The puzzle on the floor, that beautiful picture of our dreams and ambitions and that vision we saw so clearly that we had placed all the pieces in their proper order, was too fragile to be sustained without proper support. It was large and unwieldy, too quick to disintegrate under the traffic of the day, too hard to hold together in one place. It was too delicate to be real, and the pieces would tumble back into a heap because the whole structure was too frail to sustain itself against the routine wear of time.

Bobby Bowden gave us the box with the puzzle, and over the course of thirteen years of the dynasty, we had assembled it complete. It was a beautiful vision, a portrait of what we knew we could become and of what we should become in order to enrich the power of the university we all loved.

That portrait comprised of so many pieces needed to be braced and mounted on a solid base. Then it needed to be surrounded by a protective frame and covered with a clear crystal shield. Our destiny, as we had pictured it, would be assured. The glue that bound the pieces fast to the base was money. Money formed the solid, heavy frame that protected the corners and edges. The clear armor that would preserve the bright promise of our vision was also money. The truth of this was not at issue. It was our way, the way of our culture and the way of humankind.

Our magician gave us the ability to see the future, as well as the understanding and confidence that it could be achieved. Money surrounded and protected that vision, gave it substance and rendered it permanent.

So often it all seemed to be about money. Was it always about money? No, not always, but we were at a point where we had to decide. I supposed it was like being given the opportunity to become king. It's good to be the king, as one fellow said, but being king meant you also had to become part of the royal family and accept the unique culture and the responsibilities that go along with it.

Who really ever had the opportunity to become a king? Bobby Bowden had handed Florida State that opportunity. We now had the chance for our young university to join and stand in the ranks of the other great collegiate athletic programs of history, and to produce even greater opportunities for our school that such a status brought.

In 1996, Seminole Boosters asked Dave Hart to make an assessment of the entire Seminole athletic program, and determine what it would take in terms of facilities and funding to give teams and individuals in each men's and women's sports the chance to compete for championships. It was a very simple charge: How can we use Bowden's dynasty to create an overall athletics program as successful as any in the country?

Our grand vision was of an entire athletic facilities park, radiating outward from Doak Campbell Stadium, its architecture echoing the collegiate gothic style of the stadium and the older campus core. Hart produced the plan and the statement of costs. It was a wonderful plan, a plan to stir the pride of every Seminole fan. Some of the features had already come into being. The nine-million-dollar soccer/softball park, with its gothic esplanade and generous appointments, was beautiful and gave our teams and their coaches facilities that could compete against any in the country.

On September 22, 2000, the night before the Louisville football game, and in conjunction appropriately with the celebration of Bobby Bowden's twenty-fifth season as Seminole head coach, the Seminole Boosters announced the commencement of a Capital Campaign for Athletics. It was the first of its kind. The Dynasty Campaign would seek to complete all of our athletic scholarship endowments and to put all new first-class facilities and needed renovations into place.

The goal of the Dynasty Campaign was seventy million dollars. That would go a long way toward doing it all, and doing it all right. About half of that figure would be for the scholarship endowment, and half for facilities. The Boosters and Dave Hart began assembling lead gifts as part of a "quiet phase" of the campaign in 1997. Since September of the same year, more than thirty-five million had been committed toward the goal. In this new, public phase of the campaign, we worked to raise the rest of the goal.

Every campaign has a beginning and an ending. We planned to end this one in December of 2002, with a grand, triumphal celebration the Friday night before Florida State hosted Notre Dame in Tallahassee. What an appropriate resolve to this story, as the reigning glamour team of college football paid respect to the program it strived to replace.

If we could raise the money, then we could breathe life into the vision that the picture puzzle represented. But could we do it? Could our university, which was barely fifty years old, accomplish a goal that most other universities had never achieved, perhaps never even attempted? We had the chance. The opportunity that was before us was never there in the past, and it may never have been available to us again. While the dynasty still existed, while Coach Bowden led, while the passion was high, and while the emotion resonated strongest in our hearts, now was the time to take advantage.

Who would have thought it possible? What would our future have been if destiny's unseen hand had not guided events to unfold as they had? One of our good Seminole Boosters, Joel Douthett of Jacksonville, had kept a yellowed newspaper editorial tucked away for twenty-seven years. It is headlined, "FSU Football: An Autopsy." It was published on December 6, 1973, just days after our Seminoles finished the disastrous 0–11 season. It was a year fraught with unhappiness, and it was the beginning of a dreadful three-year run during which we won only three games in all.

Reflect for a moment on these observations from that 1973 editorial:

> To rebuild winning football at FSU, at this time, would require millions of dollars and it is money the University simply does not have. ... Nor is there the possibility of large sums of money coming from outside the University. There is not, at FSU, the large contingent of alumni and

athletic benefactors who contribute heavily to other, more established collegiate football programs. ... A disquieting aspect of this crisis, though, is that even if the Administration could corral enough money for a rebuilding effort, it may be too little, too late. It could never hope to collect enough cash to rebuild to the level of an Alabama, a Notre Dame, even of a Florida. The best FSU could hope for, continuing to play the kind of teams it currently plays is to gain the stature of a Mississippi State, a TCU or a Clemson, i.e., to play .400–.500 ball.

There should be other considerations. The football fan of today is a different beast than his counterpart of a decade ago. He is not as noisy, as wild or as intense ... he is more sophisticated. And with the exception of upper echelon football schools (those who play in the top 10) college football, for the first time in years, is losing popularity: attendance is dropping. The coming recession could cut even more deeply into its popularity.

Before the Administration jumps into an expensive football rebuilding program, it should think of the consequences. It should consider, perhaps, a reorientation and de-emphasis of the game. A different brand of football, maybe. The alternative could be many years of embarrassment and frustration.

The words of this editorial are painful to read and to remember, but they are instructive as to what might have been had not great leaders emerged in 1974 to re-create and reenergize the Boosters. Great leaders, with great vision for our university and for our athletics program, had emerged in recent years. They were coaches, administrators, fundraisers, and donors.

Yes, we had help from the magician named Bowden. But there was no conjurer's secret to raising money. It was simple: Every individual who loved Florida State University would be asked to give however much and in whatever way one felt he or she could. Every person who shared the powerful vision of what Florida State could achieve needed be given the opportunity to help. That done, the Dynasty Campaign would have the chance to achieve its promise: From dynasty to destiny.*

---

* Much of this chapter's material was initially published in the *Report to Boosters* (September 2000).

Bobby Bowden
Is Old-School Tough

Like each of us, Bobby Bowden is the sum of his life experiences. As a young football player, he saw weak coaches lose control of their players, and he witnessed other coaches destroy morale with their overly-harsh ideas about discipline. Bowden's life and coaching philosophy had been instructed by his moral values, which were based in Scripture.

Many fans, administrators, and pundits have weighed in on Bowden's methods of discipline. He raised four of his own boys to manhood. His son Tommy said, "Daddy believes in the compassion and forgiveness of the New Testament, but sometimes, and especially on game day, he's strictly an Old Testament man."

For the most part, we had a blessedly uneventful summer of 2000. But in late July, senior safety Derrick Gibson asked a young woman for … well, for more than her advice, and the state's sportswriters who had been dozing in the sun like drowsy toads suddenly sprang to life. And when it appeared that Bobby Bowden was not going to immediately toss Gibson's body from the top of the bell tower, the media stormed ahead with righteous glee.

I got several calls and e-mails from good Seminole Boosters who despaired at seeing our university embarrassed once again. An old friend from Atlanta was typical:

There is a column in the Atlanta paper by Terrence Moore titled "Dadgum Disgrace to FSU" concerning the litany of legal problems of FSU players and the response of Coach Bowden and the administration to Derrick Gibson's arrest, Janikowski's legal problems, and so forth.

Charlie, I have some of the same concerns as Moore sets out in his article. FSU runs the risk, if these arrests continue, with the sometimes weak-looking response from Coach Bowden and the administration, of having loyal FSU fans being embarrassed rather than proud of their association with FSU. Will good recruits begin to shy away from FSU due to the negative publicity?

That writer, as well as all FSU fans, were in the same boat. We were proud of our Seminoles, and we were also concerned about any problem that might hurt the program. We didn't like to be embarrassed by bad behavior, and we didn't like to be compared to the school down the road. That school routinely and publicly punished misdeeds by suspending players for a game or two, usually the season opener.

However, we had traveled a fair distance with Bobby Bowden, and I trusted his judgment. He was old school and he was tough, and he probably felt it was wrong to lop off someone's head, especially a young someone, just to please the howling mob. Coach had taken the position that he would handle these things internally.

There was a good chance that as long as Bobby Bowden was still in Tallahassee, we would continue to win. And as long as we continued to win, there were at least two things that would not change: First, the media would not love or protect us. And the second thing that would not change as long as we continued this wonderful success was that every transgression, no matter how small, would be blown up to front-page status.

My guess was that of all the virtues in Bowden's experience, loyalty was the most prized. Part of his method in disciplining his players out of the public eye had to do with loyalty: his to the players and coaches and theirs to him. Discipline in private did not mean lesser punishment. Hear the woeful tales of being turned over to Mickey Andrews at six in the morning to run stadium steps and perform other tasks as might amuse Mickey during that hour.

Recruiting may have actually been enhanced because of the way Bowden handled player discipline. When he looked a recruit's mother in the eye and said, "I'll discipline your son and I won't throw him to the wolves to make myself look good in public," she could embrace that as truth. Potential recruits saw Bobby Bowden as a man who would remain loyal to them as long as they abided by his rules. Everyone who survived Mickey pretty much got a second chance. But no one got a third.

There was another element in this mix, and that was Bowden's unflinchingly public acknowledgement of religious faith, and his use of morality to instruct his players. Some believed that Bobby Bowden came under greater criticism because of his Christian faith. I don't believe that sportswriters and news editors were necessarily an anti-Christian lot. What was more likely true was that because Bobby Bowden adhered to a moral code based on religion, the impulse when one of his players broke that code was to shout, "Aha!" It was human nature.

One last element was the comparison to Florida, and Steve Spurrier's practice of making a public show of suspending players. I had no criticism of Spurrier's methods of discipline. It seemed to me that both Bowden and Spurrier were consistent. What was the key difference then? Spurrier's public suspensions tended to please the fans and mollify the media. But it was also Spurrier's style to publicly berate his players' performance.

Bowden's assistants tended to stay for a decade or much longer; Spurrier's assistants tended to move on rather quickly. Bowden's star players had been inclined to return for their senior year; the other fellow's juniors tended to turn pro as quickly as they could. There was no criticism here—both men were great coaches and both led teams that hunted for championships every year.

In spite of the storm in the media over discipline, I would cast my lot with the man who placed a premium on loyalty and who disciplined his players within the context of his faith.[*]

---

[*] Much of this chapter's material was initially published in the *Florida State Times* (October 2000).

It's All about the Jimmys and the Joes

The success of Bowden's dynasty parallels the evolution of college football recruiting into the complex and highly structured affair it has become today. Defensive ends coach Jim Gladden said, "It's not the X's and O's; it's the Jimmys and Joes." Asked which was more important—coaching or player talent—Bowden laughed and said, "It's not even close. You gotta have the guys! You have to have outstanding guys. If you have good men, a coach might be able to mess it up. … But no, the real difference is the guys."

After the Clemson and Florida State players shook hands and left the field, Bobby Bowden and Tommy Bowden embraced. The father didn't want to offer hollow encouragement in the face of a crushing loss, so he whispered not sympathy but advice to his son. It was knowledge he had not come by easily: "Recruit harder," he said.

If by some chance we ended up playing Oklahoma in the Orange Bowl at the end of the season, it would close a circle that had meandered roundabout for twenty years. At the end of our first perfect 11–0 season in 1979, the Seminoles were tapped for the Orange Bowl, and what joy rang in the streets! We had never been to a New Year's Day bowl before, and at the time there were substantially fewer of those than there are now.

Our opponent was Oklahoma, one of the handful of storied programs that dominated the college landscape in those days. The Sooners were not in the national title hunt that year and seemed cranky about having to come all that way down to Miami to play against an upstart. We scored the first touchdown, but that was the end of it for us. The Seminoles were dismissed—and that word correctly conveys Oklahoma's attitude—by the Sooners 24–7. The hero of the game was the swift and elusive J. C. Watts, who would later become a congressman from Oklahoma.

The following year we had a better team, with more depth and with the No. 1-ranked defense in the nation. The reason our fans held up four fingers at the start of the fourth quarter went back to that 1980 season. During the regular season, not a single point was scored against FSU in the fourth quarter by any opponent. That was the year we beat Nebraska in Lincoln, a game considered by many of our fans to be the seminal Florida State victory in the modern era. It was then that Bobby Bowden and Tom Osborne became friends.

Another Orange Bowl invitation was bestowed on Florida State in 1980, and again, the opponent was Oklahoma, led once more by Julius Caesar Watts. The Seminoles thirsted for revenge, but there was even more at stake.

It was an odd year in college football. Freshman Herschel Walker had crashed through a wall of preseason predictions like a runaway wagonload of nitroglycerin, catapulting a decent Georgia team into the nation's No. 1 ranking. Georgia played first on that 1981 New Year's Day, and won, but it had been an ugly, patented Vince Dooley 10–9 victory, and the voters were not overly impressed.

Florida State played at night in the Orange Bowl. During the length of the season, FSU had risen from No. 13 to a No. 2 ranking in the AP poll. There were whispers that a victory over a good Oklahoma team could jump FSU into a national championship in at least one of the polls.

The score was tied 10–10 when the clock turned and the fourth quarter began. Delirious Seminole fans swayed back and forth, defiantly waving those four fingers. No one had scored on the Noles all year in the last stanza. We were fifteen minutes away from our first national title in Bobby Bowden's fifth year at the helm. It was almost too easy.

Of course it was too easy. The end of that ballgame is painful to recall. Bobby Butler recovered a bad punt for a touchdown, and the Seminoles led 17–10. Oklahoma never passed, but they were forced into throwing. And throw they did. J. C. Watts swept down the field like a zephyr. He found receiver Steve Rhodes for the touchdown, and then hit tight end Steve Valora for the 2-point conversion and the 18–17 win. For the record, with five seconds remaining, Seminole kicker Bill Capece's 62-yard field goal attempt fell 6 yards short.

Sometime later, Bobby Bowden and Tom Osborne shared a long plane ride together, and Osborne advised his friend that the only way to beat teams like Oklahoma was to recruit speed: "Sacrifice nearly everything else for speed," he had said. "Speed will carry you further and to more victories than plodding linemen and trick plays."

With offensive speed, one could beat any conference opponent. Add defensive speed to that, and one could beat anyone at all. Speed kills. "Recruit harder."

Bobby Bowden was a coach in the old-school style, and like many who had been successful, he had always been reluctant to tinker with what worked. Twenty years previously, college coaches were amazed at the fast-growing interest among fans in the process of recruiting.

Bowden said he liked the way Joe Paterno did it at Penn State. In the early 1980s, Bowden said, "When Joe signs a class of freshmen, nobody even knows their names until they show up on campus in the fall." But that was not the way it was being done at

Miami, where Howard Schnellenberger hired a full-time recruiting coordinator to direct the efforts of their assistant coaches. The coordinator facilitated player evaluations and organized communication with prospects. The Florida Gators also hired a recruiting coordinator, and in spite of a spectacular recruiting scandal under Charley Pell, the existence of any organized system seemed to afford tremendous advantage to any coaching staff employing one.

Bowden had always been cautious about change, but what distinguished his genius was that he was willing to change if he could be convinced that it was the best course. Coach Gene McDowell was our first recruiting coordinator, putting his system in place in 1984. He was succeeded by Brad Scott, then Ronnie Cottrell, and then by John Lilly.

Much of the fan interest in recruiting was sparked by the rapid rise of self-professed "recruiting gurus" in the 1980s. In 2000, those gurus offered subscription publications and elaborate websites with instant alerts and updates. They were in constant communication with high school coaches, college coaches, players' families, players' girlfriends, and with the prospects themselves. If Luther and Jasper were going to sign to play for Old Ivy, you could read about it first on any sports dot.com for just a few dollars a month.

Even in the 1980s, this fan obsession drove many sportswriters to distraction. Bill McGrotha, bless his soul, who chronicled the first forty years of our Seminole athletic program as columnist for the *Tallahassee Democrat*, despaired at what he saw as noncoaches making uniformed player evaluations, and then inflaming the fan populace by awarding meaningless rankings to opposing classes of recruits.

In the South, some said that there were three seasons: football, football recruiting, and spring football. Recruiting, which had been a process barely noticed if at all by fans at large, had become a second season of competition. Bill McGrotha was adamant in his writings that the evaluation of student-athletes was valid only when done by professional coaches intimately versed in the particular needs of their own programs. And evaluations of entire classes of recruits was laughable, said McGrotha, and perhaps even potentially harmful, because it tended to place too much emphasis on young men whose actual skills might not become evident for years.

McGrotha was a torchbearer on the issue, siding with Bowden and opposed to the relative ranking of classes of football recruits. He pointed to highly recruited players who never panned out, and to walk-ons and lightly regarded fellows who became stars. Deion Sanders, he said, was an unknown from Ft. Myers who proved to be the most talented recruit in FSU's history. Dexter Carter was another talent overlooked by all except for FSU.

Bowden was of the same mind as McGrotha, but he became convinced that there had indeed been some sort of shift in the tides of college football. He knew that a smart coach and innovator would make close examination of the changing times. A younger generation of sportswriters also agreed that the professional recruiter gurus were at least somewhat accurate in their assessments. There seemed to be too great a correlation between the schools who won on the field and the schools who also "won" the highly publicized recruiting wars.

Among those young sportswriters was Jerry Kutz, one of the founder-owners of the *Osceola*. Kutz and some of his cohorts devised their own system of evaluation. They all held McGrotha in great esteem, but they also saw the future as a wave of advanced recruiting techniques that would either buoy Florida State up toward the top, or wash it out to some sandbar where 7–4 and a good effort was the local currency.

Kutz took the names of all players on the ten-year rosters of Florida State and Florida, and placed each name into one of three categories. A Blue Chip player was one who had been coveted by FSU, Florida, Miami, and most of the other college football powers. A player was classified as a Red Chip if he had been sought actively by only two of the three big Florida schools and not universally by other powers. A White Chip player had been recruited by only one of those schools and few others. Of course, there was some factoring based on who else was in the mix. A prospect choosing between Florida State and Notre Dame was higher ranked than a player choosing between Florida State and say, Tennessee-Chattanooga.

After a cursory look at the results, McGrotha's point seemed to be made. Only 50 percent of the Blue Chip players even actually achieved starting roles at FSU or UF. However, after the numbers in all the categories were laid out, a very different picture emerged. "The obvious was staggering," said Kutz. "While only half of the Blue Chip players became starters, we found that only 25 percent of the Red Chip players managed to start and it was rare when one of the White Chip players made any significant impact."

What was staggeringly obvious was the highly recruited players were primarily the ones who became starters. Yes, many players of all descriptions might not pan out, but in a horse race you should always bet on the thoroughbred. It is a myth that Deion Sanders was not highly evaluated or not highly recruited. The Ft. Myers quarterback was not on the original Super 24 list for the Florida All-Star game (another QB was chosen), but the high school coaches later added his name as their choice. Deion was heavily recruited by all the right schools, including Florida and Georgia. Dexter Carter, one of the most talented, and certainly one of the most personable Seminole players, was, in fact, not very highly recruited out of high school. Dexter was one of those happy finds: a White Chip who rose to glory against the odds.

What became painfully obvious to ACC opponents was that Florida State's second- and third-string players all fell into that Blue Chip classification. The talent of most good teams, even great teams, falls off quickly after you get past the first string. Florida State's talent level didn't fall off at all. At FSU, the difference between the starters and the subs was experience. It was difficult for anyone who had to play us to believe that Davy Ford was our third-string tailback.

In 2000 especially, that talent difference had been frightening to behold. Victories over our previous six conference opponents had been by scores of 63–14, 59–7, 63–14, 37–3, 58–14, 54–17, and 35–6. ACC opponents welcomed a visit from the Seminoles with the same enthusiasm as if they learned that a meteor was hurtling toward earth and they were ground zero.

The upcoming recruiting class for spring of 2001 was especially critical. We had twenty-eight seniors on our team, an unprecedented high number. Somewhere along the continuum, we got out of sync. Remember that class with only nine recruits? We were overscholarshiped at the time, and in 2000 our overall numbers were dropping lower than normal. Fortunately, the upcoming class seemed to be shaping up as another splendid edition, maybe an especially talented and highly-ranked collection even by FSU standards. In the past years we had done as well as anyone in the nation, but the thing always seemed to come down to the last day.

But not in 2001. As many as fifteen nationally ranked recruits had publicly pledged themselves to sign with the Seminoles in February. Since in the past it appeared that the most highly touted recruits waited until the last minute to announce their intentions, the question arose as to whether the current group was of comparably high quality. We never had so many, so early. Could they possess true Blue Chip credentials? Kutz said that many of these early commitments were ranked among the top players at their respective positions by recruiting analysts.

What was conspicuous in the absence from 2001's early commitments was a contingent of players from South Florida,

especially from Dade County. Howard Schnellenberger laid claim
to everything south of Yeehaw Junction and pronounced it to be
the "State of Miami." There was no doubt that a broad, deep vein
of talent was located in those South Florida metropolitan areas.
But Miami players were notoriously late commitments. It seemed
to be more difficult to pry test scores and other qualifying information out of Dade County than elsewhere. I trusted we were still
in the competition for South Florida players, and that they would
show up at the finish line.

We remembered all the drawbacks that would keep a top-
ranked recruit from even considering Florida State. Bobby
Bowden's charisma and enthusiasm and coaching made up the
difference. Now we were putting all the important facilities in
place so that the next Florida State head coach would have all the
tools he needed to continue what had taken so long to build.

One young man who had announced his intention to sign
with the Seminoles was rated by some accounts as the No. 1 fullback prospect in America. He spurned offers from twenty-five
other programs to select FSU. He told the newspaper, "All of the
schools I visited were impressive, but Florida State offered the best
opportunity for me. Florida State is a school with a great tradition,
a great coaching staff, and the best of everything."

Yes. The best of everything. To a young man of eighteen,
Florida State always had a great tradition, always had the best
of everything. And, as he said, we always had a great coaching
staff. But there was no guarantee that great players and top-flight
facilities would translate into success on the field. We could name
coaches who had all the tools and talent, but they were still unable
to put a championship program together. And there were coaches
like Bobby Bowden, who used to win even with ranks filled with
mostly Red Chips and facilities badly in need of repair.

No jockey ever carried a horse across the finish line. There
was no case on record of any Division I football program

maintaining championship ambitions and seasons of victory without a deep well of highly talented players. To accomplish what Florida State had done, you would need the horses. Big horses. Fast ones.

If it was us and Oklahoma in the bowl, then we would find out just how far we had come in previous twenty years. Bobby Bowden's words to his son rang in our ears: "Recruit harder."*

---

* Much of this chapter's material was initially published in the *Report to Boosters* (November 2000).

Seminoles vs. Oklahoma in the Orange Bowl

The Orange Bowl game against Oklahoma for the 2000 national championship was the last game in the fourteenth and final year of the dynasty. The Seminoles would continue to enjoy successful winning seasons for another decade until Coach Bowden's retirement. The dynasty's perfect reign of magical heights, year after year, still remains unchallenged in its glory.

There we were, gathered like family at the annual reunion, back in Miami for another Orange Bowl. Once again. Miami, Phoenix, and New Orleans were three destinations Florida State had graced with its presence eleven times in the previous thirteen years. It was wonderful to always be among the winners at the end of the season.

We were spoiled, spoiled all the way through. We were spoiled rotten by thirteen years of top-4 finishes and ten-or-more-win seasons, national championships and conference championships, and soul-satisfying victories over darker forces who struggled against our light. Of course we were spoiled, but I didn't want to take the cure. The cure was Christmas in Shreveport. The cold turkey cure was to be revisited by the ghost of 1973. No wins, few fans, and little hope. I barely lived through it the first time; I doubted I would be man enough to survive it again.

There we were, preparing to compete in our third consecutive national championship game, our fourth such appearance in the previous five years, and our fifth in the previous eight seasons. We were cranky at the beginning of the year because the pollsters started us at the No. 2 spot in preseason and not the No. 1 position, thus denying us the opportunity to be the first team ever to go wire-to-wire back-to-back. Please don't hate us just because we were beautiful.

We did not know what would transpire when we played Oklahoma on Wednesday night, January 3, 2001, but in terms of the long success and glory of Florida State football, it mattered less than most would think. The dynasty had already been validated by the previous year's preseason to postseason wire-to-wire No. 1 run, which was unprecedented in the history of college football. The enduring strength of this program had already been tested, finally emerging in triumph after overcoming a pressure cooker of stress and controversy that would have dismantled any less solid enterprise.

Another national championship would shower still more glory on this storied program. A loss would be no less than a loss to the next national champion, taken in the title match. Chris Weinke's place in history along with that of all his teammates was secure.

Now that we knew we were going to play for another national championship in the Orange Bowl, I wanted to submit a fashion request. It was time to set aside our good taste along with our beautiful white shirts with the vibrant Seminole logos, our yellow shirts of any description, our Sunshine State aqua, green, turquoise, and chic black game wear. It was time for us to select our garnet outfits for this biggest-of-all big games.

The metallic gold of our helmets was a brilliant color, and was best worn as an accessory. Our base color was garnet, and when all troops gathered prior to battle beneath a single banner, garnet was the uniform of the day. It didn't matter that garnet would fade quickly, or that many of us had complexions that garnet didn't enhance. Nor did it matter that our best-looking outfits may be hues of other varieties. In this game and in this stadium, and in front of tens of millions of Americans, all Seminoles needed to be instantly recognizable.

Oklahoma would be all in red. They had red hats, red jackets, red shirts and skirts. No man, unless he was costumed for a masquerade ball or attempting to stab a bull in a ring, should ever wear red pants. And yet, we would witness an invasion of Sooner males strolling along North Beach resplendent in scarlet polyester double-knit golf pants, and they would do so without betraying any hint of shame.

We could not be outdone. I believed in my ability and in the ability of my fellow Seminoles to drape ourselves in outfits every bit as taste challenged and obnoxious as the fans of any opponent we would ever face. We learned our lesson in Phoenix two years before this. A tidal wave of orange swept all other impressions aside. For every Seminole wearing a nice pair of khakis and a black jacket with a Seminole head on the sleeve, there were platoons of human beings outfitted in orange hats, orange sunglasses, and orange tops, bottoms, belts. I did not know it was possible to purchase bright orange socks, but now I knew that somewhere, someone made a comfortable living manufacturing and selling such things.

Looking back on those twin Orange Bowl loses to Oklahoma twenty years before, it was almost as if our two programs had reversed roles in 2000. In 1979, we were the upstart, undefeated team challenging for national recognition. Oklahoma was the perennial dynasty-in-residence, favored to win, a little bored and unimpressed with the strength of competition we had overcome to get to Miami. But now Florida State was the program deep into the afternoon of its dynasty, and Oklahoma was the one on fire with the excitement of newly minted achievements. Bob

Stoops had done for Oklahoma what Bobby Bowden did for the Seminoles.

After defeating the Florida Gators, Florida State's strength of schedule was ranked No. 2 in the country. Oklahoma's strength of schedule stood at No. 11. That differential may not have any meaning on paper, but it encouraged on our side a sense of over-confidence that had not really benefited us in the past. Florida State was an 11.5-point favorite.

What had transpired in the last several decades was much more profound than just two teams meandering along in opposite directions. What had impacted both Oklahoma and Florida State was a fundamental change, a physical shift in the axis of college football.

In the 1970s and into the 1980s, the axis of college football was anchored in Austin, Texas. It rose to the north through Norman, Oklahoma, and reached its upper extremity inside Cornhusker Stadium in Lincoln, Nebraska. Then, as it was in 2000, there was no playoff system, but the de facto semifinal game for the national championship was more often than not settled in November between Barry Switzer's Sooners and Tom Osborne's Huskers.

Both Switzer and Osborne seemed to epitomize the public's perception of their respective programs. Tom Osborne, Bobby Bowden's close friend, reflected the solid core values of Mid-western folks who populated the vast plains of Nebraska, a state layered with family farms and small towns with white wooden churches.

Barry Switzer's autobiography is titled *Bootlegger's Boy*, which is an accurate characterization of his hard upbringing in rural Arkansas. Switzer prospered as the free-wheeling fast-talking ramrod of an Oklahoma program that exchanged NCAA proba-tion for national championships on what seemed to be a regular rotation. Oklahoma was the oil state, its landscape dotted with derricks in constant motion, like the slick and shady wildcatters who poured money into the Sooners' athletic coffers for decades. Both Oklahoma and Nebraska produced some of the finest football teams and some of the greatest players in the history of the college game. Switzer and Osborne, though vastly different in their personalities and virtues, stood as two of the greatest coaches of the twentieth century.

The decline and dissolution of the Southwest Conference, and the parallel lapse of the Big 8 Conference into a sort of clinical depression, was a slow and painful story. When the SWC collapsed, its nine members scattered among five other conferences, some of them folding into the newly created and reenergized Big 12. By that time, the axis had already shifted east. As each year of the 1990s passed, the new axis of college football became more solidly embedded in the length of the nation's fourth largest state. From Miami, it reached up through Gainesville and bore its crown in Tallahassee.

Florida became the only state in history to boast three Division I teams each winning their respective conference championships in the same year. It had happened once again in 2000. FSU, Florida, and Miami all won national championships in this decade, and all have produced Heisman Trophy quarterbacks in that span.

Here's an incredible statistic: in the BCS strength-of-schedule standings as of December 3, 2000, UF, FSU, and Miami's national rankings were No. 1, No. 2, and No. 3, respectively. And the Sooners of Oklahoma were back on center stage after a long stretch of waiting in the wings. They were talented, well coached, undefeated, and hungry to reclaim the glories of their past. They were very much like Miami was when we played them earlier in the year.

Back in October, we assumed we would win because we were the better club. Miami was desperate to win, because the stakes for them were nothing less than the validation of their return. They ached for the days of their own dynasty. The game could have gone either way and it came down to a kick. Bobby Bowden said, "Both teams played great. But if we played great, they played greater."

Did Miami deserve to play for the national title? Yes, of course they did. They earned it. Did Florida State deserve to play for the title in the Orange Bowl? Yes, absolutely we did. Did Oklahoma deserve the shot in Miami as well? They were undefeated and ranked No. 1; there was no question that the title was theirs to lose.

We had been where Miami was, and more than once. In 1989 we beat the Hurricanes in regular season and then watched in bitter resignation while Miami went on to win their third national title. The year before that we believed we were the best team in the country at the end of the 1988 season. Notre Dame had their choice of opponents to settle the title, but Lou Holtz chose to play West Virginia.

It was ironic, and satisfying in a strange sort of way, to know that if it were not for the BCS, we would be in New Orleans after New Year's instead of in Miami. We still ranked No. 3 in the two major polls, but there were eight additional polls taken into the formula, and FSU ranked No. 1 in five of those. If not for the Byzantine minutiae of the BCS's multiple polls, and for all I know their relationship with the Psychic Friends Network, we would be shut out of the title match. However, for the first time, other factors had been taken into account. Miami won ten games, but we won eleven. And Miami was paying dearly for scheduling a Division I-AA team.

Oklahoma was not just hungry—Oklahoma was starving. They were starving for what was lost. Like Florida State, Oklahoma was in the middle of a capital campaign for athletics. Mike Bristol brought a video tape to the office, a presentation tool that the Sooners used to educate their potential donors, to touch their emotions, to move them to give.

We had similar materials, and we made liberal use of Coach Bowden's image and the inspiration of his words and his character.

Oklahoma's taped presentation didn't really feature Bob Stoops, nor did it touch on Howard Schnellenberger or any of the other fellows who had led the Sooners since glory fell away. The most compelling image, the strongest voice, and the most familiar face again and again in that offering created to touch the hearts of Sooners was Barry Switzer.

I had no doubt that Barry Switzer would be on the sidelines the night of January 3rd. I imagined that he'd address the boys before they took the field. Maybe he would tell them about playing Florida State at the end of 1979 and again in 1980. I knew he would tell them about glory and national championships, and he would fire the engines of their manhood and exhort them to challenge the disrespect of those who would make the No. 1-ranked team in the nation an 11.5-point underdog.

Barry would laugh and wink and describe the magical wonder of the world at the top of the pyramid, and he would tell them just how close they were to lifting themselves back up to the lofty peak that Sooner glory claimed as their own for so many years. Then Barry would tell them to go out there and beat Bobby Bowden and the Seminoles just like he did twenty years before. But twenty years was a long time and the world had turned around. We were different now, and so were they. I couldn't tell you how much I was looking forward to the game.*

---

* Much of this chapter's material was initially published in the *Report to Boosters* (December 2000).

Epilogue

The 2000 season was the final chapter of the dynasty. FSU won its ninth consecutive ACC championship that year. Florida State vs. Oklahoma in the Orange Bowl was our third consecutive national championship game and the fifth time in eight seasons that the Seminoles had played for the trophy. The Seminoles' 2–13 Orange Bowl loss dropped FSU to a final No. 5 ranking, the first time since 1986 that the Seminoles had not finished among the top 4.

In the five seasons following the end of the dynasty, FSU won three more ACC titles, including 2005 when an unranked Seminole team upset No. 5-ranked Virginia Tech in the first official ACC championship game.

Bowden coached FSU nine more seasons before his retirement at the end of 2009. Each of those nine seasons boasted a winning record, and the nine bowl games produced an overall winning bowl record. His last day on the sidelines was a nostalgic game, a victory over West Virginia in the Gator Bowl.

Thirty-four football seasons is a long time, and those years coincided perfectly with massive growth of the university. More than 80 percent of all the alumni who had ever graduated from Florida State—going all the way back to 1851—had matriculated since Bobby Bowden became head coach in 1976. He was there long enough to have coached the sons of some of his Seminole players (Ponder, Piurowski, and Simms, as well as others).

His coaching career spanned fifty-six seasons. He had already been the head coach at three other universities before he returned to Tallahassee. That point is important because, as he said, "I probably made all the typical mistakes every new head coach makes, but my advantage was that I got to make all of them out of sight." Tenure at Samford, South Georgia College, and even West Virginia didn't expose a young coach's mistakes to the hot media glare as it would later upon the merciless national stage of championship football.

It was a match drawn by fate. When he and Ann Bowden arrived in Tallahassee, Bobby Bowden was forty-seven years old. He found himself with all the requisite skills and maturity, in possession of the perfect instrument in exactly the right place, at precisely the right moment in history.

The way things used to be, and the way it was for a long time, changed at the top of the college football pyramid as Bowden's generation of coaches passed. But unlike many of his peers, Bobby Bowden's enduring strength across the decades has been his remarkable skill at adapting to the changing social and cultural landscapes. Bowden saw the introduction of complex strategy and offenses built around the forward pass. Coach Bill Peterson is credited with introducing the pro passing game to college, but Bobby Bowden was his receivers coach and Fred Biletnikoff was the student.

Bowden was a Southern boy who saw the dawn of integration and was smart enough to understand its potential and move beyond the culture. He learned how to motivate student-athletes instead of simply yelling at jocks. He embraced the value of a professionally managed recruiting program and became an extraordinarily skilled closer. Bobby Bowden is the living proof that character does count. For all the good he represents, for all the values and virtues that he's instilled in generations of Seminole players and fans, we want to remember him always as he stood on the platform of champions.

Mike Bianchi, writing for the *Orlando Sentinel*, has earned his place as the senior sports columnist in the state of Florida. In 2004, Bianchi penned a column in which he described Bobby Bowden as "the greatest coach alive." He did not base his opinion on Bowden's win total but on the power of one man's imprint on the institution.

Much was being made at the time of the race between Bowden and Penn State's Joe Paterno for the total highest career wins. Bianchi compared the two, but of course this was before the unfortunate darkness overcame Paterno's legacy. "The ultimate mark of a coach's greatness is what the program was like before he arrived—and what it will be like after he leaves," Bianchi wrote then. "When Joe Paterno arrived, Penn State football was already good. And when he leaves, Penn State football will probably get better."

The theme was that Bobby Bowden exerted a unique influence on Florida State University, more than any other coach at any other university. Bianchi described it most eloquently in drawing the difference between Bowden and Paterno and their impact on their universities: "Bowden was the architect and builder of FSU's program; Paterno remodeled and redecorated at Penn State. Bowden poured the foundation; Paterno put up new curtains. Bowden framed the walls; Paterno hung pictures on them. Paterno painted the master bedroom. Bowden painted the masterpiece."

Bobby Bowden's FSU legacy is more than wins on the field. Those wins were the catalyst for hundreds of millions of dollars in new construction and renovations to the entire park of athletics facilities. No one knows the total amount to be counted over time.

Thank you, Coach, for who you are, and for how you have helped shape the character, the confidence, and enduring strength of the university we love so much. Emerson mused about the nature of great men more than a hundred years ago:

"When nature removes a great man, people explore the horizon for a successor; but none comes, and none will. His class is extinguished with him … ." There will never be another like Bobby Bowden.

Acknowledgments

To Connie for her love and encouragement. Very special thanks to John Corry and Andy Miller. And especially, thanks to Coach Bobby Bowden and Ann Bowden.

Also, thanks to Mickey Andrews, Scott Atwell, Mary Bailey, Ray Barbee, Patti Barber, Ed Barnes, Derril Beech, Joy Beech, Matt Behnke, Monk Bonasorte, Terry Bowden, Mike Bristol, Tom Carlson, Ken Cashin, Eric Carr, Rachel Catalano, Dexter Chase, Adam Corey, Raymond Cottrell, Julie Crump, Sandy D'Alemberte, Marcia Etheridge, Hugo deBeaubien, Gene Deckerhoff, Mary Pat Desloge, and Joe DeRoss. Thanks also to Al and Judy Dunlap, Sheri Dye, Frank Fain, Elliot Finebloom, Maria Fuller, Janice Gay, Manny Garcia, Jim Gladden, Eric Grant, Rick Grant, Sue Hall, Andy Haggard, Janice Hanks, Dave Hart, Jimmy Hewitt, Chris Holler, Betsy Hosey, Vincent Hughes, Jerry Kutz, George Langford, Lawton Langford, Brett Lindquist, Cindee Lundeen, David Lyons, Nick Maddox, Doug Mannheimer, Barbara Mason, Jim Melton, Tom McGlammory, Jim Miller, David Mobley, Russ Morcom, Garret O'Connor, Joel Padgett, Jay Peeper, Bob Perrone, Kirsten Rayborn, Jay Rayburn, Gene Ready, Karen Rich, Mark Rodin, Barry Sell, Billy Sexton, Barry Scarr, Kristi Scottaline, Gordon Sprague, Barry Smith, Larry Strom, Brian Swain, Kari Terezakis, Jennifer Terrell, Portia Thomas, Gary Thurston, Kirsten Tubeck, Bob Votaw, Cumi and Gary Walsingham, Chris Weinke, Rob Wilson, Jamie Warren, Gary Wilson, Gene Williams, Max Zahn, and many more fine Seminoles. Thanks to all of you for your kindness and support.

About the Authors

Charles Barnes was senior vice president and executive director of the Seminole Boosters until his retirement in 2012. He and Coach Bobby Bowden travelled together on the annual Seminole Booster banquet-and-golf circuit for more than thirty years, building up the Seminole Boosters organization. Barnes is a popular writer and speaker and is featured columnist for the Seminole Boosters *Unconquered* magazine. He and his wife Connie are both alumni of Florida State University.

Coach Bobby Bowden's remarkable Florida State University career began when he took over the Seminole program in 1976. The Seminoles had won just four games over the previous three seasons. Four seasons after he first walked across the campus, Coach Bowden took FSU to within one game of a national championship, posting an 11–1 record in 1979.

Among his many accomplishments, one of the most amazing is the remarkable fourteen straight top-five finishes in the AP poll from 1987 to 2000. During that run, Florida State was 152–18–1 and captured national championships in 1993 and 1999. In 1999, the team became the first team to ever go wire-to-wire as the No. 1 team in the AP poll. The Seminoles also played for the title three other times during that span.

Bobby Bowden is a committed Christian who credits his success in football to his faith. Every year the Fellowship of Christian Athletes presents the Bobby Bowden Award to the NCAA Division I football player who is a faith model in the community, in the classroom, and on the field.

Dynasty Productions Group,
in association with **Nine Times Entertainment,** presents

THE BOWDEN DYNASTY
A Story of Faith, Family & Football

• • •

Executive Producers John Corry, Rick Brawner,
Scott Davis, Michael Ortoll, Brian Hall, Brenda Heichelbech,
Les Lazarus, and John Sam Hotchkiss

Directed by Brian Goodwin and Rob Harvell

Produced by Rob Harvell

Editor Brian Goodwin

Composer Ramon Balcazar

Story by John Corry

Co-Producer Patty Kelly

Directors of Photography
Gary Johnson, Tyler Adams, and Zach Drechsler

Story Consultants Jim Gladden and Jim Joanos

Associate Producers Bob Corry, Rick Davis, Sue Hall,
Wayne Hogan, Aubrey Marcinko, Tim Paskert, Mark Rodin,
Holly Sias, Jennifer Smith, and Rob Wilson

Special thanks to Bobby and Ann Bowden,
the rest of the Bowden family, the Florida State football teams,
Florida State University's coaches and staff, the FSU
Marching Chiefs, Seminole Productions,
Florida State University, and the Florida Sports Hall of Fame

———

Special gratitude to our premier sponsor:
Visit St. Petersburg/Clearwater Convention & Visitors Bureau

Visit us!
Go to **BowdenDynasty.com**
for more information about the movie and the book.